D1590478

# HOW THE WISE MEN GOT TO CHELM

# How the Wise Men Got to Chelm

*The Life and Times of a Yiddish Folk Tradition*

Ruth von Bernuth

NEW YORK UNIVERSITY PRESS

New York

NEW YORK UNIVERSITY PRESS
New York
www.nyupress.org

References to Internet websites (URLs) were accurate at the time of writing. Neither the author nor New York University Press is responsible for URLs that may have expired or changed since the manuscript was prepared.

Library of Congress Cataloging-in-Publication Data
Names: Bernuth, Ruth von., author.
Title: How the wise men got to Chelm : the life and times of a Yiddish folk tradition / Ruth von Bernuth.
Description: New York : New York University Press, [2016] | Includes bibliographical references and index.
Identifiers: LCCN 2016018942 | ISBN 978-1-4798-2844-9 (cl : alk. paper)
Subjects: LCSH: Folk literature, Yiddish—Poland—Chełm (Lublin)—History and criticism.
Classification: LCC GR98 .B47 2016 | DDC 398.209438/43—dc23
LC record available at https://lccn.loc.gov/2016018942

New York University Press books are printed on acid-free paper, and their binding materials are chosen for strength and durability. We strive to use environmentally responsible suppliers and materials to the greatest extent possible in publishing our books.

Manufactured in the United States of America

10 9 8 7 6 5 4 3 2 1

Also available as an ebook

זכר לקדושי חלם

# CONTENTS

*Acknowledgments*                                                          ix

*Note on Orthography and Transliteration*                                  xiii

Introduction                                                              1

1. How the Wise Men Got to Gotham: The Fools of Chelm
   Take Manhattan                                                         9

2. How Foolish Is Jewish Culture? Fools, Jews, and the
   Carnivalesque Culture of Early Modernity                              43

3. Through the Land of Foolish Culture: From Laleburg
   to Schildburg                                                         60

4. Gentile Fools Speaking Yiddish: The *Schildbürgerbuch* for
   Jewish Readers                                                        77

5. The Enlightenment Goes East: How Democritus of Abdera
   Got to Galicia                                                        112

6. The Geography of Folly: The Folklorists and the Invention
   of Chelm                                                              150

7. Chelm Tales after World War One in German and Yiddish:
   "Our Schilda" and "Our Chelm Correspondent"                          188

Epilogue: The Once and Future Chelm                                      213

*Notes*                                                                   223

*Bibliography*                                                            261

*Index*                                                                   295

*About the Author*                                                        317

# ACKNOWLEDGMENTS

Many friends have joined me on the road to Chelm. I want to thank all the colleagues at the University of North Carolina at Chapel Hill who, since 2008, have made my professional life so agreeable and rewarding and who have given this project every possible encouragement. These include, in the Department of Germanic and Slavic Languages and Literatures, Eric Downing, Jonathan Hess, Clayton Koelb, Richard Langston, Radislav Lapushin, Priscilla Layne, Eleonora Magomedova, Hana Pichova, Inga Pollmann, Paul Roberge, Stanislav Shvabrin, Gabriel Trop, Ewa Wampuszyc, Christina Wegel, former colleagues Christopher Putney, Peter Sherwood, and Kathryn Starkey, and administrative manager Valerie Bernhardt; and, at UNC's Carolina Center for Jewish Studies, Yaakov Ariel, Karen Auerbach, Gabrielle Berlinger, Flora Cassen, Danielle Christmas, Marcie Cohen Ferris, Andrea Cooper, Maria DeGuzman, Michael Figueroa, Jeanne Fischer, Gregory Flaxman, Jonathan Hess, Joseph Lam, David Lambert, Jodi Magness, Evyatar Marienberg, Rosa Perelmuter, Yaron Shemer, Hanna Sprintzik, and Martin Sueldo, former faculty members Jonathan Boyarin and Christopher Browning, and communications director Karen Gajewski. Jonathan Hess, with his dual commitment to the Department of Germanic and Slavic Languages and Literatures and the Center for Jewish Studies, has been the best guide and role model possible.

The North Carolina Jewish Studies Seminar has afforded me the continual stimulus of a wide network of fellow researchers, within the Research Triangle and far beyond, thanks for which are due to its coordinators, Yaakov Ariel, Malachi Hacohen, and Julie Mell. The same is true of UNC's Program in Medieval and Early Modern Studies, under successive directors Kathryn Starkey, the late Darryl Gless, and Brett Whalen.

I am also grateful to my colleagues in the Department of Germanic Languages and Literature at Duke University, especially former colleague Ann Marie Rasmussen, and to the doctoral students of the Carolina-Duke Graduate Program in German Studies—in particular to Matt Feminella, Maggie Reif, and my exceptional advisees Janice Hansen, Annegret Oehme, and Emma Woelk, who let me divide my attention between them and the wise men. Emma, in addition, has worked with me on a separate project to translate Isaac Bashevis Singer's Yiddish Chelm tales into English.

The College of Arts and Sciences at the University of North Carolina provided various research funds. I owe an additional debt to Bill Andrews, Jonathan Hess, and Clayton Koelb for the extra support they provided while I was working on this book away from Chapel Hill. Also indispensable was my year in Jerusalem as a Yad Hanadiv visiting fellow, and for this I am deeply grateful to the trustees of Yad Hanadiv and the Beracha Foundation, fellowships officer Natania Isaak-Weschler, and my inspirational mentors, Chava Turniansky and Moshe Rosman. Invaluable, too, was the time I was able to spend at the YIVO Institute in New York as a Vivian Lefsky Hort Memorial Fellow and in Greifswald as a fellow of the Alfried Krupp Wissenschaftskolleg. Special thanks to my co-fellows in Greifswald, academic director Christian Suhm, and administrative director Freia Steinmetz, for providing such a stimulating atmosphere.

I am immensely grateful to the staff of the UNC Chapel Hill Libraries, the Jewish Division of the New York Public Library, the Bodleian Library of the University of Oxford, the Österreichische Nationalbibliothek, the YIVO Institute in New York (especially Gunnar Berg and Paul Glasser), and the National Library of Israel (especially Aviad Stollman).

I am enormously grateful, too, for numerous extended, convivial, and illuminating conversations about Chelm and Jewish eastern Europe with Avri Bar-Levav, Valery Dymshits, Dov-Ber Kerler, Moshe Rosman, and Shaul Stampfer and about European foolish cultures with Katja Gvozdeva. Monika Adamczyk-Garbowska, Rachel Ariel, Karen Auerbach, Marc Caplan, Gerd Dicke, Mirjam Gutschow, Aya Elyada, Arndt Engelhardt, Amir Eshel, David Forman, Franziska Krah, Anna Kushkova, Radislav Lapushin, Ludger Lieb, Michael Lukin, Adi Mahalel, Eddy Portnoy, Oren Roman, Amy Simon, Gabriel Trop, Miriam Udel, Claudia Ulbrich, Eli Yassif, and Ewa Wampuszyc all generously shared their expertise to answer questions or identify sources, and Martin Kober was kind enough to contribute his cartographic skills.

The journalist Matti Friedman's interest in my project and his story about it in the *Times of Israel* resulted in a number of contacts with other Chelm aficionados, some with Chelm origins, for which I am also most grateful. In Jennifer Hammer, senior acquisitions editor at NYU Press, I am very fortunate to have found someone with not only a fondness for Chelm stories but also a willingness to envision them as a suitable subject for an academic book. I would also like to thank Constance Rosenblum, Shaul Stampfer, and an anonymous reader for the NYU Press for their many valuable comments on the manuscript.

Warm thanks to numerous fellow researchers and friends for their companionship and support, among them Cornelia Aust, Elisheva Baumgarten, Christfried Böttrich, Yaacov Deutsch, Ted Fram, Rachel Greenblatt, Sharon Gordon, Debra Kaplan, Agnes von Kirchbach, Henrike Lähnemann, Astrid Lembke, Werner Röcke, Claudia Rosenzweig, Dirk Sadowski, Friederike Seeger, Curt Stauss, Ruth Szlencka, Dagmar Völker, Rebecca Wasowicz, Julia Weitbrecht, and Ido Wolff and to my esteemed Yiddish teachers Yitskhok Niborski, Sheva Zucker, and the unforgettable Pesakh Fiszman ז״ל. My greatest debt, among so many racked up in the course of this project, is to my longtime collaborator Michael Terry, who first proposed a systematic study of Chelm to me and kept urging me to pursue it and who, as interlocutor, critic, and editor, has been responsible for innumerable suggestions, corrections, and improvements, for which this book is immeasurably the better.

Finally, I owe very special thanks to Rachel and Yaakov Ariel in Carrboro, North Carolina, Elissa Sampson and Jonathan Boyarin, formerly in Chapel Hill, and Lynne and Moshe Rosman in Jerusalem, all of whom have made me and mine feel part of their family. Balancing an academic base in Chapel Hill, a home base in Berlin, and research trips all over would not have been possible without an extremely indulgent family, uncertain where in the world my foolish studies would lead me next. To Horst, Kira, Esther, Amelie, Jesko, Rosmarie, and Christoph, thank you for your support and love.

# NOTE ON ORTHOGRAPHY AND TRANSLITERATION

*Chelm* has many spellings: *Chełm* in Polish; Холм (*Kholm*) in Ukrainian and Russian; חלם (*Ḥelem*) in Hebrew; and כעלעם or כעלם (*Khelem* or *Khelm*) in Yiddish, though with an initial *khes*, not a *khof*, in the earliest Chelm tales. A similar range of options applies to the names of any number of places and people mentioned in this book—names that may be attested differently in Polish, Yiddish, Russian, Hebrew, or German settings. For the sake of simplicity, I have used common English spellings where these exist—*Chelm*, for example, instead of the Polish *Chełm*. Otherwise, I have generally tried to follow the spellings adopted in the *YIVO Encyclopedia of Jews in Eastern Europe*. Where Romanization of Yiddish is required, for example in the titles of books and stories, I have used the YIVO transcription system, devised for Modern Yiddish, modifying it slightly, where appropriate, to represent Old Yiddish.

Pennant from Chelm, 1984

# Introduction

Let me begin with a Chelm story I heard from the eminent scholar of Old Yiddish Chava Turniansky. She tells of visiting Communist Poland in 1984 with a number of other Israeli academics. Their route took them through Chelm, a city of around sixty-seven thousand today. Chelm lies in the far eastern part of the modern Polish state, near the Ukrainian border.[1] The Israeli scholars, like so many other Jews intimately familiar with tales of the "wise men" of Chelm, were excited to find themselves in a place of such Jewish cultural renown. When they spotted a kiosk open for business and selling this and that, they all rushed over to it, hoping to find something identifiably local to bring home.

No sooner had the Israelis lined up in front of the little store than growing numbers of Chelmites began converging on the spot, lining up behind the visitors, certain that some rarely available commodity had become available. This was logical enough, because that is what long lines always meant in the Eastern Bloc. The discovery that the visitors were queuing up for nothing more useful than random local objects linked to the town was likely not just disappointing but bewildering, since in non-Jewish Polish culture, Chelm as a town full of fools is unknown. The "wise men" have yet to be celebrated or exploited in postwar Chelm.

This incident symbolizes the very different meaning that Chelm has for Poles and for Jews. Among Catholic Poles, Chelm is known as a Marian pilgrimage site, while among Jews, it has played the role of the foolish shtetl par excellence since the end of the nineteenth century. The tales of its so-called wise men, a sprawling repertoire of stories about the intellectual limitations of the perennially foolish residents of this venerable Jewish town, have come to constitute the best-known folktale tradition of eastern European Jewry.

\* \* \*

What accounts for the singular Jewish association of Chelm with folly?[2] The question has been asked before, and answered this way: When God created the world, he sent out an angel with a bag of foolish souls and orders to distribute them evenly all over the world—one fool per town. But the bag tore, and all the foolish souls spilled out on the same spot. These souls built a settlement where they landed, and that settlement became the town known as Chelm.

This version of events may have an age-old appearance, but it is not to be found before 1917. Moreover, no documented association between the Jews of Chelm and foolishness appears anywhere before Ayzik Meyer Dik's 1872 Yiddish novel *Di orkhim fun Duratshesok* (The visitors in Duratshesok; *Duratshesok* is the Russian word for "Foolstown"). Nor is there any mention of the phrase "fools of Chelm" before 1873. When that phrase does make its debut, it is not in a Jewish source but in Karl Friedrich Wilhelm Wander's dictionary of German expressions.[3] However, the culturally and linguistically convoluted roots of the Chelm Yiddish folktale repertoire stretch back far past the nineteenth century to, at least, the Late Middle Ages, and this book seeks to unravel these roots.

While many people suppose that Chelm stories were meant for children, they were, like Jonathan Swift's *Gulliver's Travels*, originally written for a much broader audience, and they continue to be a source of storytelling for adults. This book also offers the first comprehensive survey of all the collections of Chelm stories and their Yiddish precursors published between 1700 and the present. The chronological approach helps to show how and why the stories developed as they did within Jewish culture and what they can tell us about Jews and their thoughts about their own society as well as their relationship to the larger society. The book argues that Chelm and its precursors have functioned for more than three centuries as an ironic model of Jewish society, both utopia and dystopia, an imaginary place onto which changing questions about Jewish identity, community, and history have repeatedly been projected.

Most importantly, the core stories of Chelm are not original to Chelm. They derive from an early modern German source, the famous *Schildbürgerbuch* (English pronunciation: SHILT-berger-BUKH) of 1598. Edward Portnoy accurately sums up the current state of knowledge in the *YIVO Encyclopedia of Jews in Eastern Europe* when he writes that "these stories first entered Jewish culture as Schildburger stories and it is unclear when they became connected to the town of Chelm."[4]

Thus, while no group of texts is more closely associated today with Yiddish and eastern European Jewish culture and identity than the "Chelm canon," neither is any other body of Jewish literature as closely intertwined with German literature and German culture. To appreciate the origins of literary Chelm, it is necessary to be aware of the corresponding German traditions, which, in the form of the *Schildbürgerbuch*, extend back to the late sixteenth century. This immensely popular work of German folly literature became popular in Yiddish during the eighteenth century and constitutes the first of several major influences that ultimately generated the corpus of Chelm tales.

This book analyzes the connections between the German and Yiddish traditions and, in doing so, challenges previous assumptions that the tales were simply transferred from the German via an Old Yiddish translation into Modern Yiddish. It demonstrates the long process of exchange between German and Yiddish literatures, from late medieval popular novels through Enlightenment texts down to ethnographic writings of the late nineteenth and early twentieth centuries. It shows early modern literature exerting a lasting effect on later modern literary production.

The history of the wise men of Chelm helps to refine our understanding of the relationship between Jewish and Christian traditions, of what is shared and what is distinctive. Moreover, the folktales of Chelm have enabled writers not simply to entertain but also to examine, with a light touch, a range of Jewish social problems. As Chelm stories were transplanted to America, even well-known writers such as Isaac Bashevis Singer used Chelm to critique aspects of Jewish society.

\* \* \*

Since the late nineteenth century, Chelm has led a double life for Jews, as both a real place and an imaginary one. The town, which in the sixteenth century was home to an important yeshiva and a golem-creating kabbalist (Elijah Baal Shem of Chelm) and in the early seventeenth century to a leading talmudist (Samuel Edels), never recovered its cultural eminence after the devastation it suffered in the Cossack-Polish War (1648–1657).

Synagogue Chelm, 8 Kopernik Street

In the nineteenth century, Chelm was regarded as a bastion of reactionism, successfully warding off efforts to establish improved schools or modern community institutions until World War One.[5] Its intellectual glory days were in the past, and its Jewish culture was regarded in progressive circles as an obscurantist monopoly. Of the town's total population in 1860 of 3,637, 71 percent were Jews, and Chelm remained predominantly Jewish until the early 1930s; but by 1939, its 14,495 Jews accounted for less than 45 percent of the population.

In 1940, the German occupiers destroyed the old synagogue and the following year erected a ghetto in the town, most of whose inhabitants were sent to the nearby extermination camp of Sobibór. After World War Two, a few hundred Jews returned; but most left again within a year, and none remain today. The cemetery still exists, though without many old tombstones. A handful of archaeological fragments of Jewish interest, found in excavations around the site of the old synagogue, are on display in the town's museum of local history.[6]

Nonetheless, the spirit of folly still, or once again, reassuringly stalks Jewish Chelm. The town's former New Synagogue, built in 1912–1914, retains a familiar outline, with the Ten Commandments still discernible over the entrance. But the building has been repurposed as the McKenzee Saloon, a western-themed bar whose walls are festooned with cowboy memorabilia and whose booths resemble covered wagons. Upstairs is a sleekly contemporary dance floor. From the spot at the far end of the room where you would expect to find an eternal light suspended before the holy ark, there hangs instead a shimmering disco ball.[7]

\* \* \*

Only a handful of studies have done more than touch on the imaginary Chelm. The Yiddish *Yizker-bukh Khelm* (Chelm memorial book) of 1954 and a second Chelm memorial book published in Hebrew in 1981 contain several articles on this topic.[8] Dov Sadan, the first professor of Yiddish literature in Israel, published two articles on Chelm, one in Hebrew and the other in Yiddish, but both are alternately ruminative and speculative.[9]

The most suggestive of Sadan's idiosyncratic "associative-linguistic" conjectures is the notion that Chelm's connection with folly may owe something to the fact that the town's name resembles the Hebrew word *ḥalom* (dream, fantasy) or, rather, its Yiddish form, *khoylem*. He further speculates that the resemblance of the word *khoylem* to the word *goylem* ("golem" in Hebrew), an automaton or dummy, is significant—"dummy" in the literal sense but also in the derogatory slang sense, as in the Yiddish expression that calls a foolish child *khoylem-goylem*.[10]

Sadan also offers the theory that the word *khakhomim* (wise men) suggested the town Chelm on account of the alliteration, but this theory cannot be supported, since the phrase *Khelmer khakhomim* (wise men of Chelm) only came into use several years after the original term *Khelmer naronim* (fools of Chelm).[11] Even so, it is likely that the ease with which the phrase *Khelmer khakhomim* trips off the tongue played some part in the runaway success of the concept.

In *The Schlemiel as Modern Hero* (1971), Ruth Wisse briefly discusses the structure of the Chelm stories, and in the article "Yitskhok Bashevis: Der mayse-dertseyler far kinder" (Isaac Bashevis: The children's story-teller, 1995) Khone Shmeruk discusses Singer's Chelm stories and compares them with earlier tales.[12] A 2009 article by Or Rogovin offers an in-depth analysis of the shtetl motif in selected post-Holocaust Chelm tales of Y. Y. Trunk.[13]

But that is the extent of the relevant literature. The Chelm stories and their origins have been conspicuously understudied. A better understanding of how these texts arose, merged with other traditions, and developed further provides insight into a narrative tradition relevant to German, Yiddish, and Jewish literature and history alike. Such a project also touches on the logic of cultural exchange, the formation of minority cultures, and the vitality of folklore.

\* \* \*

Chapter 1 begins with a discussion of the place of Chelm in postwar and contemporary American culture. It looks at examples of the Chelm literature written or performed in the United States since the mid-twentieth century, such as Arnold Perl's play *The World of Sholom Aleichem* (1953), still very familiar even if largely eclipsed by *Fiddler on the Roof* (1964).

From World War Two on, Chelm stories no longer emanated from Europe but were primarily a product of the New World, specifically New York. This is true for both the retelling of old tales and the creation of new ones and for tales told in English and Yiddish alike. Not only was New York the place where so many émigré Jewish writers ended up, but it was also a city with a foolish or manic ethos of its own. That was certainly what Washington Irving and his fellow editors at the satirical journal *Salmagundi* had in mind when they applied to New York the enduring appellation "Gotham" and referred to its residents as "the wise men of Gotham," after the proverbially foolish English village of that name.[14]

Chapter 2 travels back to the foundations of European foolish culture in the Late Middle Ages and considers the place of foolishness in Jewish culture from the fifteenth through the eighteenth centuries, so as to explain the context from which folly literature, such as the *Schildbürger-buch* and its German and Yiddish reworkings, emerged.

Chapter 3 introduces the *Schildbürgerbuch* in more detail. This German classic contains the stories that constitute the core of the Chelm canon and that establish the model for additional tales told of Chelm. This is where the story of our wise men might be said to begin, since one of the later *Schildbürgerbuch* editions provided the basis for a very faithful Old Yiddish adaptation from the German.

Chapter 4 compares all four surviving Old Yiddish editions of the *Schildbürgerbuch*, printed in Amsterdam (1700 and 1727), Offenbach (1777), and Fürth (1798).

German literature of the Enlightenment largely ignored early modern literary models and themes, but the paradox of the foolish sage expressed in the Schildburg stories was a notable exception and remained popular throughout the period. Chapter 5 analyzes the impact of German Enlightenment reworkings of the *Schildbürgerbuch* on the Yiddish and Hebrew writings of the maskilim, those who wished to spread Enlightenment values among their fellow Jews.

In another trend of the nineteenth century, imaginary foolish places started to be associated with real towns. This identification of places provides the basis for the transformation of Chelm into eastern European Jewry's national town of fools, the phenomenon described in chapter 6.

Chapter 7 explores the surge in Yiddish Chelm stories during and after World War One, a period during which major modern Yiddish writers embraced Chelm as an archetype that enabled them, in an engaging way, to appreciate or critique different kinds of Jewish society.

The epilogue takes a brief look at Chelm in contemporary Jewish life, and it concludes by identifying sources of the tales' enduring appeal. Notable among these is the opportunity they provide for writers and other artists both to entertain and also to examine a range of Jewish social problems, a function that Chelm continues to fulfill in American Jewish culture and beyond. But while the Chelm tales have proved a durable means of highlighting some of a society's concerns, they have also, more recently, provided an effective vehicle for transporting readers to an enchanted Jewish past. The book underscores throughout the complexity of religious and cultural identities and the role literature plays in shaping those identities.

1

# How the Wise Men Got to Gotham

*The Fools of Chelm Take Manhattan*

"A man journeyed to Chelm," Woody Allen says in the opening words of his "Hassidic Tales, with a Guide to Their Interpretation by the Noted Scholar," published in the *New Yorker* in June 1970, "in order to seek the advice of Rabbi Ben Kaddish, the holiest of all ninth-century rabbis and perhaps the greatest *noodge* of the medieval era."[1] How much Jewish cultural literacy does the author of this sentence implicitly expect of the *New Yorker*'s readership? Clearly, readers should be acquainted with a large enough set of American English Yiddishisms to know that the Slavic-derived word *noodge* means "a bore."[2] But, equally clearly, it is presumed that such a reader, circa 1970, could be expected to understand that a journey to Chelm would result in an encounter with folly.

Sure enough, craziness ensues. The traveler's purpose is to ask the rabbi of Chelm where he can find peace. In response, the rabbi asks the man to turn around and proceeds to "smash him in the back of the head with a candlestick," then chuckles while "adjusting his *yarmulke*."[3] Then comes the "interpretation of the noted scholar," which explains nothing at all. It only baffles the reader further by explaining that the rabbi was preoccupied with, among other things, a paternity case. In any event, according to the commentator, the man's question is "meaningless," and "so is the man who journeys to Chelm to ask it. Not that he was so far away from Chelm to begin with, but why shouldn't he stay where he is?"[4]

Allen's premise is that his audience will grasp that to be "not far from Chelm" is to be mentally not far removed from the fictitious wise men of the imaginary place in which all (Jewish) fools live. In this piece, written in part as a parody of Martin Buber's *Tales of the Hasidim*, Allen uses the fictitious foolish town of Chelm to set the frame for his tales illustrating the silliness of the mystical mind-set.[5]

A generation later, Chelm was invoked again in Nathan Englander's story "The Tumblers" (1999). Attributes of literary Chelm are also silently transferred to Trachimbrod (Ukrainian: Trokhymbrid, about one hundred miles east of Chelm), another real place made, Chelm-like, to double as an imaginary one in Jonathan Safran Foer's *Everything Is Illuminated* (2002). Numerous other American Jewish writers of recent decades have produced imaginative work wholly or partly inspired by the Chelm theme, but these have often been aimed at more limited audiences.[6] Notable among these works are Jenny Tango's 1991 feminist graphic novel *Women of Chelm*; Judith Katz's lesbian novel *Running Fiercely toward a High Thin Sound* (1992), set in New Chelm; and *Keynemsdorf* (2010), a literary novel in Yiddish by the Russian American Boris Sandler.[7]

Sandler's novel returns us to the linguistic medium in which Chelm became big in America and in which New York became the source of most new Chelm literature. As early as the 1920s, while Chelm was still a favorite topic for Yiddish authors in Europe, a parallel body of work from writers newly arrived from Russian Poland and Galicia started to form a corpus that expanded greatly after the Holocaust, while at the same time European production came to a halt.

Among the major contributors to Chelm literature in America were three writers who were close friends: Aaron Zeitlin (Arn Tseytlin, 1898–1973), Yekhiel Yeshaye Trunk (1887–1961), and Isaac Bashevis Singer (Yitskhok Bashevis, 1902–1991).[8] The three met in the famous Fareyn fun yidishe literatn un zhurnalistn in Varshe (Association of Jewish Writers and Journalists in Warsaw) at 13 Tłomackie Street, during the period when Menakhem Kipnis (1878–1942) was "the person in charge" of the club, as Trunk remarked in his condescending description of him.[9]

It was Kipnis, more than anyone else, who had popularized Chelm tales, publishing a long series of them in the Warsaw Yiddish newspaper *Haynt* in 1922 and 1923. Zeitlin and Singer published in *Haynt* as well; Trunk's books were reviewed there; and the three of them must have come across many Chelm stories in written and oral form while in Warsaw during the very years these tales were at the height of their fame.[10] All three writers came to New York in the late 1930s or early 1940s, but each contributed to the body of Chelm literature with a different agenda, at a different time, and in a different genre.

Zeitlin's play *Khelemer khakhomim* (The wise men of Chelm) was performed in 1933, six years before he arrived in the city. Trunk wrote his novel of Chelm, published in 1951, while the impact of the Holocaust was still sinking in. And Singer's first Chelm story, printed in *Forverts* in 1965, at the height of the Cold War, led to a series of political satires in Yiddish that he published in that newspaper, pieces that later, depoliticized, served as the basis for his children's literature.

These three writers exemplify the ways in which Chelm has been treated in an American climate: as a device enabling writers to explore religious questions, examine Jewish history, and discuss American and world politics. This continuing Chelm tradition also illustrates how multilingualism helped shape American culture over an extended period of time.

## Teacher on the Roof: Chelm on the Stage

When Maurice Schwartz (1889–1960), founder-actor-manager of New York's Yiddish Art Theater, asked Aaron Zeitlin to come from Warsaw to collaborate on a production of his play *Esterke un Kazimir der groyse* (Esterke and Casimir the Great) in 1939, neither man knew that this invitation would save the life of the playwright, who arrived in the U.S. just before Germany invaded Poland. The Yiddish Art Theater, which opened its doors in 1918, was the most prominent of the companies performing in Yiddish in New York after World War One.[11] Despite constant financial struggles, it maintained its commitment to the agenda of Yiddish "art theater" as articulated in Schwartz's high-minded manifesto, which appeared in *Forverts* in 1918 and insisted that the theater "must always be sort of a holy place, where a festive and artistic atmosphere should reign."[12]

In addition, this manifesto insisted that "the author should also have something to say about the play," so it is not surprising that Zeitlin had been invited to visit.[13] Nor was he unknown to the patrons and devotees of the Yiddish Art Theater on Second Avenue. His piece *Khelemer khakhomim*, which was based on a more sophisticated earlier version, *Di*

*Khelemer komediye* (The Chelm comedy), had been given its premiere there on October 16, 1933.[14]

At that time, Zeitlin was still living in Warsaw. Part of a family of writers and thinkers (his father was the Hebrew and Yiddish author Hillel Zeitlin), Aaron Zeitlin wrote poetry and prose in both Yiddish and Hebrew and was the founder and chair of the Warsaw Yiddish PEN club.[15] In 1932, he launched *Globus*, a journal that during its two years of life aspired to publish the most ambitious Yiddish literary writing worldwide. A fellow participant in the enterprise was Isaac Bashevis Singer, who, while serving as secretary of the editorial board, became a close friend of Zeitlin.

When Zeitlin's *Wise Men of Chelm* opened in New York, the play was warmly received by the Yiddish and English press alike. The *New York Times* admired its "genial lunacy," which, it suggested, "should shrink the distance between Broadway and Second Avenue."[16] The *Times* was seconded by Edith J. R. Isaacs from *Theatre Arts Monthly*, who included it in her Broadway review, stating that the play was "worth the world's attention" with "an Oriental folk quality that is amazing."[17] The *Forverts* published a detailed synopsis in Yiddish, along with a review by the paper's legendary editor, Abraham Cahan, expressing his admiration for both the play and the production.[18] *The Wise Men of Chelm* was nevertheless yet another financial flop for the Yiddish Art Theater, which had to shorten its 1933–1934 New York season and start touring the provinces a few weeks earlier than planned, but Zeitlin's "charming fable" was remembered as the "one artistic success" of the year.[19]

In the first act of the play, the Angel of Death becomes fed up with his uniquely depressing job. In the next act, he has nevertheless just carried off ten "Broder singers"—eastern European Jewish itinerant entertainers who performed in taverns and public spaces—and brought them back to the heavenly court. At his request, the group's violinist, Getzele from Chelm, performs a tune, one that he used to play for his fiancée, Temerel, while he was still alive.

Charmed, the angel decides to go down to earth, marry Temerel, and make humankind immortal by discontinuing his work. The angel heads for Chelm disguised as a certain Azriel Deutsch, ostensibly a rich merchant from German-speaking Danzig. The name Deutsch connotes *daytsh*, the Yiddish equivalent—literally "a German" but used also to mean a modern Jew, one who dressed in German, that is, western European, style.[20]

Before Azriel arrives on the scene, the audience is treated to dramatizations of a few famous Chelm stories, including the episode of the wagoner with the extralong log, which, lying sideways across his wagon, prevents him from passing down a narrow street. The rabbi of Chelm, Yoysef Loksh (Yosef Noodle), played by Maurice Schwartz himself, comes up with the obvious solution and orders that the houses be torn down—on both sides of the street.

When the outsider Azriel Deutsch arrives with the news that there will be no more death, the announcement is welcomed with joy by the Chelmites but not by the hobgoblin Yekum Purkan, who has been sent down from heaven to get the Angel of Death back to work. Yekum Purkan takes on the form of a yokel and tries to put forward counterarguments but with no success, his appearance making less of an impression than that of the affluent German Jew. Thus, Azriel marries Temerel in the presence of the whole town.

Right after the wedding, the assembled crowd wants to sanctify the new moon, an occasion for a reworking of one of the oldest and best known of Chelm tales. When, in this version, the Chelmites discover that the moon, the reflection of which they had captured in a barrel of wine, has "escaped," Yekum Purkan, with his otherworldly powers, produces another moon for the rabbi to hold up during the desired blessing. The rabbi lets go of it, however, and off it flies.

Nevertheless, Yekum Purkan is appointed superintendent of the ritual bath. The newlyweds Azriel Deutsch and Temerel move into a new home, but they can find no peace. Every night, hobgoblins and imps, roused by Yekum Purkan, Azriel's adversary, make a tremendous racket outside the couple's home—and not only hobgoblins and imps but also desperate beggars no longer receiving from mourners the alms on which they have always depended, since nobody dies and there are no mourners. Women, too, come to demonstrate, incited by Yekum Purkan to feel unfulfilled now that nobody dies and the male impulse to procreate has correspondingly vanished.

Finally, everyone is persuaded to demand that immortality should be abolished. The Angel of Death, saddened by what he recognizes as "the incorrigible folly of mankind," regretfully agrees to resume his duties.[21]

He returns to heaven, taking Temerel with him. Tried for desertion, he is acquitted through an oversight, but Temerel is sent back to Chelm to be united with Getzele's brother, Yossele, her rightful partner according to the biblical law of levirate marriage, according to which the brother of a deceased married but childless man is obliged to marry his widow.

Zeitlin's play is unique in the Chelm literature, which was and remains generally devoid both of love stories and of heavenly interventions, let alone stories of a populous spirit world, aside from the angel with the bag of foolish souls in the mythical account of Chelm's foundation. In contrast, the cosmos that Zeitlin creates around Chelm is filled with angels and fairies. Interviewed by the *Literarishe bleter* in 1933, he described his play as an encounter of a worldly Chelmishness with the supernatural world—"folksy-fantastic, playful-grotesque, with transitions from the comical to the uncanny and vice versa."[22] It matches the mood of a letter he wrote to the Yiddishist literary critic Shmuel Niger (1883–1955) in 1934, stating that the "heavenly world" was "the only reality" and was "found not only in heaven but also in the mundane world."[23]

There is clearly a point of contact here with the neo-Hasidism to which the playwright's illustrious father, Hillel Zeitlin, had become devoted, and the play resonates with echoes of European and classical Greek drama as well as the Chelm-tale repertoire. Regarding its metaphysical character, however, one precursor stands out more than others: "Der Khelemer melamed" (The teacher of Chelm, 1889), a short story by Yitskhok-Leyb Peretz (1852–1915), in which the disappearance of the *yeytser hore*, the "evil inclination," spells an end to procreation, and consequently humanity, just as the disappearance of death does in Zeitlin's play.[24] Both conclude that only a flawed humanity is viable, one infected with folly in the widest sense of that term.

When the play opened on Second Avenue in 1933, only a handful of homegrown publications, all in Yiddish, among them A. D. Oguz's story "A khokhme fun Khelemer kahal" (A piece of wisdom from the community of Chelm, 1911), B. Alkvit's "A mayse mit a shteyn" (A story with a stone, 1925),[25] and Ben Mordekhai's 1929 collection of Chelm stories,[26] were available to clue in theatergoers.[27] Most members of this audience had emigrated from Europe before the Chelm boom of the 1920s or had been born in the U.S. and therefore likely knew nothing of the town's burgeoning reputation.[28]

דער דאָרן האָט געמאַכט אין דעם זאַק אין דעם זאַק אַ ברייטע לאָך,
זײַנען די קלוגע נשמות אַרױסגעפאַלען...

Birth of Chelm, from Ben Mordekhai, *Khelmer naronim: Geklibene mayselekh* (New
York: Hebrew Publishing Company, 1929)

In addition, the Yiddish Art Theater of 1930s New York had a following among people with only a limited facility with the Yiddish language. For their benefit, the company supplied detailed English synopses for its productions. This is fortunate, because the never-published manuscripts of Zeitlin's play are believed to be lost, so that knowledge of its content must be gleaned from reviews, the Yiddish summary printed in *Forverts*, and the playbill preserved at YIVO, which includes the English-language synopsis.[29]

This synopsis was prepared by Maximilian Hurwitz, who, in his introduction, compares the prevailing spirit of Chelm to the "stupidity which English folklore ascribes to the inhabitants of the village of Gotham, in Nottinghamshire, England."[30] He explains that "the simplicity of the Chelmers and their prodigious feats of folly are celebrated in song and story, wherein the East European Jew gives free rein to his genius for mythmaking and racy, Rabelaisian humor."[31] From this, one can infer how little New Yorkers knew of literary or folkloric Chelm and also how established a cultural tradition it was thought to be in Jewish eastern Europe.

It was customary for New York–based Yiddish theater companies to play a winter season in Buenos Aires. Thus, in October 1957, twenty-four years after the New York production of Aaron Zeitlin's play, Maurice Schwartz revived *Jelemer Jajomim* at the Teatro Argentino to great acclaim, with Schwartz and his adopted daughter, Frances, singled out for their acting.[32]

Yankev Botashanski's review in the Buenos Aires Yiddish newspaper *Di prese* makes clear that the audience there required no priming to know what Chelm connoted. They were predisposed to laugh at the first hint of a familiar story, although, as Botashanski noted, the work turned out to be "not a play about Chelm folklore," as he and his fellow audience members knew it, but rather a "fantastic story" that exploits or builds on the old Chelm tales.[33]

What accounts for the apparently differing level of Chelm consciousness between New York and Buenos Aires Yiddish theater audiences? Had the eastern Europeans who emigrated to Argentina been better versed in Jewish culture or folklore? There is no reason to think so. Were the Jews of 1957 Buenos Aires less assimilated than the Jews of 1933 New York? Not necessarily. Instead, the main factor was almost certainly the passage of time. Between the early 1930s and the late 1950s, Chelm had the chance to penetrate the entire Yiddish Diaspora, spread by word of mouth and various printed formats, perhaps the most important among them being the 1951 novel *Khelemer khakhomim*, by the New York–based Y. Y. Trunk, published only in Buenos Aires.[34]

Books on Chelm aside, anthologies of Jewish humor would often feature a section on Chelm. Many collections previously published in Europe were reissued in New York, including the compendium of Yiddish jokes collected by the distinguished editor Yoshue Khone (Yehoshua Ḥana) Ravnitski (1859–1944) and originally published in Frankfurt in 1922, which appeared in expanded form in New York in 1950.[35]

Among other postwar anthologies of Jewish humor or Jewish writing that include Chelm stories are Jacob Richman's *Jewish Wit and Wisdom* (1952) and Naftoli Gross's *Mayselekh un mesholim* (Tales and parables, 1955).[36] One of the most successful English-language anthologies to feature Chelm tales was the *Treasury of Jewish Folklore* compiled by Nathan Ausubel (1898–1986), which appeared for the first time in 1948, reappeared in more than twenty printings, and contributed greatly to the development of another Chelm play, *The World of Sholom Aleichem*, which played a major role in introducing Chelm to America.

Arnold Perl's *World of Sholom Aleichem* opened in Manhattan on May 1, 1953.[37] It became an Off-Broadway hit, selling out its original run and playing for an additional nine months starting in September of that year. According to *Commentary*, "for several months now, New Yorkers in large numbers have been flocking to the Barbizon Theater," where the typical customer would "as often as not . . . buy four, five, or six tickets, inviting his parents to come along and bringing the children as well: *The World of Sholom Aleichem* has found an audience suddenly eager to discover a bond of community in reminiscences of the bygone Jewish world of nineteenth-century Eastern Europe."[38] The influential theater critic of the *New York Times*, Brooks Atkinson, called the work "humane, wise and delightful."[39] The play was subsequently performed all over the U.S. and in Argentina, Great Britain, and South Africa.[40]

That the production became such a triumph was not something that could have been predicted. Perl (1914–1971), an American-born Jew who had seen the Dachau concentration camp as a soldier and became increasingly interested in Jewish culture after the war, found himself mentioned in *Red Channels: Report of Communist Influence in Radio and Television* and was blacklisted in 1950.[41] Having lost the writing commissions on which he depended, he teamed up to form the independent Rachel Productions with the actor Howard da Silva (1909–1986), who had been blacklisted after a summons to appear before the House Un-American Activities Committee.

*The World of Sholom Aleichem* was the team's first endeavor, and they employed a whole cast of blacklisted actors, including such theatrical eminences as Morris Carnovsky and Ruby Dee; the casting of the African American Dee as an angel was enough to cause a little frisson all its own.[42] The audience, as the press agent Merle Debuskey remembers it, was made up of two demographics: "the left, the progressives," and "the people who knew and loved Sholem Aleichem."[43]

The play was criticized in some quarters for its blatant politics, and it is hard to disagree with Midge Decter's view, expressed powerfully in *Commentary*, that the sense it conveyed of Sholem Aleichem's world was partial, simplistic, and idealized. Nevertheless, the production took the milieu of Yiddish literature and literary topics to an English-speaking mass audience, somewhere it can scarcely be said to have gone before.[44]

That breakthrough was ensured not just by the play's success in theaters but also by the broadcast of a filmed performance on December 14, 1959, as part of the first season of *Play of the Week*, a prestigious showcase of the "golden age of television." Sound recordings of the play, distributed by Rachel Productions and Tikva Productions, sold widely through the 1950s and into the 1960s. The play was also appealing because of the way it translated Yiddish culture into English. Encouraged by this success, Perl went on to write more plays set in an imagined eastern Europe, among them his 1957 Sholem Aleichem adaptation *Tevya and His Daughters*.

Perl's play took its title, though little else, from Maurice Samuel's book *The World of Sholom Aleichem* (1943).[45] In fact, just one and a half of the three one-act plays that make up the entertainment have anything to do with Sholem Aleichem. While the last part of the "triptych," titled "The Gymnasium" (in the European sense of the word *gymnasium*: high school), is based on a story by Sholem Aleichem, the text adapted for the centerpiece of *The World of Sholom Aleichem*, "Bontshe Shvayg," is not his at all but one of the best-known stories of Y. L. Peretz.[46] The first act, or play, of the three is titled "A Tale of Chelm" and is announced as a "forspeiss," one of the few Yiddish words in the script, which makes sure to translate it (as "a preview, a sample").[47]

The first act begins by staging a few elements of the existing Chelm repertoire to set the tone, much as Aaron Zeitlin had. Then it segues into new material, or, rather, old jokes newly applied to Chelm, and then moves on to the pièce de résistance, a story by Sholem Aleichem about a fool who could easily have been a fool of Chelm but is not, Sholem Aleichem having preferred to invent his own fictitious location for the occasion. Because the folly involved is so much like the folly in the Chelm tales and because Chelm had, in the intervening years, acquired a monopoly on Jewish folly, Perl, or rather Perl's immediate source, Ausubel, overrides Sholem Aleichem's choice and makes it a Chelm tale, the "Tale of Chelm" of the piece's title.

The rationale for combining these three pieces and presenting them in this order, da Silva wrote in the "production notes," was to convey the idea of progression: "*Chelm* tries to laugh oppression away; *Bontche* gently condemns it; *Gymnasium* begins to combat it."[48] The play ends with an appeal to strike and in the last scene declares, "This is the dawn of a new day. No more pogroms, no ghettos, no quotas. Education is free! In this fine new world, there will be no Jews, no gentiles, no rich, no poor, no underdogs and no undercats."[49]

The play opens with the appearance not of Sholem Aleichem but of Mendele Moykher-Sforim, Mendele the Book Peddler. This is the pen name and fictional persona assumed by Sholem Aleichem's mentor, the Yiddish and Hebrew writer Sholem Yankev Abramovitsh (1835–1917). But it is not as a creative genius that Howard da Silva comes onto the stage but merely as an unsophisticated book peddler, pushcart in hand, an homage that a withering Midge Decter calls "lèse-majesté."[50]

Mendele, picking up books from his cart as ostensible aides-mémoire, serves as the play's narrator and commentator. He introduces "The Chelm Story" as "a folk story," explaining that Sholem Aleichem had gotten the idea from the people "like all great artists," before launching into the action with a rhetorical question: "What, you ask, is Chelm; or, if you know that it is a famous city in the Old Country, what's so special about Chelm? I'll tell you."[51] The angel with the bag who dropped the foolish souls over Chelm appears onstage and tells of his mishap. Then, to illustrate the consequences, there follows the old story of how the Chelmites carry the tree trunks they need for construction down the hill before a visitor from Lithuania shows up and tells them how easy it is to roll logs downhill instead of carrying them, whereupon, suitably impressed, they heave the trunks back up to the top and let them roll down.

After this introduction to the people of Chelm, Mendele presents the wisdom of individual inhabitants such as Rabbi David, who declared that "from now on every poor man will eat cream and every rich man will drink sour milk," his means of effecting this change being his decree that "from now on sour milk is called cream and cream is called sour milk."[52] The rabbi also has answers to such questions as what makes the sea salty (answer: the many herrings that inhabit it).[53]

Next up is the proverbially poor *melamed*, the teacher, who daydreams of becoming as rich as the tsar. No, he would be richer, since he "would do a little teaching on side."[54] Sent out to buy a chicken, he notes that the poulterer praises the chicken as fat, so, with impeccable Chelm logic, he decides to buy not a fat chicken but fat itself—except that he hears the fat praised as being as good as oil, so he decides to buy oil, only to change his mind again when the oil is acclaimed as being pure as water, a pitcher of which he brings home to his wife. Not that she is in much of a position to complain about faulty reasoning: according to her, two times seven is eleven, a fact she knows from personal experience. When she married the teacher, she had four children from a previous marriage, and he had four as well. Together, they had three more children. Thus, she has seven children, and he has seven children, which does indeed make eleven.

Some of this material is drawn from Chelm tales previously published in Yiddish and, to a greater extent, English.[55] Most of the stories appear to come from the English version of Solomon Simon's *Wise Men of Helm and Their Merry Tales* (1945). Also incorporated are jokes and conundrums drawn from American culture and here attributed to Chelm. This mix of Yiddish and American popular cultures, of the familiar and the unfamiliar, but the not too unfamiliar, must have appealed to the variously mixed audiences that the play attracted. Perl, not religiously inclined himself, omits any stories that presuppose even minimal knowledge of Jewish practice. Any particular eastern European Jewish flavor that remained was accessible enough not to clash with the broad claims that the play staked on behalf of oppressed simple people generally.

The climax of Perl's "Tale of Chelm" is the teacher's attempt to buy a nanny goat, which Mendele introduces as a story by Sholem Aleichem. Though Sholem Aleichem, born Sholem Rabinovitsh (1859–1916), never wrote a Chelm tale, he did write the tale that Perl now retells, and the association of this tale with Chelm is not new. In a 1929 essay, no less discerning a figure than Itsik Manger (1901–1969) stated his conviction that Sholem Aleichem "built his masterpiece 'The enchanted tailor' on one of the Chelm anecdotes."[56]

Sholem Aleichem's "Der farkishefter shnayder" (The enchanted tailor) is one of his longer stories, first published under the title "Mayse on an ek" (Story without an end) in 1901.[57] He based it on "Oyzer Tsinkes un di tsig" (Oyzer Tsinkes and the goat), a tale by Ayzik Meyer Dik (1807/1814–1893), which Dik published in 1868 in one of his many ephemeral booklets of such stories, which sold in great numbers.[58]

The protagonist, Oyzer Tsinkes, is a *melamed* (teacher) in Abdezirisok, an imaginary place whose name almost certainly alludes to the ancient Greek foolish town of Abdera.[59] Dik's locale is reworked and expanded by Sholem Aleichem into a fireworks display of fictitious place names. The protagonist—a tailor, not a teacher—is said to have "lived in Zlodievke, a shtetl near Mazepevke, not far from Khaplapovitsh and Kozodoyevke, between Yampoli and Strishtsh, right on the road that goes from Pishi-Yabede through Petshi-Khvost to Tetrevits and from there to Yehupets."[60]

The poor man, whose combined piety and simplicity is suggested by the frequent addition to his speech of Aramaisms and nonsense, is sent by his wife to buy a goat in nearby Kozodoyevke ("Goatsville"). On his way home with the creature he has bought from a *melamed* there, he stops at an inn, where Dodi, the prankster innkeeper, secretly substitutes a billy goat for the tailor's nanny goat.

The tailor's wife realizes that there is a problem when she goes to milk the animal, and so the tailor is sent back to Kozodoyevke. Each time he passes the inn, however, he stops for refreshment, and each time Dodi switches the goat for one of the opposite sex. Finally, it is all too much for the tailor, who is last seen in bed, fighting the Angel of Death. The narrator declines to report the end of the story, since it was a "very sad one." He prefers "lakhndike mayses" (funny stories) and hates stories with a moral.[61]

Among the most widely read English versions of Sholem Aleichem's story was its retelling as a Chelm tale in Nathan Ausubel's "The Chelm Goat Mystery," one of twenty-four putative Chelm tales in his *Treasury of Jewish Folklore*.[62] Referencing Sholem Aleichem and his English translators Julius and Frances Butwin in a footnote, Ausubel's version blends the "enchanted tailor" with "legitimate" Chelm, one of two stories published in Menakhem Kipnis's *Khelemer mayses* (1930) that tell of how Chelmites were induced to buy less valuable male animals instead of milk-giving females, with the inability to differentiate between the sexes illustrating admirably the foolishness of the townspeople.

One of these stories tells how the rabbi fell sick and was advised to buy a nanny goat to drink its milk. His *shammes* (assistant) goes off to a livestock market, where a peasant, realizing that he is dealing with a customer from Chelm, sells him a billy goat for the price of a nanny. When the *shammes* returns, everyone in Chelm is required to bring a plank from his floor to build a barn for this creature, which is expected to save the rabbi's life. But when the rabbi's wife enters the barn and attempts to milk the goat, the billy, understandably, kicks at her violently.

The Chelmites come up with a solution for the goat's puzzling behavior: the rabbi's wife should dress like a Gentile farmer's wife so the creature will feel at home. She does, but the billy kicks her again; and the same thing happens when the rabbi, dressed as a Gentile farmer, tries his hand at the feat. Finally, the Chelmites tie the rabbi to the billy goat and try to hold the animal still by its horns, but to no avail. On the contrary, the desperate goat tears off, pulling the rabbi with him and not stopping until it reaches Bukovina.

In Ausubel's version, which merges Sholem Aleichem and Kipnis and is told with an anti-Hasidic undertone, it is a Hasidic rebbe who falls sick, and his Hasidim who get the nanny goat, which is repeatedly exchanged by the malicious innkeeper because he has "a hearty dislike for wonder-working rabbis."[63] After much toing and froing, the Hasidim finally return with a certificate from the rabbi of the goat vendor's village, guaranteeing the animal's female credentials, plus a goat that, having been exchanged once again by the innkeeper, is, once again, male. At this point, the rabbi of Chelm invokes mystical pseudoscience to explain the inexplicable. It is "the confounded luck of us Chelm *schlimazls*, that by the time a nanny goat finally reaches our town, it's sure to turn into a billy."[64]

Perl uses Ausubel's punch line and other material from his Chelmified version, but he also makes use of material from the Butwins' translation of Sholem Aleichem, reintroducing details from the Chelm-free story into his script. Thus, Perl's protagonist is a teacher (like Dik's and unlike Ausubel's rabbi and Sholem Aleichem's tailor) but goes to a town "famous for its goats" and is victimized by an innkeeper called Dodi, both of which details accord with the Butwins' Sholem Aleichem version.[65]

Much of the credit for the effectiveness of the sketch was due to the superior abilities of the play's director, the celebrated acting teacher Don Richardson, and the blacklisted actor who played the befuddled *melamed*, Tevye-in-training Zero Mostel. Mostel's weary journeyings across the stage with the goat, or rather with just a rope, an unseen imaginary goat at the end of which drags him back and forth, are described by Atkinson in the *Times* as "the most humorous element in the sketch," a kind of dance that he considers at once "lyrical" and "imbecilic" and sufficient to convey "the foolishness of Chelm, where the people are not very bright."[66]

Midge Decter in *Commentary* would have agreed with the word "imbecilic" even if she did not see the "lyrical." For her, that world was only "the kind of Never-Never Land American Jews like to think they come from."[67] Regardless, the play broke new ground, introducing eastern European Jewish popular culture to a generation of deeply Americanized Jews and to the American mainstream. And Arnold Perl must bear all the responsibility for the persistent but entirely erroneous belief that Sholem Aleichem ever wrote anything at all about Chelm.

## The First Novel: Yekhiel Yeshaye Trunk's *Jews from the Wisest Town in the World*

One of the first scholarly evaluations of Sholem Aleichem's oeuvre was produced by Yekhiel Yeshaye Trunk in 1937. In *Sholem-Aleykhem: Zayn vezn un zayne verk* (Sholem Aleichem: His essence and his works), Trunk states that the one who wears the "little jingly fools-cap and the colorful dress of the comedian" also bears the "cup of knowledge" and that "the great masters of comedy," among whom he numbered his subject alongside Cervantes, Shakespeare, and Gogol, "had almost always the will to transform the fool (*lets*) into the transmitter of the world's profoundest wisdom."[68]

This perception also underpins Trunk's major work of fiction, his *Khelemer khakhomim oder yidn fun der kligster shtot in der velt* (The wise men of Chelm, or, Jews of the wisest town in the world), published in Buenos Aires in 1951. The intervening years had seen the annihilation of the Polish Jewish culture in whose worth he believed so completely and his own escape through Vilna (Vilnius) and across the Soviet Union to Japan and on to New York, where he settled in the Washington Heights section of Upper Manhattan in 1941.[69]

Born in 1888 in Łowicz, west of Warsaw, Trunk was educated in religious and secular subjects by private tutors in Łódź, where his family settled when he was six years old and where he grew up in a privileged milieu of mercantile wealth from his mother's side and Jewish learning from his father's, his paternal grandfather, Israel Joshua Trunk of Kutno, having been one of the most highly esteemed Polish rabbinic authorities of his time.

Trunk started writing poetry in Hebrew but changed to Yiddish in 1908 after meeting Y. L. Peretz, who urged him to switch allegiance. Affluent and very much a member of the elite, Trunk nevertheless sympathized with socialist ideas and joined the Bund in 1923.[70] He moved to Warsaw in 1925, remaining there until the German invasion of Poland in 1939. On arriving in the United States, he began work on his monumental memoir, *Poyln: Zikhroynes un bilder* (Poland: Reminiscences and images), published in seven volumes between 1944 and 1953. It is the memoir and his book on Chelm that represent his most important contributions to Yiddish literature.

Trunk considered Jewish history merely "a loyze zamlung fun farshidene geshikhtes" (a loose collection of diverse histories), with these diverse histories separated largely by language.[71] As such, he believed strongly in a Yiddish nation, a concept perhaps more meaningful to him than that of a Jewish nation. Although neither Polish Jewry nor the Yiddish nation could, without a stretch, be said to have survived the Holocaust, Trunk continued to write in Yiddish and on the Polish Jewish experience, evidently, above all, as an act of commemoration.[72]

Trunk's *Khelemer khakhomim* is the first full-scale novel to be written about Chelm. The work, an episodic novel but one with recurrent figures, consists of seventeen stories, each divided into multiple chapters. His subtitle, *Mayses fun dem Khelemer pinkes, vos men hot nisht lang tsurik gefunen oyf a boydem fun a mikve* (Stories from the record book of Chelm, found not long ago in the attic of a mikveh), reflects his desire to evoke a ruined past. The record books (*pinkasim*) maintained by European Jewish communities since the Middle Ages were official manuscript volumes containing registers of events, transactions, minutes of meetings, and judicial deliberations. An old *pinkes* of Chelm, therefore, would be the most authoritative source for the history of this, or any, Polish Jewish community.[73]

But Trunk's conception of Chelm both does and does not treat the place as akin to any other Polish Jewish community. Chelm is at once singular and universal, the paradigm for all Polish Jewish communities and all communities of whatever kind anywhere. As Trunk writes in his preface, "Khelm iz dos moshl fun der velt" (Chelm is a parable for the world).[74] In saying this, he sets out a universalizing agenda much like that of the folly literature of the late medieval and early modern period.

Trunk's *Khelemer khakhomim* resembles the European tradition of folly literature in other respects, too. The narrator often addresses the reader directly with comments on the material he is, supposedly, only transmitting, and, again as in earlier folly literature, Trunk's narrator proves to be "unreliable," presenting readers with conflicting information and going out of his way to mislead them.[75]

Thus, purely to disorient the reader, Chelm's origin is described in the second chapter of the book, not the first. Similarly, in relating the best known of all Chelm stories, the attempt to capture the waxing moon in a barrel of water, the narrator injects novelty into his telling by suppressing the familiar rationale for the attempt, that is, to enable the monthly ritual "sanctification" of the new moon, even when clouds keep it from being seen. To the contrary, Trunk insists perversely that the *pinkes* provides no justification for the Chelmites' inexplicable endeavor.

Elsewhere, the narrator claims that vital pages are missing from the manuscript because it has been consulted too often, so that the nature of the quarrel between Reb Yoysef Loksh (Yosef Noodle) and his wife must remain unknown forever.[76] In the case of another marital dispute, the narrator expresses his mistrust of the *pinkes* and contends that the alleged violent behavior of the couple may be overstated.[77] All these asides create an ambiguous account, a characteristic trait of folly literature.

For Trunk, the lover of Poland, Chelm, a city founded just after the week of divine creation, is the center of the world. He is emphatic that Adam attended the synagogue of Chelm and was a Polish Jew, definitely not a *Litvak*, a Lithuanian Jew. Moreover, according to his alleged source, a Chelmite is said to have served as the *kvater* (godfather) of Methuselah. Chelm's history takes precedence over other narratives in Jewish history, such as the Pentateuchal narrative of enslavement in and deliverance from Egypt.[78] The time frame for Chelm Jewish history in Trunk's tales is all-encompassing; distinguished visitors to the town range from Og, King of Bashan, last of the primeval giants, to Albert Einstein.

Trunk's Chelm is located in a fictionalized Poland, a monarchy whose king timelessly has his seat in Warsaw. His Chelm is an entirely Jewish town, or, rather it has one non-Jewish inhabitant, the *Shabbes goy*, who also serves as the bathhouse attendant. However, in another sign of a topsy-turvy world, when the Chelmites decide to emulate Warsaw and have a resident king, they end up electing the only Gentile in town, despite (or because of) his ignorance and habitual drunkenness.

Here Trunk has skillfully changed many aspects of a previously known Chelm tale, in which the Chelmites elect one of their coreligionists king.[79] Trunk also adds many new twists to other previously known stories. According to him, the quarrel between the teacher and his wife is inspired by the *yeytser hore*, the "evil inclination," to which he attributes a transcendent substantive reality. The *yeytser hore* adds fuel to the fire at every opportunity, feeling satisfied only when the dispute turns violent.[80]

According to Trunk, Chelm's reputation for wisdom was so great that it became the model for all the predominantly Jewish *shtetlekh* (towns) in Poland. Thus, Chelm's streets were unpaved, and the whole place was awash with *blotes* (mud) when it rained. Its wise men celebrated the situation on the grounds that the town should look just as it did at the time of Creation, when there was only wisdom in the world (and not paving). Trunk claims that it was out of deference for Chelm's preeminent wisdom that every other *shtetl* in Poland remained unpaved and drowning in mud.

Not only are Trunk's Chelmites looked up to by other Polish Jews, but their self-confidence is such that they look down on the rest of the world as foolish, more or less so depending on how different any given place is from Chelm. Two Chelmites, Reb Fayvush and Reb Leybush, decide to profit from the folly of other lands and set off "opnarn di narishe velt" (to mock the foolish world) and "ontun a spodik"—to put on it a *spodik*, a fur hat doing duty here as a fool's cap.[81]

They come first to Prussia, in the land of the "yekishn keyser" (the German emperor). Trunk intimates how far out of their depth Fayvush and Leybush are by having them describe the kaiser as *yekish*, Yiddish slang for German Jewish, not simply German.[82] The Chelmites' confusion between German Jews and non-Jews is exacerbated by the bewildering language that everyone, Jewish or not, speaks in Prussia, a language that "iz nisht yidish un nisht goyish," is not Jewish but not Gentile, that is, not Slavic.[83]

In a masterstroke of inversion, Trunk has his Chelmites believe that the touchstone of people's Jewishness is the degree to which their speech resembles that of Polish Jewry. In such a system, Gentile speakers of German are "more Jewish" than Gentile speakers of Slavic languages, Standard German being, from the Chelmite point of view, a corrupted form of Yiddish. Fayvush and Leybush can hardly believe how strange and foolish their new surroundings are. Even the houses in Germany are "oysgeputst un oysgeshleyert vi kales tsu der khupe" (dressed up and veiled like brides for a wedding), although with their red roofs they look more like "narishe indikes" (ridiculous turkeys).[84]

Arriving in the Prussian city of "Giml," they conclude that they have just crossed the legendary river Sambatyon into the land of the mythical "Red Jews," and they cannot understand why they can see no sign of *yidishkayt*.[85] By now starving, the pair pretends to be blind and beg on the streets for money, not humbled but, as true Chelmites, proud and excited to be mocking the foolish world.

The outside world also tries to fool Chelmites on their home turf. In one episode, an *Erets-Yisroel yid* (a Jew from the land of Israel) arrives in town, dressed in a white silk kaftan, a white yarmulke, and a crumpled fur hat, and insisting he can speak only *zoyer-loshn* (the language of the Zohar), the arcane Neo-Aramaic coined for medieval Jewish mysticism. These accoutrements ought to, but do not, scream the word "impostor."⁸⁶ This Jew, professedly from the land of Israel, is trying to sell land-of-Israel prayer shawls as well as phylacteries in bags made from velvet that once covered the tombs of the matriarch Rachel and the talmudic sages Rabbi Ammi and Rabbi Assi.

Reb Yoysef Loksh makes a brave attempt to converse with this man in half Hebrew, half Aramaic, and asks, of all things, whether the Turks, among whom the *Erets-Yisroel yid* lives, are the most foolish Gentiles in the world. Wonder of wonders, the holy man from the Holy Land forgets himself and answers in *mame-loshn* (the vernacular, Yiddish), declaring that the Turks have chosen Ishmael for a grandfather and commenting, "A sheyner zeyde der feter Yishmoel! Er tut gornisht, nayert zitst in der midber mit di fis oyf arunter, est semetshkes un shist mit a faylnboy-gen" (a fine grandfather that is, Uncle Ishmael!⁸⁷ He does nothing but sit cross-legged on the ground in the desert, eat sunflower seeds, and shoot with a bow).⁸⁸ Disguised in a story of an imposture, Trunk's anecdote almost certainly hints at his aloofness toward Zionism and his unhappiness at the unnatural use of Hebrew and not Yiddish as the national language of a Jewish homeland.⁸⁹

In addition to Fayvush, Leybush, and Yoysef Loksh, the *parnes* (lay leader) of the community, there are other recurrent characters in Trunk's *Khelemer khakhomim*, among them Khoyzek, the town fool, who would supposedly be reckoned a sage in any other town.⁹⁰ Trunk's Khoyzek sleeps outdoors in the market place next to the well, and he goes about in broad daylight holding a lit lantern and beating a kettledrum given him by the town's *klezmorim* (musicians).

Trunk, who was well acquainted with European literature, blends the traditional Jewish foolish figure of Khoyzek, associated with Chelm from early on, with the ancient philosopher and ascetic Diogenes, who rejects society's norms and chooses to act the fool and who is depicted in classical literature carrying a lantern at midday in search of a real man.⁹¹ But while Diogenes fails to find even one real man in ancient Athens, Khoyzek has no such problem in Chelm.

How come the Chelmites are of such exceptional caliber? In Trunk's telling of the etiological story of the angel whose bag of souls broke as he was flying over Chelm, it was not foolish souls that descended on that spot but quite the opposite. The angel was carrying not one but three bags of souls: one bag of pure fools, one bag of wise souls, and one bag containing the wisest of the wise. It was the last of these that dropped over Chelm, and this is how it came to be the wisest town on earth.

Trunk's Chelmites are unfailingly aware of their wisdom. When Chelm issues invitations to a world congress of sages ("khakhomim-kongres"), many of the most important figures in Jewish folly literature show up, among them Hershele Ostropoler and Efroyim Greydiker, two of the best-known fools in Yiddish folklore.[92] Joining them as the keynote speaker at the conference banquet is Albert Einstein, who pays handsome tribute to the wisdom of Chelm. "I look at the stars," he says to his hosts, "and I conclude that all the wheels of the world only appear to turn. All is but Purim-*shpil* and illusion. Time is a simplistic concept; on every star it babbles in a different tongue. Those who say two and two make four do not know what they are talking about."[93] Abolishing rigid distinctions of time, place, and language, Einstein becomes, as it were, an honorary Chelmite.

"Then," Trunk writes, "Einstein began to speak just like Reb Fayvke the Litvak: 'There is no world of here and now—that is what too few educated people understand. Yet I have heard tell that this is what you grasp, children as well as adults, here in Chelm. That is how you managed to capture the moon in a barrel. And that is why I . . . have come here to see for myself.'"[94]

Trunk ends his book with Hershele placing a yarmulke on Einstein's head and offering him water for the ritual purification of his hands. The great scientist is identified with the Chelmites, and implicitly, imaginary Chelm has a future, the physical destruction of Chelm Jewry notwithstanding.

Trunk was well acquainted with the Chelm stories published during and after World War One. He knew the people who collected Chelm material, such as Kipnis, and he worked briefly alongside Noah Pryłucki (1882–1941) in Vilna upon his escape from Poland.[95] He used previously published stories, retelling and often altering them, as well as inventing entirely new stories.

Though Trunk's is one the most elaborate and sophisticated of all treatments of Chelm, the work's content is little known, never having been translated into English or any other language. The same obscurity hangs over many other works of Chelm literature in Yiddish, such as the 1944 epic poem *Yosl Loksh fun Khelem* (Yosl Loksh of Chelm) by Yankev Glatshteyn (1896–1971).

After World War Two, more and more Chelm books were written in English. The Yiddish educator, writer, and dentist Solomon Simon (1895–1970) published his first book of Chelm stories, *Di heldn fun Khelm*, largely based on Kipnis's output, in 1942, hoping that it would serve as a vehicle for teaching Yiddish. A heavily edited version of this collection appeared in English in 1945 as *The Wise Men of Helm and Their Merry Tales*. Translated by Simon's son David Simon and Ben Bengal, it included a completely new opening chapter with a sequence of Chelm jokes in an almost Vaudevillian style, and it became the first widely known book-length work of English Chelm literature.[96] Pearl Kazin, writing in *Commentary*, praised it as a "parable of all Jews living in a world that is stupid and powerful. Their intelligence is materially fruitless, and their ingenuity brings no herring for their potatoes."[97] Simon ends *The Wise Men of Helm and Their Merry Tales* with the story of the destruction of Chelm and the dispersal of the Chelmites around the globe, where they "mingled with all the people of the world and dutifully spread the wisdom that was once the pride of Helm alone."[98]

In 1965, Simon published a second collection, titled *More Wise Men of Helm and Their Merry Tales*. This version was published only in English and was much more Americanized than its precursor was, even to the point of featuring the River Shore Club, "the oldest and most exclusive club in Helm."[99] Most of Simon's works, however, he published in Yiddish, editing also the New York–based Yiddish *Kinder zshurnal* (Children's journal) from 1948 to 1951.[100] Turning to Argentina as one of the largest communities of young Yiddish readers at the time, Simon published a collection of international folktales titled *Khakhomim, akshonim un naronim: Mayses fun alerley felker* (Wise men, stubborn men, and fools: Stories of many peoples) in Buenos Aires in 1959. The book included three Chelm stories, and Simon stressed in his introduction the shared roots of humankind, reflected in similar stories told all over the world. Chelm serves as just such a transcultural example, since two of his stories are introduced as an "indishe Khelem-mayse" (Indian Chelm story).[101]

Simon's widely read books reflect another trend that began in the 1940s: the adaptation of Chelm stories to serve as children's literature.

Among the many subsequent children's titles are Samuel Tenenbaum's *Wise Men of Chelm* (1965), Steve Sanfield's *Feather Merchants* (1991), and several picture books, including *The Angel's Mistake* by Francine Prose (1997) and Eric Kimmel's *Jar of Fools* (2000).[102] But no one involved in the production of this English-language Jewish-foolish children's literature has been as prominent or influential as Isaac Bashevis Singer.

## Cold War and Bedtime Stories: The Multiple Chelms of Isaac Bashevis Singer

Isaac Bashevis Singer is sometimes credited with the invention of Chelm.[103] If that is one honor too many for the Nobel laureate, he is nonetheless notable as the best known and one of the most prolific postwar writers of Chelm stories. The foolish town appears in many of his children's books, obviously in *The Fools of Chelm and Their History* (1973) but also in his *Stories for Children* (1984) and in individual stories such as "Dalfunka, Where the Rich Live Forever." In addition, a recurring character in his writing for children, the hapless Mr. Shlemiel, is often identified as living in Chelm.[104]

Singer published Chelm stories for children in both Yiddish and English and for adults in Yiddish only. His English-language Chelm children's stories, published in book-length collections with artwork by such well-known illustrators as Maurice Sendak and Uri Shulevitz, were translated into many languages and adapted for the stage as a play (1974) and a musical (1994), both titled *Shlemiel the First*.[105] By contrast, the Yiddish Chelm stories, one series for adults and another for children, both published in the *Forverts* newspaper, seem to have passed without comment, except for Khone Shmeruk's Yiddish article on Singer as children's writer.[106]

When Singer arrived in New York in 1935, he was thirty-one.[107] His older brother, the Yiddish novelist Israel Joshua Singer (1893–1944), introduced him to *Forverts*'s editor, Abraham Cahan, and soon he was making his living as a freelance writer for the paper.[108] Singer's contributions to *Forverts* between 1935 and 1987 number in the thousands, but not until thirty years after arriving in the U.S. did he publish his first Chelm story, "Der narishe khosn un di farbitene fis" (The foolish bridegroom and the switched feet), a retelling of an established Chelm tale, which appeared in *Forverts* in November 1965 under the Singer pen name Yitskhok Varshavski.[109]

Four months later, this time under the pseudonym D. Segal, another of the three identities Singer used in part to dilute his ubiquity in the columns of *Forverts*, he published the first of what was to become a series of sixteen new and unusual Chelm stories, which continued to appear until the spring of 1967.[110] These are satires, drawing unmistakable analogies to the global politics and cultural change of the time and tracing Chelm's development into a dystopia divided against itself.

The series starts with what was evidently meant to be a stand-alone piece titled "Di 'politishe ekonomye' fun Khelm" (The "political economy" of Chelm), in which Singer claims to be sharing new evidence unearthed from the archives in Chelm. This evidence consists of an account of capitalism gone wrong and the communist alternative that the Chelmites come up with, wherein money and commerce are abolished, and producers, such as the farmer and the brewer, are told to engage in barter.

When that, too, fails disastrously, a bureaucracy is devised, and government agencies are installed in Chelm to procure and distribute goods. When this fails, the Chelmites gather for seven days and seven nights but cannot agree on how to proceed. One side wants to reintroduce money and reopen the shops (and bars); the other side wants to stick with central planning. As a compromise, they divide the town into two sectors: Chelm of the shops and Chelm of the agencies, with the border patrolled by guards. West Chelmites are soon beset by inflation, while in East Chelm collectivization removes every incentive to exertion. The two Chelms blame each other, build up their armies, and make threatening noises.

Singer's biographer, Janet Hadda, has said of his work during this period that "as a social critic, Bashevis in Yiddish was harsh and conservative, completely unlike Isaac Bashevis Singer, the apolitical, wryly unworldly creature he was becoming in English. His remarks in *Forverts* seemed calculated to offend whatever Socialists still remained as readers."[111] While Singer's Yiddish Chelm series does satirize communism, and such episodes as collectivization and the ensuing famine under Stalin or the erection in 1961 of the Berlin Wall, Singer is also critical of the West—the free market and military adventurism on the right, lax law enforcement on the left—leaving the impression that he is less eager to champion any one side than to voice a pervasive pessimism.[112]

Singer's skepticism vis-à-vis all ideologies and the idea of progress itself is evident in a 1968 interview, in which he told Harold Flender of his lifelong certainty that neither "socialism or any other 'ism' is going to redeem humanity and create what they call the New Man."[113] The idea of salvation on earth Singer considers absurd; salvation, he says, is "completely a religious idea, and the religious leaders never said we would be saved on this earth."[114]

When Singer returned to the Chelm theme in *Forverts* after a lapse of seven months, again in Yiddish and using the pen name D. Segal, it was to start a run of fifteen additional pieces ridiculing the state of the world, this time even more comprehensively, by the simple expedient of attributing some of its more egregiously silly debates and decisions to Chelm. The first of these pieces about "Chelm, its history, its politics, its different epochs, its economy, its culture" was titled "Der groyser zets un di antshteyung fun Khelm" (The Big Bang and the creation of Chelm).[115] A fan of neither religious dogmatists nor dialectical materialists, Singer makes light of the science-versus-religion debate on the origins of the cosmos by reframing it as a debate about the origins of Chelm.

One faction adheres to the "biblicist" theory that "when God made the world, he also made Chelm," according to which "the Chelmites are, like all people, descendants of Adam."[116] Ranged against them are the scientists of the Chelm Academy, true believers in the theory of the Big Bang, which Singer translates into Yiddish as "der groyser zets."[117] The English term was only coined in the late 1940s and did not catch on widely in English until the 1960s, so his discussion of it was quite au courant.

According to Singer's description of post–Big Bang conditions, "it was the upper crust of Chelm that cooled first, like in a pot of porridge, where the top grows a cold skin, but inside, when you stick a spoon in, it is still hot."[118] As to the question of how long it took for Chelm to cool off, Singer maintains that it is hard to know, since "there was not a single calendar in Chelm back then, nor a watch."[119] In any case, from a blob in the Chelm River there developed the first fish, then land-based animals, and finally Chelmites. Strange but true, Singer says, "with time, a fish can become a goat, a goat a monkey, and a monkey a man."[120]

According to Singer's imaginary archival sources, the opponents of evolution prevailed in Chelm, and the champions of the Big Bang were incarcerated, until there came a time "when the proponents of the Big Bang were released from prison and those who denied the Big Bang were locked up."[121]

Singer's next target is human history, or the deterministic view of history favored by Marxists, tracing inevitable progress from prehistoric society via feudalism and capitalism to communism. First there came a prehistoric cave-dwelling proto-communist society, which he calls the "Mine-is-Yours-and-Yours-is-Mine epoch."[122] In the next stage, Chelm still operated without money, trading instead in eggs, but this meant that "poverty was particularly bad in winter, when chickens lay fewer eggs or eggs get lost in the snow."[123] Apparently it was in Chelm that a wise man first posed the question "Which came first, the chicken or the egg?"[124] To this day, however, the Chelmites have not agreed on the answer.

During this period, too, a man could buy a wife for a goose egg, but in time the bride price rose to the point that a wife cost a cow. It was then that a Chelmite called Faytl, who had but one cow, acquired a wife. Because his bride was an orphan, after the wedding she brought the cow back with her into his possession. Impressed with this result, Faytl continued to buy orphan brides until he had more than a hundred wives. Thanks to this distinction, he became king of Chelm. This meant that he did not have to swat the flies from his head because he had human fly swatters to do the job for him. Nor did he have to hold his pants up with a rope like ordinary Chelmites because he had two servants, one on either side, to perform the task.

Faytl's rise to power marks Chelm's transition into the age of feudalism. The new king is encouraged by his courtiers to behave as kings do and wage war against the surrounding small towns and villages. Casting about for a casus belli, the Chelmites hit on the idea of a *mission civilisatrice*. They declare their rustic neighbors to be uncivilized compared to the relatively urbane, rope-belted Chelmites, because they do not wear pants. War would bring civilization to "the half-wild people out there."[125] That they would also pay tribute to Chelm is, of course, a gratifying byproduct.

The war, however, does not go according to plan. As it drags on and on, Chelm runs short of basic commodities, and, as hardship increases, so does lawlessness, to the point that honest folk become an ever smaller part of the population. The wise men gather to consider how to deal with the now hopelessly inadequate town jail, finally concluding that the only solution is to let all the criminals go free and lock up the few remaining upright citizens for their own protection.[126]

With victory still eluding the Chelmites, the first of many revolutions takes place.[127] Faytl is beheaded, and a certain Dalfn seizes power with the promise of "sholem, frayhayt un briderlikhkayt" (peace, freedom, and brotherhood).[128] Autocrats come and go—"Twelve Faytls, seventeen Dalfns, and a long line of Vayzoses"—until political parties with opposing platforms are finally founded.[129] One party stands for "Chelm above all else," while the other proclaims an internationalist agenda.[130]

In the next phase, Chelm becomes so money obsessed that even theology is reconceived along capitalist lines: "God did not create the world on his own; he just hired heavenly workers and . . . wrote the check."[131] Rampant capitalism leads to so much overproduction that the Chelmites feel compelled to wage another war, this time against the nearby town of Mazl-Borsht, in the hope of coercing their neighbors to buy their surplus goods.

Mazl-Borsht is a fictitious town in the medieval tradition of Cockaigne, a land in which people devote themselves to indolence, eating, and drinking. In Mazl-Borsht, a name that combines *mazl* (fate, fortune) and *borsht* (beet soup), food is the only thing people ever think about, and their civic pride stems from the belief that they invented "borsht, sauerkraut, and sour pickles." They further say that "the first kreplach were cooked in Mazl-Borsht, in the reign of Chickeneater XVIII."[132] Finally, after many setbacks, a mass influx to Chelm of Mazl-Borshter consumers occurs, but things look more promising only for a moment.[133]

Civil war breaks out between Chelm's revolutionaries and its reactionaries, resulting in "two Chelms with two governments: two separate communities, occupying separate houses, even separate outhouses."[134] The reactionaries establish White Chelm, the revolutionaries Red Chelm, and Singer piles on the satire with a shovel, as in the case of a certain shoemaker and his family.[135] The newly enforced frontier between the two communities passes straight through the shoemaker's home, leaving the workshop on one side and the kitchen on the other. When barbed wire is run through the house, the shoemaker is forced to live in his workshop, cut off from his family. Eventually, he divorces his wife and remarries, after which the ex-wife and new wife spend their days cursing each other across the barbed wire. The outhouse is in no-man's-land, and both sides required a passport and a visa to get there. This is especially awkward for people on the Red Chelm side, since the government there does not permit its citizens to travel.

Red Chelm is a one-party state where everyone spies on everyone else, even children on their parents, and dissidents are sent to gulag-like slave-labor camps.[136] The prayer book is revised so that all references to God are replaced with references to "Bolvan the First." But if there is too much law and order in Red Chelm, there may be too little in 1960s White Chelm. Living conditions are better, but crime is rife; criminals are mollycoddled, and nothing is done about those who aid and abet the Reds.[137]

Singer's series coincided with the launch of the Cultural Revolution in the People's Republic of China, and in his sixteenth and last article, he introduces a new enemy, "Mizrakh-Khelm" (East Chelm), which poses a threat to Red and White Chelm alike.[138] White Chelm, though, is al-most too wrapped up in its own self-destructive behavior to notice. Its army consists exclusively of old women, and its culture, be it theater, music, or literature, is in precipitous decline. "Many authors decided to start their novels at the end and to tell every story backwards," Singer writes. "A novel would begin with the hero and heroine crying, 'Finally! This is the happiest moment of our lives!' Then things would start to get messed up and complications would arise, and so the novel would continue until it ended with the words, 'On a street in Chelm there lived two neighbors, one with a son and the other with a daughter.'"[139] Singer's view of the 1960s is not a happy one on any front, nor does he see the world—"Chelm"—ever improving: "There will always be a Chelm and Chelm will always have 'wise men.'"[140]

Singer's Chelm satires are almost devoid of Jewish content, with the minor exception of references to Jewish food. Otherwise there is hardly a hint of distinctively Jewish life, and as such, his series might be read as a counterstory to Trunk's tradition-steeped *Khelemer khakhomim*. Sing-er's mention in his first article of "several documents from the Chelm ar-chive" is likely a conscious allusion to the rediscovered *pinkes* of Chelm in which Trunk claims to have found his stories.[141] In Singer's version of Chelm, where the time zone is strictly contemporary and the ripped-from-the-headlines action is more squalid-foolish than charming-foolish, there may even be a friendly rebuttal of Trunk's Chelm and its nostalgic re-creation of an idealized pre-Holocaust Polish Jewish past.[142]

In 1972, Singer published a second set of Chelm stories in *Forverts*, under the heading "Nokh vegn di Khelmer khakhomim" (More about the wise men of Chelm). *Forverts* was still a daily newspaper, and the series appeared in six segments between February 21 and March 3. This time the author used the pen name Yitskhok Bashevis, which he generally reserved for his more literary and less polemical writing, and he added to the series title the subtitle "kinder-mayses" (children's stories). The tone of these stories, which is established at the outset, promised something quite different from his satirical series. Singer's Chelm tales for *Forverts*'s adult Yiddish readers had been highly politicized, thoroughly contemporary, and minimally Jewish, constituting a radical departure from the Chelm literary tradition. By contrast, the Chelm that he began creating for the paper's young Yiddish readers was neither contemporary nor overtly political and was quite Jewish.

That Singer now seemed intent on retelling traditional Chelm tales with his personal flair was apparent from his first story, subtitled "A fish an azes-ponem" (A shameless fish), which was not fundamentally new.[143] It appears in one of the earliest ethnographic collections of Chelm stories, the 1917 issue of *Noyekh Prilutskis zamlbikher far yidishn folklor, filologye un kulturgeshikhte* (Noah Pryłucki's compendia of Yiddish folklore, philology, and cultural history).[144] Singer might have encountered the story via Pryłucki or via Kipnis's Chelm series, which appeared in the Warsaw Yiddish daily *Haynt* in 1922–1923 and later in book form.[145] The older versions of the story tell how a prominent citizen of Chelm buys a carp (alive, as one did in those days) for the Sabbath. To carry it home, he tucks the fish, head down, into his shirt, as a result of which the protruding and wriggling tail slaps him across the face. For an assault this serious, the Chelmites sentence the fish to death—by drowning.

Singer's version is greatly elaborated. It describes at some length the process of buying and preparing fish for the Sabbath in the old country and how a certain poor rabbi's wife in Chelm, who could only afford the tiny fish called *shtinkers*, would stretch them with vegetables to feed the whole family. One day, however, Mendel the fisherman presents the rabbi with a fine carp as a token of thanks for freeing him from a curse. The nearsighted rabbi bends down to inspect the gift in the bucket, at which point the carp administers the slap in the face.

Despite the mild-mannered rabbi's objections that the fish is simply behaving as fish do, the more assertive lay head of the community, Groynem Oks, considers the act *a khutspe* (an impertinence) and wants the fish tried, convicted, and punished. After considering for seven days and seven nights what to do with "dem khutspedikn fish" (the impertinent fish), Singer's wise men of Chelm, echoing the original story, agree to the sentence of death by drowning.[146] To this, Singer adds a final scene, in which the sages are mortified to see the fish swim away unscathed, but Groynem reassures them that justice has been done: the fish of Chelm must have placed the impudent carp under a "kheyrem"—a ban of excommunication requiring ostracism.[147] For why else would the fish swim off to other waters?

Singer similarly elaborates a familiar story in the second of his six new episodes for *Forverts*, this one subtitled "Der Khelmer barg" (The hill of Chelm), but, thereafter, he abruptly changes tack.[148] Instead of continuing to use the European Chelm stories for inspiration, he revisits his own sixteen-part series of 1966–1967, which he sanitizes and abridges into the remaining four installments of his children's series. Gone from the source material are such unsuitable topics as excessive violence and polygamy. Gone, too, are all obvious allusions to recent events, such as the construction of the Berlin Wall. Most conspicuously absent, however, are the luxuriant descriptions of the original version, as in the section where the process of evolution is described:

Little by little the steam began to settle and become water. It became the Chelm River, which is very famous in the history of Chelm. In the beginning the water was warm. In the Chelm River there were not any carp, or pike, or tench; there were not even any of those little fish that people call stinkers. But when the water got cooler, the first living creature appeared. How did it come to be? The answer is provided for us by Professor Vayzose, a native of Chelm. The sun shone. The banks of the Chelm River turned to mud. Something in the mud started to bubble and stir, and, ever so slowly, a creature came into being. Alas, it was rather an unfortunate creature. It did not have any hands, any feet, any stomach, or any brain. It lay in the mud without even knowing that the mud was mud. The poorest pauper lives in luxury compared to this creature. But everything starts with baby steps. It was from this very creature that Chelm originated. This was the father and the mother of all the people—indeed, all the animals—of Chelm.[149]

In the children's version of the tale, all that boils down to this: "Later a river formed in Chelm. It contained many fish, and these were the ancestors of the Chelmites. This may be the reason why the Chelmites love fish, especially gefilte fish."[150] These two sentences, corresponding exactly to the Yiddish children's version, are quoted from *The Fools of Chelm and Their History*. This English-language novella for children, which Singer published in 1973, is substantially a translation of the 1972 four-part Yiddish children's précis of the 1966 original.

Singer's first Chelm story of any kind, published in Yiddish in *Forverts* in November 1965, several months before the satires, was translated into English as "The Mixed-Up Feet and the Silly Bridegroom" and was included in his first book for children, *Zlateh the Goat and Other Stories* (1966). That book was the result of a long-standing request for such a volume from Singer's friend Elizabeth Shub (1915–2004), daughter of the Yiddish writer Shmuel Niger. Shub, who met Singer shortly after his arrival in New York at her parents' literary salon, worked as a reader in the children's department of a series of publishing firms and cotranslated *Zlateh* with the author.[151]

This English-language book, preceding Singer's Yiddish Chelm tales for children by six years, contains seven stories, three of which are set in Chelm, a sign of the importance of the place in the writer's mental geography.[152] Chelm went on to serve as a location for Singer's English writing for children in three additional stories in *When Shlemiel Went to Warsaw and Other Stories* (1968), *The Fools of Chelm and Their History* (1973), and three stories in *Naftali the Storyteller and His Horse, Sus, and Other Stories* (1976), one of which had been published previously in *Cricket* and another in the *New York Times*.[153]

*Cricket* was launched in September 1973 with the hope of creating something akin to a literary magazine for children. Singer's contribution to this publication was an English version of the first of the six Yiddish

Chelm pieces published in *Forverts* the previous year, the last four of which formed the basis for *The Fools of Chelm and Their History*. These four pieces, free as they were of Jewish content, could be translated relatively easily for a general English-language young readership. "A shameless fish," a traditional Chelm tale making fun of shtetl life, was another matter. Neither the rabbi nor the *kheyrem* nor the *khutspe* survive the transition from Singer's Yiddish children's story to its English reincarnation as "The Fools of Chelm and the Stupid Carp," which follows the trend of many Singer translations, not burdening a general readership with unfamiliar, complicated, or conceivably alienating Jewish terms, concepts, and practices.[154] Instead, these translations use the most familiar or easily grasped Jewish terms—food references, for example—for undemanding and unthreatening local color and invent new plot twists in which the deletion of too-Jewish material leaves gaps that need plugging.

Thus, in the English version of this story, meant for a general juvenile audience, the traditional seven days of deliberation are expanded to six months, during which the lucky carp is given fresh water and fed with "crumbs of bread, challah, and other tidbits a carp might like to eat" and is kept under close surveillance so that "no greedy Chelmite wife would use the imprisoned carp for gefilte fish."[155]

The rabbi of the Yiddish story disappears entirely, and no one is released from anything as distasteful as a curse. Instead Gronam Ox is the lucky recipient of the largest carp in the lake at Chelm, "as a token of appreciation" for his "great wisdom."[156] When he bends down, he is slapped in the face, as in the Yiddish version, but now the fish is called not "cheeky" but "a fool, malicious to boot"; and a new concept is introduced for the young English-language readers: the wise Gronam Ox fears that if he eats the foolish carp, he will become foolish himself.[157] The conflict is pared down to the binary opposition of wisdom and folly and to just two protagonists—the foolish sage and the wise fish.

The Yiddish children's story, by contrast, features any number of sideshows and not just two protagonists, the rabbi and the carp, but also the human and piscine populations of Chelm. In this version, the wise men of Chelm prove their foolishness by accepting the fact that the carp is culpable, despite the rabbi's exculpation of the fish on the grounds that it has had none of the advantages of a traditional Jewish upbringing, never studying Torah or hearing sermons in the synagogue. Still more whimsically, Groynem Oks, speaking for the prosecution, not only holds all the fish of Chelm fully responsible for their actions but also assumes that the fish of Chelm maintain community discipline just as their Jewish neighbors do.[158]

Inevitably, the sacrifice of the particularly Jewish elements for the sake of broad accessibility leaves the English version thinner and less inspired. Thus, in the English text, the verdict of the court regarding the carp is that, in the event of a repeat offense, it will be sentenced to life imprisonment in a specially constructed pool, which amounts only to a rehashing of the earlier joke about the carp's comfortable detention while awaiting trial.

Shub's attention to the seasonal demands of the American market is evident in her urging of Singer to produce children's stories especially for Hanukkah. Accordingly, two of his three Chelm stories in *Zlateh the Goat*, "First Snow in Chelm" and "The First Shlemiel," are given a Hanukkah setting, even though Chelm tales had previously made little or nothing of the Jewish holidays.[159] Singer's 1966 English-language children's story "First Snow in Chelm," no Yiddish version of which was ever published by Singer, is an adaptation of an especially well-known traditional Chelm tale. In earlier tellings, the synagogue official charged with summoning the men from their beds to early-morning prayers avoids trampling on Chelm's immaculate first snowfall by being carried about on a table by four other individuals.

But, as with the tale of the carp eight years later, the story is made more universal. Singer reinvents the story in secular terms, free of minor synagogue officials and early-morning prayers. Now the wise men of Chelm, who could be the wise men of anywhere, misconstrue the snowfall as a shower of silver, diamonds, and pearls, a solution *ex machina* to their town's fiscal crisis. A messenger must be sent around warning the Chelmites not to trample unawares on these precious objects, but he must do so without trampling on them himself; and so it is that the wise men hit on the clever idea of carrying the messenger about on a table.[160]

In spite of all this abridgment, bowdlerization, and loss of specificity, Singer's English Chelm tales for children preserve something of the author's skepticism toward utopian societies. As Chelm's premier sage, Gronam Ox, declares in one of his speeches, "We do not wish to conquer the world, but our wisdom is spreading throughout it just the same. The future is bright. The chances are good that someday the whole world will be one great Chelm."[161]

By producing Chelm tales in different languages and for different audiences, with different content and different objectives, Singer created new traditions of Jewish storytelling in the New World, with narratives that still bear traces of both the original Chelm tales and the sources of the original Chelm tales, which lie in the rich and influential foolish culture of early modern Europe.

# How Foolish Is Jewish Culture?

## *Fools, Jews, and the Carnivalesque Culture of Early Modernity*

Once upon a time, the impoverished residents of Chelm found themselves confronted with the desperate need to provide their *shammes* (beadle) with a new pair of trousers. Reluctantly, they concluded that the only fabric available to them was their *megillah* (Scroll of Esther), handwritten on parchment—treated animal hide. When Purim came around and the Chelmites needed to read the *megillah* in synagogue, their solution for the dilemma they had created for themselves was to drape the *shammes* over the *bimah* (lectern), reading the Esther story from successive sides of his new *Lederhosen* by rolling his torso over and over again, as they would a scroll.[1]

This story is first recorded in 1920 in Heinrich Loewe's *Schelme und Narren mit jüdischen Kappen* (Rascals and fools in Jewish hats), and the phrase *Khelmer naronim* (fools of Chelm), which preceded the ironic formulation *Khelmer khakhomim* (wise men of Chelm), is significant for placing the Chelm tales explicitly within the genre of folly literature (*Narrenliteratur* in German). The Chelm tales might rank as the last bona fide creations within that major European literary tradition.

Typically, a key element of folly literature, and foolish culture generally, is the presence of what is often called the "carnivalesque," a word coined by the Russian literary historian Mikhail Bakhtin (1895–1975). If *Carnival* refers specifically to the annual Christian festivities leading up to and including Mardi Gras, which is followed by the anticlimactic austerity of Lent, then the carnivalesque, in Bakhtin's understanding of his term, includes the "total sum of all festivities, rituals, and forms of a carnival type."[2] The carnivalesque, like Carnival itself, "marks the suspension of all hierarchical rank, privileges, norms and prohibitions."[3] In the years since Bakhtin's works were translated into English, French, and German in the late 1960s and early 1970s, the carnivalesque has become a widely acknowledged "epistemological category," limited to no specific time or place and including a wide range of institutions, rituals, celebrations, performances, and texts.[4]

Carnival and the carnivalesque are historical phenomena that, as Aaron Gurjewitsch has shown, began with the urbanization of the Late Middle Ages.[5] For Bakhtin, the primary function of carnival and the carnivalesque was to provide "temporary liberation from the prevailing truth and from the established order."[6] Nevertheless, subsequent thinking has seen some refinement of Bakhtin's view, which accorded centrality to the release of tensions between high and low, official and unofficial. Carnival may have accomplished this by sanctioning a radical reversal of roles and power dynamics, but recent research suggests that more central to Carnival and the carnivalesque than the brief suspension of class distinctions was the mechanism it provided for communities to highlight perceived local problems, especially those involving sex, marriage, and gender roles.[7]

Either way, the embodiment of the carnivalesque is the fool, the symbol par excellence of transgressive behavior. The high-water mark of an extended period during which the word *folly* became synonymous with every kind of deviance was reached in the years spanning the publication of Sebastian Brant's hugely influential *Narrenschiff* (*Ship of Fools*, 1494), Erasmus's *Praise of Folly* (1515), and the anonymous *Lalebuch* (1597), which was retitled *Schildbürgerbuch* in the revised second edition (1598) and thereafter generally known as such.

Exhibitions of folly were especially prevalent in year-cycle and life-cycle events. Thus, in addition to the pre-Lenten Carnival (*Fastnacht* in German), with its carnival fools (*Fastnachtsnarren*), there was the post-Christmas Feast of Fools around the first of January and the similarly Saturnalian Feast of Asses later in the month.[8] Folly frequently accompanied rites of passage, notably weddings, and the transition between adolescence and adulthood. Young European bachelors and even married men organized themselves into confraternities known as "fool societies." In France, these groups had such names as Abbaye de Liesse (Abbey of Misrule), Abbaye de Conards (Abbey of Fools), and Abbaye de Cornards (Abbey of Cuckolds), with the leader of such groups titled, correspondingly, the Abbot of Misrule, the Abbot of Fools, or the Abbot of Cuckolds. These societies organized and participated in year-round carnivalesque performances—charivaris, masquerades, processions, and plays—that fulfilled a crucial role in the social and cultural life of the period, providing a structure for young men to rehearse masculinity.[9]

Carnival performances, court jesters, and other elements of foolish culture played a major role throughout late medieval and early modern Europe, but expressions of foolish culture exhibited considerable local variety. The heavy representation of folly in art and literature, propagated by the introduction during the fifteenth century of the woodcut and moveable type, helped spread consciousness of the varieties and possibilities of foolish culture, making its manifestations simultaneously more various and more universal.

## Jewish Foolish Studies

The crucial place occupied by folly in early modern Christian settings has been studied extensively in recent scholarship. But foolish culture as a phenomenon in early modern Jewish culture seems hardly to have been considered. The scholarship that exists has been limited to two topics: the work of professional Jewish jesters and the festival of Purim or, more specifically, Purim plays.[10]

The pioneer in the field of Jewish foolish studies is Yitskhok Shiper (Ignacy Schiper, 1884–1943), who coincidentally represented Chelm in the Sejm (Polish parliament) from 1922 to 1927 and whose *Geshikhte fun yidisher teater-kunst un drame fun di eltste tsaytn biz 1750* (History of Yiddish theater and drama from earliest times until 1750), published in Warsaw in 1923, devotes a chapter to the art of the Jewish fool of the sixteenth century.[11] Tracing the fool's evolution from the medieval *lets*, Shiper notes the changes that the figure undergoes in the sixteenth century. He does this based on inferences drawn from two manuscript collections of short texts, primarily songs. In one case, the copyist-collector is named Menakhem Oldendorf (the manuscript was completed in 1516 in Frankfurt am Main). The other manuscript was, in Shiper's time, still attributed to Isaac Wallich (Ayzik Valikh) of Worms, who died in 1632, since he is the only named author of any of the compilation's content.[12]

Shiper considers each compiler to have been a professional fool, following the occupation known interchangeably to early modern central European Jews as *badkhn* (jester) or *marshalik* (master of ceremonies), someone principally employed as a wedding entertainer. Shiper rightly recognizes that some of the texts in these two manuscripts pertain to foolish culture. However, there is no evidence to support his inference that they were professional fools. On the contrary, Oldendorf was employed as a preacher, ritual slaughterer, and copyist of manuscripts, while Wallich, son of a wealthy family, was a *parnas* (lay leader) of the important Jewish community of Worms.[13]

Maks Erik (Zalmen Merkin, 1898–1937) builds on Shiper's ideas in "Di lirik fun di 'narn'" (Lyrics of the fools), a section of his standard-setting work *Di geshikhte fun der yidisher literatur fun di eltste tsaytn biz der haskole-tkufe* (History of Yiddish literature from earliest times to the Haskalah period, 1928). Erik compares textual representations of fools in Christian and Jewish literature, concentrating on Jewish texts with Purim-related content, such as *minhagim* books (popular compendia of Jewish laws and customs) and Purim plays, and emphasizing the role of the latter in laying the foundations of Yiddish theater. Erik believes that the Purim play developed dependent on, or in close proximity to, the Christian carnival play. He also compares visual representations of fools in Christian and Jewish art and finds the costume of the Jewish fool identical with that of the "daytshn 'nar,'" the (non-Jewish) German fool.[14]

More recent scholarly works on Jewish folly follow Erik and concentrate on literature connected to Purim. In an article titled "Le 'Purim shpil' et la tradition carnavalesque juive" (The Purim play and the Jewish carnivalesque tradition, 1992), Jean Baumgarten defines Purim, with its "liberating, recreational, and regenerative function,"[15] as belonging to the "Jewish carnivalesque tradition."[16] Ahuva Belkin, in several articles, delves more deeply into the visual representation of Jewish fools in *minhagim* books and the Passover Haggadah, interpreting all these images as relating to Purim.[17] Evi Butzer's monograph *Die Anfänge der jiddischen "purim shpiln" in ihrem literarischen und kulturgeschichtlichen Kontext* (The origins of the Yiddish Purim plays in their literary and cultural-historical context) explores the many songs and plays in Hebrew and Yiddish that relate to Purim, on the basis of which she, too, makes connections to aspects of the German carnival plays.

Ever since Shiper began analyzing Jewish foolishness with his discussion of Jewish jesters as professionals, nearly all the work in this field has treated Jewish foolishness as something essentially Purim related, with scholars usually seeking parallels with the pre-Lenten Carnival. While this is a valid and valuable subject of research, it is not the whole story.

Although some scholars continue to regard carnival as exclusively bound to Christianity, the resemblance between Purim and Carnival was noted as far back as the early modern period, when the "polemical ethnographies" of Christian Hebraists and Jewish converts to Christianity routinely described Purim as the Jewish *Fastnacht* (Carnival).[18] The proximity in the calendar of the two holidays was bound to lead to this connection.[19] The nineteenth century saw a debate on Purim, Carnival, and their relative alleged excesses. The late-nineteenth-century scholar Moritz Güdemann tries to compare evidence of the extensive drunkenness during Carnival and Purim, seeking, as Elliott Horowitz puts it, "to demonstrate that Jews, unlike their Christian neighbors, had not exceeded the bounds of good taste in their pursuit of Purim amusements."[20]

The Israeli historian of Yiddish literature Khone Shmeruk (1921–1997), in a chapter on comic characters in early Yiddish theater in his 1988 book *Prokim fun der yidisher literatur-geshikhte* (English added title: *Yiddish Literature: Aspects of Its History*), takes a different approach. He proposes that Yiddish drama could only develop once European drama became less Christian, that is, less theological or less entangled with the church. One argument he makes seems particularly persuasive. Shmeruk identifies the secular stock characters that developed throughout Europe in the seventeenth century as a major influence on the Yiddish Purim-play repertoire. In particular, he finds Mordecai's persona in the Purim plays strongly influenced by the buffoonish Hanswurst (Hans Sausage) and Pickelhering (Pickled Herring), German theatrical counterparts of Mr. Punch.[21]

Notwithstanding the value of many of these studies, what is still lacking is any sense of a far more pervasive Jewish foolish culture, one not confined to Purim. In the perennial debate on the nature of the relationship between Jewish and non-Jewish cultures, nearly all commentators see Christian or Western foolish culture as the source of Jewish foolish culture.[22] Thus, Franz Rosenberg views the humor of the Purim play as "ein durchaus getreues Gegenbild" (a more or less exact match) for the German Carnival play.[23] Similarly, Erik concluded that the relationship between the Jewish fool and the non-Jewish fool was one of *nokhamung* (imitation).[24] Jean Baumgarten, too, noting the resemblance of the Purim plays to the Christian *Fastnachtspiele* (Carnival plays), with the fool playing a major part in both repertoires, states that the Christian drama provides the "antecedents" of the Jewish drama. Similarly, Belkin highlights the "affinity" of Purim rituals to the pre-Lenten Christian Carnival.[25]

Historians of Jewish culture have often aspired to locate the relationship between Jewish and Christian practices in any given situation on a continuum between embeddedness and autonomy. Compellingly, Moshe Rosman avoids the independent/dependent dichotomy and suggests that similar practices in coexisting cultures respond to a shared human need and are "cultural parallels [that] should not be seen through the prism of influence, but rather that of comparison, as two variations of a common tradition whose roots are obscure."[26]

Foolish culture, therefore, can be thought of as a set of common cultural materials structured through a "symbolic grammar."[27] These cultural materials consist of material goods, such as literary and visual representations of fools and other artifacts, and folly-related symbolic material, that is, concepts and language. The symbolic grammar of foolish culture describes the logic and rules in accordance with which rituals are performed and ideas are conceived. Thus, when a Yiddish *Seyfer minhogim* (Book of customs), printed in Venice in 1593, is illustrated with a famous woodcut of three men in a Purim procession, the image reflects a broader foolish culture. Arranged as a procession, a common element of foolish performance, the men wear outfits that feature such familiar foolish symbols such as motley, the fool's cap, bells, and donkey ears, and one carries an oversized tankard.

Recognizing the concept of "foolish culture" makes it possible to examine how Jewish foolish cultures related to neighboring Christian foolish cultures. As noted, scholarship on the subject agrees that the figure of the European Jewish fool had a strong connection with the foolish figures of Christian culture. If one assumes that all ideas, institutions, symbols, and practices relating to foolishness and the carnivalesque constitute "foolish culture," then Jewish foolish culture can draw from this reservoir of ideas and practices just as Christian foolish culture does. On the other hand, differences between these traditions can be observed.

פורים

פורים

זוען עש נצט
אין זו גינט אן
לוצטר און דן עש שמחהדו
גיין · אונ דר חזן שטראמייש
די מגילה אוני גיליין ווא אין
ברוכ לוט זי גיט איבר אנגדר
נוויקלטא · אונ גינ־ט ריבדרייא
ברכות
פון דר מגילה

Purim fools, from Isaac Tyrnau, *Minhogim*, trans. Simon Levi Ginzburg
(Prague: Ortits, 1610–1611), fol. 91v (from Johann Christoph Wagenseil's
library), Universitätsbibliothek Erlangen-Nürnberg H61/WAGENSEIL.
VK197

The occasion for the procession in the *Seyfer minhogim* is the Jewish
holiday of Purim, and it is not surprising that two of the fools have
beards to indicate their Jewishness. By contrast, none of the great number of fools in the foolish processions in the woodcuts that accompany
Sebastian Brant's *Ship of Fools* is bearded, since fools are by convention
depicted as clean shaven in Christian art.[28]

To appreciate the scope of early modern Jewish foolish culture, the
cultural milieu that is the point of departure on the route to Chelm, it is
essential to grasp the connections between Jewish and Christian expressions of foolish culture. As we shall see, there was in this period, parallel
to Christian foolish culture, a rich Jewish foolish culture that generated
a wide array of festive events, rituals, and texts.

## Folly in Jewish Graphic Materials: The Passover Haggadah

The most illustration prone of late medieval and early modern Hebrew
manuscripts and printed books is the Passover Haggadah, and most
of the important illuminated manuscripts fall into one of two groups:
those produced mainly in the fourteenth century in Spain, especially

The son who does not know how to ask, from the Rothschild Haggadah (1450), National Library of Israel, Ms. Heb 4° 6130

in Catalonia, and those produced, especially during the middle to late fifteenth century, in Germany and in northern Italy, with its influential German Jewish immigrant communities.

The most prominent of the artists responsible for these manuscripts was Joel ben Simeon, also known as Feibush Ashkenazi, who worked in Cologne and Cremona. Numerous surviving illuminated Haggadah manuscripts, whether executed by him or attributed to his workshop or to other illustrators of Ashkenazic manuscripts, include a miniature painting of a fool.[29] He is readily identifiable from the motley in which he is dressed, the foolish symbols such as the hobbyhorse given him as accessories, or his dishevelment, another unmistakable symbol of foolishness.

The placement of these images is not arbitrary, and their function is not merely decorative. Instead, the fool is depicted at the same point in each of these works. He appears alongside the passage in which the Torah is homiletically interpreted as dividing people into four types (the "four sons"). To each son, the story of Passover is to be explained according to that type's defining personality or ability. The character of each of the first two hypothetical sons—the wise son and the wicked son—proves relatively unambiguous compared to that of the other two: the "simple" son and the son "who does not know how to ask."[30]

In several of the early modern Ashkenazic manuscripts, such as the Parma Ashkenazi Haggadah (Ms. Parm. 2895) and the Rylands Ashkenazi Haggadah, the third son is illustrated as a fool. But more frequently, as in the cases of the Washington Haggadah, the Second Nuremberg Haggadah, the First Cincinnati Haggadah, the Rothschild Haggadah, the Haggadah included in the Rothschild Miscellany, and the Paris Siddur with Haggadah, it is the fourth son who wears the uniform of a fool.[31]

Characterized as unable to ask the reason for the unusual rituals of Passover night, the fourth son automatically connotes for modern readers the image of a preschool child. But for these illuminators and their audience, an inability to formulate a question suggests not infancy but "natural folly," or what modernity regards as mental disability.[32]

This interpretation of the fourth son is not limited to illuminated manuscripts or to the fifteenth century. The Mantua Haggadah of 1560, celebrated for its woodcuts, also represents the fourth son this way, modeling its depiction on the image of a natural fool executed by Hans Holbein the Younger to accompany Psalm 53 ("The fool has said in his heart, 'There is no God'"), from his set of illustrations commissioned for the Protestant Zurich Bible.[33]

## Folly in Yiddish Literature: The Case of *Till Eulenspiegel*

Among the works much appreciated by early modern Jews, as well as by early modern Christians, were the stories about Till Eulenspiegel, the great fictional foolish figure who made his first appearance in a *Schwankroman* (jest novel) printed in Strasbourg in 1510–1511.[34] The book describes his deeds in what were initially ninety-six tales arranged in loosely biographical order. The protagonist transgresses all norms of society, be it at court, in the city, or in church, vis-à-vis women and men, adults and children, Christians and Jews. Typically, Eulenspiegel manages to get away with violating the rules by interpreting expressions and metaphors in a strictly literal sense. His actions, which generally end in uproar, serve to scrutinize social conventions and mores.[35] Through the book's many editions and reworkings, it has remained a universally familiar presence in German literature, despite its bowdlerization in the nineteenth century, when, repurposed for children, it was adapted into a didactic text, entirely inoffensive and thus self-defeating.[36]

*Eulenspiegel* was translated into Yiddish at least four times, always on the basis of a contemporary German edition rather than an earlier Yiddish edition. All the Yiddish versions leave intact Eulenspiegel's persona as a trickster fool, and whatever additions and alterations are made in the Yiddish versions, the stories generally follow the German plotlines.

The earliest *Eulenspiegel*, transcribed into Hebrew script from a sixteenth-century German edition, includes 102 tales and was compiled around 1600 by the scribe Benjamin ben Joseph Merks of Tannhausen. It is part of a Yiddish manuscript held in the Bavarian State Library.[37] The text is only slightly modified from known German precursors, to the extent of omitting or rephrasing occasional patches likely to prove jarring to Jewish readers. But the book is not Judaized in any more active sense than that, and certainly the hero, or antihero, is not presented as a Jew. On the contrary, the Merks manuscript retains a reference to Eulenspiegel's *shmad*, the Yiddish pejorative for baptism, whether of Jews or Gentiles.[38]

To judge from Johann Christoph Wolf's *Bibliotheca Hebraea*, there appear to have been two editions of *Eulenspiegel* in Yiddish printed at the beginning of the eighteenth century, but if so, both are now lost.[39] Nevertheless, when Lutheran Pietist missionaries to the Jews from Johann Heinrich Callenberg's Institutum Judaicum et Muhammedicum in Halle went into the field, they often visited Jewish bookstores or talked to Jewish booksellers. In printed accounts of these travels, edited and probably embellished by Callenberg, one missionary is reported in 1731 as having seen "*Eulenspiegel, Clausnarren*, both in Yiddish, and other similar things."[40] The report, which expresses a dislike for this kind of literature, says that the missionary asked the bookseller what use Jews could have for such books, to which the bookseller apparently replied that their purpose was to keep people amused on the Sabbath.[41]

Callenberg's narrative continues with the missionary expressing incredulity that Jews had time to waste on their holy day. Was not the Sabbath created for the study of the law, which humdrum obligations made it hard to pursue on weekdays? The bookseller observes that men did indeed spend the Sabbath studying the Law and that the books about which he had inquired were for women only. The missionary then remarks that this was the trouble with the Jews: women did not study the Bible and so could not cultivate their soul.

The first surviving Yiddish *Eulenspiegel* in print was published in Prague in 1735. Remarkably, it includes five additional stories unknown in the German tradition, which give the protagonist the face of a monkey, attributed to telegenesis, the ancient belief that whatever a woman was looking at or thinking about when (or after) she conceived was liable to influence the appearance of the child.[42] The idea was likely familiar to the Yiddish translator from its preservation in the Talmud. Thus, "Aylen-Shpigel had a face like a monkey," the symbolic epitome of folly, "because his mother had looked at a monkey during her pregnancy."[43]

This edition incorporates additional stories, in which Eulenspiegel travels to distant lands, and following the ancient tradition of imagining bizarre-looking humans at the ends of the earth, encounters such fantastic types as enormously strong women, people with canine features, and others with monkey features like himself.[44] But unlike any known German version of *Eulenspiegel*, this Yiddish edition contrasts the fool's otherness with the strangeness of other "others," and he finds himself afraid of the strong women, almost eaten by the "dogs," outwitted by the "monkeys," and much relieved to be back on a ship heading to a "German land."[45]

The third Yiddish edition of *Eulenspiegel*, evidently based on a lost German version, appeared in 1736 in Homburg vor der Höhe, outside Frankfurt am Main. Except for one story featured in the German original that makes fun of a Jew, all the other *Eulenspiegel* stories are present here: it is only gratuitously Christian details that are replaced.[46] For example, an incidental reference to a *Marien spiel* (a play about the Virgin Mary) is neutralized into a *naren shpil* (a foolish play).[47] The much-abridged fourth Yiddish *Eulenspiegel* with only thirty-three stories, once again apparently based on an unknown contemporary German version, was printed in Nowy Dwór in 1805–1806.[48]

These late editions, as well as the many German editions available throughout the nineteenth century, made a great impact on the literary formation of the character known as Hershele Ostropoler, the most prominent individual fool in Jewish folklore. Tales about Hershele, said by one author to have been known as "the Jewish Till Eulenspiegel," are clearly rooted in the Yiddish and German versions of *Eulenspiegel*, in Jewish foolish culture more generally, and in eastern European Jewish oral traditions.[49] The Hershele tales' multiplicity of origins bears some resemblance to the much more complex background of the Chelm tales.[50] Hershele made his way into modern Yiddish fiction, notably in Y. Y. Trunk's book *Der freylekhster yid in der velt oder Hersheles lern-yorn* (The happiest Jew in the world, or, Hershele's apprentice years) and also appeared in a number of English stories aimed at children.[51]

## Folly in Jewish Practice: Customs, Ceremonies, and Songs

Foolish culture made its way into early modern Hebrew and Yiddish books of customs and even, pictorially at least, formal codes of law. An Italian manuscript of *Sefer ha-zemanim* (Book of seasons), the section on the events of the annual cycle in Maimonides's codification of Jewish law, *Mishneh Torah*, opens with an illustration of a Purim celebration that prominently features a Jewish fool dressed in motley.[52] The Yiddish *Seyfer minhogim* features Jewish fools in a Purim procession, also dressed in motley and carrying horns, trumpets, and other musical instruments. But some of these works contain textual as well as visual evidence of Jewish foolish culture.

Of special interest is the book of local customs written by Yuspa Shammes, the seventeenth-century beadle and scribe of the Jewish community of Worms. This work includes a vivid description of the celebration of "Shabbat ha-Baḥurim," the Young Men's Sabbath that was an annual feature of the Worms Jewish calendar.[53] On the Sabbath following Purim, older boys and younger unmarried men would gather at a house relatively far from the synagogue. The group would leave the house in procession, dressed in their Sabbath mantle and *mitron*, a miter or pointed hood, and walk in pairs toward the synagogue with their chosen leader, the so-called *knel gabbai*, dancing in front of them and acting the fool.

On reaching the synagogue, many actions that were inconceivable under normal circumstances but typically carnivalesque would ensue. The young men could sit in the women's section or occupy the seats assigned to the community elders, and they would monopolize the honorific duties associated with the reading of the Torah, duties normally reserved for substantial householders. On subsequent evenings, these householders would open their homes to the young men, hosting parties that would continue until the young men finished however much wine these prominent figures, depending on their wealth, were required by the community to provide.

All this is reminiscent of the carnivalesque traditions of the Christians of Worms on the Feast of St. Nicholas at the beginning of Advent. These similarities are especially evident in such elements such as fancy dress, masks, the crossing of normally strict boundaries, and the inversion of usually rigid hierarchies.

By analogy with the abbots and priors and other mock-ecclesiastically titled officeholders in the Gentile fool societies, the "knel gabbai" to whom Yuspa refers is clearly a mock-synagogal title corresponding to something like an "abbot of misrule."[54] The *gabbai* (Hebrew for "collector") is, historically, the lay official of a Jewish community in charge of a particular aspect of communal life, especially poor relief, including the collecting and distributing of taxes, fees, and donations. *Knel* is more problematic. The only known word to which it seems at all likely to relate is the German verb *knellen*, "to bang" (*knallen* in modern German). The Yiddish verb *knelen* means "to teach somebody," in the sense of beating knowledge into him, with a stick if necessary, a vivid reflection of the pedagogic methods of the medieval and early modern *kheyder* or Jewish elementary school.[55] In Yuspa's work, however, the reference is likely to a specifically carnivalesque title, in all probability alluding to the carnivalesque emphasis on cacophony or disorder.[56]

There are remarkable parallels between Yuspa Shammes's description of such customs in Worms and the *Oxford Old Yiddish Manuscript Songbook*, the so-called Wallich manuscript, compiled over an extended period in the late sixteenth and early seventeenth centuries, which contains more than sixty songs and plays.[57] The manuscript includes several texts steeped in the foolish culture of the early modern period, including the song "Pumay, ir libn gezelen" (Pumay, you dear companions), which reflects both the carnivalesque customs of "Shabbat ha-Baḥurim" and more widely observed carnivalesque Purim traditions.[58]

"Pumay, ir libn gezelen" is told from the perspective of a singer garlanded with bells as foolish symbols, who arrives at a party organized by a fool society. The singer is identified as a member of "the king's young men."[59] Later in the song, the "king," with a pillow to make his belly look larger, is depicted as joining the company in their rejoicing.

The Purim king, or Purim rabbi, is a carnivalesque figure with a long tradition of close association with drunkenness. Reference to such a figure is first found in parodies originating in medieval Provence, notably *Megillat setarim* (Scroll of hidden things) and *Sefer ha-bakbuk* (Book of the bottle), both attributed to Gersonides (1288–1344) and both circulating widely across Europe.[60]

The Purim king of Worms, then, derives from both a shared foolish culture in the Rhine valley and a long-standing Jewish literary tradition with roots in the Rhone valley.[61] The young men in the song that the *Oxford Old Yiddish Manuscript Songbook* preserves show support for their Purim king by joining with him in some drinking and then studying Torah. The riotous nonsense of the text evokes the young men moving from house to house for the festivities described in Yuspa Shammes's book.

The *Oxford Old Yiddish Manuscript Songbook* contains another song, unconnected to Purim, which makes sense only in relation to practices prevalent among young men's fool societies of the time. In this song, sixteen Jewish men are apparently named and shamed for having illicit sexual intercourse with Jewish and Christian girls and women.

The song was first noted as exemplifying Jewish foolish culture in early modern Yiddish literature by Yitskhok Shiper in his history of Yiddish theater and drama.[62] Shiper's assumption that the protagonists are "khsidim fun umreyner libe" (devotees of impure love, libertines) is based on Felix Rosenberg's study of the *Oxford Old Yiddish Manuscript Songbook*, published in the *Zeitschrift für die Geschichte der Juden* in 1888 and 1889.[63] Rosenberg describes the sixteen as men who pay homage to "Venus vulgivaga," that is, Venus in the character of goddess of promiscuity.[64]

For these scholars, the song falls clearly into the category of Jewish folly literature because of its *nibl-pe* (profanities) and permissiveness. Shiper considered the "Ayzik Kitel" named in the song to be its author, and he celebrates him as one of the great Jewish fools of the sixteenth century. In contrast, other scholars question whether the song qualifies as folly literature at all, given its distasteful subject matter.[65]

There is no doubt, however, that the song is rooted in the carnivalesque culture of Early Modernity. In its twenty-seven quatrains, it alludes in various ways to the foolish performances and foolish language of the time. The question remains, however, as to what exactly is foolish about this Yiddish song, which in each stanza relates, in graphic detail and with elaborate period metaphors, what amounts to the same story over and over: how each of the sixteen men had sex with *shikses* (Gentile girls), *goyes* (Gentile women), or prostitutes or how they impregnated their cook or maidservant or, in one instance, the *Shabbes goye*, the woman who helped with domestic tasks on the Sabbath so that the Jewish members of the household might avoid profaning their holy day.[66]

The foolish institution evoked in this song is the charivari, a ritual designed to expose local misconduct, particularly by writing derisive lyrics to song tunes that humiliatingly were performed in public, accompanied by raucous and discordant music.[67] The charivari was a rite staged by members of the fool societies.[68] The purpose of these performances was to deal vigilante style with breaches of a community's sexual and marital norms.

The pedagogical function of this institution as a primitive kind of adolescent or premarital sex education seems clear enough.[69] But it was not just the perpetrators of these offenses whom the charivari casts as fools. In the institution of charivari, as in this period generally, folly is seen as ubiquitous. Cuckolds, along with other seemingly innocent individuals, such as henpecked husbands and old men with young brides, are just as likely to be mocked as philanderers and seducers. Young performers even presented themselves as fools, proudly choosing foolish names for their group and its members and wearing such foolish symbols as horns.

The song in the *Oxford Old Yiddish Manuscript Songbook* reflects the ritual of the charivari in the way that it features those two groups, the ridiculed and the ridiculers. The last line of the song refers to these sixteen men as being the type who "also like to ride on such pushcarts,"[70] a remark that may suggest the ceremony of carrying the cuckold, often with horns on his head, around town in a cart.[71] Rather than literally executing this sentence, the narrator of the song gives these wrongdoers an equivalent punishment, listing them and their misdeeds in detail and thereby exhibiting them on a literary pushcart.

Yet the song is peculiar enough to raise the possibility that the real target of this charivari is not what it appears to be. Four of the sixteen named individuals have been traced in archival sources, and all turn out to have been at the center of a cause célèbre in the Jewish or civil courts during the late sixteenth century.[72] Two of these cases are of a nonsexual nature, involving a contested inheritance and a civil suit with a Gentile. Conceivably, the song's true purpose was to group together and to highlight a succession of problematic cases involving prominent members of various Jewish communities in southern Germany and Switzerland, referring to these sensitive matters obliquely through the sexualized language characteristic of charivari.

Archival sources also preserve records of named individual fools, that is, *badkhonim*, professional entertainers at Jewish weddings and other community events, such as the eighteenth-century Löb of Fürth.[73] There is also a suggestive reference to Volf Nestler as the official fool of the Jewish community of Prague, who is recorded as leading a procession of Prague's Jews to celebrate the birth of the Habsburg Prince Leopold in 1716, in a description that shows him not just acting the fool but also making use of gender-crossing foolish costume: "After this Volf Nestler, the community fool [*kahals nar*], came riding along, wearing gold sequins and a red veil of the kind favored by the women of Prague. In addition, he had on a blue coat, buttoned from the neck down and spreading out over the entire horse. The whole outfit was adorned with little horn-shaped pastries, which he would blow as if they were post-horns and consume."[74] The description, published in Yiddish with an annotated German translation, survives thanks to Johann Jacob Schudt (1664–1722), who reserves any displeasure on this occasion for the Yiddish author's choice of the word *herndlikh* for "little horns," whereas, in his opinion, the correct diminutive should be *Hörnlein*.[75] As for Wolf Nestler's performance, that passes virtually unremarked. All Schudt does in his annotation is state the obvious: that the fool blew the pastry horns before eating them to make the audience laugh. Nothing about the fool's behavior or appearance or even his existence seems to have occasioned surprise, let alone disapproval. Rather, Nestler's use of foolish symbols belonged within a shared foolish culture, and the meaning of those symbols must have been clear to Jews and Christians alike.

Fools, foolish rituals, foolish symbols, and a complex concept of folly were clearly a palpable and continuing presence in the life of early modern European Jews, within Jewish communities as well as all around them. Shared symbols and ideas of folly made a book such as *Eulenspiegel* entirely intelligible and highly appealing to Jewish readers. Another such case, as we shall see, is that of the *Schildbürgerbuch*, a work that focuses not on an individual but on exploring how an entire community succumbed to folly. The *Schildbürgerbuch* was one of the more influential books in central Europe throughout the seventeenth century, and it continued to exert an influence in the eighteenth and nineteenth centuries and even the twentieth century.

# Through the Land of Foolish Culture

*From Laleburg to Schildburg*

When the wise men of Chelm build their town, they start by felling trees on top of a hill and carrying the trunks down below. Then a Litvak (Lithuanian) comes and points out that they could have let the trunks roll down. Impressed, they carry them up the hill again in order to take full advantage of his advice.

The Chelmites, however, are by no means the world's only community of fools, nor are they the first. It was not, however, until the sixteenth century that collected tales of localized folly emerged as a feature and fixture of European literature. The first example to appear in print was the chapbook-length collection of twenty such tales published in England in the mid-sixteenth century as the *Merie Tales of the Mad Men of Gotam* by "A.B. of Phisike Doctour." The author is identified as Andrew Boorde, an English Carthusian hermit, who, having left his cell, turned perpetual European traveler and celebrated medical practitioner and wit.[1] Similar collections were published on the European continent soon after, among them "Die Lappenhewser bawren" (The peasants of Foolstown, 1558) by the Nuremberg poet and playwright Hans Sachs.[2] But the classic of the genre is another German collection, which made its print debut in 1597 under the title *Lalebuch*.

The *Lalebuch*, one of the most influential works of Early New High German folly literature, describes the antics of the wise men of Laleburg, a fictitious city "in the mighty kingdom of Utopia."[3] The book was a huge and instant success; between the end of the sixteenth century and the end of the eighteenth century, more than thirty German and four or five Yiddish editions are believed to have been published. The book's popularity continued into the nineteenth and twentieth centuries, and it inspired more than seventy German adaptations and imitations, most of them intended for children. The work also served as the major inspiration for the nineteenth- and twentieth-century tales of the wise men of Chelm.

The first edition of the *Lalebuch* was published in 1597, and the second in 1598, when it was retitled the *Schildbürgerbuch*. In the late 1690s, a substantially modernized new edition became the source for the first Old Yiddish translation. The *Lalebuch* and its derivatives are part of early modern foolish culture, with its foolish rituals and performances at one end of the spectrum and serious debates about the nature of wisdom and folly at the other.

The *Lalebuch* begins with an elaborate preamble, creating a backstory for the episodes to follow, claiming that the people called Lalen were descended from an elite group of philosophers of ancient Greece, famous for their "superior reason and excellent wisdom."[4] The author's skepticism toward these classical arbiters of wisdom is evident in the fact that this group is named Lalen; *lalein* in Greek, *lallen* in modern German, means "to babble or prattle." According to the preamble, these sages ended up being expelled from their native land by their compatriots, who ultimately found their wisdom insufferable.

These men, having deposited their wives and children in a town that became known as Laleburg, departed to take up positions as government advisers around the world. But discontent mounted again, this time among the abandoned wives, who insisted that their husbands come home and attend to their "grosse Haußhaltung" and "kleine Haußhaltung": the greater and lesser obligations of being the head of a household—in other words, their domestic and conjugal responsibilities.[5] The wise men returned and promised not to go back to their jobs, coming up instead with a plan to dissuade their employers from insisting on their return: all the sages would feign sudden madness. So well do they act crazy that before long they are no longer acting. Playing the fool has become second nature, and these intellectual titans have degenerated into blockheads.

It was mentioned at the start of this chapter that the builders of Chelm first carried their logs down the hill and then up again in order, more efficiently, to let them roll down. In this they are anticipated in the Lalen's effort to build a city hall. Here, too, they laboriously carry the logs that they need down the hill before realizing that it would have been much easier to have rolled them. In line with this insight, they, too, heave the logs back up to the top of the hill and let them roll down.

Carrying the sunlight into the town hall, woodcut from the German Filtzhut edition of the *Schildbürgerbuch*, British Library

More foolishness follows. Once they finish building the exterior of the city hall, they realize that the interior is darker than it would have been if the design had included windows. The sages eventually resolve to shovel sunlight into sacks. When they bring their sacks indoors but see no improvement, they decide to follow the advice of a malicious stranger and remove the roof of the town hall, which works beautifully in summer but less beautifully once winter arrives.

Winter also alerts the men to the absence of an oven, which they decide to build on the outside of the building, planning to keep the heat in with a dragnet, such as a hunter might use to prevent small game from escaping. Subsequent chapters describe how the wise men try to maximize the profit to be extracted from their fields by sowing them with salt, the precious "white gold" of the Late Middle Ages. A watchman is hired to protect the anticipated seedlings by keeping wild beasts at bay, but then the men worry that this guard might do more harm than good by trampling the soon-to-sprout grains of salt as he goes about his task.

To make sure that the watchman's feet never touch the ground, the sages recruit four more men to carry him around on a litter.

Next it is time for the Lalen to experiment with democracy. There follows a mayoral election, in which victory goes to the swineherd, the least educated and least qualified member of Laleburg society. This swineherd is not just any swineherd but more ominously one who lets his wife wears the pants. Chaos ensues, especially when the emperor of Utopia decides to visit. The mayor inquires of his staff whether it would be more correct to receive the sovereign on foot or on horseback, and a compromise is recommended to them. Thus, the sages go out to meet His Majesty astride hobbyhorses, contraptions richly symbolic of foolishness, childishness, and parodied knighthood, along with coarsely sexual connotations.[6] Moreover, their official gift is a jar of run-of-the-mill mustard, and the banquet consists of workaday bread and cheese. Worse is yet to come. As after-dinner entertainment, the emperor's hosts treat him to a string of rude riddles. When asked by the Lalen to grant them an imperial privilege, the emperor responds by issuing the entire town a professional fool's license.

In the book's final chapters, additional examples of foolishness are presented. Some of the Lalen, who had been sitting in a group, are unable to disperse because they cannot figure out which legs belong to whom until a stranger comes along and beats each of the jumbled limbs with a stick. Subsequently, the Lalen decide not to waste the grass growing out of the top of a wall; so they place a rope around the neck of the mayor's cow, heaving her up and wondering why her tongue is sticking out so strangely by the time they get her up to the top. When a sow is convicted of stealing from the municipal stockpile of oats and the death sentence has been carried out, the townspeople start debating who should get which parts of the pig and conclude that the most equitable option is to turn the whole carcass into one enormous community sausage. In another tale, the Lalen recall their previous experience with the logs just as they finish carrying a new millstone down into town. Accordingly, they carry the stone up again so that they can do the smart thing and roll it down. Before they release it, however, they decide that one of them should stick his head into the hole in the center of the stone so as to travel with it and report back on its final location. The designated driver, however, still attached to the millstone, meets his end at the bottom of a fishpond, leaving his fellow fools supposing that he has absconded with the stone.

A further mishap occurs when one of the Lalen is decapitated, or so it appears, except that no one can remember whether the man had anything on his shoulders before the apparent accident took place. Subsequently, another of the Lalen becomes so obsessed with trying to teach a cuckoo to cuckoo better that he climbs up a tree and remains there, oblivious to everything else, even when a wolf comes along and eats the horse he left at the foot of the tree.[7]

When the din of war draws near, the Lalen decide to save the town bell from pillage by hiding it at the bottom of their lake. They load the bell onto a boat, take it out into deep water, and drop it over the side. Then, before heading back to the shore, they make a mark on the deck of the vessel to record the precise point to which they will need to return when danger has passed and they are ready to retrieve their cherished possession. In another tale, mistaking a crab with its claws for a tailor with his scissors, the Lalen decide to place an order and hand over a fine piece of London cloth that inevitably gets ruined. The "tailor" is tried, convicted, and sentenced, luckily for it, to death by drowning. Finally, the Lalen, ever credulous, let someone sell them a dog of an extremely rare breed called the mousehound. It never occurs to anyone that they have acquired a common or garden cat. Increasingly distressed by the creature's uncanine behavior, they panic and, in a misjudged attempt to rid themselves of this by-now-terrifying creature, burn their city to the ground and flee to the ends of the earth. This is the reason that fools are everywhere, the *Lalebuch* explains, ending the book with a message that explains a lot about the world: wherever the refugees from Laleburg "settled, there they begat fools as foolish as themselves."[8]

All the silliness of these protagonists does not, however, exhaust the *Lalebuch*'s foolish content. The choicest part of the book is the manner of the telling more than what is being told, the antics of the narrator more than those of the Lalen. The *Lalebuch* distinguishes itself in terms of foolish culture by the extent to which it manages to contradict or subvert the evidence it presents. Even the title page is filled with a mix of overt nonsense and covert nonsense, such as statements that will have been discredited by the time the reader has finished. The imprint "Laleburg," for example, is not only a fictitious location but one that, ac-

Cat on the roof, woodcut from the German Filtzhut edition of the *Schildbürgerbuch*, British Library

cording to the narrative itself, was burned to the ground and abandoned forever before this account of its history was compiled.

The book provides many more conflicting arguments. The narrator repeatedly disguises his own identity as well as the source of his text. He also makes a point of blurring the boundaries between wisdom and folly, sanity and insanity.

The story is told by a thoroughly "unreliable narrator," which adds to the riddle of the author's, and his narrator's, identity.[9] This riddle is highlighted on the title page by the author's statement that, rather than supplying his name in the conventional manner, he is, as a service to his readers, providing them with a complete alphabet and the assurance that his identity may be found by rearranging some of its letters. Throughout the text, the narrator keeps playing with his readers by providing different accounts of the sources on which he claims to rely. Thus, in the preface, he says that the story was told to him by the skipper of a boat on which he was traveling during a break from a session of the Utopian parliament (*Reichstag*) that he was attending in the year 753. Later, however, he complains of the partial illegibility of his manuscript source on account of its extensive worm damage.[10]

The narrator also constantly switches narrative levels.[11] He often appears as an outside observer, and not even an omniscient one, placing himself with the readers in not being in full possession of the facts. So, for example, when a log that the Lalen are rolling breaks loose and runs amok, he says, "I do not know whether they omitted to do something and did not chain and tie it correctly, or whether the cords and ropes were too weak and so snapped, but the tree got away from them."[12]

Sometimes the narrator chooses to associate himself so closely with his audience that he addresses the reader as if he were talking to an intimate friend, as where he describes the feast hosted by the mayor and his wife and comments, "If I had been there, I would certainly have tucked in, and you, you fool, would certainly have done so, too. You would have stuffed your cheeks to get your money's worth."[13]

On other occasions, the narrator presents himself as if he were a character in his own story, witnessing the events he describes. He says, for example, "I knew perfectly well that what the Lalen thought were salt plants were really stinging nettles, for they stung ferociously. I did not wish to tell them, however, but preferred to let them carry on with their folly."[14] The alternation between detached narrator and involved narrator adds to the complexity of the book, sometimes blurring the contrast between the Lalen as fools and the narrator as the embodiment of reason.

Not only are the content of the stories and the manner of their presentation full of folly, but so, at times, is the language itself, with its insanely convoluted neologisms, such as *wunderbarnarrseltzamabenthewrlichsten*, a word that incorporates three adjectives and a noun: wonderful, curious, most adventurous, and fool.[15]

Research on the *Schildbürgerbuch* began uncommonly early—in the first half of the eighteenth century—thanks to the historian and educator Johann Christian Schöttgen (1687–1751). In 1747, using the pseudonym Johann Christian Langner, he published a "defense of the town of Schilda," in which he compared different editions of the *Schildbürgerbuch* and criticized the editors and publishers of the revised versions as intruders and mercenaries.[16] Throughout the nineteenth and twentieth centuries, scholarship on the subject was preoccupied with the relationship between the book's first edition, titled the *Lalebuch*, and the second edition, retitled the *Schildbürgerbuch*. This culminated in a long-running debate on which of the two actually came first, with the *Lalebuch* prevailing.[17] Regarding Laleburg, the jocular place of printing of the *Lalebuch*, it is unclear if either Strasbourg, and the press maintained by the heirs of Bernard Jobin, or Montbeliard, and the press maintained by Jacob Foillet, is where the book was published.[18] The question of where the fictitious Laleburg or Schildburg is located has also been an obsession for literary historians.[19]

As far back as the early nineteenth century, Wilhelm Grimm and Friedrich Heinrich von der Hagen, among others, observed that the *Lalebuch* quoted, merged, and combined earlier literary texts, such as the tales collected in Heinrich Bebel's *Facetiae* (1508–1512) and Jakob Frey's *Gartengesellschaft* (1556), as well as Hans Sachs's "Lappenhewser bawren."[20] The anonymous author of the *Lalebuch* assembles well-known stories about fools or stereotypically foolish types such as peasants, and he reassigns their foolish behavior to the people of Laleburg, incorporating these existing tales into his original story line, which starts with the creation of Laleburg and ends with its destruction.

It is also clear that the author was familiar with contemporary humanistic debates on such questions as the nature of happiness, the role of wise men in politics, and whether the cooperation of wise men can bring about *eudaimonia*, a true welfare state or great society. As Hans Rudolf Velten has shown, the text borrows ideas from Poggio Bracciolini, developed in his treatise *De miseria humanae conditionis* (On the misery of the human condition, 1455), which circulated widely in Latin and was also available in German translation.[21]

Among the many textual inspirations for the *Lalebuch*, however, one stands out: Thomas More's *Utopia*, first printed in Basel in 1516—hence the location of the action, be it in Laleburg or Schildburg, with both of them situated "in the mighty kingdom of Utopia."[22] Needless to say, every endeavor on the part of the Lalen or Schildburgers to build an ideal society goes ridiculously wrong, even though or, rather, because they abolish class distinctions, establish free elections, and hold all property in common. The *Lalebuch*, therefore, is an anti-utopian satire, with obvious references to More's classic that range from allusions in names to topics discussed to rhetorical strategies.

Other scholarly attention to the *Lalebuch* concentrated on the question of its genre. Influenced by Romanticism, Joseph Görres included the *Lalebuch* on his list of *Volksbücher* (chapbooks). This categorization is troublesome because it assumed that reading matter was intended either exclusively for the masses (or middling sorts) or exclusively for the intelligentsia.[23] The *Lalebuch* is a perfect example of how this distinction cannot be applied in the early modern context; playful, funny, and rude, the *Lalebuch* is also a highly sophisticated book, containing many allusions to humanistic debates and knowledge.

The book's sequential anecdotes (*Schwänke* in German) may make the work seem like a novel.[24] Other critics categorize the *Lalebuch* primarily as satire: Andreas Bässler, for example, concluded that the work stands in the tradition of the Menippean satire.[25] His arguments, based on formalistic features, include the characteristic fluctuation between prose and verse, a "willed lack of unity and decorum," an ironic narrator, and metaphoric inversion, by which he means that the protagonists are often shown acting out figurative expressions literally.[26]

The *Lalebuch* has also been related to contemporary political rhetoric, with critics noting that when the wise men of Laleburg are faced with any predicament, they always get together to consider their options. This process, with its emphasis on unhurried consultation and a careful balancing of competing arguments, has been described as exemplifying "deliberation," understood as an ideal form of democratic decision-making. But the *Lalebuch* demonstrates how deliberation, if it is fools doing the deliberating, can lead a community into total insanity.[27]

The richness and diversity of interpretations reflect the fact that the *Lalebuch* is considered among the most outstanding examples of folly literature of the early modern period. The figure of the fool and the various depictions and meanings of folly that emerged in the late fifteenth century had a major impact on the *Lalebuch*'s conception and execution. The fool can take on various roles, which is why the Lalen have been seen as representatives of debates on models of society, regulatory policies, or gender relations. Scholars have applied different concepts of folly to the text. So it was, for example, that the book was linked with early modern discourses on mental afflictions and humoral pathology.[28]

While scholarship has concentrated on narrative strategies, conspicuously absent from the debate has been discussion of the connection between the *Lalebuch* and the foolish culture of the early modern period. There are, however, striking parallels between the fool societies and the Lalen, who, trying to establish a community for themselves, become something very much like a fool society. An awareness of the relationship between the text and foolish culture helps explain both certain features of the *Lalebuch* and the book's enthusiastic reception. The *Lalebuch* reflects the practices of foolish culture and reworks them into literature. Thus, it is valuable to explore the connection between the *Lalebuch*, foolish culture, and, in particular, fool societies.

Groups of men, especially young men, organized in societies with names alluding to folly, such as Abbaye de Conards (Abbey of Fools), are, as we have seen, an embodiment of the foolish culture of the late medieval and early modern period.[29] The purpose of these societies was to practice maleness by highlighting misconduct, especially in matters of marriage and sexual relations.

As Katja Gvozdeva has shown, folly as practiced in these male societies has two aspects. Members of the societies employ foolish symbols and dress up as fools, using the figure of the fool to represent and celebrate their maleness. At the same time, they expose other men as fools for failing to live by the social norms of the community. When members of these societies present themselves as fools, their behavior evokes a positive perception of folly. But the victims of the foolish performances of such societies are cast as fools in a negative sense of the term.[30]

The point at which the sages of Laleburg take the decision to simulate folly so as to be released from their contracts represents the book's most conspicuous shifting of gears, as it moves from backstory to story, from setup to performance. "Performance" is very apropos here, because the rest of the text, that is, the stories that constitute the action of the book, are repeatedly evocative of the foolish performances of the fool societies that were such an important feature of early modern European social life.

It is not only the antics of the Lalen that evoke those of the members of the fool societies but also the way the narrative presents them, as if to underscore the point that the Lalen, despite their good intentions, are the ultimate fool society—not just in the broad sense but in a narrow, technical sense. They are not just the mocked fools but the foolish mockers as well.

Thus it is that the preamble to the *Lalebuch* concludes by casting the town's absentee wise men as prospective cuckolds, that favorite target of fool society pranks. The women of Laleburg summon their men home with the explicit threat that, if they do not return, they may find *frembde Vögel* (strange birds, i.e., strangers) in their nests.[31] This threat brings the men back and leads them to come up with the idea of staging an elaborate foolish performance to avoid returning to their jobs. Their resolution to act the fool brings their wives' campaign to a successful conclusion.

The main section of the book, describing the sages' all-too-successful endeavors to behave like *Narren* (fools), which follows the introduction and is punningly demarcated with the heading "Narration," continues the evocation of foolish performances in the most explicit possible way.[32] There follows a passage in verse whose whole purpose is to present the impending prose narrative as if it were a theater piece, which it calls the *Lalespil* (Lale play). This elaborate metaphor once again draws attention to the parallel between what the wise men of Laleburg decide to do and the whole purpose of the fool societies, which is to play the fool. This theatrical metaphor has another function and an important one: it draws in the readers by casting them as extras, the spectators who were indispensable to the performances—the processions, the plays, the charivaris—of the fool societies. Significantly, the *Lalebuch*'s metaphorical little poem further reinforces the foolish performance analogy by addressing itself not to everyone but to *liebe Knaben* (dear lads), as one might address fellow members, or prospective fellow members, of one's fraternity or other young males, the demographic most involved in the foolish-performance scene:

> Now come here, dear lads
> Who want a place,
> To watch the Lale play, about to start;
> To each of you I will give a spot.[33]

The paradoxical purpose of the fool societies, promoting social cohesion through ritualized social disruption, seems reflected in the directive given to each of the "dear lads" in the rest of this poem to behave "according to the customs of the country," that is, to adhere to conventions or face being "turned into a Lale" (i.e., a fool) himself.[34]

Stage plays form one kind of foolish performance. The series of events relating to the appointment of fool society leaders, including abbots or princes of misrule, form another. These appointments, culminating in burlesqued quasi-ecclesiastical investiture ceremonies, often involved competitive speech making, a pattern into which the Laleburg mayoral election, decided by poetry slam, fits easily. The various offices within the fool societies were usually filled by candidates from the correspond- ing social strata in the wider society; however, in the spirit of topsy- turvy, leading officers might also come from the lower ranks. Thus, the victory in the mayoral ballot of the swineherd, the lowest of the low, is not incompatible with the spirit of the fool societies. And it seems plau- sible that his election is meant to parallel the appointment of officers of these societies, whose titles were so often mock-religious in character. Correspondingly, the swineherd's desire to improve his social standing by becoming mayor is depicted as a matter of exchanging his *Propstei* (priory, a lesser monastery) for an *Abtei* (abbey, a greater monastery).[35]

The emperor's visit is accompanied by further foolish performances, including his initial reception at the entrance to the town. The Lalen go out to meet him riding on hobbyhorses, as the members of fool so- cieties often did in their processions.[36] Just as fool societies sought and received charters from their city council confirming their privileges, so the emperor is petitioned by the Lalen and agrees to grant them his pro- tection in pursuing their foolish "new way of life."[37] By his decree, they are all appointed as his "amusing advisers," a synonym for court fools or jesters.[38]

The presentation of this remarkable charter has been seen as marking a break from a narrative point of view. In what precedes the emperor's visit, chapters are arranged sequentially to tell an unfolding story. In what follows, the chapters are loosely arranged in no particular order, simply offering illustrations of how the Lalen behave once they have made the switch from intentionally acting the fool to their new unself- conscious state of just being fools.[39]

At the start of the narration, the sages, setting out to be perceived as fools, seem to have deliberately built their town hall without windows to get their project off to "a laudable, notable beginning" so that their changed behavior might "become obvious and well-known very soon."[40] At what point they slipped into unconsciousness of their folly is never made clear. All that is clear is that they were bona fide fools by the time the emperor visited and certified them as "amusing advisers."[41]

Where the Lalen differ most conspicuously from the fool societies is in their focus. Their antics reflect less a preoccupation with sex, marriage, and maleness than with reason and wisdom, but lacking reason or insight will make a fool of you as easily as lacking male honor or male virtue. In the nonsequential later chapters of the book, the folly of individual Lalen is ridiculed rather like the folly of the individual men chosen as victims by the fool societies—the father, for example, who expects his son to receive a complete schooling in the time it takes him to get his horse shod.

Since the Lalen no longer remember their original plan to feign folly, they cannot serve as their own audience but depend on the reader to appreciate their foolishness. This transformation is handled in the imperial privilege, which addresses not only the Lalen and their decision to live a new life but also anyone who interacts with them, since "no one, be he from the higher or lower ranks, shall question, ridicule, condemn, boo, deride, lampoon, or vex them with regard to whatever they may begin or set out to do or may already have done, neither backwards nor forwards, in word or in deed, in one way or another."[42]

The punishment to which anyone who hears or reads the stories will almost inevitably become liable is clearly spelled out. Such a person will have to wear a fool's cap; the number of bells on it will be determined by the extent of the derision in which he holds the Lalen. When folly becomes second nature to the Lalen, or, as the *Lalebuch* puts it, their "new way of life," the reader becomes more than ever a protagonist.[43] Folly can only exist in relation to its opposite, or, as Foucault concluded, folly and reason enter a "perpetually reversible relationship which implies that all madness [French: *folie*] has its own reason by which it is judged and mastered, and all reason has its madness in which it finds its own derisory truth."[44]

In that the *Lalebuch* plays on the reciprocity of reason and folly, it muddies the boundaries between them, making a fool of anyone who laughs at the fools. Thus the book's conclusion: "The name and tribe of the Lalen of Laleburg perished and was extinguished but their silliness [*Thorheit*] and folly [*Narrey*], their most valuable legacy, remained, and it is possible that you and I share a fair amount of it. Who knows if that is not true?"[45]

The *Lalebuch* was an immediate success, and a pirated second edition appeared just a year later, in 1598, printed by Paul Brachfeld in Frankfurt am Main. Still anonymous, the book had undergone two significant changes. First, the name of the locale had changed from Laleburg to Schiltburg (Shieldtown), which it remained in nearly all subsequent editions, although it was increasingly spelled "Schildburg," which was the norm by the eighteenth century. If the replacement name, "Shieldtown," had humorous intent, the butt of the joke would seem to have been the foolish pretension, amounting to a craze, of the burgher class of the time, for adopting coats of arms, precisely the hallmark that had formerly distinguished the nobility and landed gentry from their urban compatriots.[46] The second big change was the substitution of a completely new preface, one far less steeped in classical learning, which opened the book to a much wider potential audience.

## "Pomponius Filtzhut" and His Modernized *Schildbürgerbuch*

The *Lalebuch* (1597) and its second edition, the *Schildbürgerbuch* (1598), were met with great success. At least three reprints of the *Schildbürgerbuch* appeared in 1598 alone, and Schildburg even more than Laleburg became instantly ensconced in the German imagination as synonymous with an imaginary place of collective folly. Between the late sixteenth century and the late eighteenth century, more than thirty editions of the *Lalebuch* or *Schildbürgerbuch* were published, generally with only minute differences to distinguish one from another—with two exceptions.[47]

An edition of 1603 introduced a second alternative title, the ironically intended *Grillenvertreiber* (The banisher of crickets). The German expression "crickets in the head" is roughly equivalent to "bats in the belfry." This version, and the few subsequent editions also appearing under the name *Grillenvertreiber*, changed the name of the locale once again, this time to the more obvious Witzenburg (*Witz*: wit, joke). Modifications of the *Schildbürgerbuch* in *Grillenvertreiber* are less linguistic or stylistic than they are related to the narrative. Chiefly, this means adding a sequel or second cycle of adventures that befall the protagonists after the events described in the *Schildbürgerbuch* have run their course, and an expanded *Grillenvertreiber* of 1605 adds a third set of tales.

The other markedly independent version of the *Schildbürgerbuch* to appear during the book's long run of great popularity dates from the late seventeenth century and serves as the basis for all the Old Yiddish editions. Its editor calls himself Pomponius Filtzhut (i.e., Pomponius Felt-Hat), a ridiculous-sounding combination, evoking first humanist and then hick. As a Latinate nom de plume of the kind beloved by scholarly authors from the Middle Ages through the eighteenth century, Pomponius, a name borne by such intellectual luminaries of ancient Rome as Titus Pomponius and Pomponius Mela, is an impeccable choice and closely connected to the content of the book.

This pen name suggests how much the *Schildbürgerbuch* reflects the foolish culture of the early modern period and particularly the rituals celebrated by fool societies, since the name evokes the Latin *pompa*, a parade, a key venue where the young men of the fool societies acted foolishly. As for the name Filtzhut, it is not an arbitrary choice but an allusion to the emperor's arrival in Schildburg, which must be one of the *Schildbürgerbuch*'s more memorable moments. The city fathers have gone out in procession on hobbyhorses and awaited him patiently, but finally the mayor feels compelled to relieve himself. No sooner has he prepared to do so than the imperial party arrives. With no time to adjust his clothing, he makes do by holding up his pants with one hand and doffing his felt hat with the other, until the emperor extends a hand and he is obliged to shake it, a predicament that he resolves by placing his *Filtzhut* between his teeth.

Virtually nothing is known about the person behind the name Filtzhut beyond what he says of his fictional identity in his *Schildbürger-buch* edition: that he is less solvent and less respectable than one might wish to be; that he is "half-noble" (a nonsense category; you are a member of the nobility or you are not); and that he was formerly employed as town clerk and night watchman of Schildburg. He is presumably the Pomponius Filtzhut credited with the authorship of a spoof almanac, known in two versions, one for "the year of the herring 1662" and the other for "the year of the herring 1694."[48]

The Filtzhut edition is, in a sense, the opposite of the *Grillenvertreiber*. While it alters almost every sentence of the original *Schild-*

*bürgerbuch*, the changes to the narrative are negligible.[49] The novelty of his version is all about language and style. Filtzhut gives the sixteenth-century Early New High German original a comprehensive makeover. His text is sometimes less wordy and has shorter sentences and an updated vocabulary. He selectively supplements the text with passages from the *Grillenvertreiber* and other sources, and from time to time, he underscores punch lines and increases the impact of certain descriptions by giving sobriquets to some of the book's unnamed characters, for example, calling one of them the "Pied Piper of Schildburg."[50]

Occasionally, however, the editor inserts some jocular ornamentation that may compromise details of the original narrative. Thus, when the women write to their husbands calling them back from their service at foreign courts, Filtzhut has the letter signed on their behalf by a certain "Urban Querlequitzsch, associate judge and church steeple rubber."[51] A man's signature, even if it is signed "in the name of all women," somewhat undermines the story line here.[52]

Another novelty of the Filtzhut version is the suite of thirteen woodcuts that it features. For a long time, it was believed that these made Filtzhut's the first illustrated edition in the *Lalebuch-Schildbürgerbuch* tradition, but it is very likely that the undated edition titled *Lalen-Buch*, printed sometime after 1678 with the pre-Filtzhut text and the "Filtzhut woodcuts," really precedes Filtzhut, so that its illustrations serve as the models for those in his and many subsequent versions, including all the known Yiddish editions.[53] The older supposition, that Filtzhut came first, was due to the misdating of Filtzhut's undated first edition, on the basis of the mistaken belief that what was thought to be the Yiddish first edition was printed in 1637; therefore, its German source must have appeared before then.[54]

The post-1678 *Lalen-Buch* draws special attention on the title page to the fact that it is "enhanced with illustrations." These are bigger and more meticulously executed than are their counterparts in the Filtzhut edition, most of which are smaller and rougher than those in the *Lalen-Buch* and mirror images of them. All of this strongly suggests that the *Lalen-Buch*'s images were the originals.

The extremely rare first known edition of the Filtzhut *Schildbürgerbuch* features neither date nor place of publication. The catalogue of the British Library, basing itself on the uncertain evidence offered by a separate work dated 1698 with which its *Schildbürgerbuch* is preserved in a period binding, supposes 1698 to be the likely year of printing of both of the books bound together.[55] The German version of Filtzhut appeared in at least four additional editions.[56] One of the earlier Pomponius Filtzhut editions must have served as the source text for what is evidently a lost first Yiddish edition, from which the extant Yiddish editions derive. And so we are ready to examine how and why the text made its way into Old Yiddish literature, as well as the nature and contents of the Yiddish versions.

4

# Gentile Fools Speaking Yiddish

*The* Schildbürgerbuch *for Jewish Readers*

When the Chelmites built themselves a synagogue, somehow they forgot to include any windows. Their solution is to shovel sunlight into sacks. An identical tale, albeit about a town hall, not a synagogue, had already been told in the German *Schildbürgerbuch* in 1598, but it was a century before Jews could read the story in Hebrew characters.

If the English and the Americans were, as the observation attributed to George Bernard Shaw has it, two nations divided by a common language, the same might be said of various nations and the local Jewish communities of the premodern Diaspora with whom they coexisted, sharing with one another a common vernacular. Thus, a text of the *Schildbürgerbuch* produced in 1727 exclusively for Jewish readers—the second surviving edition of this kind—advertises itself as translated word for word from "hoykh taytsh" (High German) into "yudish taytsh" (Jewish German).[1]

## Hoykh-Taytsh into Yudish-Taytsh

The German character of the Ashkenazic Jewish vernacular is stressed in all the various names for Yiddish that were present from the earliest surviving references to the language, in the sixteenth century, until the early twentieth century. Throughout this period, Yiddish was referred to by the majority culture as *Judendeutsch* (Jews' German) or *Jüdisch Deutsch* (Jewish German) and, among Jews themselves, mostly as *taytsh* (German) or *yudish taytsh* (Jewish German). Only after World War One was *taytsh* displaced from its position of primacy, and the word *Jüdisch*, *Yiddish* in Anglo-American phonetic spelling, made the transition from adjective to noun.[2]

This shift reflects a change of attitude that emerged, given prevailing nationalist tendencies, in some late nineteenth-century European Jewish intellectual circles. Among German Jewish scholars, Yiddish continued to be perceived as a form of German, and exponents of the *Wissenschaft des Judentums*, nineteenth- and early twentieth-century practitioners of the academic study of Jewish history and culture, explored and emphasized the illuminating similarities between Old Yiddish and Middle High German.

Among Jews in eastern Europe, however, and among Jews in western Europe and America who had roots in eastern Europe, where the dominant culture was Slavic rather than Germanic, *Jüdisch Deutsch* began to be perceived as essentially Jewish, not essentially German. Figures such as the political activist Nathan Birnbaum (1864–1937) in Vienna and the linguist Max Weinreich (1894–1969) in Vilna, both of whom were raised and educated in German-speaking environments, promoted the distinctiveness and importance of Yiddish as a language that was decidedly different from German.[3] Both of these theories—that Yiddish was essentially an extension of Middle and Early New High German and that Yiddish was essentially a fully independent language of the Jews—were ideologically motivated.

To consider the claim of the anonymous translator-publisher-bookseller of the 1727 Yiddish *Shildburger bukh*, that he had translated the *Schildbürgerbuch* word for word from High German to Jewish German, is to realize how problematic it is. The first problem is simply that this edition is not translated from the High German text. Instead, it has been shown to derive from a now-lost true first edition of the Yiddish *Shildburger bukh*, produced around the end of the seventeenth century, on which the first extant edition, printed in Amsterdam in the early eighteenth century, also depends.[4] A second problem is that neither is the Yiddish edition of 1727 a complete word-for-word translation of any German edition, nor can it have replicated verbatim the lost Yiddish edition.

More pressing, however, is the problem posed by the translator's use of the verb *iber-zetsen*, to translate, in his claim to have translated from High German to Jewish German. The changes between the Yiddish versions of the *Shildburger bukh* and the High German source, however, are linguistically so modest as to raise several questions. What did the publisher mean when he claimed to be offering his own translation? And why, given the extreme linguistic similarity between the German and Yiddish versions, should anyone have bothered to publish a Jewish edition? Why would anyone try to sell, or want to buy, a new edition of a popular classic that boasted of how similar it was to an earlier addition? The short answer to these questions is contained in the single additional word that the translator places in parentheses on the title page of this 1727 Yiddish edition. He says, "Dizes edeles un (kuryes) shen verk hobn mir iber-zetst oyz der hoykh taytsher (galkhes) shprakh oyf yudish taytsh" (we have translated this excellent, *kuryes* [curious, i.e., remarkable, rather than odd], and beautiful book from the High German *galkhes* language into Jewish German). By a popular convention of Old Yiddish typography, parentheses were used not to indicate parenthetical ideas but to allow printers to alert readers to the fact that the word thus highlighted required their special attention, typically as a word of non-Germanic origin. It might be from another European language, as here with the word "kuryes," a Romance loanword, or, as in the vast majority of cases, from Hebrew, as with the word "galkhes." The latter ultimately derives from the biblical Hebrew verb for "to shave," so as to mean, by allusion to the practice of tonsure, the clergy and, by extension, anything Christian. In practice, however, the word's application is much narrower, being used almost exclusively to denote the Latin alphabet.[5]

Therefore, in the 1727 Yiddish *Shildburger bukh*, the publisher's claim in full is to have translated the book "from the High German Christian language into Jewish German." The issue here is one of script: "Christian German" means German written or printed in Latin characters, that is, Roman script or type or, north of the Alps, Gothic script or type, while, in the first instance, "Jewish German" signifies simply text written or printed in a Hebrew hand or font. What the editor of the 1727 Yiddish *Shildburger bukh*, therefore, means by "translation" is what we might call a transcription, even though what he does to the text is far more than that.

Even more confusing than the Yiddish editor's use of the term "translation" is his use of the term "shprakh" (language) in his reference to the High German Christian language, for language is precisely not the issue. For this Yiddish editor-publisher and others of his profession and era, and for their prospective readers, the concept of translation can be (though need not be) limited to the concept of transliteration, for which a more specific-seeming term, *oys-shraybn*, may also be found in this period.

If transliteration seems more mechanical and less creative than translation, then that is not how the anonymous entrepreneur chooses to regard the matter. On the contrary, his selling points are, first, the intrinsic merit of what he explicitly identifies as the *galkhes*, Christian, original (meaning simply the Gentile original, for the book's content is secular in nature) and, second, his exaggerated claim for the absolute fidelity of his Yiddish text, "word for word," to the Christian source.

Just in case the title page has not sufficed to make a sale, the editor-publisher of the 1727 Yiddish *Shildburger bukh* reprises his pitch in more expansive style in the remarkable full-page blurb that he provides at the end of the book, a feature that has no counterpart in any other Yiddish or German edition of the *Schildbürgerbuch*. This end matter begins thus: "To fans [i.e., fans of reading, the reading public]: Gentlemen, I humbly urge you, young and old, one and all, to hurry up and buy this book, which I have carefully rendered word for word from *galkhes* German into Yiddish, for you will find in it a lot to please you."[6] To clinch the deal with a captivating coda, he now breaks (in the Yiddish original) into the more vigorous medium of rhyming couplets:

> You will find it most entertaining and an easy read.
> It will raise your spirits.
> Come on, people!
> Take a look at this book and snap it up.
> I am not going to be staying around forever.
> Any moment now, I will have to move on—first to one place, then
>     another.
> I have no choice; otherwise some other vendor will beat me to it—
> [And] I have invested a lot of time in this.
> Dear customers, please give it your consideration.
> How shall I exist if you do not?
> I simply must make every effort to sell it far and wide.[7]

As indicated earlier, the first of the two grounds for anticipating a demand for this edition was the matter of script. It may be hard to imagine that in Jewish communities established in central Europe for seven hundred years or more, most of their members were functionally illiterate in the omnipresent script of their surroundings, but all through the early modern period, most European Christians were functionally illiterate in this script as well.[8] More remarkable may be the fact that, with the access provided by Hebrew characters, most central European Jews of this period could read Germanic literature, whereas most Christians could not. The readership within the early modern Askhenazic population for which Old Yiddish literature was intended comprised all women and children plus most men, whose command of Hebrew was insufficient to let them understand books in that language.[9] For all readers, Old Yiddish literature served to bridge the gap between Hebrew, which was, in Chava Turniansky's succinct phrase, "a language the addressees knew how to read but did not understand," and German, "a language they understood but did not read."[10]

When Paulus Fagius (1504–1549), the Protestant reformer of Strasbourg and devoted Hebrew scholar, published the Pentateuch in Yiddish translation in two editions, one for Jewish and the other for Christian readers, both in 1544, he added an informative "preface for the Christian reader," in which he explains that Jews use a different script but says nothing about a different spoken language. Jews, he says simply, "do not read anything that is not written according to their manner."[11]

A century or a century and a half later, the picture was changing. The German language had undergone tremendous development, triggered by the much-wider dissemination of printed books, which were no longer the novelty or luxury item that they were in their first hundred years. Subsequent impetus for the development of the German language came chiefly from the popularity of Luther's German Bible. Thereafter, with Martin Opitz's (1597–1639) reforms relating to poetry and the establishment of language societies, *Hochdeutsch* (High German) became the general term for standard usage. *Hochdeutsch* as "pure German" started to diverge much more rapidly from conservative Yiddish, which Goethe calls "barockes Judendeutsch" (Baroque Jewish German), using the term "Baroque" to emphasize the old-fashioned character of eighteenth-century Yiddish.[12]

By the end of the seventeenth century, Standard German had emerged fully enough for characteristics typical of "Jewish German" speech to be discernible and considered worthy of scholarly comment as a feature separate from distinctions of script. Thus, in 1699, the Protestant Hebraist Johann Christoph Wagenseil (1633–1705), in his *Belehrung der*

*Jüdisch-Teutschen Red- und Schreibart* (Instructional manual on the Jewish-German manner of speaking and writing), stresses that only a tiny minority of Jews understood Latin and that the vast majority could not even read Latin-character text. He also complains of their unwillingness to do so, a disinclination, he suggests, that derives from their fear of the Latin alphabet as the medium of Christian faith.

Wagenseil makes his observation about the Latin language to point out that any theological arguments correcting "the Jewish errors" in the language of Christian scholarship will go unread by their theoretical target audience because "the Latin language is nowhere common among the Jews."[13] Regarding Jews' literacy, he adds, in language alluding to New Testament polemics, that "our Jews are, for the most part, acquainted with High German language; they cannot, however, read what is printed in common letters, but it is hidden from their eyes."[14]

Wagenseil rightly understands that the functional illiteracy in Western script of the vast majority of the central European Jews of his time represented a self-imposed exclusion, corresponding to a cultural "comfort zone." This was, presumably, a vestige of the disapprobation of Roman script that had its moment among the more stringently separatist rabbinic authorities in the Rhineland in the twelfth and thirteenth centuries before it fell by the halakhic wayside.[15]

A concern other than conversion to Christianity is invoked in the opposition to Western-script reading matter expressed by Efrayim bar Yuda Levi, called Gumprekht Levi, the author of *Ayn nay lid ouf der megile*, a rhymed Yiddish paraphrase of the biblical Book of Esther, printed in Amsterdam in 1649. In the preface, he complains about the young people who buy books printed in Roman characters and then commission him to transcribe ("oys-shraybn") the content of their purchases into Yiddish so they can read what they have bought.[16]

In context, however, this opposition turns out to be hardly opposition at all, at least not to Western script per se. First, there may be a self-interested aspect to Levi's critique; it is, after all, an "exordial topos," a stock feature, of paratexts to criticize alternative options to the literary product being peddled. Second, the author disparages "galkhes bikher," Christian-script publications, specifically on the grounds that they are full of "nibl pe" (smut).[17] This may say more about Levi's young customers and the selections to which they introduced him than about attitudes of Jewish teachers or leaders toward mastering Western script.

A number of other sources that seem clear-cut also need to be approached with caution. At the beginning of the seventeenth century, the Jewish convert to Lutheranism Christian Gerson, describing Jewish education in his book on the customs of what he calls "the Talmud Jews," states that Jewish children are deliberately not taught other languages, to steer them away from Christian books that might result in their conversion.[18] As late as the early nineteenth century, the proponent of radical Jewish Enlightenment Peter Beer (1758–1838) wrote that his moderate Enlightenment counterpart Herz Homberg (1749–1841) neither knew the German alphabet nor was allowed to read it, as reading any non-Jewish script was considered a *Kapitalverbrechen*, a capital crime.[19] Gerson and Beer are both leading polemicists, completely engaged with their respective campaigns, so that whatever they say is rhetorical in intent.

Despite a lack of apparent enforcement from within, let alone from without, script remained a cultural frontier for most Ashkenazic Jews, as well as for most other Jews throughout the eighteenth century, and in many places beyond. Some Jewish converts to Christianity continued to use the Hebrew alphabet years after their conversion, in, for example, Christian devotional manuals that they wrote for their personal use or, in the case of the sixteenth-century Elchanon Paulus of Prague, in letters he wrote in German to various Protestant theologians. Late in life, Paulus even applied to the Holy Roman Emperor Rudolf II for a grant to hire a secretary to help him produce his works of numerological interpretation, explaining that he was "not well-versed in writing," that is, writing Western script.[20] In the late eighteenth and early nineteenth centuries, as per Peter Beer's mockery of Herz Homberg, even the *maskilim*, defined by their commitment to spreading German Enlightenment values among the Jews of central and eastern Europe, were known for their own struggles learning to read German, which the brilliant Salomon Maimon (1754–1800) is described as only "kind of deciphering."[21]

While fostered by the priorities and limitations of the educational system and reinforced by tradition and sentiment, this reticence toward Western script was fraught with ambivalence. At the same time as Ashkenazic Jews of the early modern period seem to exhibit no great desire to read Western script, and evidently did not need to do so in order to get by, the demand typified by the availability of multiple editions in Yiddish of the *Schildbürgerbuch* indicates a substantial demand for access to Western literature for pleasure.

Thus, the claim made in the 1727 *Shildburger bukh* and elsewhere, that the text was translated verbatim from *galkhes*, the Christian-script original, was expected to be received as something highly attractive. It promised an authentic experience of the text as read by Jews' Christian neighbors. It was an invitation to take part in an encounter with the German Christian culture of the time but from a position of safety within the familiar confines of Hebrew type. It is as if such books promised unfiltered access, while their nature implied enough filtration to overcome any sense of taboo, thus fulfilling two contradictory needs.

The body of Old Yiddish literature can be divided by source into three categories. First, there are translations and adaptations of Hebrew originals. Second, there are original Yiddish compositions, often prompted by current events. Third, there are translations and adaptations of European originals, nearly all of which find their source in German literature, as in the case of the Yiddish *Shildburger bukh*.[22] Old Yiddish literature uses, and sometimes fuses, everything from talmudic to Arthurian legends. Scholars of German have overlooked original works of Yiddish literature and those based on Hebrew sources. Scholars of Yiddish have tended to dismiss the European strand in this threefold cord, seeing it as un-Jewish and thus uninteresting but thereby underrating the implications of its existence and its potential as an aid to the study of Jewish cultural history.

The crucial precondition for the proliferation of Yiddish literature with German sources was the invention of moveable type in the mid-fifteenth century. Printing of texts both in Hebrew and in the vernacular using Hebrew characters resulted in a major transformation of Jewish cultural life, paralleling the transformation of the cultural life of European Christians, with both groups similarly affected by the "knowledge explosion" that accompanied increasingly inexpensive access to books and that finally made private ownership common.[23]

But while Jews were often able to print during the sixteenth, seventeenth, and eighteenth centuries, they were far less often able to do so on their own account because local authorities allowed only Christians to own printing operations. The result was frequent close collaboration between Jews, Christians, and converts on the business, editorial, and technical aspects of the trade, with all the cultural cross-pollination this collaboration encouraged. Another consequence of this new mass-production of texts was an economic imperative for wide distribution. This economic reality, which gave a strong impetus toward starting to standardize conventions of written Yiddish all over Europe, could hardly be captured better than it is in the plaintive pitch, quoted earlier, of the itinerant bookseller-publisher of the 1727 Yiddish *Shildburger bukh*.

## The Yiddish Editions of the *Schildbürgerbuch*

Sometime around 1700, the first surviving Yiddish *Shildburger bukh* appeared in print. Published in Amsterdam, it bore the title *Shildburger zeltsame unt kurtsvaylige geshikhte*, the "strange and entertaining stories of the Schildburgers," and the more flamboyant subtitle *Vunder zeltsame kurtsvaylige lustige un rekht lekherlikhe geshikhte un datn der velt bekantn Shild burger* (Wondrous, entertaining, and amusing stories and accounts of the world-famous people of Schildburg). This edition was a literal rendition of what was apparently the very recent version of the *Schild-bürgerbuch* in modernized German prepared by "Pomponius Filtzhut."

The 1727 version, the second extant Yiddish edition, also printed in Amsterdam, bears a similar title: *Vunder zeltsame kurtsvaylige lustige unt rekht lakherlikhe geshikhte unt daten der velt bekantn shild burger* (Wonderful, strange, entertaining, and highly amusing stories and accounts of the world-famous people of Schildburg). An abridgment of the 1727 version constitutes a third Yiddish edition, printed in 1777 in Offenbach, next to Frankfurt. A fourth edition appeared in Fürth, next to Nuremberg, in 1798, but this is merely an exact reprint of the third edition.[24]

The British scholar Arnold Paucker proposed that the first two surviving Yiddish editions both draw on a possible earlier Yiddish version of Filtzhut's German edition.[25] This edition could not, however, date from much earlier than around 1700 if Filtzhut's makeover of the original text appeared for the first time in 1698. As Paucker shows, the 1700 and 1727 editions contain the same tiny peculiarities not found in any German sources. For example, the editor of the German text, this "Pomponius Filtzhut," who had created a bewildering image of himself

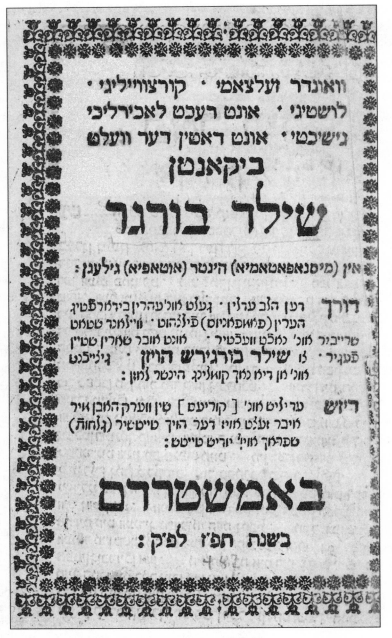

Title page from the Yiddish *Shildburger bukh* edition of 1727, Universitäts- und Landesbibliothek Sachsen-Anhalt in Halle (Saale)

by juxtaposing irreconcilably highbrow- and lowbrow-sounding components to form his nom de plume, had added to that confusion by stating his occupations as town clerk, night watchman, and *Schornsteinfeger*, or chimneysweep. In both Yiddish editions, however, he has been promoted to "ober shoren shteyn feger"—head chimneysweep.[26] Similarly, whereas the typical Schildburger is introduced ironically in the German text as having "a good memory and not a bad intellect,"[27] both Yiddish versions dispense with the irony, saying rather that the people of Schildburg possessed the "weak intellect of a cat."[28] These differences are probably not coincidental.

The Yiddish edition of 1727 is, however, as Paucker also shows, sometimes closer to the German Filtzhut text than to the Yiddish edition of around 1700, which proves that it cannot be based only on the 1700 edition and leads to his supposition of a common source in the form of a lost first edition. Where, for instance, the letter on behalf of the women of Schildburg is said to have been signed by the silly-sounding Urban Querlequitzsch, the Yiddish edition of 1700 gives his occupation as "kirkhen shrayer" (church crier), whereas the edition of 1727 gets closer to the German original by calling him a "kerkhen shayrer" (church scrubber).[29] Neither of the Yiddish translators, however, records the nonsense profession that Filtzhut actually attributes to him: "Kirchthurm-Scheurer" (church-tower scrubber).[30]

Textual indicators aside, the first and second extant Yiddish editions share a pictorial clue strongly suggesting that both are derived from a common source rather than that the second derives from the first. Both Yiddish editions feature nearly identical versions of the suite of woodcuts found illustrating German editions of the *Schildbürgerbuch* at least as far back as one printed under the title *Das lustige und lächerliche Lalen-Buch* sometime after 1678. When printed, a woodblock produces the mirror image of the scene carved on it. Therefore, an artist who, for a new edition, reproduces the illustrations that accompanied a previous edition ideally ought to create a new block showing the scene he wishes to reproduce in reverse, a skilled and expensive operation and a practice usually restricted to high-end publications.

For cheaply produced books such as these, it was normal to copy the images as they appeared and not worry that the original image would be reversed when reprinted. The images in the 1727 Yiddish *Shildburger*

ראש צעהנטי קאפיטל

וויא דיא שילדבורגר ראט שלאגטן ראש ליכט אין איז
ראט הויז צו טראגן׃      אוני׳ דיא זון מיט אלירלייא גיצייג
דורך עקסעמפיל אין דז ראט הויז מיט פיל מיא טראגטן ׃

Carrying the sunlight into the town hall, woodcut from the Yiddish *Shildburger
bukh* edition of 1727, Universitäts- und Landesbibliothek Sachsen-Anhalt in
Halle (Saale)

*bukh,* however, face the same direction as those in the Yiddish edition
of around 1700, so we should assume that they were not copied from it.
Furthermore, the 1727 edition features one of the images from the original German suite, showing the Schildburgers trying to carry the sunlight
indoors, that is missing, presumably by oversight, from the Yiddish edition of circa 1700.

It would hardly be surprising if an earlier Yiddish edition existed
and was lost without material trace, as appears to be the case, since few
copies of all four extant editions survive and nearly all of those that do
survive show signs of heavy use such as dirt stains and missing pages,
indicating that multiple readers handled these books. The paradoxical
scarcity of such mass-market publications is further exacerbated by the
fact that such books of popular entertainment were not, for a long time,
of interest to most collectors.

Greeting the emperor, woodcut from the German Filtzhut edition of the *Schild-bürgerbuch*, British Library

Greeting the emperor, woodcut from the Yiddish *Shildburger bukh* edition of 1727, Universitäts- und Landesbibliothek Sachsen-Anhalt in Halle (Saale). The woodcut shows the Schildburgers mounted on hobbyhorses to receive the emperor, while the mayor relieves himself on the dunghill. The Yiddish edition reproduces the mayor's bare behind but suppresses the feces on display in the German original.

There is little evidence of the circulation history of the Yiddish *Shild-burger bukh*. One or another edition of this title is among the 55 Yiddish books and 295 Hebrew books listed on a broadside advertising books for sale at the bookstore of the Amsterdam Hebrew printing firm of Proops around 1760.[31] For only four copies of the Yiddish *Shildburger bukh* is anything known of their provenance. Two of the most ambitious and wide-ranging Jewish collectors of the eighteenth and nineteenth centuries, respectively, David Oppenheim (1664–1736), chief rabbi of Bohemia, and Leeser Rosenthal (1794–1868), a Polish Jew who settled in Hanover, each had in his possession a copy of the first edition. Rosenthal owned a copy of the 1727 edition as well. A third copy of the 1700 edition, now in Vienna, was owned by a Christian collector, the eighteenth-century scientist Gottfried Christoph Beireis (1730–1809), in the Protestant university town of Helmstedt in central Germany.[32]

Thus, copies of the Amsterdam editions of 1700 and 1727 were to be found in private collections across the German-speaking lands through Lower Saxony and as far as Bohemia, although there is no evidence as to whether these collectors acquired their copies locally. On the basis of the evidence provided by the publisher's blurb of 1727, Proops's advertisement, and the places of printing of the 1700 and 1727 editions (both Amsterdam) and those of 1777 (Offenbach) and 1798 (Fürth), it is only possible to feel confident that, at some point during the eighteenth century, copies of the Yiddish *Shildburger bukh* must have been for sale in the city of Amsterdam, the city of Frankfurt (served by Offenbach), the villages of Franconia (served by Fürth), and other locations.

Scholarly attention to the content of the Yiddish versions of the *Schildbürgerbuch* started slowly, but the existence of such versions was noted in bibliographies from early on. The principal early modern Hebrew bibliographer, the Hamburg Lutheran pastor Johann Christoph Wolf (1683–1739), mentions the edition of around 1700, printed with no date in Amsterdam, in the fourth volume of his *Bibliotheca Hebraea*, published in 1733.[33] The next person to mention a Yiddish version is one of the earliest scholars to write on the German Schildburg tradition, Christian Schöttgen of Dresden, who examined the Yiddish *Shildburger bukh* and categorized it as a corrupted text. Schöttgen, a notable Hebraist, was the author of a highly erudite but mock-serious book-length defense of the Saxon town of Schilda from the unjustifiable charge that it was the real place that the author had in mind when he called his fictional community Schildburg.

"After I had finished this little study of mine," Schöttgen writes, "a scholar told me that he had discovered in Wolf's *Bibliotheca Hebr[aea]* ... that the Jews had printed a *Schildbürger Buch* in Judeo-German characters." He continues, "I sought out a copy and found one printed in octavo with the Jewish date of [5]487, corresponding to 1727 A D. But when I had someone fluent in Yiddish look it over, it turned out that the Jews had worked from the new ruined version with all the alterations that I described in chapter seven."[34] According to Schöttgen, then, the Yiddish Schildburg tradition was regrettably irrelevant as a textual witness because it derived not from the 1598 original *Schildbürgerbuch* but from Filtzhut's modern-language version, which Schöttgen detested.[35]

While Germany in the early eighteenth century was a last outpost of pervasive Christian Hebraism and the positive academic interest in Jews that went with it, by the nineteenth century, Yiddish was either ignored in the context of the newly founded discipline of German studies or explicitly excluded as a reflection of increasingly fashionable academic antisemitism. Not only was the Yiddish language generally ignored, but so also was Yiddish literature, including Yiddish literature with German sources, such as the *Shildburger bukh*. The latter tended to elicit a quite different reaction in the nineteenth century from that which it had elicited earlier. Whereas in the eighteenth century such books had been treated as if their existence were a matter of course, many nineteenth-century authors seem surprised to discover the existence of Yiddish literature altogether and Yiddish literature based on German texts in particular.[36]

Friedrich Heinrich von der Hagen (1780–1856), a cofounder of the field of German studies and among the first professors to teach medieval literature in Germany, was one of the few scholars of his time to touch on the subject of Old Yiddish, and in 1853 he gave a talk on "Die romantische und Volks-Litteratur der Juden in Jüdisch-Deutscher Sprache" (The romantic and popular literature of the Jews in Judeo-German). In this talk, he at least mentions the existence of a Yiddish *Shildburger bukh*, but, while including Old Yiddish literature as part of the history of German literature, he assigns it to an inferior position based on its "ignorant presentation and feral language."[37] The scholar Hermann Lotze

(1817–1871) felt obliged to assert that the idea of publishing a series of Old Yiddish texts had merit and would result in more than merely a bibliophilic curiosity item.[38]

By and large, though, mid-nineteenth-century practitioners of German studies disregarded the existence of Yiddish versions of the texts they were studying, at the very same time as the early exponents of academic Jewish studies, especially Moritz Steinschneider (1816–1907), the Berlin-based "prince of bibliographers," were busy publishing information about the existence of just such Yiddish books.

Steinschneider was passionately interested in Jewish vernaculars, and although he routinely uses the terms "Judeo-German" and "Jargon" (a way of referring to Yiddish widely used by Jews of his time, not necessarily with pejorative intent), he is also happy to refer to it as a language in its own right.[39] He includes the 1700 edition of the Yiddish *Shildburger bukh* in his bibliography of *Jüdisch-Deutsche Literatur* (Judeo-German literature) printed in installments in the influential German journal *Serapeum* during 1848 and 1849. In his many contributions to this journal, he describes item by item the incomparable Old Yiddish holdings of the Bodleian Library, the final destination of the private library of David Oppenheim of Prague; in doing so, he locates a copy of an edition of the Yiddish *Shildburger bukh* in an institutional library for the first time.[40]

Only a few years later, the criminologist Friedrich Christian Benedict Avé-Lallemant (1809–1892) included the first and only modern reprint of any portion of a Yiddish *Shildburger bukh* in his four-volume work *Das deutsche Gaunerthum* (The German underworld), published in 1858–1862.[41] Avé-Lallemant's interest is philological, not polemical, and it is in that spirit that he argues for the influence of Yiddish on the vocabulary of Rotwelsch, German thieves' cant. He presents a rich selection of Old Yiddish texts as supporting evidence, among them the seventeenth chapter of the *Shildburger bukh* according to its 1700 edition, which he prints in Yiddish type, adding footnotes in German to gloss words derived from Hebrew. His only negative remark about the Yiddish *Shildburger bukh* concerns the editor's "lavish" use of punctuation and his habit, moreover, of using it in a "completely senseless way."[42]

The attitude of the few Christian scholars who between the sixteenth and the mid-nineteenth centuries did engage with Yiddish literature from German sources is without animosity. Even the disapproval of the Yiddish *Till Eulenspiegel* emanating from Callenberg's Institutum Judaicum at Halle was a function of the antipathy of the Hallensian Pietists toward the profanity of the German literary tradition that it represented. But this early modern open-mindedness weakens as the nineteenth century progresses, and Old Yiddish literature with Germans sources fares as badly with the altered tone of the late nineteenth century as any other manifestation of Yiddish.

Discussing the source of the Yiddish *Shmuelbukh*, which he wrongly believed to be of German origin, Friedrich Zarncke (1825–1891), the well-known professor of German at Leipzig, took the opportunity to express his view that "all Yiddish adaptations of German literature have the same shoddy and crude character."[43]

Quoting Zarncke approvingly, Ernst Jeep (1867–1936) formed his own highly negative view of the Yiddish *Shildburger bukh*. In his monograph on the German *Schildbürgerbuch* and the sequels or imitations it inspired, he charges that the author of the Yiddish edition that he consulted, that of 1727, perpetrates an "Unwarheit," a falsehood, in claiming to offer a word-for-word translation, since there are copious additions, deletions, and changes.[44] As for the original feature of the 1727 edition most visible at a cursory glance, its brief promotional end matter in verse, Jeep attacks it as "shameless hucksterism."[45]

Jeep becomes even more aggressive in discussing the editor's tendency to spice things up with rhyming couplets, not just in the advertising copy at the back of the book but all through the text. He pathologizes this tendency, condemning it as "Reimwut" (rhyming mania).[46] "Our conclusion as to this translation," Jeep continues, "can only be that it is a slapdash piece of work—no more than some bookseller's opportunistic attempt to make money."[47] Nor is this Jeep's last word. He goes on to allege unpardonable abridgment, although he identifies just two small omissions (one an idiom mildly pejorative vis-à-vis Jews), on the strength of which he claims that the book exhibits the "irresponsible slovenliness" evidently characteristic of all Jewish-German literature.[48]

It is striking how little time Jeep can have devoted to the Yiddish text, even though he spent years studying the German editions of the *Schildbürgerbuch*. He seems unable to fit the Yiddish versions into his research on the textual tradition of a book that he perceives as a product of a single-language German past. His hostility is echoed by the Jewish German scholar Walter Hesse (born 1906) in his dissertation *Das Schicksal des Lalebuchs in der deutschen Literatur* (The fate of the *Lalebuch* in German literature, 1929).[49] In this work, he judges that the Yiddish text shows "an astonishing degree of corruption" and "lies on every page," by which he simply meant that it was not exactly the word-for-word translation it claimed to be.[50] Still more extraordinary, Hesse never even laid eyes on a Yiddish *Shildburger bukh* but relied entirely on Jeep.[51]

The Yiddish *Shildburger bukh* received only slight attention during the twentieth century as well. During the early decades, a Jewish commentator, Meier Schüler, who taught at Frankfurt's Samson-Raphael-Hirsch-Schule and produced several scholarly articles on medieval French and Old Yiddish literature, followed Jeep in identifying a tendency of the Yiddish *Shildburger bukh* to eliminate anti-Jewish remarks.[52] Schüler added a second tendency of the Yiddish, noting the elimination of obscenities. But this applies only to the fourth edition (1798), the one he consulted, and the third (1777), which it reprints and which had already sanitized the earthy Yiddish edition of 1727.

Schüler seems in his conclusion intent on deferring to Jeep's "establishment" opinion and then trying to temper it with a hint of apology: "Many stylistic shortcomings characterize the book as work cranked out at high speed. But the popular style of the original is preserved and a special flavor is imparted by a multitude of Hebrew words, so that the changes noted should not be regarded as a discredit to the translator."[53]

Arnold Paucker, in his unpublished doctoral dissertation of 1959 and in two articles, one in German and the other in Yiddish, was the first to survey all extant Yiddish editions of the *Shildburger bukh*. His findings, accordingly, are more finely calibrated than those of earlier authors.[54] The bulk of Paucker's contribution consists in the synoptic arrangement of divergent passages from the four Yiddish editions he examined. While his analysis of the Yiddish *Shildburger bukh* is more thorough than Jeep's or Schüler's, his conclusions are not very different.

Thus, as to whether the editions of the Yiddish *Shildburger bukh* are corruptions, transcriptions, or adaptations, Paucker's answer, like Schüler's, seems ambivalent. This conflicted feeling is especially evident in his treatment of the most distinctive of the Yiddish versions, the second edition of 1727, a book that, he seems to think, often gets things wrong and whose fondness for rhyming is degenerate. But Paucker is not unrelentingly critical; he feels that certain of the Yiddish editor's additions accord well with the protagonists' foolishness and are "sometimes not without wit or originality," while, from his perspective, the edition's blurb at the back, reviled by Jeep, seems "highly amusing."[55] Conversely, the versification, which the Yiddish editor is said by Paucker to have added everywhere, is "from a literary point of view, worthless," a problem compounded by the fact, so Paucker maintains in his Yiddish article, that "the major feature of this edition is the author's weakness for rhyming."[56] Since Paucker last published on the subject in the early 1970s, the Yiddish *Shildburger bukh* has barely been mentioned in scholarship, be it in Yiddish studies or in German studies, despite the extraordinarily large number of studies of the German *Schildbürgerbuch* that started appearing in the 1970s.

* * *

The content and structure of all forty-five chapters of the book remain the same in the Yiddish editions of 1700 and 1727 as in Filtzhut's German *Schildbürgerbuch*. Neither the beginning nor the end, that is, neither the Schildburgers' initial misguided choice of folly as a way out of their collective marital predicament nor the disastrous end that befalls their town, undergoes significant alteration. All forty-five chapters remain, in a basic sense, much as they were all the way back to the *Lalebuch* of 1597. The Yiddish edition of 1727 changes some of the individual stories' punch lines, but structurally it is much like the original.[57]

The second edition, along with the third and fourth, which prove to be more like slightly bowdlerized abridgments of the second edition than new editions in their own right, have more Hebraisms and fewer Christian references than does the first surviving edition of 1700. They also take a much freer approach to Filtzhut, often paraphrasing rather than reproducing his words.

The variations, abridgments, and occasional minor additions in all four editions can be attributed to one of three distinct tendencies. First, many of the variations are a result of differences between the Standard German and the Yiddish of the time and involve no attempt to change the meaning. Second, some changes are cultural, since the German *Schildbürgerbuch* is set in an explicitly Christian context. As with many other books translated from German into Yiddish, some of the Christian religious allusions, along with some violations of Jewish law ascribed to the protagonists, are toned down or avoided, even though these characters are not Jews themselves. Third, some alterations to the German text are introduced for literary or comic effect but with no specific Jewish motivation or connotation. Even though the Yiddish edition of 1700 is more than any of the later versions a mere transcription from German Blackletter type into the similarly Gothic Hebrew typeface almost entirely reserved for printing in Old Yiddish, it, too, is not mere transcription but translation. What makes it so are the frequent alterations in linguistic structural elements required to let the German text function as Yiddish. Paucker has stressed that the 1700 edition "adheres . . . fully, often literally, to the German text," but, although the 1700 *Shildburger bukh* usually preserves the German word order and thus differs in style from most Old Yiddish texts of the period, it nevertheless introduces several traits typical of Old Yiddish as opposed to Standard German.[58] The edition of 1727 goes further and transforms the text into a more colloquial Yiddish.[59]

Another trait of the Yiddish translations is that they use fewer Greek and Latin words than the German editions do. The heavily humanistic sixteenth-century original employs many quotations from and allusions to Greek and Latin philosophers, some of which were replaced or deleted by Filtzhut before any Yiddish translator got to work on the text. Thus, the Yiddish *Shildburger bukh* unwittingly continues a trend begun by the most far-reaching German adaptation of that time, produced in response to the need to adapt the century-old *Schildbürgerbuch* to the changes in taste and culture over that period among central European Christians.

For example, the 1700 Yiddish edition contains only the Yiddish translation, not the Latin original, of the line from Horace's *Ars poetica*, "Parturiunt montes, nascetur ridiculus mus" (the mountains groan and a ridiculous mouse is born), which is quoted in Latin and German in the German *Schildbürgerbuch* editions.[60] A few Latin words or phrases, however, still survive in Latin in Yiddish transcription in the Yiddish editions, like "suma sumarum" (*summa summarum*, in summary).[61] The reworked Yiddish edition of 1727, however, omits some Latin words and phrases found in the first Yiddish edition of 1700, such as "fide" (*vide*, see), "oudi" (*audi*, hear), and "oudi confeni" (*audi conveni*, hear and accept).[62]

Sometimes the 1700 Yiddish edition aids its intended readership by spelling out what appear as abbreviations in the German source, such as when the women of Schildburg greet their husbands with the less-than-friendly German salutation "in the name of all, etc.," a truncated expression that the Yiddish completes correctly as "in the name of all devils."[63]

Changes introduced in the Yiddish text may be less far-reaching in intent than they first appear and may be motivated by a desire to simplify or clarify the meaning for readers rather than any other agenda, such as shielding them from too much Christianity. Thus, when the Yiddish versions of 1700 and 1727 excise from the German original all mentions of the name of Sankt Velten (Saint Valentine) and replace it with the words "puts felten," this might look like a case of uncharacteristic bigotry, not just eliminating the invocation of someone holy to Christians but replacing it with something profane, since *Potz Velten* or *Potz Felten* is a popular curse in Middle and Early New High German, something like "Damn!" or "Damn you!" *Potz* came to function as a meaningless intensifier, indicating only that the word following it was an exclamation. *Velten* or *Felten*, apart from being a contracted form of the name Valentine, is considered a form of Valant (or Falant), a medieval German name for the Devil.[64] Some superstitious or genteel Christians of the time substituted the words *Sankt Velten*, "St. Valentine," in their speech when what they meant was *Potz Velten*, creating a "minced oath," like the substitution of "Darn!" for "Damn!" The Yiddish substitution, therefore, of "puts velten" whenever "Sankt Velten" occurs in Filtzhut's German text does not invert the meaning of the Christian original. It just spells it out unambiguously.[65]

The Yiddish editions of 1700 and 1727 differ somewhat in the extent of their use of Hebraisms. The 1700 edition uses about 300 Hebrew-derived words, while the 1727 edition has around 380.[66] These Hebraisms generally correspond to the Hebrew-derived words that most commonly peppered the everyday speech of the central European Jews of the period in preference to their German synonyms. Thus, the word for king becomes "meylekh," bride "kale," bridegroom "khosn," neighbors "shkheynim," finally "lesof," fear "moyre," war "milkhome," to make peace "sholem makhn," maybe "efsher," and pigs "khazeyrim."

Whereas sometimes Hebrew-derived words replace their German-derived equivalents systematically, in other cases both forms coexist indifferently in the Yiddish editions. A priest, for example, *Pfaffe* in German, may appear in the Yiddish as "pfaf" or as the Hebrew-derived "galekh." For wisdom, a highly programmatic word for the *Schild-bürgerbuch*, the Yiddish employs the Germanic and Hebraic synonyms "veyzhayt" and "khokhme" interchangeably throughout. Sometimes, the two synonyms, one Hebraic and the other not, are used together for ironic emphasis. Thus, the excellent memory of the Schildburgers is praised, in the 1727 and later Yiddish editions, as "a good *memorium* or *zikorn*."[67]

Sometimes, a word is represented by a Hebraic term in one context and a Germanic one in another. Hence, birds are generally referred to in the Yiddish *Shildburger bukh* by the Hebrew word *oyfes*, while the Germanic equivalent, *fegel*, is used more rarely. In such cases, there may be explanatory circumstances, such as when it occurs in the phrase "strange birds in your own nest," where the choice of word for "bird" is not arbitrary but results from the desire to invoke a familiar German idiom, this "strange birds" being a popular euphemism for one's spouse's lovers.[68] On the other hand, another German avian metaphor, that of a "bird trimmed and sheared," meaning a barefaced liar, a con man, survives into the 1700 Yiddish edition but is axed in 1727 in favor of the presumably more familiar "shpits bub," a rascal.[69]

As mentioned earlier in connection with the word *galkhes*, the Yiddish edition of 1727, as a signal to the reader of the Yiddish text and in line with standard practice in Old Yiddish printing, puts parentheses or brackets around Hebrew-derived words. Some French- or Latin-derived words and proper nouns are bracketed as well.[70] Very occasionally, a German word will appear within brackets, probably indicating the translator's or printer's perception of the relative rarity of the word's use in Yiddish—"ze" (German: *See*, "lake"), for example, on one occasion and "zel" (German: *Seele*, "soul") on another, the Hebrew *neshome* being a commoner word for "soul" in Yiddish.[71]

The Yiddish "shultis," corresponding to the German *Schultheiß*, meaning a mayor or magistrate, was probably bracketed on account of not being a familiar term everywhere, for example, in the Netherlands. These Yiddish translations exhibit other characteristics that look like reflections of the Dutch milieu in which the 1700 and 1727 editions were produced. These include the name changes in the Yiddish from the German "Klaus" to "Klas" (Klaas) and from "Greta" to "Grit."[72]

While the language becomes Jewish in the Yiddish *Shildburger bukh*, the protagonists—the wise men of Schildburg—do not become Jewish. They do, however, become less explicitly Gentile. The adaptations of the *Schildbürgerbuch* for a Jewish audience elicit only a mild form of "Judaization," not reworking the text in any substantial way but just omitting words or phrases that may well grate on Jewish ears—whether these involve Jewish stereotypes, offend Jewish mores, or, most often, are just gratuitously Christian. This process of cleanup becomes more far-reaching with each successive edition through to the third edition of 1777, reprinted a final time in 1798.

In the German original, the heroes, or at least protagonists, eat pork; they also visit the bathhouse on Saturday. In the 1700 Yiddish edition, they are still allowed to eat pork, although on one occasion the word "Speck" (bacon) is suppressed and replaced by the word "fet" (fat).[73] The people of Schildburg do not, however, set a bad example to their Jewish readers by bathing on the Sabbath but are represented as doing so on Sunday instead.[74] In the 1727 Yiddish edition, however, the "nice fat pig" that the Schildburgers convert into their giant communal sausage is replaced with "a nice fat cow," while an allegorical mention of a herd of pigs is converted into a less disturbing reference to a flock of geese.[75] The version of 1777 completes the job by deleting the one remaining hint of pork consumption that had made it into the previous edition. But this purging of alien practices is not in any way systematic; in all the Yiddish editions, the Schildburgers still go to church, listen to a sermon, and elect as their mayor an easygoing swineherd bearing the aptronym "Zoy Frid Ledel," which translates as something like "Mr. Pigpeace Loafer."[76]

Some of the added content in the Yiddish *Shildburger bukh* plays on the divergences between Standard German and Yiddish. Thus, when the people of Schildburg decide to elect a mayor according to the outcome of a poetry slam, they determine that the candidate, or contestant, who can keep on rhyming the longest will be victorious. Fortunately for the swineherd, he has a wife with a talent for doggerel, although the idea that she might have stood for election in her own right was one step too far even in progressive Schildburg. She excels, however, as her husband's "speechwriter," although the rhymes that she comes up with are always derogatory self-descriptions, for example, her decision to rhyme "Katrayn" (Catharein, her name) with "shvayn" (pig).[77]

When the woman's dim-witted husband is called on to deliver his poem, according to an added twist that appears only in Yiddish (and, clearly, it would not work in any other version), he can no longer recollect exactly how this couplet ends. Searching his profoundly inadequate memory, he does manage to remember that a pig is involved, but rather than letting his wife's name serve as a clue to help him retrieve the Germanic word "shvayn," he retrieves instead the Hebraic equivalent, "khazer."[78] If it ever dawns on him that the Hebrew-derived Yiddish word does not rhyme with "Katrayn," he does not allow the fact to deter him.

In the German versions and in the first Yiddish edition, even the swineherd's wife reaches the limit of her poetic powers when challenged to produce not just rhyming couplets but an *aaaa* quatrain. Prompting her husband, she succeeds in finding lines ending in "herayn" (herein), "Katrayn" (her name), and "shvayn" (pig), but the best ending she can manage for her fourth and final line is the word "most" (grape juice).[79] The joke here is that she could so obviously just as easily have referred to *vayn* and have thereby made her little rhyme work. The Yiddish editor of 1727 tweaks the story so as to let both husband and wife stay true to character, she consistently competent and he consistently incompetent. Thus, she is perfectly successful in producing a valid quatrain, with the lines ending "herayn," "Katrayn," "shvayn," and "vayn." It is Katrayn's husband, the future mayor, who messes it all up, so unable to remember or reconstruct his wife's four lines of doggerel that he manages to ruin not just the last couplet—as Katrayn does in the German original—but the first couplet as well.[80]

Here, as elsewhere, the Yiddish editor of 1727 fully comprehends and remains entirely faithful to the original intent of the *Schildbürgerbuch*, the message in this case being that the biggest fool wins. Not only is the occupation of swineherd, by convention, about as uncerebral and unprestigious as it gets, but thanks to the Yiddish editor of 1727, this swineherd is even more completely subordinate to his wife than he was in the original. And in early modern foolish culture, there is no fool like a henpecked husband.

The Yiddish editor of 1727 has an unmistakable objective in mind: to try and crank up the *Schildbürgerbuch*'s 130-year-old humor, an effort to which he applies himself with more consistency and determination than any previous editor of the book, in Yiddish or German. It always makes sense, therefore, to wonder whether any nonlinguistic change in the 1727 Yiddish edition should be attributed to the editor's clear wish to poke his readers in the ribs just a little more sharply than the text from which he was working.

Most of his changes improve the text by suppressing contradictions, adding creative detail, or supplementing the modest number of rhyming couplets in the original text. It is all small stuff in the greater scheme of things, but even so, this edition makes many more substantive changes to Filtzhut's German edition of 1698 than Filtzhut made to the 1598 first edition of the *Schildbürgerbuch*.[81]

Despite little hard information about the anonymous Yiddish editor of 1727, clearly he was thoroughly at home in foolish culture. So, too, was the anonymous editor of the 1698 revised German text on which the Yiddish versions depend, who introduces himself as "the seminoble, the honorable, Sir Pomponius Filtzhut, former town clerk, night watchman, and chimneysweep." Not only has the Yiddish editor entered fully into the spirit and meaning of the *Schildbürgerbuch*, but he has also gotten Pomponius's number as an "unreliable narrator" and has taken to him as a character, expanding his role and having him introduce first-person narratives with such phrases as "I, the town clerk." He even adds a little homage to Pomponius's unreliability at the end of the book, where, after the great conflagration has destroyed the city, including the archives with all the records of the deliberations and deeds of the sages of Schildburg, the purported author, in the 1727 Yiddish version, tells his readers not to worry about his lack of documentary sources because he, the former town clerk, is in any case illiterate.[82]

The editor of the Yiddish text of 1727 tries hard to improve the plotting of some of the weaker stories. In chapter 52, the Schildburgers are obliged to commit a levy of troops to the emperor. While they are on their way to join up, a herd of cows comes along, and one of the cows brushes against one of the conscripts. The conscript, in his new martial persona, takes this as an insult to his honor and challenges the cow to a duel, provided the cow agrees to play by the rules. The cow, however, makes no reply, and that is the end of the story as far as the German editions are concerned. For the Yiddish editor of 1727, though, this abrupt ending must have seemed unsatisfactory. In his version, the cow wanders off, which the Schildburgers take as a sign of cowardice on the cow's part and of heroism or military prowess on the part of the soldier, demonstrating their own foolishness as well as that of their colleague, whom they immediately proclaim the "Schildburger general."[83] Once again, as in the election of the swineherd as mayor, Schildburg is depicted as a society so confused that the biggest fool comes out on top.

The word for "general" appears in the 1727 Yiddish text spelled as "yeneral," in line with the practice found in Old Yiddish texts specifically from the Netherlands of using a *yod* to represent the Dutch language's highly guttural initial letter *g*, as in the Dutch word *generaal*. This is one of several instances strongly suggesting that the 1727 Yiddish *Shildburger bukh* was not simply, as per the title page, printed in Amsterdam (the world center of Yiddish as well as Hebrew printing at that time, with clients coming from all over Europe and beyond), but clues such as the spelling of "yeneral" also imply that the 1727 Yiddish editor was a Dutch Jew.

Another clue to the 1727 editor's Dutchness occurs shortly afterward, when the heroic Schildburger general decides to go home to recuperate after the fright he experiences in his first taste of battle, battle not with the opposing army but with an irate peasant, who, finding the general stealing provisions from his farm, gives chase with a pitchfork. The Yiddish edition of 1727, unlike any of the German editions or the Yiddish edition of 1700, refers to this bucolic battle with a wink as the "grose alteratsye," the great Alteration.[84] The reference is to the moment in 1578 when, in a major turning point in Dutch history, most of Amsterdam's inhabitants made a sudden switch in identity from Catholic to Calvinist, throwing in their lot as a municipality with the rebels elsewhere in the northern Netherlands who were in revolt against the Habsburgs. Because of the mildness of Amsterdam's "velvet revolution," it became known thereafter as the Alteration.

Much of the effect of this little chapter depends on its punch line, which characterizes the general's traumatic experience as less like a war and more like the Alteration, the nonwar par excellence in early modern Dutch memory. Thus, it is easy to understand why the late eighteenth-century abridged reissues of the 1727 Yiddish text (Offenbach, 1777, followed by the exact reprint of it in Fürth, 1798) omit a chapter whose central joke is too culturally specific to fathom.

In chapter 43, the Yiddish editor of 1727 again shows his determination to brighten up the storytelling, and, given the range of methods he uses to bring about this improvement, including adding rhymes, it is clear that he is motivated not by an unconscious addiction to rhyming but by a conscious desire to amuse his readers. In this chapter, one of the Schildburgers takes his thirty-year-old son to elementary school, the first visit to such an institution in the child's life or in the father's. As the father explains to the schoolmaster, his son knows nothing at all yet. But then, he adds with impeccable Schildburg logic, you would hardly expect the son to know anything at his age, when what he, the father, knows at the age of sixty-five years and a day is not worth "drek" (shit or garbage).[85]

The Yiddish editor of 1727 brings to bear several of his strategies on this story. He tweaks the original in tiny ways, such as making the father still utterly ignorant at seventy-four, not a mere sixty-five. He also adds occasional details to enrich the existing plotlines as they appear in the German and earlier Yiddish text. For example, in the original text, the father sees an assistant teacher beating a boy and, rather than construing the act as a punishment, infers that, this being a school, the act must be an instructional demonstration of caning technique. Thereupon, the father tells the principal that he does not need his son to be overeducated, but he would be satisfied if his son mastered just this one subject, caning, to the level of proficiency exhibited by the assistant teacher. The Yiddish of 1727 adds to this a rationale on the part of the father for why he does not need his son to learn too much: the delightfully redundant explanation "we are not a family of scholars [gelernte]," an addition conceivably but not demonstrably reflecting the respect accorded to learning by all socioeconomic strata in normative Jewish society.[86]

In the German text, the father now announces that he will go to the blacksmith and get his horse shod, then come back and pick up his son, having thus allowed enough time for him to receive a basic education. Whether in amusement, indignation, or both, the schoolmaster tells the father not to bother coming back but to take his son now and go. In the German Schildbürgerbuch, in the Lalebuch before it, and in the printed source from which the author of the *Lalebuch* appropriated this story (Montanus's *Gartengesellschaft* of 1560), the conclusion is simply that the father took his son by the hand and brought him back to his mother.[87] This was evidently too anticlimactic for the 1727 Yiddish editor's liking. To make the end of the story a touch livelier, he makes this last scene into a couple of rhyming couplets, which, though weak, may still seem to offer a more resonant conclusion:

> Father took his young son by the hand / and led him home to his
>   own land,
> Exclaiming: "Now's my young son / crammed with reason."[88]

It is not just a rhyme or two, though, that the Yiddish editor has added here. He has also carried the jest forward to the next level. In his version alone, the father is so foolish that he does not even comprehend that the schoolmaster, in throwing him and his son out of the schoolhouse, is reacting negatively to the suggestion that he give his prospective mature student an elementary education (plus advanced caning) all in the time it takes to shoe a horse. Instead, the foolish father blithely misunderstands the schoolmaster to be telling him that he need not bother himself to come back later but can take his son with him now because he, the father, has overestimated, not underestimated, the time required to acquire an education, the knowledge transfer having been effected while they were talking.

The 1727 editor's tendency to add rhymes is most evident in the story of the mayoral election, which even the postwar scholar Arnold Paucker condemned as an "unparalleled example of compulsive rhyming."[89] In my opinion, the extra rhymes in his text should be viewed, instead, as artifacts showing the translator making the most of his cultural capital—that is, the resources at his disposal, his talents, in this case as an expert in the foolish culture of his time, a culture in which wordplay, riddles, and rhymes were staples of entertainment in both private and public settings.

The supreme importance of rhyming for this culture could hardly be made clearer than it is in the original *Schildbürgerbuch*, where the holding of the mayoral office is determined by the outcome of a rhyming competition. For dramatic effect, both the German and Yiddish editions report that there were many contenders, but the editions reproduce the rhymes concocted by only a few of them. Excuses are given for why some other candidates' rhymes are unavailable, or the absence of their contributions is passed over without comment. The Yiddish edition of 1727 makes some slight alterations here, most conspicuously by suppressing the excuse that is given in the German text and in the 1700 Yiddish edition for the absence of contestant number 6's rhyme: that available readings could not be considered trustworthy since they could not be verified against the Rotwelsch manuscript, from which the passage in question was missing. This is just a little joke at the expense of humanist text editors, since Rotwelsch, German thieves' cant, was the least highly esteemed of all German dialects, and the supposed Rotwelsch text was the least likely to be deemed authoritative, except in the inverted world of folly literature.

Having removed the Rotwelsch explanation, the Yiddish invents as a substitute the statement that there are no rhymes from contestants 6 and 7 because they both overslept. Presumably this substitution was motivated by the Yiddish editor's concern that some of his readers, perhaps outside Germany, might not know what Rotwelsch was. Or perhaps he thought that they might know all too well what it was and be put off by a reference to it on account of the ethnic slur that it maybe carried with it. Possible Yiddish influence on Rotwelsch has been a subject of legitimate philological interest ever since the Late Middle Ages.[90]

Not satisfied with simply a revised list of candidates, the Yiddish editor of 1727 also makes a few changes in the content of their verses. This can be merely a matter of substituting a preferred synonym for a word in his source text. Thus, in the 1700 Yiddish edition, sticking closely to the German source, one candidate presents this as his best rhyming effort: "Vas zol ikh fil raymen oder zogen / ikh habe ayn fulen vanst" (How much can I rhyme or tell [ye]? / [Just] that I have a full stomach).[91] The joke intended here is not just that "zogen" and "vanst" do not rhyme but that there is such an obvious alternative way to say stomach, that is, *mogn*, that does rhyme with *zogn*, just as well as "belly" rhymes with "tell ye."

The relatively mechanical Yiddish translation of 1700 retains the wording exactly as in the German, whereas the consistently thoughtful Yiddish translation of 1727 replaces the word "vanst" with "boykh," a third Germanic word for stomach.[92] For the purposes of the joke, the word works just as well as "vanst" in not rhyming with "zogn" but also represents an improvement from the reader's point of view as being the one word among the three that is most commonly employed in Yiddish, although *mogn* would certainly have been understood by Yiddish readers. We can be sure of that, for if the use of the word "zogn" had not immediately suggested the word *mogn* as the obvious rhyming match for it, then the joke here, that "zogn" does not suffice to bring *mogn* to mind for the foolish protagonist of the story, would have been lost on these Yiddish readers.

Along with such modest modifications, the Yiddish editor of 1727 adds substantive new content. Notoriously enthusiastic rhymer that he is, it is no surprise that he enters into the spirit of the rhyming competition with gusto, choosing to stretch the *zogn/vanst* joke into two more couplets of his own devising and stepping up the foolishness with each repetition of the idea. The first of these two offerings is "Ikh hob mayn froy gelangt ayn ay / un es brekht ir in fir" (I gave my wife an egg / and she broke it in four [i.e., into four pieces]), where "in fir" (in four) fails to rhyme with "ayn ay" (an egg).[93] Were he not a fool, he could so much more easily have said not "in fir" but *entsvay* (in two), both creating a rhyme by so doing and simultaneously invoking that most normal of acts: cracking an egg in half, rather than the nonsense act of cracking an egg in quarters.

In the last couplet, the Yiddish editor introduces one more layer of complication: "Ikh hob begegent ayn vild tir / un ikh shise es in dray" (I came upon a wild beast / and I shot it in three [i.e., into three pieces]).[94] Once again, the rhyme fails on two counts. First, it does not rhyme, and, second, the act it purports to describe is absurd. Yet again, the right ending would have been not "in dray" (in three) but *entsvay*, which, as well as "in two" or "in half," also means "in (or to) pieces." The new twist this time, though, is that *entsvay* rhymes no better with "vild tir" than "in dray" does. The special foolishness evinced by the mayoral candidate here is that, faced with a difficult choice between *entsvay*, which makes sense but does not rhyme, and *in fir* (in four), a phrase that he used in the previous couplet and that this time, for a change, does rhyme even though it makes no sense, he chooses a third option, "in dray" (in three), which neither rhymes nor makes sense.

In the same spirit as that of the mayoral election, the *Schildbürger-buch* includes a passage describing a session of riddles of the "Who or what am I?" variety, arranged by the Schildburgers to entertain the visiting emperor of Utopia. Riddling is among the most prominent sources of amusement in foolish culture.[95] As is typical in folly literature, all the riddles have a blindingly obvious (and somewhat rude) solution, which always remains the road not taken, and a just possible (but ludicrously artificial) solution, which, needless to say, is the tortuous road always taken.[96]

As each of these riddles is announced, the mayor steps in to preclude any "misunderstanding" by whispering the improbable but inoffensive solution into the emperor's ear. In time, they come to the last of this series of conundrums: "I sat on a little block and gazed at the little hole. Oh, little hole, how extraordinary you are, that you like stitching as much as you do."[97] While there may be room to wonder whether the "little block" on which the speaker is seated suggests a part of an outhouse rather than a part of a husband, little else leaves scope for speculation, a point the German source underscores by offering, in this instance alone, no alternative solution, as if to say that the meaning here is so unambiguous that there can be no other explanation.

The text expresses this claim of unambiguity, however, not directly but foolish style, mock-euphemistically, saying that no alternative solution to the riddle can be provided because worms, that is, bookworms, silverfish, have obliterated precisely this little passage of the original manuscript. The translator of the 1727 Yiddish edition is so involved in the carnivalesque zeitgeist, however, that he takes the suggestion that there is no possible decorous solution to this riddle as a challenge. In response, he provides the mayor with the unimpeachably tame alternative solution that the subject of the riddle is a spider, which, finding itself on a block, a solid surface, is moved to "wish it had a stable home."[98] What, after all, is there to like about a web, which, when you look at it, is only a hole surrounded by a little stitching? The wordplay here turns on the extended meanings of the word "shtikh" (a stitch), which can also be used to mean "stitching" and, more broadly, piercing or penetration.

The German *Schildbürgerbuch* also tells of the time when the mayor and his wife arrive at church a bit late and find the congregation already spilling out because the priest was too drunk to manage more than an extremely short and obscure sermon. The Yiddish editor of 1727 modifies the narrative—not, however, in order to spare his readers unnecessary exposure to an alien religious culture but, on the contrary, to keep all that intact and simply improve the storytelling by substituting a more elegant and imaginative conclusion. In the Yiddish version, the townspeople tell the mayor that the sermon consisted of just four points, for none of which can they come up with any "oys legung" (explanation).[99] Thereupon, the mayor offers them the alternative satisfaction of a mock sermon of his own.

All this should suffice to illustrate the Yiddish editor's thoughtful and creative engagement with the text. The Yiddish editor has found an opportunity to highlight a major preoccupation, if not the central paradox, of foolish culture: the idea that folly and wisdom stand in a complex relationship and are not clear-cut antitheses. By underscoring the question of whether the swineherd mayor is a simpleton, a bit of a genius, or both, the Yiddish editor shows how much he is steeped in the thinking of a pervasive foolish culture shared by Christians and Jews.

The sanitized abridgment of the 1727 Yiddish edition, printed in Offenbach in 1777 and reprinted in Fürth in 1798, adjusts this chapter to suppress the idea of a tipsy priest, though the idea had been omnipresent for hundreds of years throughout European literature. Not only is anything sexual or scatological suppressed but also anything that could seem derogatory toward Jews or Christians. The explanation for this may have to do with the places where the first two and last two surviving editions of the Yiddish *Shildburger bukh* were printed. The first two appeared in Amsterdam, a world capital of the free press, and the last two in the more strictly regulated environment of the Holy Roman Empire with its patchwork of local jurisdictions and ecclesiastical influence.

One last elaboration of the *Schildbürgerbuch* narrative by the 1727 Yiddish editor has particular bearing on the question as to "how the wise men got to Chelm." In the tale of how the Schildburgers try unsuccessfully to carry sunlight into their windowless town hall in sacks, the German versions tell how an enterprising hobo spots an opportunity. For a consulting fee, he advises them that they need only remove the roof from their building to achieve the desired result. They proceed as advised, and their ensuing delight lasts all summer long, fading only when the weather changes, by which time the transient has, naturally, moved on. The original appeal of this story derives in part from its culturally specific context: the charivari. A favorite practice of the young men carrying out this ritual punishment would be to strip the roofing off their target's house.[100] If having the roofing removed from your home was a sign of your foolishness, then being big enough fools to pay to be talked into taking the roofing off your own town hall transports the Schildburgers to a new frontier of folly.[101]

That is where this episode ends in the German editions, as it does in the 1700 Yiddish edition, which follows them closely. This, too, is where, once again, the Yiddish edition of 1727 distinguishes itself, with its translator creatively engaged with his text and with the foolish culture of the time. He adds a little flourish as added value for his readers, unaware though they are that they are being treated to a bonus; the translator has, after all, promised his readers that what they are getting from him is the German original, word for word. However, the Yiddish version of 1727 seems, if anything, more steeped in foolish culture than any other, for it alone makes not just one allusion in this episode to the symbols of foolish culture (the removal of roofing) but also a possible second such allusion with the introduction to the story of a barrel of tar.

While, in the German version, this story concludes with the weather spoiling the Schildburgers' apparent belief that they had solved all their town hall's problems, the Yiddish version of 1727 augments their folly by having the continuing fiasco brought home to them right after they finish unroofing themselves. Once the roof is off in this Yiddish version, the vagrant adviser instructs his clients to hoist up a barrel of pitch over the exposed joists of their building and then, having made sure to capture the sun in it, to lower it back down into the town hall as a source of light.

It is possible that the content of the barrel was selected for no reason other than its special stickiness, to which the sun might credibly be expected to adhere. But tar has enough resonances in foolish culture that its selection may also have a symbolic subtext, reinforcing the point of this story: that the Schildburgers were so foolish that they did not need to be publicly humiliated by any fool society. Instead, they could be relied on to publicly humiliate themselves. According to one German proverb, "Pech und Unverstand gehen nicht von der Hand" (a lack of sense is like tar—impossible to get off your hands). According to another, "Wer Pech angreift, der besudelt sich" (if you touch tar, you get dirty), a reference to the two meanings of the word *Pech*, not only "tar" but also "misfortune."[102] Tar is also associated with the charivari, in that the young vigilantes of the fool societies might apply a little to their face as camouflage, disguise, or war paint or might apply it to a victim in a ritual punishment of tarring.

Whether or not tar alludes to folly or only to stickiness, the editor's introduction of the barrel story in the 1727 Yiddish edition corresponds in its outlines to a global folk motif that was, however, new in the Schildburg context. It strongly supports the impression that Jewish foolish culture was a part of the foolish culture shared by early modern European Jews and Christians alike, with both communities equally invested in it.

Moreover, among all the tales that recur in the many Chelm collections, none is as ubiquitous as the story of the barrel. In the Chelm versions of the barrel story, as throughout the Chelm stories, the protagonists are Jews; the barrel is full of water (or, in one version, alcohol or borsht), not tar (which by the late nineteenth century no longer evoked foolishness). And the object is not to trap the sun to illuminate the interior of the Schildburg town hall but to trap the moon and bring it back to Chelm, where prolonged local cloud cover threatened to prevent the monthly "kiddush levanah" (Sanctification of the Moon).

This ritual of talmudic origin, having been granted cosmic significance more than a millennium later by the Lurianic kabbalah, was thus of special importance to Hasidim. Still, for all the changes the barrel story has undergone in external details, in substance it is still the same story as the one told in the Yiddish *Shildburger bukh*. Thus, one can do more than simply assert the widely acknowledged general influence of Schildburg on Chelm. On the basis of both common sense and the presence in the Chelm repertoire of the barrel story, which features in the 1727 Yiddish *Shildburger bukh* and its 1777 and 1798 reissues but not in the German editions, one can suppose that the *Schildbürgerbuch* inspired the concept of Chelm specifically through the medium of the Yiddish translation rather than through transmission from the German.

This not to say that any of the writers of Chelm stories necessarily had a copy of the Yiddish *Shildburger bukh* at hand or had ever read one. Probably none of them did, given the rarity of documented copies of any edition of the Yiddish *Shildburger bukh*, with none known to have an eastern European provenance. In view of the limited cataloguing, or access to cataloguing, of holdings in libraries of former Warsaw Pact countries, however, the picture could change. But without access to printed copies, transmission must have been oral, with favorite episodes from the 1727 Yiddish *Shildburger bukh* told and retold over the 100 to 150-plus years between the publication of its three editions (1727, 1777, and 1798) and the emergence of Chelm as a foolish location.

That, however, is not the whole story. Parallel to this pathway via which the Chelm stories were inspired by the Yiddish *Shildburger bukh*, as distinct from the German *Schildbürgerbuch*, is a second pathway. Via this pathway, the *Khelmer mayses* were inspired by literary developments in the German Schildburg tradition as distinct from any oral developments in the Yiddish Schildburg tradition, as we shall see.

5

# The Enlightenment Goes East

## *How Democritus of Abdera Got to Galicia*

In 1789, the German man of letters Christoph Martin Wieland (1733–1813) published in his influential literary journal *Der Teutsche Merkur* (the German Mercury, which appeared between 1773 and 1789) an article containing his contribution to the endlessly discussed question of the moment, "What is Enlightenment?" According to him, the answer "is known to everyone who, having eyes to see, has learned to recognize the difference between light and dark, day and night."[1]

Wieland goes on to explain that light is a metaphor for the light of reason, which helps distinguish between "true and false, good and evil."[2] Thus, the author warns of "anyone who wants to give us black for white, or wants to pay with counterfeit money, or wants to conjure up ghosts, or (though this is very innocent in itself) whoever likes to follow whims, build castles in the air, or take trips to the land of Cockaigne or the Happy Islands."[3] His parenthetical concession, that irrationality "is very innocent in itself," contradicts everything else he says here and offers a broad hint of subversive intent. That his answer to the question "What is Enlightenment?" is meant as a parody of the simplistic and hackneyed answers of the period becomes clear from one word that he uses in his title, or rather from one word that he does not use but decorously represents with an ellipsis: "Ein paar Goldkörner aus – Makulatur oder Sechs Antworten auf sechs Fragen" (A couple of gold nuggets from the . . . paper, or six answers to six questions).

The fictitious context in which Wieland chooses to place his remarks is that the contents of this article came to him when he spotted "six questions about the Enlightenment" on a piece of *Makulatur* (printer's waste, a print shop's discarded mistakes or remainders), often repurposed as toilet paper, with the word "toilet" in the concept of "toilet paper" being the indecency that Wieland's faux scruples prevent him from spelling out. It is as if he were saying, in the roundabout manner of the day, that the outhouse is where many of the far too many pamphlets on the nature of Enlightenment belong. It is also as if he were saying that the thoughts he is about to express on the subject may belong there as well.

The fiction with which Wieland frames his book does not mean that he is entirely opposed to the Enlightenment. On the contrary, he is among the leading figures of the movement, to which he made substantial contributions as author, translator, and editor of a leading journal. But Wieland is a self-critical thinker who, by setting the action of "A Couple of Gold Nuggets" in a restroom, transforms it into an ambiguous essay in which the Enlightenment is simultaneously celebrated and criticized.[4] Given this sensibility, it is not surprising that Wieland, like many other writers of the Enlightenment, was interested in the German *Schildbürgerbuch*, another book that is full of ambiguity vis-à-vis wisdom and folly, reason and unreason, seriousness and laughter.

As we shall see, the German Enlightenment made considerable use of the *Schildbürgerbuch*. Wieland's *History of the Abderites* is of special note in this regard, since it proved such an attractive model for eastern European *maskilim*, the Jewish intellectuals who sought to propagate the values of the German Enlightenment, and not just the German language, among their coreligionists in the Russian and Austrian empires in the late eighteenth and nineteenth centuries. Wieland's *History of the Abderites* can also be understood as a reworked *Schildbürgerbuch*.

## Schildburg to Abdera: Christoph Martin Wieland

German literature of the Enlightenment largely ignored early modern literary models and themes. But the paradox of the foolish sage expressed in the Schildburg stories was a notable exception, remaining popular throughout the period. New takes on the *Schildbürgerbuch* that date from the late eighteenth century include Johann Gottlob Schulz's *Die neuen Schildbürger oder Lalenburg in den Tagen der Aufklärung* (The new Schildburgers, or Lalenburg, in the age of the Enlightenment, 1791),[5] Andreas Georg Friedrich von Rebmann's *Empfindsame Reise nach Schilda* (Sentimental journey to Schilda, 1793), Johann Gottlieb Schummel's *Die Revolution in Scheppenstedt* (The revolution in Scheppenstedt, 1794), and Ludwig Tieck's *Denkwürdige Geschichtschronik der*

*Schildbürger* (Remarkable history of the Schildburgers, 1796).[6] Tieck, like Wieland, reflects critically on the achievements of the Enlightenment, but Wieland's *Die Abderiten: Eine sehr wahrscheinliche Geschichte* (literally, The Abderites: A highly probable history, also cited more briefly as the *History of the Abderites*), although it uses the *Schildbürgerbuch* as only one of many sources, may be considered the most influential example of this trend.[7]

The fools in the *History of the Abderites*, first published in serial form between 1774 and 1780 in the journal *Der Teutsche Merkur* and with minor changes as a book in 1781, live in a city named Abdera.[8] Abdera was a real place, a city in ancient Thrace, whose inhabitants are singled out in some classical Greek and Latin sources for their folly. A few comic stories about them can be found in Greek literature of late antiquity, but by Wieland's time, Abdera was simply the place name remotely associated with folly by the erudite.[9] Wieland's book, therefore, which is full of new stories of his own devising, repopularized from scratch the virtually forgotten word *Abderit*, Abderite, as a synonym for fool.

Wieland's one-volume *History of the Abderites* is divided into five books, each dealing with a different facet of the town's foolishness. Klaus Manger argues that this approach is intended to cast Abdera as a mirror image of the traditional university plus its four faculties: theology, law, medicine, and arts.[10] In the first book, Wieland introduces his Abderites as all-around fools, illustrating their folly with such fictional examples as their decision to place a five-foot ivory statue of Diana on an eighty-foot column so that passersby within a wider radius might have the chance to admire it, "except that it was now impossible to discern whether it was meant to represent Venus or an oyster nymph."[11]

Other architectural follies, and this was the age of the architectural folly, include an arsenal that is vastly oversized for a tiny stock of weapons, a grand fountain emitting just a trickle of water, a grand library housing only worthless books, a gymnasium whose fencing and wrestling facilities are decorated with statues of thinking philosophers and paintings of deliberating statesmen, and a city hall, the walls of whose council chamber are covered with scenes of naked gladiators, bathing Dianas, sleeping Bacchantae, and Venus with her lover in the net of Vulcan.

Besides his evident misgivings about the grandiose tendencies of the neoclassicism that the Enlightenment championed and its frequent failure to observe the rule later formulated as "form always follows function," Wieland further identifies his Abdera with the Abdera of ancient Greece by criticizing his Abderites for the fault ascribed to them in his classical sources. That fault is the failure to appreciate the genius of their greatest native son, the pre-Socratic philosopher Democritus, who was said to have traveled the world before returning to Abdera and his compatriots' narrow-minded hostility. Wieland sees their shortsightedness as driven by the fact that if they admitted the wisdom of their philosopher neighbor, they would have to acknowledge their own inanity, since he was "their antipode in everything."[12]

In the second book, the Abderites invite Hippocrates, paragon of physicians, to visit their town and cure Democritus of what they allege is his insanity. After the great doctor examines his patient, he recommends no course of therapy for Democritus. Instead, he prescribes for all the other citizens of Abdera a regimen of hellebore, an ancient Greek herbal remedy for madness, with powerful, potentially fatal, laxative side effects.

Questions of aesthetics are discussed in the third book, where the dramatist Euripides visits Abdera and clashes with the inhabitants over their taste in theater. The fourth book contains the most famous passage in the *History of the Abderites*: the case of the donkey's shadow, a minor disagreement that grows into a major lawsuit. The dispute is over whether a person who hires an animal has also hired its shadow. The case is never resolved, since it becomes moot when the divided townsfolk get embroiled in a tug-of-war in the marketplace and end up accidentally ripping the poor creature to pieces.

Another controversy among the Abderites brings life in the city to an end. Sacred frogs, worshiped by the devotees of the cult of Latona, reproduce in such numbers that they not only upset the devotees of the opposing cult of Jason but threaten the viability of the entire city of Abdera. The only solution that the city fathers can think of is for the whole population to abandon the town, which they do.

Wieland's *History of the Abderites* was widely read in the German-speaking lands of the late eighteenth and early nineteenth centuries. Leading German writers and thinkers picked up immediately on the Abdera theme. Friedrich Schiller (1759–1805) refers to "the old story of Democritus and the Abderites" in the preface to his drama *Die Räu-*

ber (*The Robbers*, 1781), and Immanuel Kant (1724–1804), in his *Streit der Fakultäten* (*The Conflict of the Faculties*, 1798), develops a theory of historiography according to which all events and developments can be interpreted according to one of three ways of thinking, one of which he terms the "the hypothesis of Abderitism," which in his judgment involves "historical oscillation and circularity."[13] Kant singles out as the most egregious exponent of an Abderite view of history the philosopher in chief of the Berlin Enlightenment, Moses Mendelssohn.[14]

Abdera became synonymous with the idea of a foolish town, not only among such highbrows as Schiller but also among the general public. Nineteenth-century periodicals began publishing Schildburg-like stories, supposedly about the residents of such actual small towns as Schilda, Schöppenstedt, and Hirschberg, and generally doing so in a column titled something along the lines of "Stories of Abderites."

From an early date, scholars showed interest in uncovering the inspiration and sources of Wieland's satire. They started by exploring his biographical associations for clues, looking for potential echoes in the Abdera he described of his hometown of Biberach or the university town of Erfurt, where he taught, or Mannheim, where he was involved in the production of one of his plays. Wieland did indeed describe the last of these places in a letter to Catharina Elisabeth Goethe, Johann Wolfgang's mother, as the "great frog-ditch of Abdera."[15] However, he was keen to scotch the idea that he was out to write an autobiographical roman à clef or a history of any one specific Abdera, ancient or modern. In his introduction to the book, he says explicitly that he aims instead to make "a contribution, however modest, to the history of human understanding."[16] Thus, Wieland depicts folly as an anthropological constant, and therefore his work belongs to folly literature and culture as much as the *Schildbürgerbuch* does.

Schildburg and Abdera are explicitly linked once in the *History of the Abderites*, when Wieland explains the character of the Abderite townspeople. The Abderites, he says, "became a byword among the Greeks. An Abderite idea, an Abderite's shenanigans, meant to them approximately what a Schildburger's shenanigans mean to us or a Lalenburger's shenanigans mean to the Swiss."[17]

In comparing the proverbial foolishness of the Abderites and the Schildburgers, Wieland notes a similarity between the *Schildbürgerbuch* and his *History of the Abderites*, a connection that has nevertheless generally been downplayed by scholars. Thus, Fritz Martini sees a close connection between the *Schildbürgerbuch* and the *History of the Abderites* as existing only in Wieland's first chapter, where he presents one example of Abderite folly after another to prove his claim that Abdera was a remarkably foolish place. Wieland's later chapters, which are thematic in nature, have, in Martini's view, no strong resemblance to the *Schildbürgerbuch*. Volker Klotz notes that, even in the first book of the *History of the Abderites*, the differences between it and the *Schildbürgerbuch* outnumber the similarities.[18] Conversely, Manger stresses the importance of early modern folly literature for Wieland's work.[19]

Indeed, the *Schildbürgerbuch* was not the only folly literature known to Wieland. Two years after the appearance in 1776 of the first installments of his *History of the Abderites* in *Der Teutsche Merkur*, Wieland published, in the same journal, some articles on the humanist author Sebastian Brant, along with a reproduction of Jean-Jacques Boissard's engraved portrait of Brant. In a biographical sketch, Wieland praises Brant, especially his *Ship of Fools*. He devotes a second article entirely to this book and to the sermons of Johann Geiler von Kaysersberg (1445–1510), the famous Strasbourg theologian who used the *Ship of Fools* as a point of departure for his preaching.[20]

Wieland was, however, not only conversant with the *Ship of Fools* and its translations from the original German into Latin, French, and English but also with the work of other writers of the early modern period, such as Georg Rollenhagen (1542–1609) and Johann Fischart (1545–1591). He also discusses in the *History of the Abderites* a much more recent book in the tradition of folly literature: Laurence Sterne's *Tristram Shandy* (1759). Wieland held this book in such high esteem that, according to the eighteenth-century German novelist Jean Paul, his personal copy was completely worn out.[21] Wieland also collaborated in 1774 on a second edition of Sterne's book in German.

Even allowing for all the differences in preoccupations and style attributable to the different periods from which the books date, the connection between the *Schildbürgerbuch* and the *History of the Abderites* as two linked classics of folly literature is unmistakably apparent in multiple closely analogous structural features. First, both works are about a foolish society; even though both works contain individual protagonists, neither book is *about* individuals. Further parallels that point to the *Schildbürgerbuch* as Wieland's primary model include the ancient Greek background invoked in each case, the conception of folly that they share, the strikingly similar role of the narrator, and, the clincher, the strikingly similar conclusion to both books.

The inhabitants of Schildburg and Abdera alike trace their origins to Athens, the thinking person's supposed ideal city. Both groups have degenerated, or have at least come down in the world, so that in each case their home is now some minor settlement in the middle of nowhere. As explained in the *Schildbürgerbuch*, "habitually, the Greeks expelled these [the Schildburgers] and others out of perverse ingratitude for the benefits that they had received from them, and packed them off to foreign parts."[22] The refugees who settled in Schildburg, somewhere in the land of Utopia that is beyond Misnopotamia (a blend of *Mesopotamia* and *mis-*, as in *mistake* or *misadventure*) are similar to those inhabitants of the Greek city of Teos, in Ionia, who, according to the *History of the Abderites*, originated in Athens and ended up in remote Abdera in Thrace.

Furthermore, just as Schildburg is located by its author in Utopia—literally, "no place" in particular—so Abdera is intended as any and every place. As Wieland said in a letter published in his journal *Der Teutsche Merkur* in 1778 to avoid misunderstandings and the taking of umbrage at his provocative text, "it is not possible to say, here is Abdera, or there is Abdera. Abdera is everywhere."[23] His objective, he explains, was simply to write "ein Märchen von Narren und Närrinnen," a fairy tale about foolish men and foolish women.[24]

Greece is chosen as the place of origin of the Schildburgers and the Abderites for the same reason: as a byword for the highest standards of wisdom, from which standards the fools of both cities declined. However, whereas the Schildburgers deliberately abandoned their wisdom after lengthy deliberation, the *History of the Abderites* states simply that "no sooner had the Teians turned into Abderites than they began to degenerate."[25] Wieland's Abderites do, however, evidently retain a latent capacity for wisdom, since it is suggested that a few children from Abdera be isolated from their parents and educated by a learned man so that they may become wise again. Wieland's contention here is presumably that nurture alone, just as nature alone, can make one foolish or wise.

Wieland uses Greece as a source of inspiration for another reason. Given his preference for moderation in all things, even moderation in enthusiasm for the Enlightenment, he cannot help wanting to moderate the inclination of his contemporaries, influenced by the German archaeologist Johann Joachim Winckelmann (1717–1768), to idealize classical antiquity as the zenith of civilization. Wieland has reservations about the prominence of classicism in the intellectual and artistic life of the German-speaking lands in the late eighteenth century. It is his intention, therefore, to poke fun at the glory that was Greece by reviving awareness of its silly side.[26] He therefore localizes the *Republic of Fools*—the title of the 1861 first English translation, by Henry Christmas, of the *History of the Abderites*—in an ancient Greece that seemed to him overglorified by his contemporaries.[27]

The *Schildbürgerbuch* and the *History of the Abderites* also share a similar concept of folly. In both, foolishness is a matter of faulty reasoning leading to wrong conclusions as to how to solve problems. "The Abderites never lacked ideas," Wieland says, "but rarely were their ideas suited to the situation to which they were applied, a fact that did not occur to them until the occasion was past."[28] The Schildburgers are the same: if they do finally see sense, it will be too late—although "too late" is a concept they have trouble grasping, as evident in their belated recognition of the merits of log rolling over log carrying.

In addition, the Schildburgers and Wieland's Abderites share the fallacy that performing well in one field predicts excellent performance in another. Thus, the Schildburgers elect the swineherd as mayor because he, or his wife, can keep a rhyme going longer than any of the other candidates. Almost identically, the Abderites elect the best singer in town as their *Nomophylax* (guardian of the laws).

The narrators of both the *Schildbürgerbuch* and the *History of the Abderites* are "unreliable narrators," providing their readers with conflicting information, deceiving them, and sometimes addressing them as if they had a long-standing personal acquaintance. All this is done with disorienting intent, so the reader is frequently forced to wonder which parts of the text are meant as true and which as false, which parts are meant to make sense and which nonsense, who is wise and who foolish.[29] Like the town-clerk-cum-chimneysweep narrator of the *Schildbürgerbuch*, the narrator of the *History of the Abderites* often represents himself as engaging in lively dialogue with and even berating an imaginary reader, the questions in whose mind he likes to anticipate.

Both authors also use the narrator to create confusion about their sources. The narrator of the *Schildbürgerbuch* first claims that he is transmitting an oral account, then complains about the wormholes in his manuscript source, while Wieland's narrator apologizes for being unable to provide all the details of the controversy over Democritus's disputed sanity "because the records of the entire case were long ago devoured by mice."[30]

Earlier in the *History of the Abderites*, Wieland also creates the impression that he is relying on, or claiming to rely on, documentary sources when he lists a string of ancient authorities for his information on Abdera, including Herodotus, Diogenes, Lucian, Cicero, and Horace, but then undermines himself by urging any reader who "does not wish to look them up" to consult the entries on "Abdera" and "Democritus" in the standard Enlightenment encyclopedia of the time, Pierre Bayle's *Dictionnaire historique et critique* (*An Historical and Critical Dictionary*, 1697).[31]

Later, Wieland returns to this theme, pretending to rebuke his readers for not paying enough attention to what he has to say about Abdera or not delving deeply enough into the sources but letting themselves get distracted by such relative trivialities as studying, teaching, traveling, or getting married. Again, he promptly undermines his position by complaining that he had wasted time researching the history of Abdera simply "because it did not occur to [him] in time to look up the article in Bayle."[32] The jest here is that if the reader takes the advice given and consults Bayle's articles on Abdera and Democritus, it will become clear that Wieland extracted the whole of the small kernel of historical information that he has from Bayle or the sources cited by him, so that his *History of the Abderites* required virtually no research, just a lively intelligence.

Not done with sowing confusion, Wieland offers yet another source for the *History of the Abderites*. When he published his journal articles about Abderites as a book in 1781, he added a "Key to the History of the Abderites," whose fictitious editor (Wieland himself) describes the author of the *History of the Abderites* in paradoxical terms as "a writer little known . . . but much read since the year 1753."[33] In the "Key to the History of the Abderites," he explains that the writer of the *His-*

*tory* found evidence of the survival of the ancient Abderites in a treatise by the scholarly writer Hafen Slawkenbergius. This is a reference to Laurence Sterne's novel *Tristram Shandy*, in which Sterne refers to Slawkenbergius, a German scholar of his own creation. Sterne credits Slawkenbergius with writing the exhaustive treatise *De nasis* (On noses), a work that seems to rely heavily on the widespread belief in the nose's kinship with the penis and the potential therefore for double entendre in any reference to it.[34] Sterne offers little insight into the content of the "extremely scarce" *De nasis* other than to report its account of a visit to still-German Strasbourg by a stranger named Diego. This Diego has an enormous nose, and his presence throws the entire community, including the most respectable housewives, nuns, and even university teachers, into such a turmoil that the French are finally able to conquer the place.[35] Slawkenbergius's treatise and the way it is presented in *Tristram Shandy* can be read as a form of foolish performance in which the author mocks the cult of virility and credits it with far-reaching and potentially catastrophic results, as at Strasbourg, where the folly inspired by Diego's nose turned one of the most important German cities into a French provincial backwater.

What connection, then, does Wieland, in his "Key to the History of the Abderites," wish to make with Slawkenbergius of *Tristram Shandy* fame? How do the themes of the two works relate to each other? It is the theme of folly that unites these works, folly that causes the ruin of Strasbourg as much as of Abdera. For the reference to Slawkenbergius to be effective, Wieland needs and expects the audience for his "Key to the History of the Abderites" to be familiar with *Tristram Shandy* so that he can play with and then frustrate readers by offering no new information on "noses" but only on Abdera, "the paradise of fools and frogs," whose inhabitants maintain their foolishness so firmly that "it has never been possible to perceive the least essential alteration in the Abderites, wherever they were transplanted and however much they mixed with other people."[36] In short, "they are still the same fools they were a thousand years ago in Abdera."[37]

The most striking analogy between the *Schildbürgerbuch* and the *History of the Abderites* is the ruin of both communities, Schildburg and Abdera—both books end similarly and provide the same explanation for the universal presence of folly.

The inhabitants of both cities are forced to abandon their homes because animals take over and the hierarchical order of nature is turned upside down. It is the infestation of mice, followed by the acquisition of the "mousehound," whose behavior so unsettles the Schildburgers, that finally brings their community to an end. Abdera ends much the same way, when the sacred frog population becomes so enormous as to attract countless rats and mice. Here, too, the inhabitants lose control of their environment and feel compelled to disperse. Wieland gets his infestation of rats from Bayle's entry on Abdera, to which he adds mice on his own initiative. Wieland further fleshes out the skeletal Abdera tradition by adding that the mice started appearing in an alarming profusion of colors, not just mousy brown but yellow, green, blue, and blood red. The crisis is turned over to the enlightened natural philosophers of the Abdera Academy of Sciences, who respond with a report concluding that a mouse is a mouse, regardless of color. This information is no doubt valuable but not in itself something that offers the town a way out of its predicament.

The *History of the Abderites* not only parallels the account in the *Schildbürgerbuch* of the decline and fall of the city. It also exactly parallels the consequence of the fall of the city as described in the *Schildbürgerbuch*, with the departure and dispersal of the town's foolish inhabitants and the resulting spread of folly throughout the world.

The author of *Schildbürgerbuch* and Wieland share a fear not just of folly but of its pervasiveness. The *Schildbürgerbuch* ends with the warning that folly can be transmitted by heredity or contagion. Wieland's "Key to the History of the Abderites" concludes by asserting that "the *History of the Abderites* can . . . justly be regarded as one of the truest and most reliable mirrors, and, just for that reason, a faithful one, in which the moderns can look at their countenance and, if they only wish to be honest with themselves, can discover in what respect they resemble their ancestors" (i.e., the Abderites).[38]

The mirror, which lets people see themselves as they are, as a first step toward wisdom, is a metaphor that Sebastian Brant famously used in his *Ship of Fools*, a book that he referred to as a *Narrenspiegel*, a fool's mirror.[39] The *Schildbürgerbuch* and the *History of the Abderites* both see folly as part of human nature. And they see wisdom, therefore, as something "unnatural," something to be achieved and something requiring continuous attention to maintain. This sentiment is summed up in the quotation from Horace that concludes the "Key to the History of the Abderites": "Sapienta prima est stultitia caruisse," the beginning of wisdom is to have eschewed folly.[40]

The mirror is one of the principal symbols used in the texts and images of early modern foolish culture. It is found, for example, on the façade of the town hall in Nördlingen, held up toward the observer in the sculpture of a fool, which bears the caption, "That makes two of us." As Brant and the author of the *Schildbürgerbuch* and Wieland believe, the boundaries between Schildburgers or Abderites and the inhabitants of "normal" towns, and between the fools in the text and the readers of the books, is fuzzy.

The *Schildbürgerbuch* and the *History of the Abderites* agree that wisdom is a treasure that needs careful preservation. Wieland modernizes the discourse on folly, and he also introduces a new type of person in his narrative: the exceptional individual who seems to possess just the right degree of self-awareness, for example, Democritus and Hippocrates. They are characterized as authentic sages, or "cosmopolitans" as Wieland calls them, creating with the *History of the Abderites* a new concept of cosmopolitanism in European discourse.[41] The cosmopolitans belong to an ancient order to which Wieland devotes an entire chapter in the second book of the *History of the Abderites*. This invisible society is so secretive that hardly anything is known about it except that, though its members have neither a constitution, nor symbols, nor solemn rites, they maintain a stronger solidarity among themselves than any other order or fraternity in the world.[42] Cosmopolitans are citizens of the world who recognize one another regardless of differing ethnic or religious backgrounds. Their main aim is to promote "the perfection of the whole."[43] This idea of the cosmopolitan surrounded by a foolish world proves so appealing to the aficionados of Jewish Enlightenment that they identify with it strongly and adopt Abdera as their model foolish society, a society that, as we shall see, finally evolves into Chelm.

## Abdera to Brody: Mendel Lefin and Joseph Perl

The *History of the Abderites* proved highly attractive to maskilim, not especially to the Mendelssohn circle in Berlin but to their devotees, the second generation of modernizing Jewish intellectuals, who had grown up in eastern Europe, continued to live there, and sought to bring Enlightenment values to their coreligionist neighbors in the late eighteenth and early nineteenth centuries.

Wieland's book was read in Germany as a parody of the mentality of small-town Germany in general, but it was widely believed, too, to be a parody of one or another such town in particular, despite the author's denial.[44] The maskilim, however, found it all too easy to identify with the persecuted philosopher Democritus and to identify the persecuting Abderites not with narrow-minded small-town Germans but with their own opponents in the narrow-minded small-town Jewish communities of eastern Europe: dogmatic community rabbis, irrational Hasidic rebbes and their credulous followers, and even differently enlightened maskilic rivals. This is the background against which the first tales of the wise men of Chelm emerge.

During the late eighteenth and early nineteenth centuries, the influential early eastern European maskil Mendel Lefin (1749–1826) was at work on an extended study in Kantian philosophy, which he titled *Nachlass eines Sonderlings zu Abdera* (The literary remains of an eccentric of Abdera). In doing so, he identified himself with Democritus, whom other Abderites considered an eccentric.[45] Born in 1749 in Satanów in Podolia, a southeastern province of the Polish-Lithuanian Commonwealth, Lefin spent time between 1780 and 1784 in Berlin, the center of the Jewish Enlightenment, before returning to Podolia.[46]

In Berlin, Lefin came to know many of the proponents of Haskalah, among them its two leading figures, Moses Mendelssohn (1729–1786) and David Friedländer (1750–1834). Back in Poland, he settled for a while in Mikołajów, a town on the estate of Prince Adam Kazimierz Czartoryski (1734–1823). Czartoryski was a leading protagonist of the Polish Enlightenment, and he became Lefin's patron, supporting him intellectually and financially, with housing and a lifelong stipend. He sponsored Lefin's publications and appointed him tutor to his sons, whom Lefin accompanied on their travels as far as the Russian court at St. Petersburg.[47] In return, Lefin dedicated his *Nachlass eines Sonderlings zu Abdera* to Czartoryski's wife, Izabela, a patron of the arts and his hostess in Sieniawa, another residence of this noble family.

Lefin started writing his *Nachlass eines Sonderlings* in Sieniawa in 1794 and finished it in Mikołajów in 1806. Dissatisfied, he then reworked his text and did not feel ready to publish until he had completed a final revision in 1823, by which time failing eyesight obliged him to employ an amanuensis. He complained that all his work had been in vain since he was now aged and ailing, unable to give it the final polish that he felt it needed.[48] The manuscript, accordingly, was never published and remained with Lefin's student Joseph Perl (1773–1839) in Tarnopol. Only fragments amounting to twenty pages have survived and are now in the National Library of Israel in Jerusalem.[49] Yisroel Vaynlez was, however, able to read the entire manuscript while it was still in Tarnopol, on the basis of which he published a brief description.[50]

Lefin must have encountered Wieland's *History of the Abderites* in Berlin or through his patron Czartoryski, whose sixteen-year-old son, Adam Jerzy Czartoryski, passed through Weimar in 1786, writing that the city was "already known as the German Athens."[51] In Weimar, the young Czartoryski met his father's pen-friend Johann Gottfried Herder (1744–1803), as well as Johann Wolfgang von Goethe (1749–1832) and, eventually, Wieland.

Wieland made a prosaic impression on the young prince, who described his demeanor as "anything but poetical; he was short, rather stout, somewhat advanced in years, wrinkled, and wearing a sort of nightcap which he seldom took off."[52] This impression did not deter Lefin, Czartoryski's tutor, from adopting Wieland's literary model: a town populated by ignorant fools, excepting only the writer, whom the others disparage as a fool or dismiss as an eccentric.

Abdera and its relationship with its famous son Democritus appealed to Lefin because Wieland depicted the ancient philosopher as a thinker interested in questions much like those that Lefin tackled in his *Nachlass eines Sonderlings zu Abdera*. Vaynlez has transmitted a table of contents for each of the six chapters of this now essentially lost book. The first chapter, titled "Reveries of a Fifty-Year-Old Disciple of Kantian Metaphysics," comprised, or was intended to comprise, eight essays on human reason, addressing the ideas of Kant and of Mendelssohn's *Phaedon* (1767), from which it quotes extensively.[53] The remaining five chapters of the *Nachlass eines Sonderlings* deal with questions of perception, language, and ethics.

In Lefin's identifying as an eccentric and locating himself in Abdera, the hostile environment that he has in mind is Podolia, home to such places as Sieniawa and Mikołajów. But Lefin was less preoccupied with the backwardness of Podolia than with the culturally retarding effect on his coreligionists of the Hasidic revivalist movement, which was born in these Podolian towns shortly before his birth and against which he fought all his life.[54]

This region was the home of several major Hasidic centers, including Międzybóż, the birthplace of the movement. It was to Międzybóż that Israel Baal Shem Tov (1700–1760), the founder of Hasidism, moved in 1740, remaining there until his death.[55] Lefin also lived briefly in Międzybóż, though much later, in 1791.[56]

One of the earliest accounts of Lefin's concerns about Hasidism and thoughts on how to fight it is the document in French "Essai d'un plan de réforme ayant pour d'éclairer la nation Juive en Pologne et de redresser par là ses moeurs" (Plan for a reform intended to lighten the Jewish nation and to improve its habits). He drafted the essay in 1791 at the request of his patron Czartoryski, to help the latter as a member of the Sejm, the Polish parliament, which met in Warsaw from 1788 to 1792.[57] Published anonymously and addressed to the National Education Commission, it was, as summarized by Nancy Sinkoff, both "an apologia on behalf of Judaism and . . . a proposal for the reform of the Jewish community."[58] In this "Essai d'un plan de réforme," Lefin described Hasidism as "a new sect" built on a basis no stronger than a "weak spider's web," for all it amounted to was the crediting of prophetic and miraculous powers to the sect's leaders.[59]

A similar view is found in an anonymous prayer against the Hasidim found in the Joseph Perl archive, according to which the followers of the Baal Shem Tov "plot against your people to make them forget your Torahs [laws] and even to make them negate human understanding."[60] For Lefin, the clownish antics of the rebbes and their Hasidim constituted the greatest obstacle to the progress and happiness of the Jews of eastern Europe. He and others saw in Hasidism a folly similar to the foolishness of the Abderites, who also had implicit faith in the supernatural, thus despising Democritus, one of the earliest exponents of scientific thought.

In Lefin's last round of revisions of *Nachlass eines Sonderlings zu Abdera* in 1823, he added a remark regarding his good fortune at having finally moved "beyond the borders of Abdera" to a place "where someone engaging in scholarly work is not necessarily branded as an eccentric."[61] At some point after 1808, Lefin had left the Russian-ruled governorate of Podolia and settled in Galicia, where he lived at different times in Brody (Austrian since 1772) and Tarnopol (Austrian 1772–1809, Russian 1809–1815, and Austrian again from 1815).[62] Because both towns were important centers of Haskalah, Lefin had less reason to feel misunderstood or dismissed as an eccentric.

In the "Essai d'un plan de réforme," Lefin contended that ridicule was the best way to fight Hasidism, and to describe his Podolian milieu as Abdera was clearly to ridicule it. Nevertheless, insofar as one can surmise much about *Nachlass eines Sonderlings* from the table of contents prepared by Vaynlez or the few surviving pages of the manuscript, the targets of his satires and polemics sound more like abstract proponents of irrationality than Hasidic rebbes and their followers.

Lefin's major disciple Joseph Perl, however, did have Hasidic rebbes and their followers explicitly in mind when he invoked the name Abdera in one of his books. Perl was familiar with a wide range of the European literature of the Enlightenment and felt a particular affinity with the work of Wieland.[63] Born into a wealthy family in Tarnopol, he was fascinated from childhood by Hasidism but quickly found the movement so problematic that by the age of thirteen he had composed a damning indictment in the form of a German pamphlet titled "Über das Wesen der Sekte Chassidim" (On the nature of the Hasidic sect, 1786). Perl became a committed maskil, who founded and directed an enlightened Jewish school in his hometown, in the archive of which Lefin's *Nachlass eines Sonderlings* was preserved.

Perl shared Lefin's belief in moderate Enlightenment, which tried to strike a balance between religious and secular knowledge. His life as an activist, however, differed from Lefin's, partly because he was operating in Austrian Galicia (whereas Lefin's activism had been mainly in prepartition Poland) and partly because he belonged to the generation after such opponents of the rebbes as Lefin and Elijah of Vilna, and by his time the Hasidic bandwagon looked as if it might crush all other Ashkenazic life beneath it.

Perl's masterpiece is the satire *Megale temirin* (Revealer of secrets, 1819), a collection of fictitious letters edited by a certain "Obadiah ben

Petaḥiah."[64] The letters Obadiah is credited with finding were ostensibly written to one another by Hasidim and caricature their ideas, manner of expression, and flamboyantly ungrammatical use of Hebrew.[65] The downside of Perl's choice of Hebrew was that it limited the number of prospective readers, particularly among the followers or potential followers of the rebbes; accordingly, in pursuit of his practical objective, he also translated his book into Yiddish.[66]

In the mid-1820s, Perl wrote a sequel to *Megale temirin* titled *Boḥen tsadik* (Test of the righteous), which remained unpublished until 1838, when it appeared in Prague.[67] It is in this work of Perl's that the town of Abdera and its foolish inhabitants make their appearance.[68] This time the plot has a magical aspect to it, albeit—and this is the point—nothing out of the ordinary by the standards that Hasidic enthusiasts applied to their religious beliefs.

Obadiah ben Petaḥiah, the fictitious editor of the fictitious letters that make up *Megale temirin*, reappears in *Boḥen tsadik* as the narrator. Obadiah has now come into possession of a *shraybtafel*—a writing tablet—with speech-recognition and audio-surveillance capabilities. Specifically, it has been programmed to intercept and transcribe private conversations about *Megale temirin*.

As we join Obadiah, his device has reached the limit of its storage capacity, and he is desperately seeking someone who can transfer the data so he can delete it from his tablet and resume the recording of further conversations. This is what forces Obadiah to hit the road, hoping to find the help he needs, the essential qualification for performing the task being not specialist know-how but basic integrity. Obadiah wanders from one Jewish community to the next, "Abdera" included, seeking and failing to find anyone with enough genuine decency to be able do the job, to pass "the test of the righteous." Finally, after much traveling, he does find such a person, a farmer on one of the progressive or utopian new Jewish agricultural settlements in Russia.

When Obadiah visits Abdera, however, he finds a town very much like Wieland's Abdera. The entire population is composed of ignoramuses, be they peddlers, merchants, rabbis, or putative maskilim.[69] The inhabitants act like fools by being "empty and devoid of any kind of wisdom, knowledge, or morals" and consider everyone possessed of intellectual or scientific curiosity as *epikorsim* (heretics), just as Democritus was regarded in Abdera of old.[70] Obadiah's description of Abdera is notable for singling out the town's economic and educational elite.

Abdera is a prosperous town where commerce is king and even well-educated business leaders are so engrossed by trade as to forget their religious duties. "They do not even have a fixed mealtime," he writes, "and on the Sabbath and festivals they are oblivious to what they are eating and drinking." In short, "they literally do not know in what kind of world they go about."[71] Having singled out this class of successful businessmen with a strong grounding in Talmud study, a demographic whose members consider themselves Abdera's maskilim, he further singles out as his prime example one especially wealthy businessman-cum-advanced-scholar, whom he describes only as "a certain well-known person."[72]

*Bohen tsadik* was not well received by all maskilim, especially those from Brody. When Solomon Judah Rapoport (1790–1867), the Galician-born chief rabbi of Prague and before that the rabbi of Tarnopol, had written a positive review of *Bohen tsadik*, he had added to the book's notoriety by making overt what Perl had left covert and naming the "certain well-known person" as Ephraim Zalman Margulies (1760–1828).[73] Whereas Rapoport, a pioneering critical scholar of Jewish literature, was the most prominent strictly observant Ashkenazic rabbi of the time to identify with the maskilim and oppose the Hasidim, the equally eminent Margulies, a highly successful banker and a leading authority on Jewish law, chose the delicate, if not impossible, position of sympathizing with the maskilim and with the Hasidim. In Perl's version, Margulies is charged with hypocrisy, adopting the practicable but not courageous position of sympathizing with the maskilim among the maskilim and with the Hasidim among the Hasidim.[74]

By identifying Abdera's "certain well-known person" as Margulies, Rapoport identified Abdera as Brody, a community famous, alongside Perl's hometown of Tarnopol and almost in competition with it, as one of the great centers of Jewish Enlightenment in eastern Galicia.

*Bohen tsadik* was a roman à clef, in which Perl often encoded the names of people and places with one or other tool of rabbinic hermeneutics, such as numerological equivalence or anagrams. Even if Rapoport had not spilled the beans about Margulies, it would not have been hard to guess which Galician community, pervasively flawed despite what seemed to be powerful maskilic influence, Perl had in mind, since the consonants of Abdera coincide with those of Brody. Perl's Abdera, his city of fools, is characterized by the universality of its folly. In his view, all sections of this proud and reputedly enlightened community are corrupted, from the gullible devotees of charlatan rebbes to the materialistic pseudointellectual elite. If reports of Margulies's hypocrisy and his appeasement of the purveyors of folly were correct, even the town's leading light proved to have an incoherent position and thus to be a fool.[75]

If Schildburg in Yiddish translation is the first town full of fools in Jewish literature, Abdera, as represented by Lefin and elaborated on by Perl, is both the first town full of Jewish fools and the first foolish town in original Jewish literature. As such, it stands as a milestone on the road to Chelm.

We are getting close now; Chelm is only one hundred miles northwest of Brody as the crow flies. The road taken, however, was not as the crow flies. To get there, we must make one more stop, this time in Vilna, then in the western provinces of the Russian empire, now Vilnius in Lithuania.

## Abdera to Chelm, via Duratshesok and Khes: Ayzik Meyer Dik

Perl's *Boḥen tsadik* appeared in Hebrew only, and Abdera only just squeaked into Yiddish literature by way of a volume titled *Sipure ḥakhme Yavan* (Tales of the Greek sages) by the Galician Judah Leib ben Ze'ev (1764–1811), an important Hebraist of the German Jewish Enlightenment in Berlin and later Breslau and Vienna. Years later, his book was translated from Hebrew into Yiddish by Ayzik Meyer Dik, famous as the first full-time professional writer in Yiddish, who issued it in a bilingual edition in 1864. Abdera is mentioned here as the hometown of the laughing philosopher Democritus, but no connection to Chelm is drawn.[76] Dik, however, went on to become the first Yiddish author to write about the fools of Chelm and before that about a town that he mock discreetly calls just by an initial—the Hebrew-Yiddish letter *khes*.[77]

The Vilna-born Dik is not only responsible for the first known documented linkage of Chelm and folly, but he is also the acknowledged pioneer of popular modern Yiddish belles lettres, responsible for an enormous and varied output, published in the literary sections of newspapers and as inexpensive books and booklets.[78] He received a traditional Jewish education and was well versed in rabbinic literature as well as in the European literature of the Enlightenment, the latter fostered by the German lessons that he took in secret with a Catholic priest.[79] He was a deeply committed maskil, and his antipathy to Hasidism was equally heartfelt, although it did not prevent him from contracting a second marriage with the daughter of a Hasidic family from Nesvizh.[80]

Writing, in Hebrew and especially in Yiddish, was a calling and a livelihood for Dik. His relationship with the Vilna printing and publishing firm Romm, later famous for its 1886 Talmud edition, ensured the precarious survival of writer and publisher alike. But there was a third dimension to his writing: the opportunity it gave him to propagate Enlightenment values and polemicize on their behalf through satire.

Literary publishing in Yiddish in eastern Europe was still unusual in Dik's time, its development delayed by the strict censorship imposed by the Austrian authorities in Galicia and the Russians in Congress Poland and the Pale of Settlement.[81] Dik, however, was a Russophile, a strong supporter of government initiatives aimed at modernizing the education received by Jews, and he was on good terms with Vilna officialdom.

Steeped in Jewish and European literature, he specialized in combining the two, Judaizing what he borrowed more comprehensively than had been done in any earlier Yiddish literature adapted from European sources. He did this by setting his stories in a contemporary eastern European Jewish folk milieu and populating them with Jewish protagonists.

In 1867, Dik published anonymously a little book titled *Blitsende vitsen oder lakhpilen* (Brilliant jokes, or, laughing pills). This collection of anecdotes includes a group of six that are devoted to the wisdom of "a certain town" that he calls Khes—that is, just the initial Hebrew letter of the place name, as if not to shame the locals by naming it in full.[82] These anecdotes of Dik's are cited by the Polish Jewish historian Filip Friedman as the origin of Chelm's notoriety, in a Yiddish essay on the history of Chelm that he contributed to the *Yizker-bukh Khelm* (1954).[83] As to where the stories came from, Friedman says categorically that foolish tales entered Yiddish folklore with the name "Shildburger mayses" via the translation of the *Schildbürgerbuch* into Yiddish, adding by mistake that this text was available in Yiddish as early as 1597, the year the original version was published in German as *Lalebuch*.

Friedman's next question is, "When did they become 'Khelmer may-ses'?"[84] His reply is, "For this we do not have a real answer in our scholarly literature. It is known that in the nineteenth century several Jewish communities were renowned for their folly, for example, Posen. With the passage of time, the whole body of foolish stories coalesced around Chelm. Several Khelmer mayses were printed for the first time ca. 1867 in a small booklet of 32 pages, printed in Vilna and titled *Blitsende vit-sen*."[85] Friedman adds that Noah Pryłucki (his Polish Jewish folklorist colleague) was of the opinion that the booklet bore all the signs of Dik's work, and this is now accepted as authoritative.[86] What matters most about this for present purposes is that Friedman names "the wisdom of a certain town Khes" and describes it unhesitatingly as representing the first appearance in print of an association between Chelm and folly.

Since these stories are very brief, have not been translated, and are not available in a modern edition even in Yiddish, here they are in full:

The Wisdom of a Certain Town Khes

(1) One winter, the sky was so overcast that it was impossible for the townsfolk to perform the Sanctification of the Moon for several months in a row. But when one of them went out of town and was fifty miles away, he could see the moon bright and clear. He tilted a barrel of water toward it, and when the reflection of the moon shone brightly on the surface of the water, he quickly put a lid on the barrel and sent it back to Khes.

(2) Once, as the count drove through Khes, the town that he owned, a wheel of his carriage broke. When the nobleman wanted to pay for the rope used to fix it, the townspeople refused to accept a single kopek, saying, "You deserve the rope."[87]

(3) Once, when there was worldwide famine, they decided at a meeting to eat on alternate days.[88]

(4) Once on a Friday night that fell on the Ninth of Av, their rabbi told the *shammes* [the beadle of the synagogue] to call out a reminder to people to conduct themselves in accordance with the rules concerning private things. He answered him, "Rabbi, I had better call out tomorrow, since no one is in there today."

(5) Once, when it snowed in Khes for the first time in anyone's experience—since it snows only once in a hundred years in those

countries—the townspeople were reluctant to trample on the snow. But the *shammes* had to do the rounds to wake people for synagogue, so they decided to carry him about on a bed.

(6) Once, one of their fellow townsfolk was visiting another town and wrote them that he had recognized their moon over there. They should send him money, and he would inquire.[89]

Dik's miniature tales of Khes contain the nucleus of the whole literature of the wise men of Chelm. Some of these stories are Schildburg tales or clearly related to them, while others offer distinct variations on the theme of a town whose inhabitants have in common a particularly foolish way of thinking and acting. Dik's anecdotes open with the famous story of capturing the moon, which finds its way into almost all the subsequent collections of Chelm stories. It seems to be the key story for Dik, as if it were the perfect depiction of the foolish wise man mentality. Not only is it placed first in his set of six stories of Khes, but it returns, in variant form, as the last of the six.

The folly of trying to capture the moon, or failing to differentiate between the thing and its reflection, is one of the most universal and ancient of folktales, documented in multiple locations.[90] The attempt of a bunch of monkeys to rescue the moon when they saw that it had fallen down a well is recorded in China as early as the fifth century, and at least one version was in circulation among Yiddish speakers in nineteenth-century Europe before its appearance in Dik's "Wisdom of a Certain Town Khes." In Hirsh Lion Dor's *Brivnshteler* (1851), a child makes everyone laugh by lamenting his failure to catch the sun in a bucket.[91] Dik's moon stories differ little in spirit from the tale of the Schildburgers' attempt to shovel sunlight into sacks; his stories bear an even closer resemblance to the version, original to the 1727 Yiddish *Shildburger bukh* and reproduced in the later Yiddish editions, that involves placing a barrel of tar on top of the town hall and catching the sun in it before lowering it down into the building as a light source.[92] The Yiddish *Shildburger bukh*'s protagonists, however, are Gentiles, while Dik's protagonists are Jews, and his telling of the story is gracefully adapted to a distinctively Jewish milieu; now it is not the sun that they wish to capture in a barrel and bring indoors but the waxing moon that they are after, so as to have the chance to perform the monthly prayer ritual of "sanctification" that requires its visible presence.

Dik's one-liner of a story about the people of Khes convening an "asife" (meeting) so as to consider how best to handle a shortage of food is not strictly a Schildburg story, but *structurally* that is just what it is.[93] First, there is a problem. Next, a town meeting is called to come up with a solution. Then there is exhaustive deliberation, and after all that, the decision taken could not be more idiotic. Even if neither the overarching narrative of the *Schildbürgerbuch* nor its underlying message, a critique of Renaissance utopianism, especially Thomas More's, is preserved intact in the Chelm stories, the Schildburg tradition is responsible for elements that are fundamental to the construction of Chelm's foolish society.

When the fools of Schildburg are faced with any predicament, they always get together to consider their options. The meeting takes the form of an open and thorough debate; the pros and cons of any proposal are thrashed out to everyone's satisfaction before a decision is taken. This Schildburg process, with its emphasis on unhurried consultation and a careful balancing of competing arguments, has been described as exemplifying "deliberation"—deliberation understood as an ideal form of democratic decision-making.[94] The *Schildbürgerbuch* and, in its wake, Dik's "Wisdom of a Certain Town Khes," demonstrate how deliberation, if it is fools who are doing the deliberating, can point a community onto the road to chaos.

Dik's story of the attempt by the people of Khes to keep the snow pristine is, like the capturing of the moon, in substance a Schildburg story—the story of the Schildburgers' attempt to protect their salt plants, again adapted to a Jewish milieu. The watchman who has to patrol the fields is transformed into the characteristically Jewish role of the *shulkloper*, who went from house to house summoning people to prayer by rapping on their shutters, window, or door.[95] Little could be more evocative of a shtetl scene somewhere in eastern Europe, so that the letter *khes* (*ḥet* in standard Hebrew) with a *segol* could very easily stand for Chelm. "Ḥelem" is the standard spelling in Hebrew and, in the nineteenth century, often in Yiddish, too, although the initial letter *kaph* becomes more common in twentieth-century standard Yiddish orthography.

Again, the aristocratic title "count," which features in the second story of Khes, is a strictly European one, and the image conjured by the noble owner of a carriage and a largely Jewish private village or small town on his estate fits comfortably with eastern European local realities. All the same, while a village or small town might belong to an individual landowner, Chelm was a small city, the kind of place where property ownership was much more diverse.

Dik's Khes stories include one detail that argues forcefully against an eastern European location: the statement that snow (anything but a rarity in Chelm or for hundreds of miles around) was so rare in Khes that the people were awestruck by their first-ever experience of it. It is possible that Dik's literary education included that favorite of earlier eastern European maskilim, Wieland's *History of the Abderites*, and it is just possible that the Greek location of Abdera may have left its mark on Dik, at least to the ex tent of suggesting a warm climate.

Just as the Khes story led straight to the Chelm stories, it seems plausible that the name Khes led straight to the name Chelm. If Dik's readers had asked themselves which Jewish community he could have had in mind, in other words, which well-known Jewish community or communities began with the letter *khes*, they would have found that they had few choices; add the vowel that Dik provides, *segol*, and Chelm is the only contender. Other Jewish communities beginning with *khes*, for example, Chmielnik, had most or all of the same features that militate against identifying Khes with Chelm (such as heavy snowfall), plus the fact that it was not a well-known place.

Certainly, the meteorological inconsistency of the snow story did not prevent many subsequent Jewish folktale collectors and writers, among them Noah Pryłucki and Shmuel Lehman, Menakhem Kipnis, and Itsik Manger, from including this tale in their compilations of Chelm stories. That they were aware of the problem, though, is evident from the fact that they all remove any reference to the novelty of snow and thus must propose an alternative explanation of the Chelmites' reluctance to set foot on it. In the collection of Chelm stories complied by Pryłucki and Lehman, the Chelmites are implicitly credited with an aestheticism such that they cannot bear to contemplate sullying the scenery. Manger takes a similar line but explains that the wise men of Chelm wanted to preserve the pristine prospect because they were adults with the mind-set of children.[96]

Kipnis invents an elaborate paradox for his explanation. It had been an aberrant winter, he claims, with only one light snowfall, so the wise

men were determined to save what little snow there was from destruction. Otherwise there would be nowhere for a "shlitveg" (sled run) for
the farmers to bring food into town as they did every winter, a conclusion that ignored the fact that the roads were now passable.[97]

Perhaps the most striking of Dik's non-Schildburg Khes stories is that
of the foolish rabbi. It is a joke about Jewish law and, as such, enough
of an in-joke to say something about the cultural literacy of Dik's anticipated readers. The story revolves around the regulations that apply
when the Fast of Av clashes with a Sabbath. In that case, the pleasures
of the Sabbath take precedence over the mortifications of the fast day—
eating and drinking, washing, and so on. Abstention from all these, and
from sexual intimacy, is deferred to the twenty-four hours following the
end of the Sabbath but permitted on the Sabbath itself, except for sexual
intimacy, from which one must abstain on the Sabbath *and* during the
twenty-four hours following it.

After Friday-night prayers in the synagogue, the rabbi of Khes wants
the *shammes* to make an announcement reminding people "to conduct
themselves in accordance with the rules concerning private things," that
is, reminding them of the prohibition of marital relations on the Sabbath
when the Ninth of Av falls on that day of the week and observance of the
fast day is in other respects deferred to the following day. The rabbi is
not just too *frum* (pious) to do the job himself but too squeamish even
to spell out for the *shammes* what he means.

If the *shammes* in this story is a fool for not understanding the rabbi's
meaning, the rabbi is an even greater fool, not only for his excessive
scruples but also for expecting the *shammes* to catch on to his circumlo-
cution. Instead, the *shammes* supposes from the rabbi's reference to "the
rules concerning private things" that he is meant to make an announcement through the outhouse door reminding occupants to observe the
laws and customs governing behavior therein, hence his reply: "Rabbi, I
had better call out tomorrow, since no one is in there today." This story is
the predecessor of many more tales in the Chelm canon that make fun of
spiritual leaders in the Jewish community as well as communal officials
such as beadles and teachers.

Dik's 1867 Khes stories may not, strictly speaking, be Chelm stories,
but they contain key elements of the future Chelm stories and are the
unmistakable immediate precursors of the first known bona fide Chelm

stories, also written by Dik not many years later and included in his novel *Di orkhim in Duratshesok* (The visitors in Duratshesok), published in 1872.[98] These are not only the first documented stories anywhere of the fools of Chelm; they also represent the first proper evidence of any notion of an association between foolishness and the Jews of Chelm. And they bear definite traces of *Schildbürgerbuch* stories.

Dik's novel, an anti-Hasidic satire, was inspired by Mordekhai Aharon Gintsburg (1795–1846) with his mock-kabbalistically titled *Tikun Lavan ha-Arami* (Rectification ritual of Laban the Aramaean), unambiguously subtitled "a narrative poem against the Hasidim" and first published in 1864, long after the author's death. *Di orkhim in Duratshesok* is a satire set in the imaginary town of Duratshesok, an allusion to the Slavic word *durak*, meaning "simpleton" or "fool."[99] The name Duratshesok reflects the fashion in nineteenth-century eastern European fiction of creating place names with symbolic meanings, as in the case of the Russian writer Mikhail Saltykov-Shchedrin's Glupov, in his *History of a Town* (1870).

Examples from Yiddish literature include Loyhoyopoli (Nowhereville), the setting for Yisroel Aksenfeld's (1787–1866) *Dos shterntikhl* (The headband, written in the late 1830s or 1840s, published 1861), and the evocation of a foolish town by the Hebrew and Yiddish writer Sholem Yankev Abramovitsh with his Hebrew-named Kisalon (Foolsville), rendered Glupsk in Yiddish.[100] Sholem Aleichem appropriated Glupsk as a name for one of his locales, along with other foolish names of his own devising such as Narrenberg (Fools' Hill). In 2010, the Russian American writer Boris Sandler published a new Yiddish novel in this tradition, titled *Keynemsdorf* (Nosuchville).

The inhabitants of Duratshesok are indeed simpletons or fools, cheated by two impostors who stop at the town, ostensibly for the Sabbath. One of these visitors presents himself as a cantor named Zundl Kreyehon.[101] The name Kreyehon, "crowing cock," would have been unpropitious enough given his chosen profession, but the word also has the equally discouraging idiomatic sense of "loudmouth." The other visitor styles himself Reb Borekh Bal Shem Tov, an itinerant *vunder rebbe* (wonder rabbi, or miracle worker).[102]

For the visitors to win the confidence of their victims, Zundl pretends to treat Reb Borekh with disrespect, so that Reb Borekh can feign anger and cast a spell over Zundl, whereupon Zundl can complete his role by feigning demonic possession, thereby managing to scare the whole population of Duratshesok, even the town's maskilic schoolmaster. Dik gives Reb Borekh all the attributes of a caricature rebbe; by his intercession, infertile women become pregnant and long-vanished husbands return to their abandoned wives; fortunes are told, promising imminent recovery, an easy death, or a place in the world to come. Not only the Jews but even the Christian women of Duratshesok are eager to stand in line to hand over their money and jewelry to the rebbe in exchange for his blessings and amulets. Only after the Baal Shem and, a few days later, the cantor, have departed do the Duratshesokers realize that they have been duped by a pair of experienced fraudsters; they "even began to feel embarrassed about the [apt] name of their town."[103]

This is the moment when Dik addresses his "dear readers" and suggests that if Duratshesok seems like a very foolish place, one might say the same of Chelm, "which is not at all far away" (although the fact that Duratshesok is an imaginary place makes its proximity to Chelm also imaginary). Chelm, he says, has long had a reputation for "vilde narishkeytn" (wildly foolish behavior).[104] Dik proceeds to give examples of the folly of Chelm, and these examples turn out to feature stories from the *Schildbürgerbuch* and other stories in which the Chelmites exhibit characteristic traits of the Schildburgers.

Just like the Schildburgers in the *Schildbürgerbuch*, the people of Chelm in Dik's *Orkhim in Duratshesok* sow their fields with grains of salt, reckoning, in Dik's version, that it would be more lucrative than using the land as a cemetery. The consideration they give to the nonagricultural option of a cemetery may suggest that Dik's Jewish protagonists were not experienced farmers, making their decision to sow salt almost plausible. As in the *Schildbürgerbuch*, the salt harvest is thought in Dik's Chelm to be at risk from wild animals.[105] In the *Schildbürgerbuch*, this is why the Schildburgers carry a watchman around on a litter. That story line is not used by Dik with regard to Chelm, but then he had already used it in "The Wisdom of a Certain Town Khes," in the story of protecting the snow from the *shulkloper*.[106]

Dik ends his story of sowing salt in Chelm by saying that the salt plants were lost because wild beasts licked them all up, whereupon, in a twist all Dik's own, the Chelmites convened a public meeting, just as they do at moments of crisis in Khes and Schildburg, and decided to declare war against the wild beasts. The conflict ends with casualties on both sides, including one headless Chelmite, an image that derives from the *Schildbürgerbuch* and its tale of the headless man who may never have had a head to begin with, but no one can remember.[107]

Dik, in accordance with his method, elaborates with details peculiar to Jewish life. One of the rabbis of Chelm having disappeared during the fighting, his wife believes that the headless corpse is her husband. The judges of the rabbinical court, however, require a corpse to have a head to be eligible for positive identification unless witnesses can testify that the body had no head to begin with. This is a matter of real practical concern to the apparent widow, because unless she can identify the corpse as her husband's, she will remain in marital limbo, unable to remarry, as an *agune*, a "chained woman," tied to her first husband, who may or may not be dead. Nevertheless, she cannot in good conscience tell the court for sure whether her husband had a head before he went missing, because he was always out studying all day and she never saw him in the light.

The court turns to the synagogue's Talmud-scholar habitués, but neither they nor even the *shammes* can help, for the rabbi was particular always to study as well as to pray under his prayer shawl and was never seen to remove it. When the judges ask at the bathhouse, where nudity was the norm, the attendant there cannot help either, because the dense cloud of steam always limited his view. As a last resort, the judges remember that their colleague had written many works of religious scholarship, and they realize that by studying them carefully, they will be able to determine whether he did or did not have a head. The head as a metonym for intelligence is reflected in numerous Yiddish proverbs, for example, "Az men hot nit keyn seykhl darf men keyn kop nit hobn" (If you do not have common sense, intelligence is not much use—or, literally, you do not need a head).[108] After a thorough review of the rabbi's oeuvre, the rabbinic court is finally satisfied that he could not possibly have had a head, a happy conclusion, since the headless man is therefore recognized as the rabbi and the rabbi's wife is free to remarry.

Dik is thus either the first person to record an existing folk or oral association between foolishness and the Jews of Chelm or the inventor of the association of the Jews of Chelm with folly. If the latter, why Chelm? David Roskies has documented Dik's strong identification with the Russian state, and especially the policies of Tsar Alexander II, and has found in him a characteristically Russian tendency to look down on the restive Russian colony of Congress Poland.[109] That might at least suggest why Dik should have picked on a town in Congress Poland rather than in the Pale of Settlement, the Polish-Lithuanian territories fully annexed by Russia at the end of the eighteenth century. Dik's specific choice of Chelm might even owe something to the fact that Chelm was often in the Russian news in the 1860s and 1870s, for political reasons having nothing to do with the town's Jewish population, namely, an attempt to de-Polonize and Russify the city and surrounding region by suppressing the Uniate or Eastern Rite Catholic Church, loyal to Rome, whose last remaining Polish diocese was the Eparchy of Chelm. The move was strenuously resisted by many people, priests as well as laity, and the ensuing antics were sufficient to lend the town a temporary reputation as a wild and crazy place. All this was happening in the years during which Dik published "The Wisdom of a Certain Town Khes" (1867) and *Di orkhim in Duratshesok* (1872), and it came to a head in 1875 with the involuntary reunion of the Orthodox and Uniate churches.[110]

In 1877, when Dik published his novel *Der shivim moltsayt* (The seventieth anniversary feast), he included a chapter on the situation of the Jews in Poland as well as general remarks on Polish history. He is as dismissive about Polish Jews as he is toward the Polish government. When he discusses the Sejm, the Polish parliament, he concludes that the members never agree on anything and disagree even more when they part than when they assemble. Dik writes that the Jews (exactly which Jews he does not say) use the bon mot "Khelem a shtot un Poyln a medine" (as Chelm is to towns, so Poland is to countries), meaning, presumably, that both are a laughingstock, or should be.[111]

This analogy represents the second time that Chelm and foolishness are associated in Jewish literature; either it suggests that Dik expected his readers to be familiar with Chelm's reputation for folly, or he was using this as an occasion to complete the hatchet job he had begun ten years earlier in "The Wisdom of a Certain Town Khes" and continued five years after that in *Di orkhim in Duratshesok*. Supposing a preference on Dik's part for making fun of a stereotypical Hasidic town in Russian Poland rather than one in Russia, then Chelm, a relatively large, relatively well-known, thoroughly Hasidic town, where the Jewish Enlightenment had made no inroads at all, was a natural choice. While these Hasidic Jews who constituted a large majority of the town's population will have had no direct involvement in Chelm's ecclesiastical warfare, it is possible that the coverage of this continuing trouble contributed to Dik's consciousness of the place.

Writing in the *Yizker-bukh Khelm* (Chelm memorial book), Filip Friedman says, "How it came about that a town renowned for its *lomdus* [learning] and Torah became the butt of mockery in folk humor to this day has never been the subject of scholarly research."[112] Since Friedman goes on to identify Dik's *Blitsende vitsen* as the earliest appearance of Chelm mockery in Jewish literature, his question as to "how it came about" must for him be a question as to the source of what Dik records. The fact that he has no idea is noteworthy in view of his encyclopedic knowledge of Polish Jewish history. It greatly diminishes the likelihood that any "fools of Chelm" tradition existed before Dik's 1872 novel *Di orkhim in Duratshesok* or, at most, before 1867, when readers of Dik's *Blitsende vitsen* could speculate about the identity of Khes.[113]

In the absence of a better explanation for Chelm's fate as an object of ridicule than its extrapolation from an arbitrarily chosen Khes, two propositions are likely to be true. The first is that Dik's reference in *Di orkhim in Duratshesok* (1872) to Chelm as a place with a reputation for "vilde narishkeytn" (unrestrained folly) is a reputation of his own inventing. The second is that the appearance of the phrase "Chelmer narrunim," fools of Chelm, in the third volume of Wander's dictionary of German expressions, *Deutsches Sprichwörter-Lexikon*, which appeared in 1873, implies only that his Jewish expert informant Ignatz Bernstein had reported an association in the culture between Chelm and fools, something that might mean no more than that such an association existed in Dik's novel of the previous year.[114]

Neither of the two remaining very early writers of Chelm stories, both of whom use the town as a location for anti-Hasidic satire, could be suspected of laughing at Chelm out of anti-Polish prejudice. The obscure Herts Bik (Herz Bick) was evidently a Galician—he published his book in Lemberg (Lviv)—and Y. L. Peretz came from Zamość, the closest place of any size to Chelm. In each case, it is possible that jocular rivalries might be involved, between Austrian and Russian sectors of historical Poland in the case of Bik or between neighboring communities in the case of

Peretz, and these might have lent an extra charm to the denigration of Chelm. However, absent any documentary evidence, we can assume that these writers' choice of Chelm as the place to mock was simply a matter of following Dik's precedent, adding thereby intertextual richness.

## The Sagacity of the Rabbinic Sages of Chelm: Herts Bik and Y. L. Peretz

The first book in whose title Chelm and wisdom are mentioned together is *Der Khelemer khokhem* (The wise man of Chelm), by Herts Bik, published in 1887. This is also the first book in which Chelm and its fools enjoy the starring roles. Chelm and its fools appear only in a supporting role in Dik's 1872 novel *Di orkhim in Duratshesok*, receive the briefest of mentions in Wander's *Lexikon,* and are mentioned once in passing in another of Dik's works of fiction, *Der shivim moltsayt* in 1877. All of this shows what an outlier Dik was and suggests how slight a reputation for folly Chelm must have had before he came along, and even for years afterward, if it had any such reputation at all, and there is no compelling evidence to suppose that it did.

It is fifteen years from Dik's reference to, and illustration of, the folly of Chelm as comparable to that of Duratshesok until, in Bik's book, a single Chelmite appears again in any further foolish escapades, and this time it is in a work of maskilic parody, almost lost without trace but surviving in at least two copies, one in the National Library of Israel and the other at Harvard.[115] This modest little book was printed by Jacob Ehrenpreis in Lemberg, so Chelm is mocked in print first in Vilna, capital of the Russian empire's governorate of Lithuania, and next in the capital of the Austrian empire's province of Galicia.[116] Nothing is known of the author, Herts Bik—whether, for example, he was connected to the prominent Galician Bik family, whose leading member, Jacob Samuel Bik (1772–1831), was Mendel Lefin's student.[117] Not only his first name, Herts (rather than the less central-European-sounding Yiddish equivalent Hirsh), but also the substance of his book reveal his alignment with maskilic ideas and opposition to the superstition and ignorance of an eastern European Jewry dominated by the Hasidic movement.

*Der Khelemer khokhem* is a satire directed against the narrow-mindedness inculcated by backward towns and the Hasidic lifestyle. On its title page, the book describes itself as "a geretenish fun a Khelemer vos er hot gemeynt az er iz a khohkem" (a cornucopia from a man of Chelm, a self-styled sage), adding, "un man muz lakhn az men leynt di kluge eynfele fun a Khelemer khokhem" (and one has to laugh if one reads what passes for wisdom with a wise man of Chelm).

The book contains five anecdotes, which make fun of a rabbi from Chelm and his wife. The couple is easily tricked, has a limited sense of the laws of nature or even an awareness that the world operates in any predictable fashion, and is always ready instead to attribute events to miracles. The anecdotes describe Chelm just as it was at the time: a Russian-ruled town with a minor Hasidic court, a major Russian garrison, and the Jewish businesses that depended on serving it. Thus, the stories do not present a timeless super-shtetl, an imaginary place of exclusively Jewish life, but reflect conditions in a contemporary midsized town with a mixed population of Christians and Jews.[118] The book does not, however, aim for an exact depiction of Chelm, despite certain parallels between the stories and the real-life situation of the town at the time. Rather, it seeks to present a realistic environment from which the rabbi and his wife are detached because of their narrow-mindedness, stupidity, and belief in miracles.

Bik's book tells, for instance, of how the rabbi's wife bought the same chicken thirteen times over from a Cossack vendor whose accomplice then proceeded to steal the creature back from her home again and again, until finally the two Cossacks tired of exploiting her and set off with their hen to find some other dupe. The rabbi tells himself and his wife that they have nothing to worry about because the two Cossacks will undoubtedly spend all the money they stole from her on liquor, as if that meant that the rabbi and his wife would end up suffering no loss.

Equally absurd are the rabbi's opinions as expressed to the parties to a dispute in the rabbinic court between an army contractor, who had paid for five thousand sacks of flour, and the miller, who had then failed to deliver on time. The situation proves way over the rabbi's head; rather than deciding damages, he starts berating the contractor for placing such an order. What, after all, would anyone want with such a quantity of flour? The two parties, realizing that they are never going to get anywhere, abandon the hearing.

On another occasion, the rabbi is sitting in the outhouse, a structure on stilts projecting out into the lake in Chelm. Suddenly, he hears a shot, from which he infers that he must have been mortally wounded. His pants still down, he runs into the study house and is finally pacified, taken home, and put to bed. When the doctor cures the rabbi by taking a *kneydl* (matzah ball) out of his head, a variation on the medieval and early modern European practice of cutting a supposed stone out of the head of a fool, a kind of proto-lobotomy, he is greatly relieved. But his relief lasts only until Passover, when his wife serves him *kneydlekh* (matzah balls), whereupon he runs from the house screaming, "Gevalt, di rebitsin hot mikh gevolt dershisn" (Woe is me, the rebbitzin wants to shoot me dead), at the sight of which people gather to giggle at "dem klugn rov" (the clever rabbi).[119]

On another occasion, the rabbi, traveling in winter, takes off his shoes and places them neatly on the ground before climbing aboard a sleigh and into its fur sack, and then he wonders why the shoes are not waiting for him when he reaches his destination. This is very much in the spirit of Schildburg, not differing greatly, for example, from the story of the Schildburgers who, after dropping their town bell into the lake, made a mark on the side of their boat at the point from which they threw it so that they could return to the same spot at some later date to retrieve it.

The first and longest story in *Der Khelemer khokhem* is one of the two stories of Bik's that became part of the "Chelm canon." It represents a type of a tale well known in Russia, Poland, Lithuania, and eastern Europe.[120] The rabbi decides that he would like to visit the rebbe in Zinkev for Shabbes. Zinkev (the Yiddish spelling of Zenkov, Poltava, now Zinkiv, Ukraine) was an important Hasidic center, the seat of the Zinkover rebbes, descendants of the eighteenth-century Rabbi Abraham Joshua Heschel of Apt. Between Chelm and Zenkov lies the whole width of the Pale of Settlement, over five hundred miles, which suggests that when the *Der Khelemer khokhem* notes that it was "two miles away," it does so ironically, as if trying to inhabit the mind of the geographically challenged rabbi.[121]

The rabbi gets into a horse-drawn carriage whose driver recognizes "vos far a khokhem er iz" (what kind of wise man he is), so he earns his fare for the long trip by just driving around Chelm for fifteen minutes before dropping the rabbi off on the opposite side of the market square from the spot where he picked him up.[122] The rabbi, as expected, believes himself to be in Zinkev, and so unshakable is this belief that he cannot assimilate any evidence to the contrary. All sorts of complications ensue until finally he falls ill and is nursed in his own home by his wife, whom, since he is still sure he is in Zinkev, he is unable to recognize. When he finally recovers, he is convinced that a sorcerer must have brought him back from Zinkev. As a result, he becomes more devout than ever, fasting every Monday and Thursday and each year commemorating the anniversary of his miraculous return with a special Purim, a personal celebration at which he relates all the *nisim* (miracles) that he experienced during his extraordinary journey.

The Zinkev story is often retold in later accounts of the wise men of Chelm, with minor variations; the protagonist may, for example, go to Warsaw instead of Zinkev.[123] Bik's satire about an individual wise man of Chelm is set in a town whose other inhabitants, his wife excepted, do not exhibit foolishness. The focus of Bik's mockery is solely the rabbi and his rebbetzin, in line with the maskilic preoccupation with the negative social effects of reactionary community leaders and Hasidic culture (or lack of culture). The reader is invited to laugh along with the other Chelmites, who, in several of the stories, appear as the audience for their rabbi's antics. The mockery of rabbis, their wives, and their staff or colleagues is a big part of the older maskilic satirical tradition as represented by Joseph Perl. In the late nineteenth and the early twentieth centuries, this polemic against Jewish authorities and institutions became a prominent part of the Chelm literature, appealing to such major Jewish thinkers and writers as Yitskhok-Leyb Peretz and David Frishman (1859–1922).

Frishman uses the wise men of Chelm and their ludicrous deliberations to express dismay at the proliferation of grandiose Jewish organizations.[124] Similarly, in a political article published in 1894, Peretz criticizes the proto–Religious Zionist Ḥoveve Tsiyon, a pioneering movement that encouraged the building of agricultural settlements in Palestine.[125] Peretz reports that letters received from the settlers, describing blossoming gardens and anticipating imminent redemption, have been contradicted by an emissary of the organization who has discovered that there is nothing to be seen at one of these supposed settlements but rocks and bones and that all the allocated funds have gone.[126] Peretz further reports that the rabbinic leaders of Ḥoveve Tsiyon have hushed up the scandal, and this he compares to an episode in Chelm in which a bowl of milk once went missing. According to Peretz, the cat in the house where the incident occurred had recently died and was thus off the hook; the householders had just eaten meat and were thus temporarily debarred by custom from consuming milk; and the rabbi was ready to vouch for the maidservant's whereabouts. Therefore nobody at all could be responsible for the crime.

Peretz's Chelm parable expresses the same critique of the rabbinate as Bik's *Khelemer khokhem*, but, like most of Bik's anecdotes, it does not seem to influence later Chelm literature, unlike Peretz's three proper Chelm stories, which went on to make a discernable impression on Aaron Zeitlin, Yekhiel Yeshaye Trunk, Itsik Manger, and others.

Rabbis and teachers are the main protagonists in all three stories set in Chelm by Peretz: "Der Khelemer melamed" (The teacher of Chelm, 1889), "Iber a shmek tabak" (On account of a pinch of snuff, 1906), and "In alt Khelem: A Khelemer maysele" (In old Chelm: A little story from Chelm, 1911), the date of the first of them placing him as third behind only Dik and Bik in the chronological sequence of writers of Chelm stories. Although Peretz is one of the most prolific, esteemed, and studied of modern Yiddish writers, his contribution to the fledgling Chelm literature is rarely discussed.[127]

Peretz was born in Zamość in Russian Poland, thirty-five miles south of Chelm. He received a traditional schooling but also showed an early interest in Polish, Russian, German, and French literature.[128] He practiced as a lawyer in his hometown until settling in Warsaw in 1887. In 1891, he was appointed to a paid position in the Warsaw Jewish community, and his house became one of the most important meeting places for Yiddish writers. In the years immediately before that, he was employed by Jan Bloch to work on a statistical survey of Polish Jewry. This required him to travel throughout Poland, and his encounters with so many Jews and manifestations of Polish Jewish culture and folklore greatly influenced his literary work. It may even have helped inspire him to produce his few Chelm stories and also, perhaps, to answer Dik's anti-Polish description of the Chelmites with something less dismissive.

In the earliest of Peretz's Chelm stories, "Der Khelemer melamed," the weight of humanity's sins threatens the survival of the world.[129] But the "thirty-six righteous men," the unwitting superheroes of kabbalistic and especially Hasidic mythology, are able to capture the *yeytser hore*, the "evil inclination," the inclination to do wrong, here incarnated as a demonic figure, which they kill and burn. Without evil (for example, in the form of envy or jealousy), there is no interpersonal or intercommunity tension, and the world is at peace. Then again, without evil (for example, in the form of lust or insecurity), nobody feels motivated to marry or procreate.

So the world would have ended anyway, and the intervention of the thirty-six would have been unavailing, but for the *melamed* of Chelm, who had been living for the past seven years as a hermit in the forest to deaden the evil inclination that had taken hold of him.[130] He seemed to have succeeded in this and was returning to civilization when a speck of ash from the burning corpse of the *yeytser hore* flew into his eyes. From there, it infected his entire body, and ultimately by contagion it reinfected the entire world—Peretz's own mythological explanation for the global phenomenon of evil or folly. Peretz ends his story with the narrator referring to his grandfather, who told him the story and who used to credit the *melamed* of Chelm every time he attended a wedding, circumcision, or redemption of a firstborn son, taking the view that now "in each of us there is a part of the teacher of Chelm."[131] Neither folly nor wisdom is mentioned, but submission to and rejection of the inclination to transgress are much the same thing as folly and wisdom, be it in the "wisdom literature" of the ancient Near East and the Hebrew Bible or the "folly literature" of the Late Middle Ages and Early Modernity.

In Peretz's second story, "Iber a shmek-tabak" (On account of a pinch of snuff, 1906), Peretz describes a rabbi in Chelm who has never once sinned, much to the annoyance of Satan, whose acolytes set out to trip him up. The rabbi is accustomed to walk out to the edge of town and prepare himself for the Sabbath with a recitation of the Song of Songs, and here a demon awaits him, dressed as a *daytshl*, the mocking diminutive of a *daytsh*.[132]

The rabbi is about to treat himself to a pinch of snuff, but before he can inhale, the demon imperceptibly blows the snuffbox to the ground. When the rabbi bends down to pick it up, the demon blows again. The rabbi goes to retrieve the box from where it now lies, but the demon blows again, and so on until the rabbi loses sight of the bigger picture and fails to notice the onset of the Sabbath or the fact that he has crossed the boundary of permitted Sabbath travel. The Chelmite's temptation is explicitly reminiscent of the temptation of Job, except that Job withstood terrible pressure and did not crack, while the rabbi let his perfect score be spoiled by a trifle. Peretz's moral: "Nobody ever stubs his toe against a mountain. It's the little lusts that bring a man down."[133]

In the last of these three stories, titled "In Old Chelm," the protagonist is the communal rabbi of Chelm, who, when asked for advice, proves of no practical use whatever, much as in Bik's *Khelemer khokhem*. The rabbi, seated one day in his *bezdn shtub* (courtroom), is pondering the wonders of God's creation, especially the wonders of such creatures such as "yidelekh un, lehavdl, andere" (Jews, and—not to mention them in the same breath—others [i.e., Gentiles]).[134]

Still lost in contemplation, the rabbi is visited by Yankele, a poor householder. Yankele complains that the Shabbes goy has just knocked out three of his teeth. The rabbi considers the matter and pronounces that Yankele's perfectly healthy teeth must have been defective, since Jews do not have strong teeth, something he knows because he has been having dental problems himself. When all is said and done, he explains, "The basic fault lies in the teeth."[135] Therefore, Yankele is to never again to expose his teeth to a Gentile.

Yankele keeps his mouth shut as instructed, but before he knows it, the Shabbes goy has crept up on him in the street, knocked him unconscious, and taken a bite out of the loaf he was carrying. Yankele returns to the rabbi, exclaiming that "there is no justice in this world," where "the murderer goes about scot-free."[136] The rabbi pronounces that bread is the source of all evil, citing in support the dictum that "a man sins on account of a crumb of bread."[137]

When Yankele runs into the Shabbes goy once again, this time behind the bathhouse, he is severely beaten by him. Yankele tells the rabbi how close he came to death, but the rabbi once again rallies to the Shabbes goy's defense.[138] Behind the bathhouse, he divines, must be the place where Cain killed Abel; thus, the place is imbued with danger, and people who go there do so at their peril.

Finally Yankele returns yet again. This time he had encountered his nemesis behind the synagogue, and the Shabbes goy had broken almost every bone in his body. The out-of-touch, ineffectual rabbi continues to deny that Yankele has a problem, on the grounds that any and every Jew in Chelm might also be in danger. On this basis, however, his under-reaction turns to overreaction, and he perceives that come Yom Kippur, when everyone is crowded into the synagogue and the Shabbes goy comes to light fresh candles to illuminate the closing service, he could easily seize the opportunity to set fire to the place and wipe out the entire Jewish community of Chelm all at once.

Accordingly, the rabbi calls a public meeting, has Yankele give an account of his experiences, and then pronounces his ruling: First, Yankele is to be banished from the town, because the Shabbes goy has a grievance against him, and, therefore, Yankele is a danger to the community. Second, the Shabbes goy is to get a raise from the community and an increased allowance of bread and liquor. Taken together, these things may be enough to placate the fellow.

The rabbi's twisted, mystically flavored thought processes prevent him from relating to poor Yankele as a real person in real need or from considering the possibility that the simplest explanation of any situation may well be the right one—in this case, that the Shabbes goy is the problem, not Jewish teeth, nor bread, nor the aura exuded by the site of Abel's murder. The rabbi is every bit the Chelmite sage of maskilic satire, and that Peretz has a maskilic agenda is clear from the moral with which he ends his story: "Laughable? Even so, there is a little of the rabbi of Chelm in each and every one of us."[139]

It is just like the moral of each of Peretz's other Chelm stories, the tale of the teacher ("in each of us there is a part of the *melamed* of Chelm") and the tale of the pinch of snuff ("It is the little lusts that bring a person down"). For him, just as for early modern folly literature, to be human is to err. Folly is contagious, and no one is immune. Peretz's Chelm stories are as much didactic as entertaining. They promote the cause of self-awareness, functioning as what the early modern German writers called a *Narrenspiegel* (fool's mirror). Even though the subjects of Peretz's Chelm tales are the classic maskilic targets of backward religious and educational functionaries, his message of universal foolishness goes beyond the narrow scope of maskilic satire and opens up the Chelm story to fresh ideas and ambitious literary treatments, of the kind that were to follow in the twentieth century.[140]

# 6

# The Geography of Folly

*The Folklorists and the Invention of Chelm*

Once there was modern Jew, a *daytsh*, living in Chelm, who showed no compunction about driving his car around town on the Sabbath. The wise men came up with a plan; they would strap themselves inconspicuously to the front of the vehicle, causing it, so they supposed, to tip over when it moved. The modern Jew could break a bone, which might be just the thing to give him pause. The driver, however, failed to notice their presence, and it was not he but they who came to a sticky end.

This story was included in a widely read and highly influential chapter of Chelm stories in the second volume of *Noyekh Prilutskis zamlbikher far yidishn folklor, filologye un kultur-geshikhte*, which was also one of the earliest collections of Chelm stories in the new field of ethnography.

When the writer and ethnographer Friedrich Salomon Krauss (1859–1938) submitted the dissertation for his *Habilitation* (the second doctorate traditionally required in central European universities before appointment to a regular academic position) at the University of Vienna in 1887, it was rejected. Krauss, a trained classicist who was an industrious collector of epic poetry and songs, especially in the Balkans, and of ethnographic material relating to sexuality, encountered much opposition thanks to both his subject matter and his research methods.[1] As he summarized the grounds for his rejection, which put an end to his professional advancement, the feeling was that "old women's stories and beggars' songs . . . have no place in scholarship."[2] His case reflects many of the difficulties that practitioners in the emerging field of ethnography encountered in the nineteenth century. In that period, not only was the suitability of the material contested, but so was the reliance its exponents placed on oral accounts.[3]

Undeterred, Krauss continued collecting and publishing his material despite never obtaining a permanent academic job. Among his many readers was Sigmund Freud. Between 1890 and 1898, Krauss was the editor of one of the earliest ethnographic journals, *Am Ur-Quell* (At the source), published monthly in Hamburg.[4] It was the first of the journals in the new disciplines of ethnography and folklore to publish a collection of stories about Chelm, which appeared in 1892 under the title "Abderiten von heute unter den Juden" (Modern-day Abderites among the Jews).[5]

Under the far-reaching influence of Wieland's *History of the Abderites* (1781), the name Abdera had become established as a generic term for a town full of foolish inhabitants. The idea of such a place, or many such places, took hold as a popular subject of oral and written storytelling, maintaining that hold through the nineteenth century and giving rise to a genre of *Schildbürgerbuch*-inspired literature known as Abderite tales and often set in Schilda. Soon repertoires of variant Abderite tales came to be viewed as local or regional patrimony, along the lines of Eric Hobsbawm's notion of "invented tradition," which, as he puts it, seeks "to inculcate certain values and norms of behaviour by repetition, which automatically implies continuity with the past."[6] Thus, Schilda, in its capacity as a spiritual heir of Abdera, became a symbol of German national pride, even though what it symbolized was German folly.

This new trend in the late eighteenth and the nineteenth centuries of locating folly on the map, which started out as Schöttgen's erudite joke and was adopted in various Enlightenment reworkings of the *Schildbürgerbuch*, which named their location Schilda rather than Schildburg, was next taken up by the practitioners of the new, increasingly nationalistic field of German studies, especially scholars of German philology and ethnography. When Jewish nationalism developed as a response to European and especially German nationalism and to the antisemitism that was its corollary, a need was perceived for Jews to have a foolish town of their own. It is this need that largely explains Chelm's notoriety.

European scholars and writers began assigning real-world geographical locations to fictitious foolish towns and collecting stories about them. Jewish collections of such stories appeared in ethnographic journals, chiefly in German and Yiddish but also in Polish. These ethnographic accounts were published in the late nineteenth and early twentieth centuries, both as individual tales in newspapers, periodicals, and antholo-

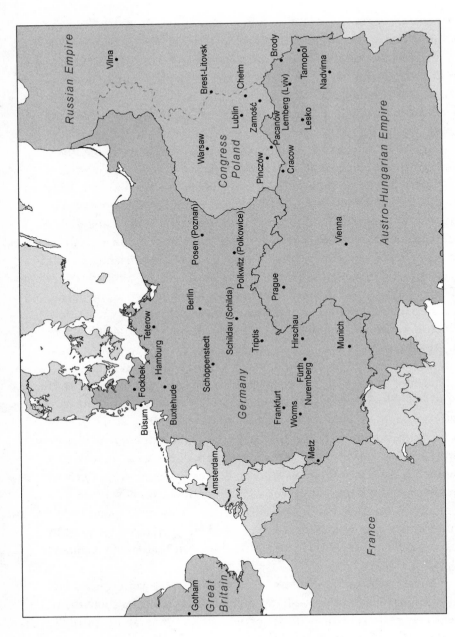

Foolish towns of pre–World War One Europe (Martin Kober, Hamburg)

gies and in book-length treatments by a single author, and they represent the point of departure for the proliferation of Yiddish Chelm stories.

During and after World War One, eastern Europe, especially Poland, started to become much more widely perceived among German Jews as the location par excellence of authentic Jewish culture, and as a result, literary Chelm frequently came to function as a representative Polish Jewish community, sometimes introduced to German-language Jewish readers with explicit reference to the German *Schildbürgerbuch* tradition. As a parallel phenomenon, Chelm stories in Yiddish, rooted in the ethnographic collections, started to proliferate after 1922–1923, when Menakhem Kipnis contributed a series of Chelm columns as a Friday feature in the Warsaw-based Yiddish daily newspaper *Haynt*.

## How Schildburg Became German

That Schildburg was to be understood as an imaginary place is clear from the fact that it was located by its creator in the fictitious kingdom of Utopia. This detail is retained in more than thirty editions of the *Schildbürgerbuch*, from the earliest, printed in 1598, through the eighteenth century.[7] Not until 1747 is there any definitive evidence of the invented name Schildburg being associated with the town of Schilda in the district of Torgau in Saxony, and even then, it was only in jest.[8] Schilda, a minor market town near Leipzig that has nowadays settled on the alternative spelling Schildau, was first mentioned in 1184 but always remained a small place, with only 81 houses in 1551 and 128 in 1747.[9] Any association between Schilda and the foolish deeds of the Schildburgers in these early years seems tenuous.

Closest to being explicit with regard to such a connection is Martin Zeiller (1589–1661), who refers in his *Itinerarium Germaniae Novantiquae* (1632) to "Schilda in Meissen, which, together with Hirschau, gets mocked a lot," although mocked for what he does not say. He says much the same in his voluminous *Topographia Germaniae* (1642–1654), a series best known for its engravings by Matthäus Merian (1593–1650). In the second edition of this work, published by Merian's sons in 1690, it is finally made clear that the two towns were renowned only for their "silly, ridiculous deeds."[10]

The connection between Schilda and Schildburg took off only in the mid-eighteenth-century when Johann Christian Schöttgen published his *Vertheidigung der Stadt Schilda* (Defense of the town of Schilda, 1747). Schöttgen, the preeminent early modern historian of Saxony, was born in Wurzen, just a few miles southwest of Schilda, and studied theology, Oriental languages, history, and philosophy at the University of Leipzig. Before becoming rector in 1728 of the famous Kreuzschule, the cathedral choir school in Dresden, he served in a similar capacity as an educator in Frankfurt an der Oder (Brandenburg) and Stargard (Pomerania).[11]

Schöttgen's one-hundred-plus publications made important contributions to many subjects, among them pedagogy, the history of the book, the history of Pomerania and Saxony, Christianity, and Judaism, this last including an influential work on the Talmud and Christian origins and a journal titled *Der Rabbiner* (The rabbi).[12] His magnum opus is his edition of unpublished archival documents titled *Inventarium diplomaticum historiae Saxoniae superioris* (Inventory of the historical records of Upper Saxony, 1747), featuring more than twelve thousand selected items. In contrast to Zeiller, Schöttgen offers no hint of Schilda's reputation for folly in his references to the town in his major historiographical works.[13]

The same year Schöttgen published his immense *Inventarium*, however, he also found time to publish the relatively slender *Vertheidigung der Stadt Schilda*, under the pseudonym Johann Christoph Langner. The sixty-year-old polymath adopted not only a fictitious name but also a fictitious occupation and age, declaring himself to be "juris practico," a lawyer, and one at the beginning of his career.[14] He attributed his inexperience to the lack of "clients at the bar" that left him free, so he said, to take up the defense of a client "outside the bar," namely, the town of Schilda, or Schildau.[15]

Schöttgen's treatise has always been read as a serious scholarly work, one that argues exhaustively that the Saxon town of Schilda could not possibly be the place originally intended by the name Schildburg. He compares geographical, historical, and linguistic facts about Schilda with whatever he can glean about Schildburg from a close reading of the *Schildbürgerbuch*, noting all the discrepancies between the real Schilda and the Schildburg there described.

*Vertheidigung der Stadt Schilda* contains a comparison of various editions of the *Schildbürgerbuch*, including an edition of 1659 that closely resembles the first edition of 1598, as well as the undated revision by "Pomponius Filtzhut" and, very briefly, the Yiddish edition of 1727. Schöttgen's scholarly discussion of editions and source texts constitutes the first scholarly work on the *Schildbürgerbuch*. On the other hand, the author's disguise in the frame story as an inexperienced and unsuccessful young lawyer, as well as the acknowledged motivation for writing this defense, that he expected it to provide him with "a pleasant pastime," adds a facetious dimension to the treatise's serious scholarship.[16]

On the title page itself, the author announced his less-than-fully-serious intentions, stating that he had written the defense in "idle hours."[17] Hence, the booklet has a set of double meanings and includes both genuine scholarly arguments about the *Schildbürgerbuch* and its origins as well as mock arguments faux-indignantly refuting the claim that the book alluded to the town of Schilda. The *Vertheidigung der Stadt Schilda* is, therefore, a kind of highbrow sequel to the *Schildbürgerbuch*. Schöttgen's ironic tone has the effect of turning his purported defense of the town into an accusation against the place and its values.

When Schöttgen compares the edition of 1659 and the undated Filtzhut edition, he picks choice examples, selected as much for their entertainment value as their philological interest and often presented in a way that undermines rather than strengthens the case he is supposedly making. At one moment, he is rebuking Filtzhut as "a stupid guy" on account of the "Sauglocke" (literally: sow's bell; figuratively: indelicacy) that he introduces into the text by changing the innocuous statement of the original *Schildbürgerbuch* that the clock struck one to the nonsensical and impolite claim that it struck *vierzehn* (fourteen). This is nonsense inasmuch as the twenty-four-hour clock was still used by astronomers only and is impolite inasmuch as he does not spell fourteen as *vierzehn* but as "fürtzen," inevitably conjuring up the verb *furzen* (to fart).[18]

In another instance, however, Schöttgen complains that Filtzhut has altered the question that the Schildburgers ask the emperor after the meal to which they treat him. Rather than inquiring, as in the original text, if he would care to pee (*flötzlen*), Filtzhut's Schildburgers ask if he would like to smoke. Schöttgen's objection is that tobacco was an anachronism in Schildburg, a place that flourished at an unspecified but distant and certainly pre-Columbian point in the past. This sort of thing showed up Filtzhut's text as not so much emended as corrupted.

While Schöttgen's objection to the Filtzhut edition as inferior to the original is genuine, his objection to "sows' bells," indelicacy, is not. It is not just that he defends the presence in the text of the informal verb *flötzlen*. Rather, he dwells on it and, while pretending to be unfamiliar with its meaning, does so in such a way as to make sure that the reader understands what it was that the Schildburgers were really asking the emperor after dinner, namely, not whether he would care to relieve himself but whether he would like to urinate recreationally.

Schöttgen, listing the words in the *Schildbürgerbuch* that are not used in the Saxon dialect of German, states that "we [Saxons] do not know what kind of game or amusement is intended by *Flötzlen*."[19] His claim not to know "what kind of game or amusement is intended" is Schöttgen's oblique way of telling the reader what was going on in the original: that this was a reference to the phenomenon of the pissing contest, part of the cultural practice of the fool societies.[20] All this shows the *Vertheidigung der Stadt Schilda* blending scholarship and comedy, a mixture characteristic of early modern culture, in which foolishness played such a prominent part and of which Schöttgen's book is one of the last literary witnesses.[21]

Schöttgen's defense did not succeed in saving Schilda from identification with Schildburg. On the contrary, it succeeded in putting Schilda on the literary map and turning the town into a synonym of Schildburg. Several other German towns had names similar to Schildburg, among them two places called Schildberg (now Štíty, Czech Republic, and Ostrzeszów, Poland), another Schilda in Brandenburg, and Schiltach in Swabia. Schöttgen mentions the latter and suggests a connection with the notion of Swabians as fools as expressed in the term *Schwabenstreich* (Swabian antics). Nevertheless, from the late eighteenth century on, the Saxon Schilda was the most renowned foolish town in Germany, and today it is the one place in Germany that retains and cultivates such a reputation in a major way.[22]

Schilda's reputation was helped by various *Schildbürgerbuch*—inspired Enlightenment works that mentioned the town of Schilda in their title. These works include Rebmann's *Empfindsame Reise nach Schilda* and its sequel, *Leben und Thaten des jüngern Herrn von*

*Münchhausen, wohlweisen Bürgermeisters zu Schilda* (Life and deeds of Baron von Münchhausen, wise mayor of Schilda, 1795), as well as Friedrich Christian Laukhard's *Annalen der Universität zu Schilda oder Bocksstreiche und Harlekinaden der gelehrten Handwerksinnungen in Deutschland* (Annals of the University of Schilda, or, Antics and harlequinades of the learned craft guilds in Germany, 1798–1799) and Tieck's *Denkwürdige Geschichtschronik der Schiltbürger*, all of which place the action in Schilda. By the end of the eighteenth century, the fame of Schilda had eclipsed that of Schildburg.[23]

References in various literary works often drew a connection between multiple imaginary foolish towns, as when Jean Paul explains in his novel *Der Titan* (The titan, 1800–1803) that the way to progress as an author is not to read a lot but to write a lot: "a man may read thirty years with less improvement than he would gain by writing half [as long]. It is just in this way that we authors mount to such heights; hence it is that even the worst of us, if we hold out, become somewhat [proficient], at last, and write ourselves up from Schilda to Abdera, and from there away up to Grub Street," meaning, apparently, that one may begin as a fool, progress to being a slightly more refined kind of fool, and end up as a hack.[24]

Many writers of the Enlightenment considered Abdera and Schildburg/ Schilda to be interchangeable, the one the prototype for the other, even though Wieland talked only of a similarity, not a lineage. An Abdera-Schildburg equivalence is apparent in the entry headed "Schildbürger" in the *Wörterbuch der deutsche Sprache* (Dictionary of the German language, 1807–1811), by the writer and linguist Joachim Heinrich Campe (1746–1818), a favorite author of the eastern European maskilim.[25] He observes that the word *Schildbürger* is commonly understood as meaning "citizen/s of Schilda[u]," but, he says, this is a misapprehension, since one never takes the name of a town and attaches the word *bürger* (burgher/s, citizen/s) to it to describe its inhabitants. Campe also says that the term is used figuratively to describe a person whose behavior is characterized by tomfoolery, so that *Schildbürgerstreich*, Schildburger tomfoolery, means simply "tomfoolery," the same being true of *Abderitenstreich*, "Abderite tomfoolery."[26]

In an 1813 supplement to the dictionary, Campe proposes replacing *Abderitismus* (Abderitism), Kant's own term for circularity as one of his models of history, with the term *Abderitenglaube* (Abderite faith) or *Abderitenlehre* (Abderite doctrine).[27] In a broader sense, he feels, *Abderitismus* could also be replaced by *Abderitenstreich* (Abderite antics).[28] In an addendum, he recalls a discussion with a friend who suggested replacing *Abderitismus* altogether with *Schildbürgersinn* (Schildburger thinking) or *Schildbürgerstreich* (Schildburger antics), because those terms would come more readily to "unlearned Germans, who had certainly heard of the Schildburgers but not of the Abderites."[29]

Even though Campe balks at recognizing "Schildburger antics" as a new word, both *Schildbürgerstreich* and *Abderitenstreich* became standard terms used synonymously during the nineteenth century. Campe's dictionary reflects the merging of different discourses at the beginning of the nineteenth century, with the commingling of the terms *Abderiten* (from Wieland and the elite milieu of Enlightenment satire, with *Abderitismus* coined as a philosophical concept by that most serious of writers, Immanuel Kant) and *Schildbürger*, a name and a connotation with which ordinary Germans, too, were familiar.

Not only had the association with Schilda fixed Schildburg geographically within Germany, but the recent reworkings of the *Schildbürgerbuch*, with their Enlightenment agenda, also reschedule the action, so that both time and place have moved, from nowhere in particular and some time in the remote past to contemporary Germany. Abdera's location in far-off Greece was well understood by early nineteenth-century German readers but all the more meaningful given Germany's national self-image in this period as the clear successor to ancient Greece.[30]

Carnivalesque events also played a role in inventing a German foolish tradition for Schilda. Thus, when the annual Cologne carnival was reestablished in 1823 as part of a German nationalist revival after the Napoleonic occupation, each year's celebrations were thoroughly documented in a special commemorative publication. The festivities used old carnivalesque symbols such as fools' caps, bells, and hobbyhorses and revived foolish stock characters, but there were also innovations, especially a new emphasis on political satire, often evoking anti-French sentiments. The carnival's theme in 1825 was the fight between happiness and sorrow. As a new feature, foolish towns were represented, as allies of happiness, and the carnival almanac for that year supplies a list of foolish towns in alphabetical order:

In the realm of fools the following towns are famous: From antiquity Abdera, situated on the coast of Thrace and described in detail in Wieland's *Abderites*; Beckum in Westphalia, Bouchain and Bruges in France; Kashmir in India; Cleves in the Lower Rhine; Cochem on the Moselle; Dijon in Burgundy; Dülken in the Duchy of Jülich; the entire province of Gascony; the little town of Großelfingen in Hechingen; Lille in France; Mazandaran in Persia; Paris; Polkwitz in Silesia; Przelautsch in Bohemia; Rome; Schilda in Saxony; Schöppenstädt in Wolfenbüttel; York in England; Valenciennes in France; Venice; Weinheim in Swabia.[31]

This list of foolish towns brings together everywhere from Wieland's Abdera to German towns with such renowned carnivalesque institutions as the fool society of Cleves and the court of fools in Grosselfingen, to towns beyond the German-speaking lands famous for their carnivalesque performances, including Dijon in France, with its "mère folle" (Mother Folly) and celebrated fool society, the Infanterie Dijonnaise.[32]

In the 1825 Cologne carnival, representatives from these foolish towns took part in various major events, such as processions and comical public disputations. This making of the representation of foolish towns into a feature of the Cologne carnival performances was widely discussed as a notable innovation in various German journals.[33] This carnivalesque development evidently suited the zeitgeist, being well received and helping spread the notion of foolish towns within Germany and beyond.

Another factor that helped to foster the concept of foolish towns was the emerging field of German philology, closely connected to the nascent German national movement of the early nineteenth century. In this period, German Romantics rediscovered the charms of such older popular literature as the *Schildbürgerbuch*, which August Wilhelm Schlegel (1767–1845) listed in his Berlin lectures of 1803–1804 among "the books of the folk"—a basic misconception, since early modern prose novels originated among and were popular with all social classes.[34]

Inspired by Schlegel, Joseph Görres (1776–1848), hailing the *Schildbürgerbuch* as "in its way infinitely masterly and accomplished," included it in his collection of German "Volksbücher" (chapbooks), a series that was meant to form a kind of German national canon.[35] Referring explicitly to Görres, the first professor of *Germanistik* (German studies), Friedrich Heinrich von der Hagen, included a reprint of the

*Schildbürgerbuch* among the four works of German folly literature that he published in his *Narrenbuch* (Book of fools, 1811), describing them as the "ancient patrimony of the German nation."[36] Discussing the *Schildbürgerbuch* in his introduction to this collection, von der Hagen makes the remarkable assertion that "every country has its share of amusing people, more so in Germany than anywhere else, on account of their innate disposition to a superb wit and sense of humor."[37] Thus, he says, every tiny region and district in Germany has a town with a reputation for folly, although pride of place goes to Schilda in Saxony.

Von der Hagen is also the first to identify the anonymous author of the *Schildbürgerbuch* as a Saxon—wrongly, Schöttgen having already demonstrated that whoever the author was, he was not a Saxon. Von der Hagen, however, failed to appreciate his case and became Schöttgen's imaginary target long after the event by being the first scholar to explicitly identify Schildburg with Schilda, finding in the playful name Misnopotamia, the land beyond which lay Utopia (according to the *Schildbürgerbuch*), an allusion to the Saxon Margraviate of Meissen.

Even though von der Hagen discusses Schöttgen's *Vertheidigung* at length, he makes no attempt to refute Schöttgen's case that Schilda cannot possibly be Schildburg.[38] He also discusses the origins of the *Schildbürgerbuch*, which are, he declares, "enshrouded in darkness." Darkness notwithstanding, he claims, without producing any proof, that the antics described had already enjoyed a long life "in the people's mouth" before they were committed to writing.[39] He sees the *Schildbürgerbuch*, or the oral prehistory that he alleges for it, in the same spirit as that in which many other Romanticists approached medieval and early modern German literature, as part of a mythic past, a tradition in large part of their own inventing.

Von der Hagen's *Narrenbuch* was neither a best-seller nor welcomed by all scholars of German literature, including the Grimm brothers, who published a harsh critique anonymously in the *Leipziger Literatur-Zeitung* in 1812. The Grimms were particularly peeved because they had told von der Hagen in 1809 of their intention to produce a scholarly edition of the *Schildbürgerbuch*, two years after which he had forestalled them by issuing this quick and dirty reprint of a previous edition.[40]

The brothers accused von der Hagen of bad faith and pointed out a string of mistakes just in the brief bibliographical note that he had added.[41] Furthermore, they reproached von der Hagen for failing to place a "men only" warning on the book in view of the occasional indelicacy of the language.[42]

The Grimms, whose review provided many sources for the content of the *Schildbürgerbuch*, called for research on its influence, since its stories had spread across "more than thirty regions" in Germany, as well as among the Germanic "related tribes" and the Slavs and as far as Hungary, England, and France.[43] Even though the brothers do not talk specifically of multiple foolish towns, their emphasis on the far-reaching influence of the book aligns them with von der Hagen and the general interest of the moment in locating folly on a larger European map.

While von der Hagen's publication created little excitement except among the Grimms, his identification of Schildburg as Schilda in Saxony was referred to in many subsequent nineteenth-century histories of German literature. So it was that Schilda acquired a prominent role in German popular culture as a place strongly connected to German identity, symbolizing during the tumultuous first half of the nineteenth century an imaginary unified Germany of the past. Thus, the poet, literary historian, and politician Ludwig Uhland (1787–1862) said in his 1831–1832 lectures on the *Sagengeschichte* ("mythistory") of the German and Roman people that even if Germany had no real historical unity, the *Schildbürgerbuch* furnished an "imaginary unity of foolish Germany."[44]

Other leading scholars named Schilda as the home of the Schildburgers in their literary surveys. Among them were the philosopher Karl Rosenkranz (1805–1879) and Georg Gottfried Gervinus (1805–1871) in his *Geschichte der poetischen National-Literatur der Deutschen* (History of the poetic national literature of the Germans, 1836), published in multiple editions throughout the remainder of the nineteenth century.[45] Schilda, along with other towns in Germany such as Buxtehude, Schöppenstedt, Teterow, and Tripstrill, were so commonly associated with folly in the second half of the nineteenth century that the literary historian Karl Friedrich Goedeke (1812–1887) concluded, in his landmark work *Grundrisz zur Geschichte der deutschen Dichtung aus den Quellen* (Compendium on the history of German literature from the sources, 1862), that local *Stichelschwänke* (mocking jests) were spread thickly all over Germany, with the *Schildbürgerbuch* as the model for such literary treatments of "traditional local simple-mindedness."[46]

The consolidation of Schilda's position as the German foolish town par excellence was also furthered in publications aimed at general audiences, partly as a function of the Romantic agenda and partly through the rapid growth of literature for young readers. In contrast to the reworkings of the Enlightenment, the new editions of the *Schildbürgerbuch* in the nineteenth century made no attempt to relate the book to contemporary parallels. Instead, these editions followed the original structure of the book.

Between 1836 and 1878, ten new editions appeared in print, sometimes with multiple impressions and often as part of larger series of *Volksbücher* (chapbooks). Some of these editions were just reprints of earlier editions, including von der Hagen's. Others, among them the most successful by the poet and Romanticist Gustav Schwab (1792–1850), abridged the book, cutting some chapters out entirely, which mainly served to remove obscenities. Schwab's sanitized *Schildbürgerbuch* was included in his *Buch der schönsten Geschichten und Sagen* (Book of the best stories and legends, 1836), issued in many reprintings through the nineteenth and twentieth centuries and to the present day. Schwab's version, directed mainly at young readers, placed the *Schildbürgerbuch* among the books of "Germanic national poetry," which, in the Romantic view, nourished the ordinary people "alongside the hymn book and the Bible."[47]

Still other reworked editions, following the same trend toward deleting all perceived obscenities, included *Der Schildbürger wunderseltsame, abenteuerliche, unerhörte und bisher unbeschriebene Geschichten und Thaten* (The Schildburgers' wondrous, adventurous, unknown, and previously undescribed stories and deeds, 1838) by Gotthard Oswald Marbach (1810–1890) and the 1843 edition of Karl Simrock (1802–1876), though the latter is less radical and simply replaces some obscene words with dashes.[48] Simrock and others included illustrations, many of them showing an idyll of small-town life. Some editions also incorporated one or two additional stories, such as that of how the Schildburgers moved their church, which had its origin in a sixteenth-century tale by Hans Sachs.[49] The first to appropriate Sachs's tale on behalf of the Schildburgers was Ludwig Aurbacher, whose rhymed and richly illustrated Schildbürger stories (under the old title of the Lalenbürger) were published in the Munich satirical journal *Fliegende Blätter*.[50] This publication had a large and widespread circulation, and its many readers included Sigmund Freud.[51] In Aurbacher's version, the church must be moved because it is not symmetrically aligned with the newly built town hall. The story later was incorporated in various versions into the Chelm canon, as the story of how the Chelmites moved their synagogue—or moved their city's hill.

Scholars of German philology, especially many independent scholars, were not only interested in the literary history of the *Schildbürgerbuch* and other early modern prose novels but also in German proverbs and expressions, which Simrock conceived of as "a treasure accumulated over the past thousand years."[52] New collections of sayings, often based on early modern collections, included some that mentioned Schilda or the Schildburgers. The first modern collection of German proverbs, by Wilhelm Körte (1776–1846), recorded references to Schilda, the Schildburgers, and their antics under the lemma "Schild" (shield).[53] Simrock records, "He is from Schilda!" in his collection of expressions published in 1847.[54]

Collecting such sayings became a prominent part of the new practice of folklore in the second half of the nineteenth century, and many collectors combined material drawn from earlier printed sources with contemporary oral material gathered in the field. Among them were the independent scholars Otto von Reinsberg-Düringsfeld (1822–1876) and his wife, Ida von Reinsberg-Düringsfeld (1815–1876), who made research trips through Europe. Otto published a volume of proverbs and expressions associated with specific countries, regions, and towns titled *Internationale Titulaturen* (International epithets, 1863), and Ida published a corresponding volume titled *Das Sprichwort als Kosmopolit* (The proverb as cosmopolite, also 1863). Otto's book placed Schilda and the Schildburgers together with other foolish towns. Some of the allegedly foolish locations he records had never previously been listed.[55]

Schilda, Polkwitz, Schöppenstedt, and other foolish towns became so familiar that they appear without needing explanation in the *Ideen: Das Buch Le Grand* (Ideas: "Book Le Grand") of Heinrich Heine (1797–1856), published as the second part of his *Reisebilder* (Travel pictures, 1826–1827). There, the narrator emphasizes that he, like Heine, was born in Düsseldorf. "Yes Madam, that is where I was born," he says, "and I point this out expressly lest after my death the seven cities of Schilda,

Krähwinkel, Polkwitz, Bockum, Dülken, Göttingen, and Schöppenstedt compete for the honor of being my birthplace."[56] In this ironic reference to Homer's seven birthplaces, Heine replaces them with six very familiar names of foolish towns in Germany and a seventh place name, the renowned university town of Göttingen, a place the author hated.

When Heine lived in exile in Paris, he continued to use the word *Schilda* to connote German folly and provinciality, exclaiming, "Oh Schilda, my fatherland" when commenting on the Hambach Festival as a missed chance to claim unity and liberty for Germany in 1832.[57] But Heine also uses Schilda to express his longing for a home, parodying both his own life in France and the contemporary Germany of the Biedermeier era, as in the poem "Anno 1839":

> O Deutschland meine ferne Liebe,
> Gedenk ich deiner, wein ich fast!
> Das munter Frankreich scheint mir trübe,
> Das leichte Volk wird mir zur Last.

> (Oh Germany, my far-off dear,
> I all but weep to think of thee!
> Light-hearted France seems drab and drear,
> Her giddy race depresses me.)[58]

Folly enters in the second stanza, where the narrator longs for Germany's "Narrheitsglöcklein, Glaubensglocken" (foolscap jingles, church-bells' chime), by which he means the Germans' "Grobheit" (lack of sophistication) as against the French excess of it; the taciturnity of the German woman "who comes to bed without a word" as against France's "smiling women, always prating"; and Germany's quiet stagnation as against the constant change in France, where "everything is whirling, flailing."[59] Thus, the narrator imagines Germany as a backward country in which he hears "Nachtwächterhörner" (nightwatchmen's horns), "Nachtwächterlieder" (nightwatchmen's songs), and the song of the nightingale.[60]

Finally, the last stanza transports the poet to Schilda, which stands, along with the oaks, for Germany:

Dem Dichter war so wohl daheime,
In Schildas teurem Eichenhain!
Dort wob ich ich meine zarten Reime
Aus Veilchenduft und Mondenschein.

(In foolish Schilda's oaken grove
The poet's mood was so serene!
That's where my gauzy rhymes I wove
From violet scent and lunar sheen.)[61]

Heine senses the nineteenth century's new meaning for Schilda as the location of the *Schildbürgerbuch*, serving as an apt symbol of Germany and its national pride, be it on account of its folly or its provincial smugness, which Heine mocked but claimed to miss. But for all Heine's consciousness of the irony of celebrating folly as a major symbol of a fledgling national identity, its perversity was not persuasive enough to deter other Jews from seeking out Jewish foolish towns as part of their desire to form a national identity of their own.

## Proverbial Jewish Fools of Prague, Poznan, and Chelm

When the Austrian lexicographer and biographer Constantin von Wurzbach (1818–1893) published his collection of proverbs *Glimpf und Schimpf in Spruch und Wort* (Tolerance and insult in maxim and word, 1863), he explained under the keyword "Schildbürger" that the Jews had their equivalent of the small German towns associated with folly, such as Schilda, Polkwitz, Schöppenstedt, and Teterow, although "their Schildbürgers live in quite stately cities, and the Jews of Prague, Worms, Frankfurt, Metz, and Fürth are the Jewish Schildaers."[62] As evidence for Prague, he provides a paradoxical and enigmatic expression, "Der Dorf-Narr zu Prag sein" (literally: to be the village idiot of Prague).[63]

According to von Wurzbach, this phrase is used to describe the "village-idiot" Jews of Prague. Von Wurzbach relied heavily on the collection of Jewish expressions complied by Abraham Tendlau (1802–1878), *Sprichwörter und Redensarten deutsch-jüdischer Vorzeit* (Proverbs and idioms of the German Jewish past, 1860). But the saying about

Prague that Tendlau supplies, "Der darf Narr zu Prog sein!" (He must be a fool in Prague), is not quite the same as the one recorded by von Wurzbach.[64] Von Wurzbach uses the phrase "Dorf-Narr sein" (to be a village idiot) and Tendlau the phrase "darf Narr sein" (must be a fool), a discrepancy based on a misapprehension of von Wurzbach's, who understood the Yiddish verb *darfn* (must, need) as the German *Dorf* (village). Insofar as this misunderstanding suggests mishearing, it may mean that the expression was in circulation in Cracow or Lemberg in the 1840s, when von Wurzbach was stationed there as an Austrian officer before leaving the army and becoming a librarian. During his period of military service in Galicia, he was also collecting Polish expressions and Ukrainian and Polish songs.

Tendlau, the son and grandson of successive rabbis of Wiesbaden, was inspired by the Romantic movement to collect proverbs and fairy tales. He became a pioneer in publishing Jewish legends and sayings in German, based on oral informants as well as the Talmud, Midrash, medieval and early modern sources, and especially such Old Yiddish texts as the *Mayse bukh*.[65] In his collection of proverbs "recorded from the mouth of the people," Tendlau reports that the Jews of Prague, Metz, and Fürth were spoken of by other Jews as the Jewish "Schildabürger" (burghers of Schilda).[66] This seems to be the first indication of Jews of specific towns being associated with folly.[67] Tendlau's comparison of the Jews of Prague, Metz, and Fürth to the foolish inhabitants of Schilda reflects, of course, the nineteenth-century conflation of Schildburg and Schilda.

In addition, Tendlau records the epithets of other towns such as "Frankfurter Gées" (egos of Frankfurt) and a "Wormser Ness" (Worms miracle), the latter alluding to the collection of stories of miracles titled *Mayse nisim* (1696) by Yuspa Shammes of Worms.[68] By oversight, von Wurzbach includes Frankfurt and Worms on his list of Jewish foolish towns, even though they are mentioned by Tendlau for reasons other than foolishness. What Tendlau intends is to record that Frankfurt Jews were proverbial for their arrogance and that the reputation of Yuspa Shammes's book made a *Wormser nes* the German Jewish equivalent of what came to be known in eastern Europe as a *bobe mayse*, a tall tale.

Although Tendlau published his *Sprichwörter und Redensarten* in German, he often recorded the sayings in Yiddish or with Yiddish components, but all in Latin characters. This reflects the script shift that German Jews underwent in the early nineteenth century, in line with which German Jewish literature took over the role that Yiddish literature had previously played.[69] Tendlau expresses reservations about incorporating Yiddish, partly because he accepted the period view of Yiddish as "a corrupted German idiom" and partly out of concern lest his collection be misused for anti-Jewish polemics.[70] Nevertheless, he chose to record these expressions as closely as possible to their original form to preserve the characteristic traits of the *Mundart* (dialect) spoken in the Jewish communities of Germany and beyond.

Despite Tendlau's misgivings, his collection of sayings was well received among non-Jewish readers. Dictionaries, encyclopedias, and anthologies seem to have provided a forum for the exchange of ideas and information at a time when other arenas of intellectual exchange, such as the German universities, excluded Yiddish language and literature as topics of potential interest. Early folklorists and collectors of proverbs, however, often worked outside the universities, as librarians, schoolmasters, and merchants, and were little affected by academic fashions or politics. They tended to share their research with one another and to disregard differences of religious or ethnic background.

Among Tendlau's eager readers was Karl Friedrich Wilhelm Wander (1803–1879), who, between 1867 and 1880, compiled and published the largest of all these collections of German proverbs, the *Deutsches Sprichwörter-Lexikon*. Wander, a teacher who had been suspended for political reasons, had emigrated to the United States in 1850 but returned a year later and spent most of his life in Silesia as a spice merchant. His collection not only became the standard work on German expressions but also included the contributions of collectors of Jewish sayings in both central Europe and, for the first time, in eastern Europe, too, Wander treating Yiddish language and culture as a legitimate and important part of German language and culture.

Wander includes many of Blass's and Tendlau's Yiddish proverbs, not in standard German but in the original spelling, and the Jewish foolish towns of Prague, Metz, and Fürth are therefore discussed in his dictionary, along with another, previously undocumented Jewish foolish town, this time outside of Europe but evidently spoken of as such a place by European Ashkenazim, namely, Nazareth.[71] Wander includes a number of previously unpublished Yiddish expressions on the basis of correspondence with the great collector of this material Ignatz Bernstein (1836–1909), then living in Warsaw. Thus, Wander's dictionary, whose subtitle promised it to be a "Hausschatz für das deutsche Volk" (Home treasure trove for the German people), proudly featured the sayings collected by Bernstein in eastern Europe, usually marked as *Jüdisch-deutsch* (Judeo-German), treating Yiddish as a subcategory of German alongside other subcategories that he includes, such as Swiss German and Low German.

Wander's *Sprichwörter-Lexikon* provides evidence of a culture in which stories about foolish towns circulated orally in eastern Europe. It is Wander who refers, for the first time anywhere, in his 1873 volume, to the phrase "Chelmer Narrunim," the fools of Chelm, citing information supplied by Bernstein as his source for the expression. Wander's explanation closely connects Chelm to the German discourse on foolish towns: "Because of its inhabitants, the town of Chelm in Poland has a reputation similar to that of Schilda, Schöppenstedt, Polkwitz and other [places] in Germany. Many amusing stories are in circulation, which are comparable to the antics of the Abderites and to what has been written about Schilda."[72]

In addition to the expression itself, Wander records an example of its use that was sent to him by Bernstein, namely, that the people of Chelm were said to have taken steps to secure their (built-in, thus unstealable) communal oven from theft by placing above it an inscription that read, "This oven belongs in the synagogue of Chelm."[73]

The Chelmites, however, are not the only Polish Jewish fools in Wander's book. The Jews of Posen, now Poznań, then in the Prussian-ruled sector of historical Poland, are similarly fools—"posener Narren" or "Pojsner Närrunim" (fools of Posen).[74] A passage in the autobiography of Solomon Maimon (1754–1800), his *Lebensgeschichte* (1792–1793), fashioned as if an ethnographic account of a Jew from the Polish-Lithuanian Commonwealth who found his way into Enlightenment circles in Berlin and elsewhere, evidently served as a source for Posen's reputation.[75]

When Maimon was prevented by residence restrictions from settling in Berlin in 1779, he spent some time in Posen working as a teacher. At the end of his time there, an event occurred that he records in his book. A pair of antlers were mounted on a wall in the town's Jewish community hall, and all the Jews of the place, he says, believed that anyone who touched this object would die. One day, the preenlightened but increasingly independent-minded Maimon said to some of his coreligionists, "You Posen fools, do you really believe that anyone touching these antlers will drop dead on the spot?" Maimon thereupon touched the antlers but, failing to drop dead, found himself confronted with such hostility and "fanaticism" that he felt he had no choice but to set off a second time for Berlin and try his luck there once again, hoping to "destroy by Enlightenment the remnant of superstition which still clung to [him]."[76]

This same conflict, between West-facing maskilim and other Jews, whose beliefs and actions were not based on reason, furnished the background for the first literary evidence of Chelm tales. However, before the term "fools of Posen" entered Bernstein's collection, it was altered, and the story was stripped of any overt tension between enlightened and traditional Jews and turned into an account of a simple prank. The Maimon figure now becomes the poor *shammes* of Posen—not longing for Enlightenment, just desperate for money. Therefore, he secretly writes in Hebrew on the Torah ark in the synagogue the words, "Do not touch, lest you die."[77]

The frightened community orders its employee, the *shammes*, to erase the inscription, which he consents to do with the proviso that first he be permitted to raise a fund to benefit his family, whom everyone expects to momentarily lose their breadwinner. After pocketing a substantial sum, the beadle proceeds to erase everything except the Hebrew word "pen" (lest), that is, he leaves just the Hebrew characters *peh* and *nun*, which, he gleefully explains, stand for "*Posener Narren*."[78] This "folktale" is the source given for the expression "fools of Posen" provided by Bernstein and published by Wander.

When Bernstein, with the help of Binjamin Segel (1866–1931), published the results of his collecting activity in 1908, he still included the proverb "Poyzner naronim" but this time only with a brief note stating that the Jews of Posen were famous for being fools because of an incident in which their beadle had gotten the better of them.[79] The dictionary, published in Yiddish and German, adds in a German note that the beadle obviously was not from Posen.

If the space devoted to Posen's folly contracts in Bernstein's own publication compared to its treatment in Bernstein's contribution to Wander's dictionary, the attention Bernstein gives Chelm in this later work of his expands. Along with the expression "Chelemer narrunim," he offers three examples of Chelm's proverbial use in Yiddish, including an expression connoting a fool of the most extreme kind; such a person one might call "der shvants funem Khelemer khazn's indik"—the tail of the turkey of the cantor of Chelm. The phrase strings together four things that eastern European Jews had come to associate especially with foolishness: tails, turkeys, cantors, and Chelmites.[80] In fairness to tails, however, it should be noted that Yiddish, like German, uses *shvants* also in the extended sense of "penis."[81]

In another Chelm expression recorded by Bernstein, though, it seems to be regarded as a normal kind of town, since it is not the community as a whole that acts the fool but an individual who acts the fool at the expense of the community. "Khoyzek nar vil oyshungern Khelm" (Khoyzek the fool wants to starve Chelm into submission) is an expression that, courtesy of Bernstein, is also featured in Wander's collection. It derives from an anecdote about how Chelm was once besieged by a single fool named Chojsik (Khoyzek), sometimes also called "Khoyzek nar" (Khoyzek the fool), who believed that he could starve the town into submission just by lying down in front of the city gate.[82] In the end, it was he who almost died of starvation, while the rest of the population failed to notice his siege at all.

This tale was frequently told of natural fools in German literature as early as the sixteenth century.[83] Khoyzek, the etymology of whose name is uncertain, is a foolish Jewish stock character from eastern Europe.[84] He is mentioned as early as Maimon's autobiography (1792–1793), in which the author tells a similar story, although here the one-man siege takes place in Lemberg, not Chelm. Maimon compares the fool's siege and its failure with the Hasid Yossel of Kletsk's attempt to accelerate the coming of the Messiah.[85] The name Khoyzek also functions as an abstract noun denoting the kind of activity to which his disposition gives rise; the word was translated in a German-Yiddish dictionary of 1733 as "Belustigung" (merrymaking).[86]

Khoyzek is, nevertheless, a figure whose kind of folly is not that of the "artificial fool," the professional entertainer who chooses to play the fool, but that of the "natural fool," who cannot help his behavior. His folly is thus like that of the Chelmites. As a result, some stories about Khoyzek are eventually easily adapted to Chelm, such as the tale of his unsuccessful attempt to enter his house while carrying his stick sideways, which becomes the tale of the Chelmites who try to drive down a street on a wagon onto which they have loaded their logs sideways. After much struggling, they decide to solve the problem by demolishing the houses that stand in their way.[87]

Another Yiddish saying featuring Khoyzek that Bernstein records suggests the extent of the folly attributed to him: "Khoyzek nar hot zayn eygn vayb nit derkent" (Khoyzek the fool did not recognize his own wife). This notion is much like the one in Bik's story of how the rabbi of Chelm thought he was in Zinkiv although he was still in Chelm and thus was not in the right frame of mind to recognize his wife.[88]

The last example recorded by Bernstein maintains that "the Chelmites are not fools; it is just that they and folly always coincide with each other." The same thought is applied not to the Chelmites but to Khoyzek in the collection of Galician Jewish expressions published in 1923, seventeen years after Bernstein's book, by the Yiddish linguist Alfred Landau (1850–1935). Apropos of this saying and its Chelmite equivalent, *Jüdische Sprichwörter und Redensarten* observes that "countless anecdotes are in circulation about Chelm that are reminiscent of the Abderites' antics."[89]

The connection between Chelm and Abdera had been articulated earlier by Bernstein's collaborator Binjamin Segel, whose 1892 contribution to the emergence of Chelm stories via the journal *Am Ur-Quell* is key to the history of "how the wise men got to Chelm." This contribution is embedded in continuing fights over the practice of Jewish folklore and questions of assimilation versus dissimilation and Zionism versus anti-Zionism.[90]

## The Abderites of Chelm: Categorically Foolish and Distinctly Jewish

When Friedrich Krauss, editor of the journal *Am Ur-Quell*, published his "Merksprüche für Folkloristen" (Mnemonics for folklorists) in 1899, he urged his readers to remember that "mankind has a unitary origin. Its path was basically similar everywhere from the beginning, . . . and its development has exhibited the greatest resemblance in all groups [nations], insofar as they have reached the same level of civilization."[91]

It was understandable, therefore, that when Max Grunwald (1871–1953), rabbi in Hamburg and Vienna until his emigration to Palestine, founded the Gesellschaft für jüdische Volkskunde (Society for Jewish Ethnography) in 1898, aiming to "obtain an insight into the inner lives of the Jews," Krauss decried this emphasis on Jewish ethnography and culture in isolation as "Stuss" (nonsense).[92]

Krauss also states that "ethnography is neither Jewish nor Christian nor Muslim nor Buddhist nor German nor Slovak nor English nor Chinese but a science of the human." He continues by questioning whether there is a Jewish people at all "except in the fantasies of the Zionists, the inverted antisemites who deny the character of Judaism and its exclusively religious-societal significance."[93] Krauss's provocative stance and that of *Am Ur-Quell* may not have been popular in all quarters, but the journal was recognized as setting the standard in folklore studies at the end of the nineteenth century.

One area of interest that Krauss promoted through his journal was "modern-day Abderites," a topic that stimulated a succession of articles, ten in all, which appeared between 1891 and 1893 and whose contributors exemplify Krauss's view of proper ethnographic writing. The resulting assembly into a single series of mainly contemporary tales of foolish towns spanning Europe, Asia, and Africa and a range of religious identities including Judaism, Christianity, and Islam helped vindicate his premise of the unity of humankind, with what was deemed foolishness looking much the same everywhere.

The comparative ethnographer and geographer Richard Andree (1835–1912), noted for his occasionally controversial work on Jewish communities, was the first to contribute to Krauss's Abderite series.[94] Andree recognizes that Abdera is the world's first known foolish town. But offering examples from around the world, from a village in Senegambia to another in Anatolia, another in Syria, and yet another, Handschuhsheim, near Heidelberg in Germany, in all of which he finds both universal and local characteristics, he takes the view that telling jokes and comic stories about one's neighbors is part of what it is to be human, part of a "Völkerpsychologie," part of the psychological makeup shared by all people.[95] Andree thus aligns himself with Krauss's position that "the human spirit functions even in this regard [making fun of neighboring towns, tribes, and nations] everywhere in the same way."[96]

The similarities in Andree's examples are explained by a shared mentality of all human beings, whereas the divergences are explained as originating in local conditions or in specific events at a particular time in a particular place. Abderite antics, in other words, may be said to be categorically foolish but distinctly local.[97] Many contributions to research journals from the end of the nineteenth century and into the twentieth followed this line, emphasizing similarities between the tales as well as identifying local traits.[98]

Andree's article was followed by nine more on the Abderites. Most concentrated on specific foolish towns such as Büsum and Fockbek in northern Germany, whose pronounced local distinctiveness included their Low German dialect, coastal setting, and a cuisine in which herring and eel reign supreme.[99] These north German fools are also more markedly Christian; it is not their town hall that they build without windows but their church.

Two of the *Am Ur-Quell* articles were contributed by the literary historian Ludwig Fränkel, who talked in one them about tales of "Abderites in Old England" and in the other about his research on the *Schildbürgerbuch*, as well as a collection of Neo-Latin comic tales from the eighteenth century that he also connects to the Abderite motif.[100]

In the midst of this Abderite enthusiasm among pioneer folklorists, an article titled "Modern-Day Abderites among the Jews" appeared in the third volume of *Am Ur-Quell* (1892), contributed by Binjamin Wolf Segel, using the pseudonym Wolf Benjamin Schiffer.[101] Segel, who became a leading figure in German Jewish journalism, was born in the Galician village of Łopuszna near Rohatyn in 1866.[102] He studied science, art history, and philosophy in Lemberg, Vienna, and Berlin before beginning his career as an ethnographer, journalist, and writer.

No one else published as many articles in *Ost und West* (East and West, 1901–1923), the journal published by Leo Winz (1876–1952) that promoted eastern European Jewish culture to German Jewish readers and whose editor in chief Segel became.[103] But Segel also published in other German Jewish publications, such as *Der Morgen* (1925–1938), a review closely associated with the scholars of *Wissenschaft des Judentums* and others oriented toward a more general readership, including *Im deutschen Reich* (the journal of the Centralverein), the *Gemeindeblatt der Israelitischen Gemeinde Frankfurt am Main*, and the Austrian Jewish journal *Die Wahrheit*.[104]

Segel's articles in *Am Ur-Quell* are among his first publications, always signed with the pseudonym Benjamin Wolf Schiffer, though he uses additional noms de plume in later life, among them A. Benesra, Bar Ami, B. Friedberg, B. Samuel, A. Warszawski—and Doubting Thomas. Before submitting his article on Chelm, Segel had already published an article in *Am Ur-Quell*, titled "Sündenkauf" (Dealing in sins: On Jewish notions of paying for the remissions of sins), and he must have been familiar with previously published articles on the subject of Abderites.

Segel observes that both Jewish and Christian Abderite towns exist in Poland, Russia, and Lithuania, but never does a single town have both a Jewish and a Gentile Abderite reputation. Jews in these lands, he maintains, think of a town as being foolish only in terms of its Jewish population. As his example of a Christian foolish town, he names only Pacanów in southern Poland, which seems an ironic choice of Gentile Abdera given that most of its population at this time was Jewish.

Segel's three Jewish examples are Nadvirna, a Hasidic center in eastern Galicia (now Ukraine); Lesko, or Linsk in Yiddish, also in Galicia (now Poland), an old Jewish community where Jews accounted for a substantial majority of the population; and Chelm, which he describes as the best-known foolish town of the three. "Of all these towns," Segel says, "almost the same stories are told."[105] He then goes on to relate seven stories, all of which he tells about Chelm. In the *Am Ur-Quell* tradition, he finds them noteworthy because of their similarity to other stories of Abderites.

Two of the tales he relates had already been told by Dik: the tale of the *shammes* in the snow and a version of the story of capturing the moon, this time, though, in a barrel not of water (as in Dik's "Wisdom of a Certain Town Khes") but of liquor; both of these stories of Dik's derive from the Schildburg tradition, as discussed in chapter 4.[106] Four of the other anecdotes that Segel presents are again genuine Schildburg stories, not found in Dik. Moreover, the narrative style of the stories recorded by Segel is very similar to that of the German Schildburg stories, differing only in details. Sometimes these changes make the story more Jewish: in Schildburg, the wise men build a town hall; in Chelm, they build a synagogue. But, for the most part, the stories are the same: in Segel's Chelm, almost as in Schildburg, the men carry stones down the hill and then up again; in Chelm they forget to include windows in the synagogue, just as in Schildburg the townspeople forget to include windows in the town hall. In Chelm as in Schildburg, their solution is to shovel sunlight into sacks. These four stories look as if they were adapted from the *Schildbürgerbuch* to a Jewish milieu by Segel himself, with a view to fleshing out the still-embryonic Chelm tradition as a Jewish counterpart to other ethnicities' Abderite traditions.

While the later German versions of the *Schildbürgerbuch* tend to sanitize the stories, in the Chelm adaptations there is a tendency to go in the opposite direction and make them a touch more risqué. This feature would no doubt have met with the approval of Krauss, who controversially specialized in collecting risqué folk material, especially in the Balkans and Japan. Thus, there is the Schildburg story of the man who appeared to have been decapitated, except that no one, not even his wife, could be sure if he ever had a head to begin with. In the Jewish version recorded by Segel, the question is whether the headless body is that of the rabbi, and it is his wife who cannot be sure on the question of whether he ever had a head. Then comes this embellishment: the rebbetzin does remember searching him on one occasion for lice; the trouble is that she cannot remember whether the hair that she picked through was on his head or elsewhere.

Finally in Segel, we find for the first time a story that was to become one of the Chelm stories most often repeated in print. It tells of the time that the wise men of Chelm decided to move their synagogue. They took off their coats and started pushing, but while they pushed and pushed, to no actual effect, their coats got stolen. Looking back and not seeing their clothes, however, their reaction was to congratulate themselves on how far they must have moved the building. This is an old story but not part of the old Schildburger tradition. Instead, it originates in a sixteenth-century tale by Hans Sachs, which, surprisingly, had not been retold until the nineteenth century.[107] However, the story reappeared in print in 1847 in one of the revised versions of the *Schildbürgerbuch*, and it evidently reentered oral culture at this point because only thereafter do folklorists encounter it at all.[108]

That this story, resurrected in the nineteenth century, was attributed to Chelm confirms what the absence of any pre-1872 references to the fools of Chelm implies: that the Khelmer mayses are a product of the late nineteenth century. There is not a hint of even a single tale or remark before then in which the Chelmites appear even momentarily foolish, while there is one such tale from the 1790s (Salomon Maimon's) regarding Posen and two such references to Brody, disguised as Abdera, from the first half of the nineteenth century (Lefin and Perl). Dik does not, or does not clearly, associate Chelm with folly in 1867, but he does in 1872, when he is the first to articulate it. The theme remains a presence in Yiddish literature, though not a well-defined one, until Segel's seven stories, published in 1892 in the German-language journal *Am Ur-Quell*, define and establish the future Chelm genre.

Segel also included in this seminal article a list of twenty-seven epithets of other towns, some obscure, such as "Janower—Beigel," an association that leaves unclear both which of the many Janóws is intended and just what being "Bageltown Janow" implies.[109] While also uncertain, "Bóbrkaer—Levanah (moon)" plausibly enough associates Bóbrka, Galicia (now Bibrka, Ukraine) with the well-known Chelm tale of trying to capture the moon. If so, this is more probably a tale first told of Bóbrka and then reassigned to Chelm than the reverse, in line with the tendency to relocate foolish tales to a single designated foolish town. Bóbrka would thus be one of the multiple lesser Jewish foolish towns of Russian Poland, Galicia, and thereabouts to whose existence Segel all too briefly refers, communities to which at least one foolish story may have been attached, if not a fully fledged foolish reputation, during the years that such stories were much in vogue across a great swath of Europe before their consolidation uniquely around Chelm.

The likelihood of this scenario is reinforced by another article in *Am Ur-Quell* (1892), published a few months after Segel's, in which other Yiddish epithets for towns were presented by J. A. Charap, among them "Chelemer Chachumim" (wise men of Chelm) and "Brodyer Narunim" (fools of Brody), the latter perhaps a relic of Lefin's and Perl's maskilic polemics.[110] In accordance with a new emphasis in scholarly publications on involving and identifying local correspondents as sources, the article acknowledges a certain Salomon Wieser of Nowy Sącz in Galicia as an informant.

In Norbert Krause's *Am Ur-Quell* article on the Abderites in Büsum, northern Germany, he includes a story similar to the one about the

Chelmites' attempt to move their synagogue.[111] This time it is a church that needs moving and a Jew who advises the fools of Büsum to put a coat on the spot to which they wish to move the church, as a marker. Instead of watching the coat as asked, the Jew takes advantage of their foolishness and steals it. The Büsumers happily believe that they must have deposited their church on top of the coat.

It is no surprise that *Am Ur-Quell* publishes an anti-Jewish story, given Friedrich Salomon Krauss's commitment to comprehensive and comparative documentation, to which this is testimony. Krauss, however, who as a writer was also active in rebutting antisemitism, adds on this occasion a low-key editorial note recording that he had heard almost the same story from his South Slavic informants, differing only in that it lacked any reference to a Jew, casting as the rogue just a passing journeyman.

Segel also follows the idea that Andree had developed in the opening article of the Abderite series and presents Chelm as a fully developed Jewish Abdera—categorically foolish but distinctly Jewish. Growing up in Galicia and studying in Austria and Germany, Segel had many opportunities to encounter Schildburger-style stories, since tales about foolish towns were widely published in the nineteenth century, many versions for young readers and others for a general audience, and they were part of the oral culture as well as of interest to researchers and their readers. But his eventual serious interest in them accords with, or is driven by, his ideological point of view. The stories of the Jewish fools of Chelm that Segel collected or invented are very similar to stories of the Gentile fools of other Abderite towns, suiting his purpose of persuading German Jews and non-Jews through his writing that Jews had a culture comparable with that of Christians and also persuading German Jews that eastern European Jewish culture was comparable to theirs.

Segel's view becomes unmistakable in his later publications. In the last issue of *Ost und West*, he stated that "never have two peoples, a very large and a very small one, permeated each other more deeply than Jews and Germans."[112] Segel was a fierce opponent both of injustice to Jews in the Russian empire and of prejudice against eastern European Jews on the part of central Europeans, Jews and otherwise. Thus, he takes a simultaneous swipe east and west when describing the pogroms of the 1880s as the application by Russian "Chuligans" (hooligans) of German antisemitic theory.[113] He also wrote a polemic against the German Jewish philosopher and public intellectual Theodor Lessing (1872–1933), who became famous for a book he wrote many years later on Jewish self-hatred.

Lessing had published a series of articles titled "Eindrücke aus Galizien" (Impressions from Galicia), published in 1909 in the *Allgemeine Zeitung des Judentums*. Segel's rejoinder took the form of a pamphlet that he titled sarcastically *Die Entdeckungsreise des Herrn Dr. Theodor Lessing zu den Ostjuden* (Dr. Theodor Lessing's expedition to the eastern Jews, 1910), in which he dismisses Lessing's tendentious description of Jewish life in Poland and Russia.[114] He polemicized, too, against the Frankfurt-based Jewish feminist Bertha Pappenheim (1859–1936) and what he considered to be her patronizing view of Jewish women in eastern Europe.[115] Segel's polemical talents were also employed on a long and thoughtful critique of the *Protocols of the Elders of Zion* published in 1924, a popular abridgment of which he produced in 1926.[116]

Segel's Chelm stories of the 1890s are not combative in tone, but they, too, are programmatic, fitting in with his pronounced universalism. He later reveals a strong antipathy to the idea of a Jewish nation, or a "Nationaljudentum" (national Jewry), as he calls it in his essay *Die polnische Judenfrage* (the Polish Jewish question, 1916). This is mainly a critique of the cultural illiteracy of the German Jewish leaders of the Komitee für den Osten (Committee for the East), a Zionist-initiated effort begun in 1914, in coordination with the German and Austrian governments, to persuade Jews in Russia and Russian Poland to support and assist the Central Powers in exchange for postvictory recognition and representation as a nation. As World War One continued, the committee, while maintaining its political objectives, also became German and Austrian Jewry's major relief agency for Jews in the eastern European war zone. Segel's opposition to the Komitee, therefore, left him a rather isolated figure, according to his friend Chajim Bloch's 1931 obituary for him.[117]

For Segel, Jewishness was primarily a "Religionsgenossenschaft" (religious collective), whose members shared, in addition to the rites and dogmas of the religion, some characteristic traits that, far from indelible, disappeared within a generation after leaving Judaism.[118] It is not surprising, therefore, that Judaism plays a major role in the stories that Segel presents in his article (building the synagogue, moving the synagogue, the *shammes* in the snow, the rabbinic court's review of the missing rabbi's writings). Segel's stories are not told as maskilic parody, which targeted the ignorance of rabbis and rebbes and their followers. Instead, it is the town's population as a whole that is foolish—that is, its Jewish population, because in Chelm there are no non-Jews in sight.

As the German foolish towns have distinctively Christian marks of identity, Segel's Chelmites have distinctively Jewish marks of identity, but that is not what is depicted as foolish about them, any more than churchgoing is what is depicted as foolish about the Schildburgers. By introducing Chelm as the Jewish foolish town, Segel alludes to a common tradition of European foolish towns. Using the stories as part of a Jewish foolish culture and locating it in one of the largest towns with a Jewish majority, a kind of super-shtetl, he establishes folly as an extra dimension of Jewish cultural identity.

Why did Segel publish his stories in German when they are so clearly set in a Yiddish-speaking environment? In an earlier essay on the Polish Jewish question, Segel declares his love for Yiddish, although he criticizes the Yiddishist movement.[119] Even though Yiddish is Segel's preferred language in social settings—he even liked to converse with his Christian friends in Yiddish, teaching it to them so that they could appreciate its subtleties—he is convinced of its current decay and unsuitability as a medium for scholarly publications and intellectual debates. He does not expect Yiddish to flourish in the twentieth century, but he does anticipate a great role for the language as a "Kulturträger" (cultural resource). Toward that end, he has, he says, translated some of "its best results" into German and Polish.[120]

Segel evidently considered the Chelm stories to be among those "best results," and he published examples in both German and Polish. Only a year after his article in German on "Modern-day Abderites among the Jews," he published nine stories of Chelm in Polish in a volume of ethnographic material that he collected in eastern Galicia.[121] Seven of these stories are almost the same as the Chelm stories that he published the previous year in *Am Ur-Quell*. Of the two Chelm stories that he had not published previously, one is a version of a well-known Slavic folktale that had already appeared, in a different form, in Bik's *Khelemer khokhem*. In Segel's version, a man takes a nap on his way to a fair. Someone moves him while he is asleep, so that when he wakes up, he is facing in the opposite direction. He continues on his way, failing to realize that he is now taking the road by which he came. When he reaches the town, he wonders why everything about it seems exactly the same as back home; there is even a woman who looks and behaves just like his wife.

These Polish-language Chelm stories of Segel's were reprinted in a 1898 collection of Jewish humor, which includes additional Chelm tales, compiled by Henryk Lew, the ethnographer husband of the harpsichord revivalist Wanda Landowska. This section of Lew's book is titled "Nasza Abdera" (Our Abdera) and provides further variants on the synagogue-construction story (the building now lacks even a door), includes a few previously unpublished stories, and makes the connection between Chelm and other foolish towns of the world.[122]

Ethnographers of all stripes became interested in Chelm. Segel in *Am Ur-Quell* (1892) was followed by the doyen of Jewish ethnographers, Max Grunwald, who recorded two Chelm stories and the epithets applied to several European Jewish communities, "Chelemer Narrunim" (fools of Chelm) and "Posener Narronim" (fools of Posen) included.[123] These appeared in the first volume of Grunwald's journal, *Mitteilungen der Gesellschaft für jüdische Volkskunde* (1898). The material came from respondents to a questionnaire developed and sent out in 1896 by the Society for Jewish Ethnography, which Grunwald headed. The Chelm stories (the *shammes* in the snow and the moon in the barrel) are recorded much as they appear in Dik's Khes tales.

In 1924, more than thirty years after first publishing on Chelm, Segel returned to the subject, but this time openly promoting his political views and expressing his anti-Zionism in a Chelm piece that he contributed to the Vienna-based weekly *Die Wahrheit*. Titled "Das Brillantendiadem" (The diamond tiara), the piece begins with a recap of some of the best-known Chelm stories. He then adds tales of his own whose agenda is unmistakable.[124] He starts by mentioning Chelm's ancient and beautiful synagogue, built long ago by the Chelmites' wise ancestors. Their descendants, however, he says, with an obvious reference to the philistinism of contemporary Jewish leaders, are ashamed of such an old-fashioned building. Hence, they remodel the interior with paperboard, which promptly catches fire, and the building burns to the ground.

Segel's next story is about a widow, left with six children. Her husband, a rich man, was the biggest benefactor of the Jewish community in

Chelm until he lost everything in a business failure and promptly died. The widow had to sell all her belongings, starting with her diamond tiara; but eventually there was nothing left to sell, and she and her children went about malnourished and barefoot. When a stranger, appalled by her conditions, petitioned the community to provide her and the children with shoes, the Chelmites decided that shoes were not enough. Rather than buying shoes, they would buy her anew all the things that she had been forced to sell, and they would replace them in the order in which she had sold them. They located a tiara just like hers in Vienna and ordered its delivery. Calling at her house to see how their gift had been received, they were puzzled to find the precious tiara untouched on the table, while the widow and children were dead from hunger and cold.

Segel's parable is meant to illustrate the plight of the great numbers of Jewish indigents and refugees in and from eastern Europe, dislocated by World War One or the Russian Civil War that followed. To the behavior of the Chelmites in this story, he contrasted the work of Keren Ha-Yesod, the Palestine Foundation Fund. Segel had been commissioned by the Centralverein deutscher Staatsbürger jüdischen Glaubens (Central Association of German Citizens of the Jewish Faith) to write a piece on the Fund, established in 1920, which was having great success in Germany and throughout the more affluent parts of the diaspora in raising funds for Palestine development projects.[125] Segel's view of Zionism as pretentious folly becomes apparent when, sounding much like Wieland's critique of the Abderites for their overblown neoclassical Enlightenment construction projects, he simply lists a selection of Keren Ha-Yesod's planned projects: a university, a national library, a national museum, a national theater, a national opera, and a national academy of sciences in Palestine.

In Segel's view, these are people who have gotten their priorities badly wrong. What they are doing is like collecting money for a diamond tiara while the widow and her children are perishing in the cold. Segel is extremely disturbed by what he sees as the absence of any comparable commitment on the part of central or western European Jews to the relief of their distressed coreligionists to the east, and he signs his essay Doubting Thomas, in honor of Thomas the Apostle, who did not trust in the resurrection of Jesus. The essay was reprinted in *Die Wahrheit* to mark Segel's death in 1931, with an editorial commenting on his general perceptiveness, but the provocative signature was not repeated.

Although Segel was an ethnographer, for him Chelm was not only a cultural artifact but part of a living culture in which it could usefully be invoked in contemporary debates: "Chelm is everywhere, in every town a smidgen."[126] Thus, it was Binjamin Segel more than anyone whose varied contributions defined the range of ways in which Jewish literary Chelm has functioned ever since.[127]

Segel was not only a pioneer. He also had a strong influence on a younger generation of Jewish ethnographers, including those associated with the Vilna-based Yidisher Visnshaftlekher Institut (Yiddish Scientific Institute, YIVO). One of the members of the inner circle of YIVO's ethnographic commission, Naftole Vaynig (1897–1943), refers to Segel as the "altmayster fun der yidisher entnografye" (doyen of Jewish ethnography).[128] Especially prominent among Segel disciples was the ethnographer, scholar of Yiddish, and political activist Noah Pryłucki. Born in Berdichev, Volhynia (now Berdychiv, Ukraine), Pryłucki spent most of his life in Warsaw, until he fled the German occupation and settled in Vilna, where he worked for YIVO until he was killed by the Gestapo in 1941.

Pryłucki was passionate about transcribing Yiddish songs, stories, proverbs, and other ethnographic materials wherever he could find them and for organizing his many collaborators to do the same. Between 1909 and 1912, he assembled a group of young ethnographers, among them A. Almi, Shmuel Lehman, and Pinkhes Graubard in Warsaw, who committed themselves to the collection of Yiddish folkloric material.[129]

Despite the differing convictions of this group—Lehman was a supporter of the Bund (the non-Zionist Jewish labor party) and Graubard was a Labor Zionist, while Pryłucki was a Diaspora Autonomist or Folkist—they were united in identifying with the Yiddish language and culture. Pryłucki acted as their mentor, and when the group did split, it was over their approach to the standardization of Yiddish.[130] Pryłucki was notorious for his insistence on transcribing Yiddish so as to reflect as accurately as possible the idiosyncrasies of his informants, giving the fullest possible weight to variations in dialect and regional accent, a form of pedantry that elicited humorous comment from a number of writers.[131]

Pryłucki, for his part, regarded Segel as offering an exemplary model of Jewish ethnographic practice. He relied heavily on Segel's work, published and unpublished. Segel, for instance, sent him one hundred Yiddish songs that he had collected in Galicia, many of which were included in Pryłucki's book *Yidishe folkslider* (Yiddish folk songs, 1911 and 1913).[132] It is not surprising, therefore, that when Pryłucki and his collaborator Shmuel Lehman published the chapter of Chelm stories in the second volume of *Noyekh Prilutskis zamlbikher far yidishn folklor, filologye un kultur-geshikhte*, several of the stories they included were translations into Yiddish of stories that Segel had published in German in *Am Ur-Quell*.

In the first volume of *Prilutskis zamlbikher* (1912), Pryłucki and Lehman had published a remarkable list of more than four hundred expressions or sayings about the supposed characteristic attributes of the Jews of specific towns, with the attribute of foolishness ascribed not just to Chelm but to other places as well. When Ber Borokhov (1881–1917), the Labor Zionist leader and scholar of Yiddish, published his critical review of Pryłucki's work in 1913, he acknowledged that the author had a good idea in this study but contended that his methodology was so poor that it should be "thrown into the garbage."[133] Borokhov's point is that Pryłucki undermines the value of his research by according equal weight to anything that one or more informants may have told him, so that Chelm, Żelechów (between Lublin and Warsaw), and Zakritsh (presumably Zagórz in Galicia) were all represented as equally foolish towns. For Borokhov, this is scandalous, for whereas Zshelekhover and Zakritsher fools are unknown outside Pryłucki's article, and even Pryłucki produces no "folklor-shtiklekh" (folktales) about them, "Khelemer naronim" are so famous that "the entire world makes fun of them and recounts innumerable anecdotes."[134]

Indeed, nine of the four hundred expressions in Pryłucki's collection refer to Chelm, some of them taken from Bernstein and others previously undocumented, and, in the second volume of *Prilutskis zamlbikher* (1917), Pryłucki writes that hundreds of Chelm stories are in circulation. Something of the reported scale of this repertoire is conveyed in the chapter titled "Khelemer naronim" (Fools of Chelm), which includes thirty-nine Chelm tales, which Pryłucki categorizes in his postscript as *Abderiten* (Abderite stories), placing them thus in the European Schildburg/Abdera tradition.[135]

Some of the material that Pryłucki included was sent to him by Alter Goldberg, who later compiled his own book of Chelm stories. Another informant, identified only as Korman, lived in Chelm itself. But most of the tales were recorded in Lublin, presumably by Shmuel Lehman. The collection is remarkable for being the first ethnographic collection of Chelm stories entirely in Yiddish, inspiring a succession of Yiddish writers to take up the theme. Also remarkable is the fact that half the stories reported by Pryłucki are new, demonstrating that between the start of the twentieth century and the Russian Revolution, the Chelm story concept went, as it were, viral in the Jewish oral culture of Poland and the Pale.

The thirty-nine Chelm stories can be divided into two groups: first, stories from the Schildburger tradition and, second, new stories of foolishness in Chelm, often strongly characterized by their Jewish cultural references. Among the Schildburger stories are those from Segel's collection in *Am Ur-Quell* as well as other tales of Schildburg not previously applied to Chelm, notably the episode of the mousehound that was really a cat, which concludes the *Schildbürgerbuch* and which, not until more than three hundred years later, is recorded for the first time as explaining the imaginary destruction of Chelm.[136] Many other Chelm stories focus on the construction or improvement of the synagogue, which, variously, has no door, is too small, or needs to be moved. Pryłucki ends his article with numerous stories extracted from other articles in *Am Ur-Quell*'s Abderite series, such as an account of how the Friesian fools of Büsum built their church. He also provides a Yiddish abridgement of Andree's introduction, emphasizing the Chelm stories' international analogues and accepting Andree's view that the Abderite story is a function of basic human psychology.

The tales in this collection that are new often feature traits of specifically Jewish life in eastern Europe and are also often characterized by a contemporary touch, as in the story of the modern Jew who drove his car on Shabbat. But most of the new stories center on religious life and several include a degree of cruelty, such as the one about how to count a minyan in Chelm. Not only must the Chelmites stick their tongue into a box, but they are also to put something unkosher in there to deter anyone from sticking his tongue in twice.

The headless rabbi, illustration by S. Faygenboym, in Falk Heilpern, *Hakhme Helem* (Warsaw, ca. 1926)

Many stories are centered on religious buildings—the synagogue, certainly, but also the mikveh. The latter often serves as a crime scene, for instance, when there is a pig wandering Chelm's marketplace, which nobody wants to touch.[137] The rabbi comes up with a plan to put a rope around the animal's feet and drag it into the mikveh in order to drown it. But the pig lies down on the steps of the mikveh and refuses to move. The women cannot perform their ritual immersion, and the only solution the wise men can come up with is to burn down the bathhouse. The pig's consequent death is only one of many casualties in these stories of Chelm. In other tales, the carpenter drowns in the mikveh, the *shammes* is made to jump from the roof of the synagogue, and the rabbi's head is split open by some overeager Chelmites determined to free him of the annoying fly on his scalp.[138]

Another new story, embellished in many later versions of the Chelm stories, is told about a *melamed* (elementary school teacher or private tutor) and his wife.[139] It fits into a new trend in the later stories, which often focus less on the community as a whole than on particular members, especially such functionaries as the rabbi, the *shammes*, and the *melamed*. Here, the impoverished teacher visits a pupil's house, sees a strudel in the kitchen, and asks what it is. The servant explains it to him, and when the teacher gets home, he gives his wife enough money for her to bake a strudel as well. The teacher's wife, however, uses the money to buy shoes for their child.

When the teacher next comes home and there is no strudel, he and his wife start to fight, and both finally end up inside their storage chest, which has wheels, a custom common in Poland in order to be able to evacuate one's house quickly, if necessary, along with one's most precious belongings. Naturally enough, an underpaid *melamed*'s chest is empty, so the teacher and his wife fit inside easily. As they continue to fight, the lid closes on them, and the chest starts rolling downhill toward the market place. The Chelmites are so frightened by this unknown driverless vehicle that they close their shops, rush into the synagogue, and blow the shofar. God, it seems, intervenes, because the chest comes to a standstill. When the rabbi and elders open it, out step the teacher and his wife. Thus, it comes about that the wise men of Chelm enact three *takones* (amendments), thereafter permanently posted inside the town's synagogue:

1. Teachers may not live on a hill.
2. They may not own a chest with wheels.
3. They may not eat strudel.

Another of the new stories collected from informants, again reflecting Jewish tradition but this time not in conflict with modernity, contains an entirely original and subsequently well-known attempt to answer precisely our question of how the wise men got to Chelm. The germ of the story is an idea in Jewish angelology that goes back to a midrash, one of the Rabbis' expositions of the Bible, preserved in Genesis Rabba, a compendium of such teachings from around the fifth century.[140]

The idea in question, with which the tale as presented by Pryłucki begins, is that "yeder malekh hot zayn shlikhes" (every angel has its mission), that is, it exists for one specific purpose.[141] Using this tradition as a prop, some creative individual dreamt up the narrative that an angel was sent out by God with a sack of foolish souls. Its mission was to distribute these souls evenly all over the world, one fool per town; but the angel's sack came undone, and instead they all fell out on the single spot that is Chelm. These stories that Pryłucki and Lehman assembled from a mix of printed and oral sources can be seen as the starting point for the proliferation of books and anthologies of Chelm stories written in Yiddish, Hebrew, German, Polish, Russian, English, and other languages during the twentieth century.

7

# Chelm Tales after World War One in German and Yiddish

## *"Our Schilda" and "Our Chelm Correspondent"*

Once a plague of mice threatened the town of Chelm.[1] A stranger from Königsberg, a German city near the Russian border, offers to help and sells the townspeople a cat. He has to leave town by the next train, but the Chelmites suddenly become anxious to know what the creature will eat once it has finished with the mice. So they rush to the station, find their man, and pose their question to him in Russian.

In a state of confusion, he replies, "Was?" (pronounced *vas* in German—"What?"), but the Chelmites assume he is answering in Russian. The Russian *vas* (you) throws the town into turmoil, and the Chelmites, fearing for their lives, manage to catch the cat and bind it to the *shammes*. Next, intent on throwing the cat to its death, they carry it up to the roof of the synagogue, still bound to the *shammes*. The cat survives the fall, but the *shammes* is not so lucky. The desperate Chelmites trap the cat again, put it inside the synagogue, and set fire to the building. But the cat escapes to the neighboring house, which the Chelmites, like the Schildburgers before them, also burn, and so on until the entire town is incinerated; but "di kaz lebt bis hajntigen tog" (the cat lives on to this very day).[2]

When, during and after World War One, eastern Europe, especially Poland, started to become much more widely perceived among German Jews as the location par excellence of authentic Jewish culture, literary Chelm came to function frequently as a representative Polish Jewish community, sometimes introduced to German-language Jewish readers with explicit reference to the German *Schildbürgerbuch* tradition.[3] But in the heart of Yiddish culture, in such places as Warsaw and Vilna, Chelm tales also started to proliferate and inspired many collectors and writers.

With the difficult situation in interwar Poland, folklore was a flowering enterprise, into which Jews could venture, and the folksy Chelm

Catching the cat, illustration by S. Faygenboym, in Falk Heilpern, *Ḥakhme Ḥelem* (Warsaw, ca. 1926)

tales were ideal material to record, retell, and rewrite.[4] However, without Menakhem Kipnis's series in the Warsaw newspaper *Haynt* in 1922–1923, Chelm would probably never have gained the popularity it has retained until today. It was with and following Kipnis's series that the prolific publication of Chelm stories in Yiddish, Hebrew, German, English, Russian, and other languages took off.

## "Our Schilda": Chelm Stories in German after World War One

German-language collections of Jewish jokes and anecdotes published after 1918 reflect the new interest of many German Jews in eastern European Jewish culture, while at the same time making connections to the German culture of these readers. One of the most prolific writers in German of popular books on eastern European Jewish topics was Chajim Bloch (1881–1973).[5] Bloch, remembered now mainly for his book on the golem of Prague, which he based on the controversial writer Yudl Rozenberg's *Sefer niflaʾot Maharal* (Miracles of the Maharal), worked as, among other things, a book dealer whose clients included Salman Schocken and Martin Buber.[6]

Buber served Bloch not only as a source of income but also as something of a literary role model. In 1921, Bloch published *Hersch Ostropoler:*

*Ein jüdischer Till-Eulenspiegel des 18. Jahrhunderts* (Hersh Ostropoler: A Jewish Till Eulenspiegel of the eighteenth century). His subtitle interprets the Jewish fool Hershele for a German Jewish audience in terms of the familiar fictional German fool Till Eulenspiegel.[7] In the introduction, Bloch expresses his opinion that the "Polish Jew" as a type and a topic had become such a "favorite of western [European] Jewish readers" because there is "much outlandishness in him."[8] In line with this demand for eastern European Jewish outlandishness, Bloch announces his intention of issuing more collections on foolish figures, such as Shayke Fayfer, Froyim Greydiger, Khoyzek, and the fools of Chelm. None of these projects was ever realized, but other writers took on the task of presenting Chelm stories to German Jewish readers, often referring to the German Schildbürger tradition, while stressing the distinctiveness of the Polish Jewish milieu.

Thus, twelve Chelm stories are included in a collection of jokes and anecdotes titled *Schelme und Narren mit jüdischen Kappen* (Rascals and fools in Jewish hats, 1920) by Heinrich Loewe (1869–1951). A prolific writer, Loewe was one of the leading early German Zionist activists and a principal proponent of what became the Jewish National and University Library, now the National Library of Israel. His Chelm stories include a couple of tales that were previously unknown. Loewe is also the first to tell what became the often retold story of the *shammes* who complains of his inability to do the rounds on his own, knocking on every shutter to rouse the whole town in time for the predawn *selihot* prayers before the High Holidays.[9] He asks for an assistant, but the sages of Chelm have a better idea: they collect all the shutters in a central location so that the *shammes* can do his job unassisted.

Most of Loewe's other stories are already present in Dik, Segel, or Pryłucki and Lehman, but they differ here in many details, which may be understandable, given his reliance largely on a single oral informant from Płock, in central Poland. This suggests that Chelm stories were known across Poland after World War One even before Kipnis's transformative intervention. Similar versions of one of Loewe's two new stories—that of the *shammes* and the shutters—appear in a few collections published two years later in 1922, Kipnis's among them.[10] Though Loewe's collection is written in German, many words, and especially punch lines, are in a transliterated Yiddish, which serves both to present the narrative as a verbatim account and to underscore its eastern European setting.

Loewe notes in his introduction that there are many Jewish foolish towns, but he says that Chelm is, like Schilda in German culture, the most important. His Chelm is located in "Jewish Poland" near Pinczew (Pińczów, in western Galicia), which is, like Chelm, a real town, albeit a relatively small one, but nowhere near Chelm.[11] Since it makes no sense to locate a place in terms of its supposed proximity to a far more obscure place, Loewe's jocular purpose was likely to highlight Chelm's remoteness from civilization and the randomness of its selection: it is interchangeable with any number of Polish Jewish towns.

Loewe's Western perspective is evident from the contrast between this deliberately cavalier attitude toward Polish geography and his attentiveness to the geography of Germany and its foolish towns. The Khelmer mayses resonate especially well for him because of the many connections he can draw to the German narratives with which he is so familiar, and his article mentions many Schildbürger stories as well as tales attributed to other German foolish towns, such as Triptis and Teterow.

For all Loewe's Zionism, he is not driven by a Jewish nationalist agenda to be especially interested in original or distinctively Jewish aspects of the Chelm stories. On the contrary, Chelm in his view fitted nicely into the position on the emergence and nature of Yiddish language and culture that he had expressed in print. In 1915, for example, he produced a survey of *Die jüdischdeutsche Sprache der Ostjuden* (The Jewish-German language of the eastern Jews) on behalf of the Komitee für den Osten (Committee for the East), in which he stated that Yiddish is a "deutsche Mundart" (German dialect), which the Jews took from their German home to eastern Europe in the Late Middle Ages and which they had preserved like a "sanctum" so that they never lost touch with German culture.[12]

Similarly in his earlier publication *Die Sprachen der Juden* (The languages of the Jews, 1911), he stresses the primacy among eastern European Jews of the "German mother tongue as the language of domestic, social, and business communication" and notes its adoption by the "non-German-speaking" Jews whose ancestors lived in eastern Europe before the German Jews' eastward migration.[13] Loewe deeply regrets the fact that Germans, and especially scholars of German history, underrate and even reject "Judendeutsch" (Jews' German). In so doing, he says, they fail to recognize that "twelve million German-speaking Jews, of which ten million speak Jewish-German [and only two million speak standard German] constitute a strong basis of support for Germanness abroad."[14] According to Loewe, Jews took the Schildbürger stories from their German "Judengasse" (Jewish street) to their Polish ghetto.[15] They adjusted the old stories to their new milieu and added new stories, so that "diese Narren tragen jüdische Kappen" (these [German] fools wear Jewish caps).[16]

Loewe was not the only one to spell out the connection between the German *Schildbürgerbuch* and the Chelm stories. The link was also mentioned in one of the earliest examples of Chelm stories told for children, a series published anonymously in 1923–1924 under the title "Aus dem Buche der Narrheiten" (From the book of follies) in the Vienna-based *Menorah*, a lavishly illustrated journal framed as a "Familienblatt" (family paper). The Chelm series started in the second issue of the journal, in the "For our little ones" section, and continued intermittently until the tenth issue, printed in October 1924.

The children's literature of Chelm, the one area of Chelm literature where publishing activity continues unabated, with new titles in many languages including Yiddish, Hebrew, English, and Russian, using the town and its sages as a pedagogic tool to teach and reinforce Jewish identity, is a relatively late starter. The children's series in *Menorah* sets the tone, conspicuously scaling back the elements of black humor and cruelty in the older Chelm stories, so that, for example, the *shammes* who is induced to jump from the roof of the synagogue holding the cat merely breaks his leg and is permitted to live in the juvenile version. (The cat, of course, survives to fight another day in both versions.)

The prologue to the Chelm series in *Menorah* follows the post–World War One trend in German Jewry of locating authentic Jewishness in eastern Europe. The stories are framed by a narrator who purports to travel to Poland and to find, hidden in an attic, *Das Buch der Narrheiten* (The book of follies), an imaginary old book "in the language that is spoken by the Jews in Poland," an intriguingly indirect way of referring to Yiddish.[17] The narrator assumes that his readers have heard of the *Schildbürgerbuch* and *Till Eulenspiegel*. But now, he continues, he proposed to tell stories "von unseren Schildbürgern" (from our Schildburgers), invoking with the "our" a unified identity of Jews in East and West. Young Jewish readers, familiar with the German tradition, are thus encouraged to substitute for it now the Chelm tradition as their authentic heritage.[18]

The *Menorah* account of how Chelm came into being is clearly inspired by the German *Schildbürgerbuch*. Now, though, it is not Schildburg but Chelm that used to be a place of great wisdom and Chelm scholars, not Schildburgers, whom everybody asked for advice. The many visitors so disturbed everyday life that the Chelmites decided to behave stupidly, and thus foolishness became their habit. Subsequent stories serve to teach traditional Jewish practice. The moon is captured (with a net) in order to teach about the ritual sanctification of the new moon. The shofar is introduced in a new story, set on Rosh Hashanah, in which the community decides that because the synagogue is getting old, they need a new building. Three members of the community come forward, each offering to donate a suitable plot of land. It is decided that the honor will go to the most pious of the three, this to be determined by which of them builds the most admirable sukkah—a pretext, once again, for indirectly and humorously teaching a little something about Judaism, this time the holiday of Sukkot.

When *Menorah*'s Chelmites finally get around to building their synagogue, the pedagogical subtext is polemical instead of ritual. The wise men of Chelm refuse the help of a qualified bricklayer since he is not pious enough. Instead they proceed on their own "like children," simply piling bricks one on top of the other. Only later do they realize that they should have used mortar, but instead of taking professional advice, they go ahead and make their own from flour and water. Even when they start over yet again, this time using mortar made from sand and lime, their walls fall down because they have omitted to lay any foundations.

Finally, they accept the advice of the bricklayer, who tells them that they need to lay foundations, but not a word more than this are they willing to hear from him. Instead, having planted the foundation bricks in the earth, they sit back and wait for their edifice to grow. After two years, the foundations have still not produced any shoots, let alone a synagogue, and they are forced to go back to the bricklayer after all. The story, then, is a parable about the reservations of traditional eastern European Jews concerning modern or western European Jews and Jewish organizations, a major tension in contemporary Jewry that *Menorah* tried to mitigate.

Among the earlier German-language publications promoting this new appreciation for eastern European Jewish culture, *Das Buch von den polnischen Juden* (The book of the Polish Jews, 1916) by Shmuel Yosef Agnon and Ahron Eliasberg, contains two Chelm stories, one previously published by Segel and the other by Grunwald.[19] Since there was hardly anything published in Yiddish on Chelm at the time, Agnon and Elias-berg had to rely on the German ethnographic collections.

Chelm stories were also among the selections from Yiddish litera-ture made available in Romanized Yiddish—Yiddish in Western-script transliteration geared toward assimilated German-speaking Jews—as in Immanuel Olsvanger's *Rosinkess mit Mandlen* (Raisins and almonds, 1920). Olsvanger collected the stories from Jewish students and refugees who came to Switzerland from Russia and Galicia. Along with the best known of all Chelm stories, the one about capturing the moon, he also includes the story of the supposedly man-eating cat.

Between the wars, the Chelm fools make their debut in Jewish ency-clopedias. While the American *Jewish Encyclopedia* (1901–1906) and the Russian *Evreiskaia entsiklopediia* (Jewish encyclopedia, 1906–1913), the latter substantially based on its American precursor, both feature articles on Chelm, neither mentions the town's still-embryonic reputation for folly.

The entry by Jakob Pinchas Kohn, a teacher at the Talmud Torah in Leipzig, and Ludwig Davidsohn, a journalist in Berlin, on "Jewish humor and wit" in the German *Jüdisches Lexikon* (1928), however, states that Chelm is "a sort of Jewish Schilda," before adding obscurely that Chelm is preferred by Jews since it possesses "den Vorzug der tieferen Gedanklich-keit, die den Schildbürgern ermangelt" (the advantage of conceptual depth, which is lacking in the Schildburgers).[20] This entry goes on to as-sert inexplicably (having just referred to the German *Schildbürgerbuch*) that the Yiddish *Shildburger bukh* is the earliest collection of eastern Eu-ropean Jewish humor to appear in print.[21] A separate article in the same encyclopedia, under the heading "Chelmer Narronim," states briefly that the motives of the German Schildburger tradition are, in the Chelm stories, applied to Jewish community life and institutions.[22] The author of this short entry is Michael Berkowicz (1865–1935), who translated

Theodor Herzl's *Judenstaat* into Hebrew, and his sources include Bernstein, Loewe, and, chiefly, Kipnis's Yiddish articles in *Haynt*.

If the *Jüdisches Lexikon* was geared to a general audience, the German-language *Encyclopedia Judaica* aimed to represent the findings of "Wissenschaft des Judentums" (academic Jewish studies) at a higher level. Nevertheless, Mark Wischnitzer's article on the history of Chelm refers to our subject only to the extent of concluding that Chelm's "inhabitants are the designated representative fools in Jewish folktales, just like the Schildburgers in German popular culture."[23] Whether the *Encyclopedia Judaica* ever planned to elaborate on the wisdom of Chelm, perhaps in an article on Jewish humor, is unclear; publication of later volumes was put on hold in 1934 and never resumed.

The last significant German-language writing on Chelm appeared in Felix Weltsch's *Jüdischer Almanach* (Jewish almanac) of 5696 (1935–1936). The author of the piece was the prominent journalist Ezriel Carlebach (1908–1956), who grew up in Leipzig, studied in Lithuanian yeshivas, emigrated to Palestine, and later returned to Europe. He contributed to *Haynt*, for which he wrote in Yiddish, although it was not his mother tongue; published in many German-language journals, such as *Menorah*; and became editor of the *Israelitisches Familienblatt* in Hamburg.[24] Returning to Palestine in 1937, he worked for *Yediot Aḥronot* and later founded *Ma'ariv*.

Carlebach's critical descriptions of the conditions of Jewish life in the Soviet Union as well as Nazi Germany, published under the pseudonym Levi Gothelf in *Haynt*, earned him a formidable reputation as well as enemies and death threats.[25] At the height of his engagement with reporting on German and Russian totalitarianism for the Polish Yiddish press, he also found time to publish a collection of Chelm stories for a German Jewish readership. Titled "Vollständige Historie der ehrenwerten Stadt Chelm" (Complete history of the venerable town of Chelm), this feature in the *Jüdischer Almanach* started with "Preliminary Remarks of the Compiler," in which Carlebach declared that it was "our privilege," but also "our obligation," to have "our Schilda."[26]

Chelm as the Jewish Schilda, Carlebach maintained, rehabilitates the Jews, since they would otherwise be associated only with "stereotypical Jewish humor: bright, excessively bright, excessively pointed, self-ironizing."[27] By contrast, Carlebach equated the foolishness of Chelm, like that of Schilda, to simple *Blödheiten* (stupidities) that everyone could laugh at, a gentle foolish humor that is neither dazzling nor hair-splitting but corresponds precisely to the reputation that Schildbürger stories enjoyed in Germany at this time.[28]

Carlebach emphasized the folksiness of the Chelm stories, which are, he said, told among the simple people in eastern Europe. He claimed that he had altered nothing, so as to maintain "the rough, unedited text of childish stories," and, moreover, that these stories had never previously been published in such a complete collection. He had gone much further than Menakhem Kipnis, he said, who had published what was hitherto the largest collection of Chelm stories ever.[29] Carlebach's twenty-three stories, however, are nonetheless translations from Kipnis's oeuvre, with only minor alterations. His "Complete History of the Honorable Town of Chelm" marks the end of Chelm stories in German, a phenomenon that built on the audience's familiarity with the Schildbürger tradition and their interest in previously unfamiliar eastern European Jewish folk culture.

The readers of these collections were either killed in the Holocaust or forced to leave Germany, so that their descendants would read Chelm stories, if at all, in Hebrew, English, or other languages. The wise men of Chelm were rarely mentioned in German literature after 1945, but Salcia Landmann introduced some stories in her West German best-seller *Der jüdische Witz* (The Jewish joke, 1960),[30] and East German readers encountered them briefly in Fred Wander's literary memoir of the Holocaust *Der siebente Brunnen* (The seventh spring, 1971).[31] Isaac Bashevis Singer's *The Fools of Chelm and Their History*, translated from the English and published in 1975, was the first German-language volume to be dedicated entirely to this one subject.[32]

## "Our Chelm Correspondent": Chelm Tales in Yiddish after World War One

In 1922, when the well-known Yiddish singer, musicologist, folklorist, and journalist Menakhem Kipnis (1878–1942) started to publish Chelm stories in *Haynt*, the leading Yiddish daily newspaper in Poland, the event became the turning point in the transformation of Chelm stories into a full-fledged popular phenomenon.[33] He expanded the material and devised a format that served as a model for subsequent writers. Kipnis was already such a favorite among *Haynt* contributors that, as *Haynt* editor Khayim Finkelshteyn remembers, "there was no Jewish household in which Kipnis' name was not mentioned with a happy smile."[34]

Kipnis was born in a family of cantors in Uzhmir, Volhynia, and was employed as principal tenor in the chorus of the National Opera in Warsaw. According to legend, on at least one occasion the Days of Awe coincided with a run of performances at the opera, so that he spent the period dashing back and forth between the theater and the Nozyk shul, where he was also performing in a professional capacity.[35] He was also heavily involved in various ethnographic projects before World War One, as an avid photographer and collector of Yiddish folk songs. He later performed these songs throughout Europe, often with his wife, Zimre Zeligfeld (ca. 1900–ca.1942).[36] In collaboration with her, he published two popular collections of Yiddish folksongs, in 1918 and 1925, based on their personal collection, subsequently lost in the Warsaw ghetto, where Kipnis died and from where Zeligfeld was sent to her death at Treblinka.[37]

The appearance of Kipnis's Chelm stories in *Haynt* evoked differing reactions among his readers. Years later, in August 1967, the composer Henekh Kon remembered, in an article on Kipnis in *Der tog–Morgn zshurnal* (The day–Morning journal), that while his Chelm stories were a "big sensation," with many readers eagerly awaiting the next Friday edition, others would have liked to see the series discontinued. Kon recalled the editor receiving several letters from mothers in Chelm who begged him to stop printing these stories, which they saw as so damaging to their community's reputation that they feared for their daughters' prospects and foresaw a town full of "alte, farzesene moyden" (old maids left on the shelf).[38] A reporter from *Haynt*, Yoysef-Shimen Goldshteyn, remembered in fall 1972 that Kipnis and his wife had been loved in Chelm as everywhere else but became extremely unpopular there once the Chelm series appeared. The folklorist and Yiddishist Moshe Lerer, who later worked at YIVO, also intensely disliked Kipnis's Chelm project.[39]

A total of sixty-seven stories appeared, one almost every Friday between July 1922 and March 1923.[40] According to Kon, when the series ended, some devotees of the Kipnis Chelm stories threatened to cancel their *Haynt* subscription and were appeased only when Kipnis began a new humor column, this time without specific reference to Chelm. It seems doubtful that Kipnis stopped making fun of Chelm out of concern for those who felt victimized or offended by his columns, since in 1930 he reworked them into a book, which, with ninety-two stories, is one of the largest collections of Chelm stories ever produced.[41]

Kipnis's Chelm columns were titled "Fun der kluger shtot . . ." (From the wise town . . .), and the earliest stories also carried the subtitle "Ayndrikn fun Khelm gufe" (Impressions from Chelm itself), amended after the second story to "Khelemer mayses oyfgenumen in Khelm gufe" (Chelm stories actually recorded in Chelm). This underscores one of the original features of the columns that contributed greatly to their popularity. In them, Kipnis presented himself as the paper's special correspondent in Chelm, on assignment to research the history of the town and the antecedents of its perfectly normal-seeming present-day Jewish community.

The first story, published on July 14, 1922, establishes the period of the wise men of Chelm as belonging to the past, with little or nothing to do with the new Chelm. In the old days, so this first story says, people were ashamed to admit that they were from Chelm, but nowadays people are proud to be from Chelm and will even more proudly recount stories of its sages. The narrator claims that he could not find any continuity between old Chelm and new Chelm, the current Chelm Jewish population having no historical memory, being descended from migrants from Volhynia, Belorussia, and even Lithuania—a tongue-in-cheek disclaimer that he deliberately contradicts as soon as the second story, published in the same issue as the first story.

The narrator claims to have heard this second story from an aged Chelmite, who insisted he got it from a reliable source. But yet again Kipnis establishes himself as an "unreliable narrator" by turning to his readers, taking them into his confidence, and confusingly admitting "tsvishn unz geret" (just between us) that the old stories are nonsense: "nisht gestoygn un nisht gefloygn" (they do not have legs—literally, they could neither stand nor fly).[42] He also adds that while many stories have been attached to Chelm, no one knows why. Nevertheless, these stories, which he has just said may have no connection to Chelm, sound best when they are heard in or from Chelm directly.

Having categorized Chelm stories as purely fictitious, the narrator continues to have it both ways, artfully weaving into his stories facts about the real town of Chelm—its people, its history, and its physical features. Kipnis, the twentieth-century Yiddishist from the Pale, posing as an investigative reporter, seems compelled to do just what the anonymous sixteenth-century original author of the *Schildbürgerbuch* (or *Lalebuch*) and "Pomponius Filzhut," the seventeenth-century modernizer of the German text (the latter posing as Schildburg's town clerk and archivist), had done before him in sending alternating messages of "Believe me" and "Don't believe me."

Kipnis's manner of relating the story of Chelm's foolish origins exemplifies his method of embellishing and enhancing his storytelling with historical and geographical details. Chelm Hill, with its hilltop Basilica of the Birth of the Virgin Mary, a major pilgrimage destination, was and remains the town's one famous monument, and as such, it is appropriate that the hill should play a key part in the parallel universe of Jewish foolish Chelm. As reported briefly by Pryłucki, all the world's foolish souls landed in Chelm because the angel's sack in which they were traveling came undone over that spot. In Kipnis's elaboration, this accident is not random but the result of superhuman error: the angel was flying too low and thus tore the bag on the famous Chelm Hill that rises unexpectedly out of the surrounding flatlands. This is what Kipnis assures his readers he was told by an old Chelmite, who guaranteed that it was from a "truthful source."[43]

The "reporter"-narrator investigates the celebrated "gorka" (Russian: hill) and finds it to be central to other stories. This is the hill that the wise men of Chelm try to push, and this, too, is said to be the hill down which they carry the logs for their synagogue-construction project, only to carry them up again when told that they should have rolled them down instead. This last story, Kipnis says, he finds hard to believe; nevertheless, it is undoubtedly true that the "hill of the story is there," on top of which, before the Great War, was the home of the "shvartser galekh Yevlogi" (black priest [i.e., black-robed, Orthodox priest] Eulogius), he says, who lived in the monastery next to the basilica.[44] In this way, he pursues his literary agenda of muddying the waters by introducing entirely correct but entirely irrelevant details of Chelm history. The detail rings true, suggesting authenticity while simultaneously managing transparently to prove nothing at all with respect to the truth of the Jewish Chelm stories. The reference in this case, incidentally, is to Bishop Eulogius Georgievsky, from 1905 on a driving force of a separatist movement promoting the secession of Chelm and its surroundings from Russian-ruled Catholic Poland and its adhesion to Orthodox Russia proper; he was a figure so hated by Polish nationalists that he needed constant police protection.[45]

Elsewhere, Kipnis invokes such small details of other monuments in Chelm as the hooks on the exterior walls of the old synagogue. These, he claims, are the remnants of shutters that the community mounted in front of the synagogue windows back in the day of the wise men, to reduce the chances that the Torah's wisdom might escape. The narrator comments that the story must be true, since the hooks are still visible, and history "has not invented the story for nothing."[46]

Other stories dwell on one or another real or ostensibly real feature of the town. One long narrative tells of how a blacksmith came to town. Since he had a dark complexion, the backward Chelmites, mired in superstition and prejudice, supposed he might be a gypsy and thus perhaps a criminal.[47] Accordingly, they all assembled to plan precautions to avoid losses from their shops. Since break-ins were more likely to take place after dark, they first resolved to open their businesses at night and close them during the day. They quickly abandon this scheme upon discovering that none of their potential customers was awake during the new trading hours. Instead, they hire a night watchman, but he, it turns out, is scared of patrolling for fear of catching a cold.

The Chelmites deliberate and decide to give the night watchman a sheepskin coat; but the community treasurer complains that he alone is entitled to wear such a garment, and if the night watchman were allowed to do the same, people might mistake the lowly watchman for the distinguished treasurer. They come up with a solution whereby the night watchman is to wear his coat inside out, which again leads to complications, when, after nightfall, a wolf mistakes him for a sheep.

The night watchman somehow survives, and the Chelmites decide to raise him up out of harm's way on a horse. He is not a skilled equestrian, however, and cannot stop his mount from wandering out into the open country beyond the town. So the Chelmites decide to tether the horse to a post outside the old bathhouse. The same night, a gang of robbers come into town and strip all the shops, but when this is discovered the next morning and the night watchman is asked why he did not blow his horn, he answers that he did not want to disturb the sleep of the Chelmites. For this thoughtful (in)action, his salary is doubled.

This story, which Kipnis repeated in a different version a month later, in September 1922, was, he wrote on that occasion, one that had been in circulation for a while without any association with Chelm.[48] True to his Janus-like narrative strategy, however, he also provided the contradictory information that the post to which the night watchman's horse was tethered could still be seen outside the old bathhouse in Chelm up until World War One, when the Germans occupied the town and the post was uprooted, their horses being so much stronger than Chelm horses.

Kipnis's stories are distinctive for elaborating on the connection with the real town of Chelm, but they are equally distinctive for the stylization and the heightened sense of unity among the stories introduced by his use of often repeated formulae. On this account, he, too, like Dik and Segel before him, might be said in some sense to have established the Chelm tale genre.

The structure of such a tale develops as follows: a problem arises among the Chelmites, either discovered internally or introduced from the outside. The townspeople or elders gather together, deliberate endlessly, and ultimately come up with a surprising and silly solution. This structure, new in the Chelm tales but long prevalent in the Schildburg tradition, becomes reinforced by Kipnis's invocation of such stock phrases as "hot men gemakht an asife un s'iz geblibn" (they called a meeting and came to a decision) and the frequent repetition of words and actions, as in "hot men gemakht an asife un men hot getrakht un getrakht" (they called a meeting and pondered and pondered) and "hot men getrakht zibn teg mit zibn nekht" (they pondered for seven days and seven nights). These features serve as markers of the town's communal action, and through their repeated use, they offer the reader a sense of familiarity while offering the writer an easily adopted formula still commonly used in many modern Chelm tales in various languages.

Kipnis used three kinds of sources for his Chelm collection, each of which he acknowledges in a different way: existing literary and ethnographic collections, stories sent in by readers, and popular tales not previously attached to Chelm. Although Kipnis never refers explicitly to previously published collections, he sometimes includes such indications as "di legend dertselt" (the legend recounts) or "dertselt di folks-legende" (the folk legend recounts).[49] His broad conception here of a folk source follows the same lines that he pursues in his collecting of folk songs. As Itzik Gottesman has noted, Kipnis included anything in his song collection that was "beloved and considered authentic . . . by the people," even if it was written by well-known authors, such as Y. L. Peretz or Avrom Reyzen (1876–1953).[50] His main criterion, which also applied in his Chelm collection, is that the song or story should be told by the Jewish folk, which "includes the intelligentsia as well as the uneducated Jew."[51] Thus, Kipnis is familiar with, and uses, stories from the Pryłucki and Lehman collection, and he repeats Dik's Chelm stories from the *Orkhim in Duratshesok*.

A new and major source for Kipnis's collection is Alter Druyanov's comprehensive Hebrew-language *Sefer ha-bedihah veha-ḥidud* (Book of jokes and wit), published in 1922, the same year that Kipnis started his Yiddish Chelm series in *Haynt*. Druyanov's compendium is the first to assemble Chelm tales in that language. Druyanov (1870–1938), born in Druya, on the outskirts of Vilna, attended the Volozhin yeshiva and became an editor, writer, and Zionist. Before settling for the second time in his life in Palestine, he initiated, in Odessa in 1918, the ethnographic journal *Reshumot*, with his friends Ḥayim Naḥman Bialik (1873–1934) and Yoshue Khone Ravnitski, another keen collector of Jewish jokes.[52] Druyanov's collection of jokes, expanded into three volumes in a later edition in Palestine, became a classic and remains widely known in Israel. The first edition of *Sefer ha-bedihah veha-ḥidud* includes twenty-five Chelm stories, many of them not previously recorded, and later editions added many more.

Any differences between Druyanov's Hebrew Chelm tales and the Yiddish corpus to that point can be attributed to the inherent difference between the language of scholarship and the vernacular and to the typically more advanced yeshiva education of writers and readers of Hebrew as against readers of Yiddish. Accordingly, the discourse of Druyanov's wise men may sometimes sound more like that of twisted talmudists than mere simpletons, even if the conclusions they reach are the same. Druyanov's account of a debate over what to do with the floorboards in the new bathhouse (whether to sand them for greater comfort or leave them rough for greater slip resistance) may feature Aramaic terminology and some of the verve of talmudic argument, but the characteristically Chelmite compromise (sand one side, leave the other side rough, and install the floor with the smooth side facing downward) is as half-witted as anything in the Yiddish Chelm repertoire. Kipnis includes this story of Druyanov's, minus its learned language but including the comment, on the part of his journalist narrator, that he felt he had to verify the story by lifting one of the floorboards, which he did clandestinely, having been refused permission by the synagogue leadership. What he found when he did so, he teasingly declines to say.

Kipnis included five more Druyanov stories in his book, all of them differing only slightly from his source, including a Chelm-versus-modern-technology story. This tells of the *shammes* who used the town's proudly acquired fire hose as storage space for, among other things, lettuce for the Passover seder and garlic for medicinal purposes. The result was that no water at all came out of the hose when it was used on the next fire. After long debate, the Chelmites reached a compromise whereby the *shammes* might continue to store things in the hose, if he promised to remove them well before any fire.[53]

In the book based on the *Haynt* columns, Kipnis also added Sholem Aleichem's popular "Iber a hitl" (On account of a hat, 1913), retelling it as a Chelm story. And in Kipnis's "Der melamed in generalske kleyder" (The teacher in a general's uniform), a *melamed* (teacher) from Chelm (substituted for Sholem Aleichem's unsuccessful businessman Sholem Shakhne) mistakenly puts on the clothes of a general who happens to have slept next to him in a cheap hostel in Warsaw.[54] When the teacher arrives at the train station, he wonders why people treat him with so much more respect than in Chelm, until he catches sight of himself in a mirror on the train and realizes that the porter at the hostel had failed to wake up him, the poor teacher, but must clearly have woken up the general instead.

Though the original subtlety is not preserved in Kipnis's short retelling of the story, he nevertheless sets a trend here in which stories by Sholem Aleichem become merged with Chelm stories, so that the famous fictional Kasrilevke, a "symbolic-satirical place," as Dan Miron states, and its quality of "Kasrielism, . . . defined as poverty and provincialism softened, even redeemed, by a sense of humor, a happy-go-lucky attitude," are now combined with Chelmite stupidity and ignorance, something Sholem Aleichem did not have in mind.[55]

If Kipnis does not explicitly acknowledge his published sources, he gladly mentions direct and genuine informants. Two-thirds of the way through the series, between the section subtitled "Khelemer mayses oyfgenumen in Khelm gufe" (Chelm stories actually recorded in Chelm) and the section subtitled "Khelmer mayses, gezamelt un bearbayt" (Chelm stories collected and reworked), there appears an intervening story, subtitled "A Khelmer folks-mayse" (A Chelm folk story), sent to him by Garel Rozenband from Vladimir-Volinsk, fifty miles from Chelm.[56] Rozenband assured him that the story was well known in Chelm and in such nearby places as Zamość, Hrubieszów, and his own Vladimir-Volinsk.

This long tale, titled "Where Did the Fools of Chelm End Up?," tells how a "yishuvnik" (villager) named Berel outsmarts the Chelmites by selling them a supposedly money-excreting horse, a rabbit capable of performing the duties of a *shammes*, and an egg that can bring about the resurrection of the dead. On account of the last of these, the Chelmites decide that they can save themselves the expense of a doctor, and when the rabbi's wife dies, they rejoice that they will now be able to put their egg to work. When it fails to revive her, they hunt down Berel, capture him in a sack, and are about to toss the sack, with him inside, into the river, when his wits rescue him from this unpromising predicament. Gathering that a nobleman is passing by in his carriage, he cries out in Polish, "I do not want to become king."[57] The nobleman infers that the speaker has been placed in the sack to coerce his acquiescence and, seeing an opportunity for himself, volunteers to change places with him. Thus it is that he is drowned in the river while Berel drives away from the scene in the nobleman's carriage. Not content with this triumph, the cheeky villager returns to Chelm a month later with stories of how "yene velt" (the world to come) is brimming with gold, silver, and diamonds. So convincing is Berel the Undead that masses of Chelmites across the social and intellectual spectrum, from the bath attendant to the rabbi, go down to the river, throw themselves in, and drown.

This story reverses both the conventional contrast between urbanized or even small-town Jews, liable to have access to a rabbi, an elementary education, and some level of organized Torah study, and the *yishuvniks*,

Jewish country bumpkins who might have none of these opportunities, as well as the prevailing power dynamic between Jews and Gentiles and patricians and plebeians.[58] Kipnis was evidently taken with the story's radicalism, for he uses it to conclude the first sequence of his serialized reports on the "old Chelmites about whom the people tell lovely stories and splendid folk legends."[59] Eight years later, when he edited his columns into a book, he moved the story into final position so it could serve as his explanation of how the original Chelm Jewish community became extinct.

Later stories in the *Haynt* series naturally included a higher proportion of variants on stories printed earlier in the series as well as new stories sent in by readers, reflecting Kipnis's open-ended and participatory notion of popular culture. One contributor of several stories was Rokhl Leye Ayzenshlos from Łódź (presumably related to the Yiddish writer Alter Ayzenshlos, who died in Łódź in 1925).[60] Some of her contributions resemble the corresponding Pryłucki and Lehman versions, but in other cases, her version is substantially different, as in the episode in which the Chelmites try to count each other.[61] In its original incarnation, the context of the story was synagogal: the need to ascertain the presence of the quorum of ten men required for public prayers. In Ayzenshlos's secular retelling, however, we find nine wise men of Chelm in the river taking a swim and anxious to make sure that they have not lost one of their number. When they start to count "nisht eyns, nisht tsvay, nisht dray" (not one, not two, not three), following the opposition in Jewish law or custom to the direct enumeration of people, they always come up one short.[62] Each of them leaves himself out of the reckoning and thus counts only eight until a stranger passes by and manages to count them all. The swimmers are so relieved that, leaping for joy, they run through town, oblivious to the fact that they are all stark naked.

Others among Kipnis's informants were inspired to create their own texts, among them Moshe Lindeman, who felt a special connection to the material, having been stationed in Chelm as an Austrian soldier in World War One, and who submitted seven chapters in rhyme on the alleged history of the old Jewish cemetery in Chelm.[63] Other correspondents wrote in to say that they had heard Chelm stories long ago as small children while they were still in *kheyder* (elementary school).[64]

Kipnis removes the references to correspondents that he had featured in his newspaper articles from the compilation of these columns that he edited into a book, which he published in 1930. He also eliminates the persona of investigative journalist that he created as a framework for himself as narrator when crafting these stories for *Haynt*. And he removes the elaborate references to the real town of Chelm that he had previously taken such care to introduce. Instead, he says in his foreword, Chelm is now the universal foolish town for Jews the world over. The town has become so popular among the people, he adds, that if there is any "comical and absurd foolish story, one attributes it to Chelm."[65] If it sounds as if he regrets that development, the fact is that he had used this technique himself in his newspaper series and does so even more conspicuously in the book version.

In particular, Kipnis incorporates stories about the foolish trickster figure Efroyim Greydiger, simply by having the fools of Chelm serve as his targets. When Efroyim Greydiger once visited Chelm, so Kipnis has it in *Haynt*, he saw the Chelmites struggling to carry a cow up to a hayloft. Betting with them that he could accomplish single-handed what they could scarcely do as a group, he scampers up the ladder, throws down a bale of hay, and calls out, "You Chelm fools, why carry the cow up to the hay if you can toss the hay down to the cow?"[66] This short and simple exchange opens up a new line in Chelm stories in which some outsider, "normal" or otherwise, visits Chelm and endures a brief encounter with the local wisdom.

Kipnis's 1922–1923 series in *Haynt* and his 1930 book released an outpouring of Chelm tales in print—new and old, literary and less so—in stand-alone volumes and Jewish humor collections. Among Chelm-only works of this period are Gustav Kaftal's *Naye oysdervelte Khelmer mayses* (New selected Chelm tales), published in Warsaw in three editions (1929, 1936, and 1937), and Alter Goldberg's *Khelmer mayses*, published in Biłgoraj in 1931.[67] Sholem Mirer included "Khelmer geshikhtes" (Chelm stories) in his book *Antiklerikale folks-mayses* (Anticlerical folktales), published in Moscow in 1940. His Marxist program is visible in the way he retells existing Chelm stories. It is not the people of Chelm who are fools but the rabbi—the Jewish "cleric"—who urges the Chelmites to sow salt, dances while they push the synagogue, and believes that the moon has escaped from the barrel because it is not "bashert" (meant to be) and because people do not deserve the "holy moon."[68]

As in the German-language Chelm literature, Chelm stories also entered children's literature in eastern Europe and, to a much greater extent, were used for Hebrew- and Yiddish-language pedagogic purposes.[69] One energetic user of the Chelm motif for such purposes was Shloyme Bastomski (1891–1941), the Vilna Yiddish writer who founded the Naye Yidishe Folkshul publishing house to cater to the growing Yiddish-language secular elementary school movement and was the founder-editor of two popular Yiddish children's magazines, *Der khaver* (The friend) and *Grininke beymelekh* (Little green trees).[70]

Bastomski's *Mayselekh vegn Khelemer naronim* (Little stories about the Chelm fools) contains almost two hundred short stories and jokes. The collection is a bit of a hodgepodge. Alongside some older Chelm tales, there are jokes similar to the kind sometimes told in America about "Little Johnny," here arbitrarily set in Chelm. Other, more didactic parts of his collection are not strictly speaking Chelm tales either. Understandably, Bastomski's collected Chelm stories and ostensible Chelm stories, which he published between 1938 and 1940 as three issues of *Grininke beymelekh*, received mixed reviews.[71]

However, one of Bastomski's coeditors at *Grininke beymelekh*, Falk Heilpern (1876–1945), produced one of the most influential collections of Chelm tales to be written in Hebrew.[72] Heilpern, born in Nesvizh, worked as a teacher, writer, and translator from Russian, German, and English into Hebrew and Yiddish. His *Ḥakhme Ḥelem: Bediḥot ve-halatsot ʿamamiyot* (Wise men of Chelm: Folk japes and jests) was published around 1926 in Warsaw, and *Ḥelm ve-ḥakhameh: Meḥubar be-ḥelko lefi mekorot ʿamamiyim* (Chelm and its wise men: Complied in part from folkloric sources) appeared in 1937 in Tel Aviv, where Heilpern had settled after emigrating to Palestine in that year.

Heilpern's collections became classics of Hebrew literature for children and are still reprinted in illustrated editions in Israel today. His first collection, *Ḥakhme Ḥelem*, was illustrated by Shaye Faygenboym (1900–1942), a leading Warsaw Jewish cartoonist who published in that city in *Moment* and *Haynt* and was the art director of *Illustrirte vokh*.[73] Faygenboym's memorable illustrations of the wise men, gesticulating wildly, for example, about the moon in the barrel, add a whole extra dimension to the Chelm tradition.

Capturing the moon, illustration by S. Faygenboym, in Falk Heilpern, *Ḥakhme Ḥelem* (Warsaw, ca. 1926)

In December 1928, in this period when Chelm stories figured so prominently in Polish Jewish cultural production, the young Itsik Manger arrived in Warsaw, where he stayed, with occasional breaks, until 1938. According to David Roskies, it was during this time that Manger's "self-transformation into a folk bard" took place.[74] For someone well versed in German literature but aspiring to create a "Yiddish folk epic," a literary topic as popular as Chelm would have been a natural subject in which to take an interest.[75] So it is not surprising that just six months later, in May 1929, Manger published an essay titled "Di Khelemer may-ses" (The Chelm tales) in the Warsaw journal *Literarishe bleter*. This was one of the most important literary journals in Yiddish, edited by Melekh Ravitsh (1893–1976), Perets Markish (1895–1952), Israel Joshua Singer, and Nakhmen Mayzel (1887–1966). Manger's article may be considered the first scholarly look at the Chelm genre.[76]

Manger's familiarity with German literature is evident in his article, which he opens with a reference to the Swiss author Gottfried Keller (1819–1890) and his fictional Schildburg-like Seldwyla.[77] Manger is familiar with the older German tradition and recognizes that the Chelm tales have "most likely been influenced from the German Schildbürger" literature.[78] However, according to Manger, the Chelm tales are different from their German source because they present an "apopteoz fun tmimes" (apotheosis of naïveté), which is, in his view, their defining trait: "Chelm is child. A child with beard and ear-locks, clumsy and naïve. And from all its afflictions and sorrows there emanates the aroma of the cross. It is where golden childish naïveté is crucified on the bitter, sophisticated, perverse crossbeams of the world."[79]

If the Chelmites, in Manger's view, represent the apotheosis of naïveté, then Manger's view represents the apotheosis of Chelm. Exactly where he is going with this image he never elucidates, but certainly the Chelmites have come to be infinitely more for him than just frivolous figures of fun. They are figures of pathos and paradox: children with beards. This is 1929, ten years before the outbreak of war, nine years before Kristallnacht, which evoked Chagall's *White Crucifixion*, four years before the Nazis came to power, and before his own experiences of heightened antisemitism in 1930s Poland. It is not plausible that he means to suggest that the Jews collectively have something Christlike about them. He does, however, seem to say precisely that of the Chelmites, although with what seriousness he means to propose a Chelmo-centric theology is anyone's guess. This passionate but oblique utterance does not feel like a throwaway line, and Chelm is a topic to which he returns repeatedly in the 1930s. Noticeably, however, he never mentions it again in his wartime and post-Holocaust writing.

In what other sense might the Chelmites strike Manger as exuding in their afflictions a whiff of the cross? There may be a parallel between the foolishness of the Chelmites as valorized in the Chelm tales and the theoretical Christian tendency to valorize the paradoxical, to embrace folly and seek it out.[80] The source for this value is Paul, in whose letters the New Testament's references to fools and foolishness are largely concentrated. Key here is the First Letter to the Corinthians. As Paul is forced to endure hardship and persecution for his faith, he both accepts his suffering and comes to regard the "imitation of Christ," joining Jesus on the path to martyrdom, whether literally or symbolically, as the proper way to live the Christian life.[81] The actions of Christian holy fools, notably the holy fools (*iurodivye*) in Russian Orthodox Christianity, however bizarre they may seem, are always supposed to contain a hidden truth. So it is for Manger with the Chelmites. Only Chelm (and children) can attain the truths that no wise man is able to perceive.

It is from this perspective that Manger tells of how the Chelmites send out emissaries to seek justice. They find it with an innkeeper, who offers to sell them a barrel of justice to take home. When they get the barrel back to Chelm and the rabbi opens it, the entire town square fills with a vile odor, and the rabbi cries out, "Jews, justice stinks."[82] For Manger, this is a perfect description of the justice of this world, one that should be "engraved in golden letters on the marble walls of the League of Nations."[83] It is not the Chelmites that are foolish but the rest of humanity. Chelm stories are not about how the Chelmites are fooled but about how, like a child, they have access to eternal wisdom.

The definite meaning of another line in Manger's 1929 essay is equally elusive: "Khelem iz a shtot un got a foter" (Chelm is a town and God a father).[84] It sounds reminiscent of Dik's quip that as Chelm is a town, so Poland is a country (that is, both are ridiculous). Manger, however, is not making a political point as is Dik but appears rather to be opening up a transcendental dimension of Chelm. Four years later, he has recourse to the same expression in a ballad, his preferred poetic form, published in his volume of poems *Lamtern in vint* (1933).[85] The poem is titled "Khelemer balade" (Ballad of Chelm) and opens with the lines "Khelem iz, vi ir veyst, a shtot und got iz, vi ir veyst, a foter" (Chelm is, as you know, a town, and God is, you know, a father).[86] His persona, the last Chelmite, retells the story of how the people of Chelm captured the moon. In the last verse, the special relationship between Chelm and God is evoked when he addresses God in intimate form as "tate-foter" (Daddy), imagining a father figure playing an old melody for a blind tomcat—*koter* in Yiddish, rhyming with the *foter* of "tate-foter" in the line above.

Manger was one of the first to introduce Chelm and poetry to each other, but he was followed by other eminent Yiddish poets, such as Mani Leib (1883–1953) and Miryam Ulinover (1890–1944). Ulinover, the first woman to write about Chelm, Kipnis's informants aside, published eleven Chelm-themed poems in 1938, some in *Haynt*, where they appeared as "Lider fun Khelm" (Songs from Chelm), and others in the monthly journal *Inzl*.[87] Her Chelmites are again naïve or childlike, confusing their "fiselekh" (little feet) with one another or wondering about the purpose of telegraph poles and concluding that they must be meant for the swallows to sit on. In her poem "Tey un tilim" (Tea and psalms), Ulinover takes an exalted "theological" view of Chelm, not unlike Manger's, seeing it as a special place for perceiving the presence of the divine in the quotidian.[88]

In 1937, a year before Manger left Warsaw for Paris, he published the story "Der Khelemer zatsa'l" (The rabbi of Chelm, of blessed memory) in the *Naye folkstsaytung*. He included the story again in *Noente geshtaltn*, a book of essays first printed in that journal, for which he also wrote a foreword. The theme of the collection was "the literary past," and his story of the rabbi of Chelm finds itself in good company with essays on the collector of texts Isaac Wallich from Worms, the writers Ayzik Meyer Dik and Avrom Goldfaden (1840–1908), and the jester Hershele Ostropoler.[89]

Manger's rabbi, the protagonist of his story, knows well the reputation of his hometown, full of "naïve children with beards and side curls who cannot even tie a cat's tail."[90] The rabbi sees himself as single-handedly responsible for saving Chelm from the fate of being more foolish than any other foolish town in world history. Were it not for him, "Chelm would look like Abdera, the Ionic Greek town of long ago. Or, not to mention them in the same breath [the year of writing was, after all, 1937], like the German town of Schilda."[91] It was he, so he said, who had suggested carrying the *shammes* to protect the pristine snow. It was he who had settled the question of whether to beautify the synagogue with murals or have the walls be white lest the interior resemble a church. You can do both, he had pointed out; first paint the walls, then whitewash them.

Even now, the rabbi was still busy upholding Chelm's reputation, awaiting the return of emissaries he sent out to seek justice. Manger then repeats this story as he had first told it in his essay on Chelm in 1929, but with an enhanced ending.[92] When the rabbi opens the barrel and the horrific stench of justice wafts out, he commands everyone to go home, wash their hands, and recite *asher yatsar*, the prayer to be said after using the toilet, and let them remember that "justice" often stinks. When the rabbi gets back to his study, he finds that he is "not crushed by his disappointment regarding human justice."[93] It is, after all, only human justice, not the "justice of the creator of the universe" in whom he still has faith. Hasid that he is, in the end he joins his own shadow in a mystical dance of praise. The rabbi of Chelm, the most Chelmish of the Chelmites, might be considered the biggest fool on earth, but Manger thinks otherwise and dissociates himself from "scoffers elsewhere" who may be inclined to call him and his community "Chelm fools."[94]

Manger's inversion of Chelm may be arresting in its intensity, but it is hardly without parallels before or after him. Uncertainty about wisdom is intrinsic to folly literature; that is what it is about. It is present in the sixteenth century, in Brant, Erasmus, and the *Schildbürgerbuch*, and it is likewise present in the hugely popular modern Yiddish folksong "Tshiribim," associated especially with the Barry Sisters, stars of 1940s and 1950s New York radio. The last verse of the lyrics, which have been borderline nonsense throughout, begins by recalling Chelm's dubious reputation, juxtaposes this with the contention that its inhabitants seem to laugh all day and night, and ends with the question, "Zogt ver zaynen di narishe, ver zaynen di khakhomim?" (Tell me, who are the foolish and who the wise?).

# Epilogue

## *The Once and Future Chelm*

Three of the children of Chelm are discussing the *volkn-kratsers* (sky-scrapers) of New York. The first kid imagines that, because they are so tall, the snow must never melt on their roofs. The second adds the supposition that a special oxygen supply must be needed up there in order to breathe, and the third concludes that the baking of *matse* for Passover must start around Hanukkah so as to allow enough time for the delivery man to take the elevator up as far as the top floor.[1]

This little Chelm fantasy, recorded nowhere else, is told in *College Yiddish*, a textbook published by YIVO in New York in 1949. Its author was the then only twenty-three-year-old Uriel Weinreich (1926–1967), who fled with his father, Max Weinreich, from Vilna to New York during the Second World War and later taught Yiddish at Columbia University. Intended as "an introduction to the Yiddish language and to Jewish life and culture," it remains the standard textbook for English-speaking students of Yiddish to this day.[2] *College Yiddish* launched something new by setting out to teach Yiddish as a foreign language to adults, as well as simultaneously educating students in eastern European Jewish culture. Weinreich's book represented a shift in thinking about Yiddish, moving "from 'mere' *mameloshn* [mother tongue] to a cultural asset available to everyone."[3] Singled out for praise was its "abundant use—as is only appropriate in a book dealing with Yiddish—of folk humor and folk sayings."[4]

Chelm is Weinreich's preferred location for illustrating this "Jewish humor,"[5] and he presents the word "Khelemer" (Chelmite) as meaning both an "inhabitant of Khelem" and Yiddish folklore's "proverbial fool."[6] Moreover, he marks the word with an asterisk, his method of indicating words of critical importance to the language, which ought to become part of the learner's "active vocabulary" and should, accordingly, be memorized.[7]

Even though Chelm tales became widespread in Yiddish and German as of the late 1920s, they were only beginning to appear in America when Weinreich presented them to an English-speaking audience in his textbook. Along with Solomon Simon's *Wise Men of Helm and Their Merry Tales* (1945) and Nathan Ausubel's selection of Chelm stories and jokes in his *Treasury of Jewish Folklore* (1948), *College Yiddish* helped to establish Chelm as part of American Jewish culture.

Weinreich includes a variety of Chelm tales in the course of his book.[8] Among them are some of the oldest stories, such as "The Khelem Jews build a synagogue," in which students are required to translate from English into Yiddish an account of how the Chelmites carried their logs down the hill and up again.[9]

Each lesson in *College Yiddish* starts with a reading text, which sometimes helps illustrate life in the old country, for example, the joke Weinreich tells about traveling without a ticket on Russian trains. This practice was so widespread as to be a frequent topic in travelogues about tsarist, Soviet, and even post-Soviet Russia.[10] Rather than paying full price for a ticket, passengers might pay a small bribe to the conductor to turn a blind eye to their presence and to tip them off if an inspector should happen to come aboard. Weinreich tells of a Chelmite taking a train trip and guilelessly buying himself a legitimate ticket. When the conductor enters the compartment to warn that an inspector is coming down the train, the Chelmite dives under the seats like all his fellow passengers. Unlike them, however, he omits to take care that the toes of his shoes should not stick out. Inevitably, the otherwise-unsuspecting inspector spots him, yanks him out, and demands to see his ticket. This, to the petty official's consternation, the Chelmite readily produces. For what possible reason, then, the inspector wants to know, could he have wanted to hide when he was perfectly entitled to travel. "Because," says the catastrophically innocent Chelmite in an entirely unconscious breach of solidarity against the unloved regime, "all the others did."[11]

The Chelm tales in *College Yiddish* demonstrate the range of stories then in circulation. They include stories based on medieval and early modern precursors and stories invented in the late nineteenth and early twentieth centuries, the latter often stressing the backwardness of the Chelmites in adapting to a modernity represented, for example, by rail transportation. And they include new stories that bridge the old and the new worlds, such as Weinreich's original jest about New York skyscrapers. In other words, *College Yiddish* includes representative samples of the whole Chelm repertoire, rooted in the Late Middle Ages and continuing to be written and rewritten to the present day.

Chelm's reputation spread worldwide through twentieth-century emigration from eastern and central Europe. From the 1930s onward, Chelm literature can, roughly speaking, be divided into four categories. First, there are collections dependent for their Chelm content on preexisting ethnographic and folkloric publications. Collections that included Chelm stories had various foci, including Jewish humor. Second, there are Chelm-themed literary creations by accomplished writers. Third, there is a new trend in the twentieth century toward treating Chelm as a subject for children's literature, which started in German and Yiddish but then spread to other languages, including Hebrew, Russian, and, most notably, English. And fourth, there are Chelm stage plays and films, the latter generally animated and usually made for television.

Chelm's presence in contemporary performing arts can be seen in the award-winning Canadian short film *Village of Idiots* (1999) as well as in an opera by Robert Strassburg and other musical works, including the "klezmer musical" *Shlemiel the First*. The town's name is currently invoked by klezmer bands: the Chelm Feelharmonik, What the Chelm!, and 7 Wise Men of Chelm. Chelm also has a certain presence on social media, specifically in the blogosphere and on YouTube.

Illustrated children's books featuring Chelm tales have been fairly common since the 1970s. Chelm can even be found transplanted to the Wild West in a graphic novel that combines Jewish folklore and western Americana to tell stories about "Rabbi Harvey," the rabbi of the fictitious cowboy community of Elk Spring.[12] Other illustrated children's books focus on Jewish holidays, notably Hanukkah and Passover, as in David Adler's *Chanukah in Chelm* (1997) and Linda Glaser's *Stone Soup with Matzoh Balls* (2014). Some of these books use the Chelmites' characteristic confusion to discuss their young readers' likely confusion regarding religious and cultural distinctions, especially as regards Christmas, as in Eric Kimmel's *Chanukkah Tree* (1988) and Jon Koon's *Confused Hanukkah* (2004).

The evocation of Chelm has been a trend in children's literature be-yond the United States as well, showing up, for example, around the same time as Singer's Chelm stories for children, in the very popular Russian book *Khelomskie mudretsy* (Wise men of Chelm, 1969; expanded edition 2004). This was supposedly written by the Yiddish writer Shike Driz (Ovsei Driz, 1908–1971) and was certainly translated, if not also writ-ten, by the avant-garde poet Genrikh Sapgir (1928–1999).[13] In the book, the Soviet secular equivalent of Santa Claus, Ded Moroz (Father Frost), visits Chelm one cold winter day to see for himself if the wise men are as wise as they are reputed to be. Sapgir, whom the authorities would allow to be published only as a children's author, favors extravagant or absurd images, describing, for instance, the snow-covered houses of the "mestechko" (shtetl) as being as if dressed in headscarves, shawls, and felt boots. According to Sapgir, Chelm's assembly of wise men, whose youngest member was only 150 years old, decided to build an oven out of ice, and when this failed, they tried again, this time using butter.[14] An-other of Sapgir's ostensible Russian translations from the Yiddish merges the Passover song "Chad Gadya" with the old story of Chelm's plague of mice. Sapgir's influential work served as a basis for more reworkings in Russian, including a musical, performed at the Twelfth World Festival of Youth and Students in Moscow in 1985, and an animated short film of 2005. Sapgir's reappropriation of Chelm, as well as other Soviet Jewish reworkings and performances of Chelm tales, including Moyshe Gersh-enzon's *Di Khelmer khakhomim* (The wise men of Chelm), performed at the Yiddish theater in Vilnius in 1960, require further research as to their political and aesthetic significance.

Chelm also plays a major and still-unexplored role in Israeli popular culture and literature and is frequently invoked even in newspapers and current-affairs broadcasting with reference to parliamentary, govern-mental, and institutional mismanagement and folly.[15] Daniella Ashke-nazy's blog *Chelm-on-the-Med*, for instance, is a periodic aggregator of more or less absurd soft news stories from Israel, called what it is "be-cause in so many ways, Israeli public and private life seem modeled after Chelm."[16] Chelm does appear to be regarded as one of Israeli culture's richer natural resources, well adapted to the population's widely vary-ing linguistic and cultural backgrounds and the misunderstandings to which this is liable to give rise. Writers who have continued to publish in Israel on Chelm in Yiddish include Yosl Lerner in his *Fun Khelemer pinkes* (From Chelm's community minute book, 1975), Borekh Mordkhe Erlikh in his *Khelemer dertseylungen* (Chelm stories, 1977), and Khayim Zeltser in his *Shtern oyfn yarid oder di festung fun khokhme* (Stars over a fair, or, The fortress of wisdom, 1985). There is also a considerable repertoire of Israeli Chelm literature and Chelm-inspired literature in Hebrew, including Ephraim Sidon and illustrator Yossi Abolafia's *Ma'aleh Karahot* (1980), about goings on in a hair-hating town translated as Baldy Heights. Chelm has appeared in Israeli music, too, as in Yossi Banai's popular 1968 record of songs and stories, as well as in theater and television productions.[17]

Recent years have shown a new global trend in Chelm reworkings, which have started to merge Chelm stories with other legends of Jewish or non-Jewish origin. Produced for audiences that are increasingly multicultural and/or increasingly deracinated, these versions present Chelm as a fictitious place of the past or of another world.

An example of this is *The Real Shlemiel*, an animated children's film from the late 1990s. It tells how an orphan boy named Aaron comes to Chelm to live with his uncle. Soon after the boy's arrival, the town is threatened by a golem created by an evil sorcerer. Though the boy cannot stop the destruction of Chelm, he still manages to rescue the townspeople, who then disperse to every inhabited part of the world. The film was distributed worldwide, its title adapted into many languages, with different allusions to religious traditions or national folklore. In Spanish, it was presented as *David y el gigante de piedra* (David and the stone giant), in German as *Die Schelme von Schelm* (The fools of Schelm), in French as *Le Monde est un grand Chelm* (The world is a big Chelm). The Belgian-Israeli maker of this film, Albert Hanan Kaminski, amalgamated the golem legend and other legends with Chelm stories, some but not all of them based on the children's stories of Isaac Bashevis Singer, whose Nobel Prize credentials are trumpeted in the opening credits and on a number of the posters.[18]

*The Real Shlemiel* illustrates how Chelm tales have been reworked for a young audience from various traditions. Some old Chelm themes survive, at least in outline, such as the idea of the Chelmites' dispersion after the town's destruction as a way of accounting for the omnipresence of fools. But Chelm's destruction as depicted here also draws on Holocaust narratives and the annihilation of eastern European Jewry, as well as the story of earlier Jewish emigration from that part of the world. In spite of this, the humor is very basic, with the comical effects achieved in the traditional manner of Chelm literature, albeit in highly simplified form, just by depicting the town's inhabitants as stupid and naïve.

Some of the topics presented in *The Real Shlemiel* are also part of a play by Boris Zilberman, *The King of Chelm*, which premiered at KulturfestNYC in 2015. As in *The Real Shlemiel*, in *The King of Chelm*, a young boy called Aaron comes to rescue the town, and in the play, too, different traditions are merged. The events unfold in a different way, however, and the topics are treated with more sophistication. Aaron, an American who wishes he were "Captain Power," is bored by the company of his elderly grandfather, who, to keep him amused, gives him an old book titled *The King of Chelm*. Simply by opening the book, Aaron becomes part of the story and is transported to Chelm in the form of his fantasy superhero Captain Power, causing chaos as he tries to help the townspeople. This he proposes to do by rescuing their magic "tree of wishes," which the boorish richest man in town wants to chop down. Instead of depicting Chelm as a community of fools, this Chelm is a magic world with its own logic, inhabited by such idiosyncratic figures as the philosopher Shimele, the hippie yoga teacher Lilly, the Master of Cakes, and the Master of Hats; the Master of Hats wears three different items of headgear to represent three personae: a general, a professor, and an old lady. Aaron learns to accept his limitations and realizes that the magic tree can be rescued only in cooperation with the inhabitants of Chelm, however offbeat these good people may at first appear.

Loosely based on Sapgir, the play has been a success in New York. The actors often engage with the audience and include them in decisions they have to make as the plot unfolds. In one of the performances, when Aaron complained about the weirdness of Chelm's citizens, a child from the audience helpfully interjected, "But New York City is weird." And this is very much what Chelm is about; whether meant as a fantasy or a parody of the real world, it is a place with which an audience can identify, drawing connections to their own surroundings.

Nevertheless, in mainstream European or American circles, in the performing arts and in pop culture as in traditional literary forms, the Chelm theme is hardly recognized and cannot be said to serve there as an inspiration for new creativity. Treatments of the subject, whether in novels, humor collections, comic strips, children's books, or oral transmission, have been primarily aimed at, or have primarily reached, Jewish audiences and have only rarely transcended this demarcation. But while the Chelm stories have stayed largely within the confines of Jewish culture, within that sphere, Chelm has proved, and continues to prove, an enduring inspiration for storytelling of many kinds, religious and secular alike.

\* \* \*

The collected tales of the wise men of Chelm constitute the best-known folktale tradition in Jewish culture. The story behind the Chelm stories illustrates a whole range of developments and shifts in Jewish culture over the past three hundred years. The prehistory of the Chelm tales exposes a rich vein of evidence for dynamic negotiation between different cultures and different languages, especially between German and Yiddish. Even though Chelm as a foolish place proves to be an invented tradition that did not gain momentum until the twentieth century, the Chelm phenomenon and its backstory suggest that Jews, like Christians, participated in a shared European foolish sensibility, and it is from this sensibility that the Chelm tales emerged.

As early as the fifteenth century, Yiddish versions of popular, secular works of European literature were being produced. The source language for this literature, at least until the end of the early modern period, was overwhelmingly German. This is where the story of Chelm might be said to begin, since one of the later editions of the *Schildbürgerbuch* provided the basis for the Old Yiddish adaptation of that staple of German culture.

But it was not simply engagement with non-Jewish cultures that helped to establish Chelm as a literary Jewish "utopia." Also at work was a trend toward disengagement or separatism. The Chelmite became Ashkenazic Jewry's own figure of fun, whether heightening or defusing internal Jewish tensions, between, for example, Russian and Polish Jews at the end of the nineteenth century. In addition, both eastern and central European Jewish cultural nationalists of the late nineteenth and early twentieth centuries, some Zionists included, had a tendency to seek authentic forms of Jewishness in eastern Europe, especially in

Poland and the Pale of Settlement, rather than in the German-speaking lands, and this perception also did much to put Chelm on the map.

The prehistory of the Chelm tales also reveals how great a part Hebrew literature played in the emergence of the stories, as well as how much these Hebrew writers were inspired by German literature of the Enlightenment and how greatly, in particular, they were taken with the Enlightenment's special fondness for satire. The history of the stories shows, too, how entangled Yiddish, German, and Hebrew literature were in the eighteenth and nineteenth centuries.

Modern Yiddish literature was a late starter, but Chelm was part of it right from the beginning. Indeed, the first professional Yiddish author, Ayzik Meyer Dik, is evidently the originator of the idea of foolish Chelm. For him and many after him, Chelm was not only an exercise in literary entertainment but also a means of expressing ideological positions and criticizing others' viewpoints.

Chelm's symbolic value is that it allows ideas and opinions, feelings and ideologies to be expressed and questioned at the same time. It has always functioned as well as a satirical model for the illustration of prevailing questions of Jewish identity and community, history and memory, place and time.

Mainly published in booklets and newspapers, Chelm stories in their heyday represent the culture of reading prevalent among Jews in the nineteenth and early twentieth centuries.[19] The backstory of Chelm also shows how a "folk" fiction was invented, much like such analogous Jewish legends as the golem.[20] Chelm tales are, however, not confined to the limits of Jewish popular culture; avant-garde and modernist Jewish writers having taken them up and produced literature of consequence.

Chelm stories and their precursors do not only travel through time, sometimes surprisingly unaltered, but they also travel through Jewish spaces. Mass circulation of Chelm tales first came out of Warsaw in the interwar period and as such was destined to be short-lived. Yet in postwar New York, they enjoyed, and continue to enjoy, a second wind, comparable in strength to the first, as integral to the revival of Yiddish and eastern European Jewish culture.

New York is also the place in which a language shift occurs, with the tales, originally so conspicuously told and predominantly written in Yiddish, being translated and, with increasing frequency, written in English. These developments in Chelm literature also showcase the Americanization of Jewish culture. Still, many Chelm stories have been written in America in Yiddish as well as English. Isaac Bashevis Singer's Yiddish Chelm stories, published in Yiddish in the *Forverts* in the late 1960s and early 1970s, along with his Chelm stories for children in English published around the same time, exemplify this trend, making American Chelm literature an excellent illustration of the multilingual Jewish culture of North America.[21]

Even if many of the Yiddish Chelm stories no longer find readers in their original language and wait for translations to bring them back to life, these tales remain one of the most viable vestiges of Yiddish culture. Chelm stories continue to be revived, not only through literary translation but also via oral transmission into languages currently spoken by large numbers of Jews, and they are made accessible in plays, songs, animations, children's literature, and elsewhere. Sometimes they bear traces of a postvernacular Yiddish, that is, a language whose evocation carries symbolic meaning, even for those who no longer use it to communicate.[22] They are "tales my zayda told me," tales inhabited by the shlemiels, shlimazels, and shmendriks of a sometimes Disney-like shtetl.[23]

In the short film *Village of Idiots*, based on an old Chelm story, Shmendrik sets out to visit another town, falls asleep on his way, forgets from which direction he came, unwittingly walks home, and concludes that there is another Chelm, identical to his own.[24] But since he finds no exact counterpart there for himself, he concludes that new Chelm's Shmendrik must have set out for the old Chelm. His sleep is disturbed by such disconcerting thoughts as the realization that while he is in bed with the doppelgänger of his own wife, his doppelgänger must unintentionally be in bed with his real wife. With daylight, however, he reaches the conclusion that the whole world is one enormous Chelm. Therefore, as a pragmatic kind of man, he need not wear out his shoe leather going all the way back to somewhere in practice no different from where he is already.

Many writers and artists have told and retold many Chelm stories in the less than 150 years of their existence. Like Shmendrik, each of these writers and artists, in seeing the stories from a different perspective, discovers a new Chelm. Shmendrik's actions, like the actions of any Chelmite, seem foolish and laughable, since in reality he never goes anywhere, but his folly, nevertheless, leads to wisdom, insight, and understanding. And as long as Chelm stories continue to serve both as a meaningful model for some aspect of the evolving world and as cause for laughter, there seems little reason to doubt that they will continue to be retold and rewritten and live happily ever after.

# NOTES

INTRODUCTION

1. The Slavic root of the name means "hill."

2. On other, scarcely remembered, Jewish foolish towns, see for instance the collection of Efim Raïzé (1904–1970) on which Dymshits based his article "Les nigauds de Khelm, de Tipchichok et de Koulikov." See also Dymshits, *Evreĭskie narodnye skazki*.

3. Wander, *Deutsches Sprichwörter-Lexikon*, 3:930, no. 1173. The noun *naronim* in the phrase that Wander records—"Chelmer Narrunim"—is neither Hebrew nor German but the encapsulation within a single word of the fusion of the two languages that constitutes Yiddish. The occasional Hebrew inflection of non-Hebrew words—in this case the German word *Narr*, "fool"—is a classic example of the merging that makes Yiddish what the linguist Max Weinreich termed a "shmelts-shprakh" (fusion language). Weinreich, *History of the Yiddish Language*, 2:622.

4. Portnoy, "Wise Men of Chelm," 2:2027.

5. On the history of Jewish Chelm, see Wodziński, "Chełm." See also Virtual Shtetl, the collaborative website of Polin: Museum of the History of Polish Jews and the Jewish Historical Institute in Warsaw, "Chełm" (accessed March 14, 2016, http://www.sztetl.org.pl/en/city/chelm/).

6. In 2010, the museum mounted an exhibition on the Jews of Chelm, but the companion volume makes only passing reference to the wise men. See Mart, *Żydzi w Chełmie*.

7. See Schaechter, "Absurdity Returns to Chelm."

8. Bakaltshuk-Felin, *Yizker-bukh Khelm*; Kanc, *Sefer ha-zikaron li-kehilat Ḥelem*. For a critical review of the 1954 Chelm memorial book, see Shatzky, "Review of Yizker Books—1955," 73–74. Shatzky's negative judgment is discussed by Jack Kugelmass and Jonathan Boyarin, in the introduction to *From a Ruined Garden*, 25. Kugelmass and Boyarin also include a translation from *Yizker-bukh Khelm* of Yisroel Ashendorf's "The Ancestors' Merit and the Blessings of Laughter," 171–172.

9. Sadan, "Ḥakhmey Helem"; Sadan, "Arum Khelem un der khelmyade."

10. Many thanks to Dov-Ber Kerler for his nuanced, qualified defense, in a personal communication, of Dov Sadan's approach. See also B. Weinreich, *Yiddish Folktales*, 405n3: "In a class on Yiddish folklore at U.C.L.A. in 1948, Dr. Max Weinreich offered as a possible explanation for Khelm's status as archetypal Jewish town of

fools the fact that the first story of the creation of a golem in Eastern Europe was set in Khelm."

11. The town is spelled with an initial letter *khes* in the earliest Yiddish Chelm stories, like the Hebrew-derived *khoylem* and *khakhomim*. Later Yiddish spelling of Chelm, however, employs an initial letter *khof*.

12. Wisse, *Schlemiel as Modern Hero*, 10–12; and Shmeruk, "Yitskhok Bashevis," 259–270.

13. Rogovin, "Chelm as Shtetl."

14. Washington Irving, William Irving, and James Kirke Paulding, *Salmagundi; or, The Whim-Whams and Opinions of Launcelot Langstaff, Esq. and Others*. The magazine was published in twenty numbers between January 1807 and January 1808. New York was referred to as Gotham as early as the second issue and repeatedly thereafter. The "wise men" of Gotham appeared in the third issue (February 13, 1807). See Burrows and Wallace, *Gotham*, xii–xiv, 417–418.

## CHAPTER 1. HOW THE WISE MEN GOT TO GOTHAM

1. Allen, "Hassidic Tales," 31.

2. On Yiddish in contemporary American culture, see Shandler, *Adventures in Yiddishland*, esp. chap. 5, "Absolute Tchotchke," 155–176.

3. Allen, "Hassidic Tales," 31.

4. Ibid.

5. Allen's sixth tale is a reworking of Buber's "Der Schatz" (The treasure). See Buber, *Die chassidischen Bücher*, 532–533. The collection was translated by Olga Marx as *Tales of the Hasidim* and published by Schocken in New York in two volumes in 1947 and 1948.

6. For fiction in English, see Sapir, *The Last Tale of Mendel Abbe*, in which the attributes of Chelm and New York are merged for a post-9/11 story. For Chelm-themed children's literature in English, see, for instance, Adler, *Chanukkah in Chelm*; Binder, *Brothers Schlemiel*; Binder, *Hanukkah Present!*; Binder, *Matzah Mishugas*; Freedman, *It Happened in Chelm*; Glaser, *Stone Soup with Matzoh Balls*; Kimmel, *Jar of Fools*; Koon, *Confused Hanukkah*; Sanfield, *The Feather Merchants*; Schwartz, *Yossel Zissel and the Wisdom of Chelm*. Of a psychological, educational, or spiritual bent are Mandelbaum, *Chelmaxioms*; Shatin, *Simple Wisdom*; Rossel, *Wise Folk of Chelm*; and S. Schachter, *Laugh for God's Sake*, 133–141.

7. On Sandler's novel, see Krutikov, "Postmodern Yiddish Satire."

8. Singer, whose brother Israel Joshua was named after Trunk's grandfather Israel Joshua Trunk of Kutno (Shiyele Kutner for short), liked to play tricks on Trunk. See Hadda, *Isaac Bashevis Singer*, 61–63.

9. Trunk, *Poyln*, 7:50. Trunk had already encountered Kipnis at Y. L. Peretz's home. On Singer and the association, see Cohen, "Yitskhok Bashevis-Zinger."

10. See chapter 7.

11. On the Yiddish Art Theater and Maurice Schwartz, see Sandrow, *Vagabond Stars*, 261–274.

12. Schwartz, "Manifesto," quoted in Sandrow, *Vagabond Stars*, 262.

13. Ibid.

14. Zeitlin's play was not published, and no manuscript has been located. I could find only the playbill at YIVO in New York, in the Maurice Schwartz Papers, YIVO, RG 498/4, 33. On the two versions of the *Di Khelemer komediye* and the *Khelemer khakhomim*, see Szeintuch, "Aharon Tsaitlin ve-ha-te'atron be-yidish," 40–46.

15. On Zeitlin, see Krutikov and Pinsker, "Zeitlin Family."

16. S[chack], "Genial Lunacy in Theatre."

17. Isaacs, "Good Playing A-Plenty," 12–13.

18. Cahan, "*Khelemer khakhomim fun Arn Tseytlin in Moris Shvarts's kunst teater.*"

19. Schack, "Yiddish Season Ends." On Zeitlin's reaction to the failure, see his letter to Yoysef Opatoshu on January, 14, 1934, in Szeintuch, *Bi-reshut ha-rabim uvi-reshut ha-yahid*, 231.

20. Niborski and Vaysbrot, *Yidish-frantseyzish verterbukh*, 211.

21. Playbill, in Maurice Schwartz Papers, YIVO, RG 498/4, 33.

22. "Arn Tsaytlin vegn zayn nayer pyese 'Khelemer naronim.'"

23. Quoted in Faierstein, introduction to *Poems of the Holocaust and Poems of Faith*, xii.

24. See chapter 5.

25. Chelm-born Eliezer Blum (1886–1914) used the pen name B. Alkvit when he published his story in *Kinder zshurnal*.

26. Ben Mordekhai's volume presented mainly a reworked selection of Menakhem Kipnis's stories from Warsaw's *Haynt*. A second and third edition was published under the title *Khelmer khakhomim* in 1929 and 1933.

27. One of the first Chelm tales in *Forverts* appeared under the headline "Vodevil vitsn" (Vaudeville jokes) on February 25, 1923. See also the short entry "A Khelemer maysele" in *Forverts*, July 8, 1928.

28. Even in Europe, the first widely distributed stand-alone Chelm books only appeared in the late 1920s; see chapter 7.

29. See Szeintuch, "Aharon Tsaitlin ve-hate'atron be-yidish," 40.

30. Maximilian Hurwitz, "Synopsis of Aaron Zeitlin's 'The Wise Men of Chelm,'" in playbill of *Khelemer khakhomim*.

31. Ibid.

32. Playbill of *Jelemer Jajomim*, in Maurice Schwartz Papers, YIVO, RG 498/4, 33.

33. Botanshanski, "Di Khelemer khakhomim viln lebn."

34. Another, somewhat later, Buenos Aires publication devoted entirely to the Chelm stories was Volf Merkur's *Di velt iz Khelem* (1960). Merkur had played Zanvel, one of the Broder Singers, in the New York performance of Zeitlin's play, and a typed list of all the plays performed by the Yiddish Art Theater between 1918 and 1960 and compiled by Merkur is to be found in the Maurice Schwartz Papers, YIVO, RG 498/1, 12.

35. See Immanuel Olsvanger's *Röyte Pomerantsen* (Red oranges) in transliterated Yiddish, which was previously published by Schocken in Berlin and was edited by

the same publisher in New York in 1947. See also Olsvanger's *L'Chayim! Jewish Wit and Humor*, 129–131, nos. 162, 163, 165.

36. Gross's book was translated into English as *Studies in Jewish and World Folklore* by Haim Schwarzbaum (1968), who provided the text with exemplary annotations.
37. Ben Shahn had created the poster for the premiere and published a booklet with sketches of the play.
38. *Commentary* 17 (1954): 389.
39. Atkinson, "Three Short Plays."
40. Solomon, *Wonder of Wonders*, 69. On the play, see also Mahalel, "We Will Not Be Silent"; Dauber, *Worlds of Sholem Aleichem*, 344–353.
41. American Business Consultants, *Red Channels*.
42. Solomon, *Wonder of Wonders*, 61–64. On Ruby Dee, see "Ruby Dee Heads Yiddish Play Cast."
43. Interview with Merle Debuskey, in Frommer and Frommer, *It Happened on Broadway*, 80.
44. Negative judgments include a long review by Decter in *Commentary* and several articles in *Counterattack* in 1953. See Solomon, *Wonder of Wonders*, 69–70.
45. On Maurice Samuel's *The World of Sholom Aleichem*, see Shandler, *Adventures in Yiddishland*, 106–107.
46. On "Bontshe Shvayg" and its translations into English, see Norich, *Writing in Tongues*, 97–102.
47. Perl, *World of Sholom Aleichem*, 5.
48. "Production Notes," in ibid., 50. See also Solomon, *Wonder of Wonders*, 67–68.
49. Perl, *World of Sholom Aleichem*, 45–46.
50. Decter, "Belittling Sholom Aleichem's Jews," 390.
51. Perl, *World of Sholom Aleichem*, 5–6.
52. Ibid., 7.
53. See S. Simon, *Wise Men of Helm*, 4.
54. Perl, *World of Sholom Aleichem*, 7.
55. The stories were available in English. See S. Simon, *Wise Men of Helm*; and Spitz, "Chelm—The City of Fools."
56. I. Manger, "Di Khelemer mayses," 376. Sholem Aleichem's story had been used for a Chelm play by Eliezer Shteynbarg as early as the 1920s.
57. The Yiddish word *farkisheft* has been translated variously: "The Enchanted Tailor" (trans. Julius and Frances Butwin); "The Haunted Tailor" (trans. Leonard Wolf); and "The Bewitched Tailor" (trans. Bernard Isaacs).
58. Dik, *Oyzer Tsinkes un di tsig*, 2–9. There is a digital copy at the Bavarian State Library, Munich. See Roskies, *Bridge of Longing*, 160.
59. See chapter 5.
60. Sholem Aleichem, "Der farkishefter shnayder," 3. The translation follows for the most part Roskies, *Bridge of Longing*, 161. See also Sholem Aleichem's story "A frier peysekh," first published in *Der fraynd*, April 9, 12, and 13, 1908, which is set

in the German town of "Narrenberg" (Fools' Hill). It has been translated by Adda Birman as "A Premature Passover."

61. Sholem Aleichem, "Der farkishefter shnayder," 51.

62. Ausubel, *Treasury of Jewish Folklore*, 327–331.

63. Ibid., 328.

64. Ibid., 331.

65. Perl, *World of Sholom Aleichem*, 9.

66. Atkinson, "Three Short Plays."

67. Decter, "Belittling Sholom Aleichem's Jews," 389.

68. Trunk, *Sholem-Aleykhem*, 22. See also B. Davis, "Yehiel Yeshaia Trunk."

69. On Trunk, see B. Davis, "Yehiel Yeshaia Trunk"; Schwarz, "Trunk, Yekhiel Yeshaye"; Schwarz, *Survivors and Exiles*, 171–180; and Roskies, *Bridge of Longing*, 312–318.

70. On Trunk and the Bund, see Gorny, *Converging Alternatives*, 148–156.

71. Trunk, *Yidishe kultur-fragn*, quoted in Gorny, *Converging Alternatives*, 149.

72. See for instance *Kvaln un beymer: Historishe noveln un eseys* (Sources and trees: Historical novels and essays, 1958) or *Meshiekh-geviter: Historisher roman fun di tsaytn fun Shabse Tsvi* (Messiah storms: Historical novel from the times of Shabbetai Tsevi, 1961).

73. Rogovin, "Chelm as Shtetl."

74. Trunk, *Khelemer khakhomim*, xix.

75. See chapters 2–4.

76. Trunk, *Khelemer khakhomim*, 109.

77. Ibid., 210.

78. Ibid., 53.

79. See Kipnis, "Khelmer keyser in goldene shikh."

80. Trunk, "Elfte mayse: Der yeytser-tov un der yeytser-hore in Khelm," in *Khelemer khakhomim*, 197–222. Trunk has literary precedents for adding an angelological or demonological touch to his version of Chelm, with the Angel of Death appearing in Zeitlin's *Khelemer khakhomim*, Satan appearing in Peretz's "Iber a shmek-tabak," and the evil inclination itself, again depicted as an external force, in Peretz's "Khelemer melamed."

81. Trunk, *Khelemer khakhomim*, 297.

82. Ibid., 299.

83. Ibid., 300.

84. Ibid.

85. On the Red Jews in Yiddish literature, see Voß, "Entangled Stories."

86. Trunk, *Khelemer khakhomim*, 94.

87. Ishmael, that is, the Jews' uncle, the brother of their father, Isaac.

88. Trunk, *Khelemer khakhomim*, 95–96.

89. Gorny, *Converging Alternatives*, 151–152. Trunk especially disliked the Sephardic pronounciation of modern Hebrew, since "the Sephardim have no common

spiritual and psychological ground with the overwhelming majority of Ashkenazi Jews" (ibid., 152).

90. Trunk, *Khelemer khakhomim*, 68.

91. On Diogenes of Sinope, see Branham and Goulet-Cazé, *Cynics*.

92. Two years after *Khelemer khakhomim*, Trunk published *Der freylekhster yid in der velt oder Hersheles lern-yorn* (The happiest Jew in the world, or, Hershele's apprentice years).

93. Trunk, *Khelemer khakhomim*, 341. The translation follows for the most part Rogovin, "Chelm as Shtetl," 266.

94. Trunk, *Khelemer khakhomim*, 341.

95. With Yisroel Rabon, Trunk and Pryłucki edited *Untervegns: Almanakh far yidisher literatur* (Underway: An annual of Yiddish literature).

96. Many features of the Yiddish text, such as repetitions, alliterations, and rhymes, as well as references to Judaism, are omitted. On the other hand, the English translation often includes a longer moral, as well as a number of playful names, such as Mottel the Mayor, Shloime the Scientist, and Berel the Beadle.

97. Kazin, "Wisdom of Fools," 95.

98. S. Simon, *Wise Men of Helm*, 135. Simon's original conclusion adds an idea found in Y. L. Peretz's Chelm stories, that "in each one of us is a small piece of a Chelmite." See chapter 5.

99. S. Simon, *More Wise Men of Helm*, 111.

100. Tozman, "Kinder zshurnal," 86.

101. See S. Simon, *Khakhomim, akshonim un naronim*. The first of the two Indian Chelm tales, "An ofene tir" (An open door), is set in Chelm. The other, "Der kligster fun ale naronim" (The wisest of all fools), is set in the Indian village of "Hazhra." The collection ends with a third Chelm tale, "Shir an umglik in Khelem" (A real mishap in Chelm).

102. For an annotated bibliography of Jewish children's stories in English, including Chelm stories, see Elswit, *Jewish Story Finder*.

103. See for instance Lahr, "Bring Back the Clowns," 75. He refers to "the imaginary town of Chelm, a village of fools invented by Isaac Bashevis Singer for his children's stories."

104. A New York–like Chelm is the setting for "The Day I Got Lost: A Chapter from the Autobiography of Professor Schlemiel," a story about an absentminded professor who forgets his own address, first published in *The Puffin Annual* for 1975 and reprinted in *Stories for Children* (1984). On the figure of the *shlemiel* (loser) in modern Jewish literature, see Wisse, *Schlemiel as Modern Hero*.

105. Singer himself worked on a dramatization of *Ven Shlemiel iz gegangen keyn Varshe* (When Shlemiel went to Warsaw). See Cohen, "Isaac Bashevis-Singer's Attitude to the Yiddish Theater," 59. In 1974, the Yale Repertory Theater produced *Shlemiel the First*, based on Singer's Chelm stories.

106. Shmeruk, "Yitskhok Bashevis."

107. On Singer, see Hadda, *Isaac Bashevis Singer*; Roskies, "The Demon as Storyteller," in *Bridge of Longing*, 266–306; Wolitz, *Hidden Isaac Bashevis Singer*; Denman, *Isaac Bashevis Singer*; and, with further references, Sherman, "Isaac Bashevis Singer."
108. On Singer and *Forverts*, see Hadda, "Bashevis at *Forverts*."
109. The story was translated into English as "The Mixed-Up Feet and the Silly Bridegroom," in *Zlateh the Goat and Other Stories*. Easy access to Singer's Yiddish Chelm oeuvre is made possible by the meticulous and revelatory bibliographic work of Roberta Saltzman. See her *Isaac Bashevis Singer*.
110. On Singer's pen names, see D. Miller, "Reportage as Fiction, I."
111. Hadda, *Isaac Bashevis Singer*, 137.
112. A critical view of the series is included in Shmeruk, "Yitskhok Bashevis," 269.
113. Flender, "Interview with Isaac Bashevis Singer," 43.
114. Ibid., 44.
115. All translations from *Forverts* are by Emma Woelk and me.
116. Singer, "Der groyser zets."
117. Ibid.
118. Ibid.
119. Ibid.
120. Singer, "Kapitlekh fun der Khelmer geshikhte."
121. Singer, "Der groyser zets."
122. Singer, "Kapitlekh fun der Khelmer geshikhte." The phrase "Mine-is-Yours-and-Yours-is-Mine," quoting a familiar formulation from Mishnah Avot 5:10, represents a rare Jewish touch in Singer's Chelm satires.
123. Ibid.
124. Ibid.
125. Singer, "Khelm bashlist tsu firen milkhome."
126. Singer, "Tsores in Khelm un a kluge eytse."
127. Singer, "Di revolutsye in Khelm." See Singer, "Di naye partey fun di Khelmer komitetn": "There was no more beautiful word in Chelm than 'revolution.' Every young man was supposed to be a revolutionary. If not, he was not allowed to go to university. He also could not get a date."
128. *Dalfn* in Yiddish, *dalfon* in Hebrew, is a term for a pauper but also the Persian name of the second of Haman's ten sons. See Esther 9:7.
129. *Vayzose* (Vayesata): the tenth of Haman's sons and a particular figure of fun in the early modern Yiddish Purim literature. The name Vayzose can also, by extension, denote a fool—or a penis. See Niborski and Vaysbrot, *Yidish-frantseyzish verterbukh*, 262.
130. Singer, "A naye epokhe in Khelm."
131. Ibid.
132. Singer, "Khelm un Mazl-Borsht."
133. Singer, "Vi azoy es hot gearbet di Khelmer demokratye."

134. Singer, "Di Khelmer revolutsye un vos zi hot gebrakht."

135. Singer, "Di tseteylung fun Khelm un di rezultatn derfun."

136. Singer, "Bolvan der ershter un zayn ayzerne hant."

137. Singer, "Di parteyen in vaysen Khelm un zeyere makhlokesn."

138. Singer, "Der sakh-hakl fun der geshikhte fun Khelm."

139. Ibid.

140. Ibid.

141. Singer, "Di 'politishe ekonomye' fun Khelm."

142. Singer published two more stories in *Forverts* in 1967: "A kapitel Khelmer geshikhte" and "Vi azoy Khelm iz geblibn on gelt."

143. Singer, "Nokh vegn di Khelmer khakhomim: A fish an azes-ponem."

144. See Pryłucki, "Khelemer naronim" (1917), 197, no. 26.

145. Kipnis, "LX: Farmishpet dem fish."

146. Singer, "Nokh vegn di Khelmer khakhomim: A fish an azes-ponem."

147. Ibid.

148. Singer, "Nokh vegn di Khelmer khakhomim: Der Khelmer barg."

149. Singer, "Der groyser zets."

150. Singer, *Fools of Chelm*, 4.

151. Allison, *Isaac Bashevis Singer*, 17. On Singer's longtime reluctance to write stories for children, see Shmeruk, "Yitskhok Bashevis."

152. Singer, "The First Snow," "The Mixed-Up Feet and the Silly Bridegroom," and "The First Shlemiel," in *Zlateh the Goat and Other Stories*.

153. "Dalfunka, di shtot vu gvirim lebn eybig" (*Forverts*, March 7, 1974) was translated as "Dalfunka Where the Rich Live Forever: A Story for Children" (*New York Times*, March, 28, 1976). Singer, "The Fools of Chelm and the Stupid Carp," *Cricket*, November 1973, 77–84. They are reprinted, together with "Lemel and Tzipa," in *Naftali the Storyteller* and in *Stories for Children*.

154. The story is also included in his *Naftali the Storyteller* and again in his *Stories for Children* (1984).

155. Singer, "Fools of Chelm and the Stupid Carp," 81.

156. Ibid., 77.

157. Ibid., 78.

158. Singer, "Nokh vegn di Khelmer khakhomim: A fish an azes-ponem."

159. Berkley, "Isaac Bashevis Singer."

160. Singer, "The Snow in Chelm," in *Zlateh the Goat and Other Stories*, 30. Singer's English-language stories of Chelm, in which the place is sometimes referred to as a village and sometimes as a town in English—such is the effort that has been made at consistency—are not alone in the Singer oeuvre in being dumbed down for a broad readership unacquainted with Jewish customs. See for instance Wolitz, "*Der yid fun bovl.*"

161. Singer, *Fools of Chelm*, 57.

## CHAPTER 2. HOW FOOLISH IS JEWISH CULTURE?

1. Loewe, *Schelme und Narren*, 55.
2. Bakhtin, *Problems of Dostoevsky's Poetics*, 122.
3. Bakhtin, *Rabelais and His World*, 10.
4. Stallybrass and White, *Politics and Poetics of Transgression*, 6. See Bakhtin, *Rabelais and His World*, 218.
5. Gurjewitsch, "Bachtin und der Karneval," 425.
6. Bakhtin, *Rabelais and His World*, 10.
7. Stallybrass and White, *Politics and Poetics of Transgression*, 1–26.
8. For a comprehensive study, see Harris, *Sacred Folly*.
9. N. Davis, "Reasons of Misrule."
10. Leading studies on the foolish culture and literature of Christian Europe include Welsford, *Fool*; Könneker, *Wesen und Wandlung der Narrenidee im Zeitalter des Humanismus*; N. Davis, "Reasons of Misrule"; Billington, *Social History of the Fool*; Bachorski and Röcke, "Narrendichtung"; Burke, *Popular Culture in Early Modern Europe*.
11. Yitskhok Shiper, *Geshikhte fun yidisher teater-kunst un drame*, chap. 5, "Di kunst fun 'yidishe narn' beysn 16tn yorhundert," 66–80.
12. The manuscript was sold in two stages during the nineteenth century, with the result that one part is now the Bodleian Library's Ms. opp. add. 4° 136 (*Oxford Old Yiddish Manuscript Songbook*), while the other constitutes the Frankfurt Stadt- und Universitätsbibliothek's Ms. hebr. oct. 219. Both manuscripts are edited in Matut, *Dichtung und Musik im frühneuzeitlichen Aschkenas*, 1.
13. See also the entry by Shiper on Yiddish literature in the German *Encyclopaedia Judaica*, in which folly literature plays an important role: Shiper, "Jiddische Literatur."
14. Erik, *Di geshikhte fun der yidisher literatur*, 138. Erik here follows the line taken by Franz Rosenberg, Moritz Güdemann, and others in the late nineteenth century.
15. Baumgarten, *Introduction to Old Yiddish Literature*, 360.
16. Ibid., 359.
17. Belkin, "*Habit de Fou* in Purim Spiel?"; Belkin, *Ha-purim shpil*.
18. The idea that carnival is distinctively Christian was argued by Dietz-Rüdiger Moser in his critique of Bakhtin. See Moser, "Lachkultur des Mittelalters?" On the term "polemical ethnography," see Deutsch, "Polemical Ethnographies." On Christian Hebraists' description, see for instance Christiani, *Amme seudat Purim*; Matthaei, *Beschreibung des Jüdischen Purim-Festes*. See also Güdemann, *Geschichte des Erziehungswesens*, 3:270–274.
19. For more on the dependence of the moveable date of Easter on the date on Passover and its corollary, the routine proximity in February–March of the Passover-contingent date of Purim and the Easter-contingent date of Carnival, see Elisheva Carlebach, *Palaces of Time*, 8–11, 36–38, 117–119.
20. Horowitz, *Reckless Rites*, 249. See also his chapter 9, "Purim, Carnival, and Violence," 248–277.

21. Shmeruk, *Prokim fun der yidisher literatur-geshikhte*, 206–207.

22. For a thorough discussion, see Moshe Rosman, "Hybrid with What?"

23. Rosenberg, "Ueber eine Sammlung" (1888), 277.

24. Erik, *Di geshikhte fun der yidisher literatur*, 138.

25. Baumgarten, *Introduction to Old Yiddish Literature*, 366; Belkin, "*Zmires purim*"; Belkin, *Ha-purim shpil*; and Belkin, "*Habit de Fou* in Purim Spiel?," 40.

26. Rosman, *How Jewish Is Jewish History?*, 142.

27. See Gvozdeva, "Spiel und Ernst," 195. On symbolic grammar, see Keesing, *Kwaio Religion*, 214–215.

28. See, for instance, the title page of Brant's *Narrenschiff*, 2.

29. On Joel and his illustration of the Rothschild Haggadah, see Zirlin, "Joel Meets Johannes," 281.

30. On the four sons, see M. Friedman, "Four Sons of the Haggadah"; Metzger, *La Haggada enluminée*, 138–171.

31. On the fool in the Washington Haggadah, see Katrin Kogman-Appel, "Illustrations of the Washington Haggadah," 93–96.

32. Premodern fools were assigned to one or other of two categories: "artificial fools" and "natural fools." The artificial fool is the professional wit, comic, or clown, best exemplified by the court jester. Natural fools were widely considered to belong to their own order of creation, almost another species. Far from being pathologized, these natural fools were deemed miraculous and oracular. See von Bernuth, *Wunder, Spott und Prophetie*.

33. *Die gantze Bibel*, fol. dd iiijr. Holbein's images for the Zurich Bible circulated widely in separate editions such as *Historiarum veteris instrumenti testamenti icones*.

34. The first extant complete version was published in Strasbourg in 1515. For a general introduction and an overview of the differences among the many editions in various European languages—there were more than a hundred such editions—see Lappenberg, *Dr. Thomas Murners Ulenspiegel*. For a more recent introduction, see Tenberg, *Die deutsche Till-Eulenspiegel-Rezeption*. See, too, the comprehensive introduction by Paul Oppenheimer in his English translation, *Till Eulenspiegel: His Adventures*.

35. For a comprehensive interpretation of *Eulenspiegel*, see Röcke, *Die Freude am Bösen*, 213–265.

36. Lindow, *Ein kurtzweilig lesen von Dyl Ulenspiegel*.

37. Bayerische Staatsbibliothek Munich, Cod. hebr. 100, fols. 134r–191r. One folio is unnumbered, resulting in a manuscript of forty-nine leaves. See Steinschneider, "Jüdische Litteratur und Jüdisch-Deutsch," 39–41, no. 388; Paucker, "Yiddish Versions of the German Volksbuch," 232–233. See Erik, *Di geshikhte fun der yidisher literatur*, 329–230; he argues that Benjamin Merks based his Yiddish text on the German edition of 1586, but John A. Howard supposes that a different version, deriving from the Erfurt 1532 edition, was used: Howard, "Little Known Version of *Til Eulenspiegel*." Müller, in contrast, believes a Frankfurt edition to have been

the source: Müller, "Eulenspiegel bei den Juden," 36. Howard's study includes an edition of the text in an idiosyncratic transcription, using the Latin alphabet expanded with special characters: Howard, *Wunderparlich und seltsame Historien Til Eulen Spiegels.*

38. Merks, *Vunderparlikh und zeltsame historien Til Aylen-shpigelz,* fol. 134r.

39. J. Wolf, *Bibliotheca hebraea,* 2:1255, no. 27; 3:86, no. CCXIVb. See Müller, "Eulenspiegel bei den Juden."

40. Callenberg, *Achte Fortsetzung seines Berichts,* 197. Another of the Hallensian Pietist missionaries recalled encountering an itinerant Jewish bookseller in 1730, who "carried around *Clauss Narren* and other nasty books of the kind translated into Yiddish, who, by so doing, had strewn the devil's semen among the Jews, which had already seduced so many Christians." See Callenberg, *Anderer Theil der dritten Fortsetzung seines Bericht,* 13. The Pietists disliked any kind of folly literature, even Wolfgang Büttner's *Historien von Claus Narren* (Stories of Claus the Fool), whose Lutheran pastor author composed this volume of tales, ostensibly about the antics of Claus, as a vehicle with which to convey Protestant ethics. There is no other hint of a Yiddish version of *Claus Narr* ever having existed, and it seems most unlikely that a book relying so heavily on Christian ideas and allusions would have been translated into Yiddish.

41. On Callenberg's narrative, see von Bernuth, *"Das jischev fun Nar-husen,"* 133–134.

42. Babylonian Talmud Bava Metsia 84a.

43. *Aylen-shpigl* (1735), quoted here from Neugroschel's translation "Five Stories about Till Eulenspiegel," 92–93. On the Yiddish text, see Müller, "Eulenspiegel im Land der starken Weiber, der Hundsköpfe und Anderswo."

44. On the classification of marvels and marvelous people, see Daston and Park, *Wonders and the Order of Nature.*

45. Neugroschel, "Five Stories about Till Eulenspiegel," 96.

46. In contrast, Benjamin Merks's manuscript does not feel compelled to omit or modify this story.

47. *Aylen-sphigl* (1736), quoted in Paucker, "Yiddish Versions of the German Volksbuch," 240–241.

48. There is a fifth edition from Breslau (Wrocław), which shows close resemblance to the Nowy Dwór print. See Müller, "Eulenspiegel bei den Juden," 40. A copy was recently acquired by Yale University Library, which still needs thorough examination. The Nowy Dwór *Vunderlikhe und komishe geshikhte fon Ayln-shpigl* survives as a unicum in a pamphlet volume held in Frankfurt am Main's Stadt- und Universitätsbibliothek (Jud. Germ. 777).

49. Bloch, *Hersch Ostropoler.*

50. On Hershele Ostropoler, see Schwarzbaum, *Studies in Jewish and World Folklore,* 266–274; Liptzin, "Ostropoler, Hershele."

51. Trunk, *Der freylekhster yid in der velt oder Hersheles lern-yorn.* See also Shtern, *Hershele Ostropoler un Motke Khabad;* Manger, "Di balade fun Hershele Ostropoler mit der levone"; Holdes, *Mayses, vitsn un shpitslekh fun Hershl Ostropoler.*

52. *Mishneh Torah*, Northern Italy, mid-fifteenth century, Vatican City, Biblioteca Apostolica Vaticana, Ross. 498, fol. 85v.

53. Hamburger and Zimmer, *Minhagim de-Kehilat kodesh Vermaysa*, 258–269. The Worms *minhagim* book is preserved in three different manuscripts. See Epstein, "Die Wormser Minhagbücher"; Eidelberg, *R. Juspa*; Baumgarten, *Introduction to Old Yiddish Literature*, 372–373. On the long history of the Jews in Worms, see Römer, *German City, Jewish Memory*.

54. The title *knel gabbai* is still found in the late eighteenth century, if not beyond, borne by the most prominent figure in the life of a confraternity within the Jewish community of Frankfurt am Main known as Rodfe Tsedakah. Married men were permitted to join or remain members; but the society's activities were primarily organized by and for young unmarried men, and only bachelors were eligible to become officeholders. The group managed to combine charity (e.g., distributing firewood to poor widows) with conviviality, getting together once a week at a pub. See Sulzbach, "Ein alter Frankfurter Wohltätigkeitsverein."

55. On the use of *knelen*, "to teach someone," see Neuberg, *Pragmatische Aspekte der jiddischen Sprachgeschichte*, 152.

56. See Daxelmüller, "Jewish Popular Culture since the Middle Ages," 45–46.

57. Matut, *Dichtung und Musik im frühneuzeitlichen Aschkenas*, 2:364. The name Yuspa Shammes appears in the secondary literature in a variety of transliterations, including "Yuspa Shamash" and "Yozpe Shames." See Max Weinreich's *History of the Yiddish Language*, 1:A195. The most common spelling, "Yuspa Shammes," is the one used here.

58. For an extended discussion of this manuscript, see von Bernuth, "The Carnivalesque in Early Modern Ashkenaz."

59. Matut, *Dichtung und Musik im frühneuzeitlichen Aschkenas*, 1:86–87.

60. See Davidson, *Parody in Jewish Literature*, 26–31, 115–147.

61. Demonet-Launay, "Le nom de Bacbuc."

62. Shiper, *Geshikhte fun yidisher teater-kunst un drame*, 66–80.

63. Ibid., 73. On Rosenberg and his work, see Matut, *Dichtung und Musik im frühneuzeitlichen Aschkenas*, 1:1–6.

64. Rosenberg, "Ueber eine Sammlung von Volks- und Gesellschaftsliedern" (1888), 258.

65. See Butzer, Hüttenmeister, and Treue, "*Ich will euch sagen von einem bösen Stück.*"

66. Matut, *Dichtung und Musik im frühneuzeitlichen Aschkenas*, 1:141–149.

67. On the pan-European ritual of charivari, see N. Davis, "Reasons of Misrule"; Le Goff and Schmitt, *Le charivari*; Thompson, "Rough Music"; Gvozdeva, "La procession charivarique en texte et image."

68. On fool societies, see N. Davis, "Reasons of Misrule."

69. Gvozdeva, "Karnevaleske Statuten."

70. Matut, *Dichtung und Musik im frühneuzeitlichen Aschkenas*, 1:151.

71. See also Thompson, "Rough Music."

72. See Butzer, Hüttenmeister, and Treue, "*Ich will euch sagen von einem bösen Stück.*"

73. Würfel, *Historische Nachricht von der Judengemeinde*, 141.

74. Schudt, *Jüdisches Franckfurter und Prager Freuden-Fest*, 47. On Schudt and other early modern writers on Jewish rituals, see Deutsch, *Judaism in Christian Eyes*; Elyada, *Goy Who Speaks Yiddish*.

75. Schudt, *Jüdisches Franckfurter und Prager Freuden-Fest*, 49.

## CHAPTER 3. THROUGH THE LAND OF FOOLISH CULTURE

1. Boorde, *Merie Tales of the Mad Men of Gotam*. This is the first extant edition, based on a now-lost edition of around 1540.

2. Sachs, "Die Lappenhewser bawren." He published the *Schwanck* (jest) "an der faßnacht" (on Carnival) of 1558. See ibid., 383.

3. Ertz, *Das Lalebuch*, 10.

4. Ibid.

5. Ibid., 20.

6. Gvozdeva, "Hobbyhorse Performances."

7. The German word *Gauch* has the same extended meaning as the corresponding English word, "cuckoo."

8. Ertz, *Das Lalebuch*, 138. The first edition of the *Lalebuch* includes an appendix, as promised on the title page, containing stories allegedly culled from "the latest news sheets from all over the world." Although these mock reports are an integral part of the book as originally conceived, no subsequent edition of the *Lalebuch* has reprinted them, the modern critical editions included. Neither Ertz's edition of the *Lalebuch* nor Karl von Bahder's includes the appendix. Von Bahder, *Das Lalebuch (1597)*. See Bachorski, *Irrsinn und Kolportage*, 267–269.

9. See Booth, *Rhetoric of Fiction*, 339–347. For the *Lalebuch*, see Bachorski, *Irrsinn und Kolportage*, 261–274. Attempts to credit authorship of *Lalebuch*, published anonymously under both titles, to Johann von Schönberg, Johann Fischart, or anyone else have not been found persuasive.

10. Ertz, *Das Lalebuch*, 99.

11. See Bachorski, *Irrsinn und Kolportage*, 271–274; Emmelius, "History, Narration, Lalespil," 241.

12. Ertz, *Das Lalebuch*, 37.

13. Ibid., 80.

14. Ibid.

15. Ibid., 30.

16. Schöttgen, *Vertheidigung der Stadt Schilda*, 10. On Schöttgen, see chapter 5.

17. The *Schildbürgerbuch* was favored by Peter Honegger, in *Die Schiltburgerchronik und ihr Verfasser Johann Fischart*. His arguments were refuted by Stefan Ertz, in *Fischart und die Schiltburgerchronik*. For a summary of the debate, see Kalkofen, "*Lalebuch* oder Schiltbürger, Anonymus oder Fischart?"

18. Von Bahder, introduction to *Das Lalebuch (1597)*, lxii. For an extended discussion, see Fay, "Mannskopf in Arabesken."

19. For a summary of the location debate, see Wunderlich, "*Schildbürgerstreiche*"; Könneker, *Satire im 16. Jahrhundert*, 205–222. On recent scholarship, see Schny-

der, "Bibliographie zum Prosaroman des 15. und 16. Jahrhunderts," 574–575; and
Dicke, "Lalebuch."

20. Wunderlich, "*Schildbürgerstreiche*," 660–661. On the relationship of Sachs and the *Lalebuch*, see Seelbach, "*Die newe Zeitungen auß der gantzen Welt*," 101n12.

21. Velten, "Die verbannten Weisen," 726–734.

22. Ertz, *Das Lalebuch*, 10. On the relationship of More's *Utopia* and *Lalebuch*, see Dicke, "Morus und Moros."

23. Görres, *Die teutschen Volksbücher*, 183–187.

24. Wunderlich, "*Schildbürgerstreiche*," 647–649.

25. Bässler, *Sprichwortbild und Sprichwortschwank*, 321.

26. Bässler refers to Dronke, *Verse with Prose from Petronius to Dante*, 5.

27. Dröse, "Formen und Funktionen politischer Rhetorik." Other approaches linked the *Lalebuch* to contemporary debates on feudalism and especially to the contemporary tensions between princes and municipalities, as well as to questions of family and gender relations. See Bachorski, *Irrsinn und Kolportage*, 275–295.

28. Schmitz, "Consuetudo und simulatio." It is arguable whether the Lalen are indeed depicted as melancholics. See Schmitz, "Die melancholischen Schildbürger." Recent scholarship has also shown that folly is even reflected in the narrative structure of the text. See Emmelius, "History, Narration, Lalespil."

29. N. Davis, "Reasons of Misrule."

30. Gvozdeva, "La procession charivarique en texte et image."

31. Ertz, *Das Lalebuch*, 24.

32. Ibid., 31.

33. Ibid., 32.

34. Ibid.

35. Ibid., 70.

36. Gvozdeva, "Hobbyhorse Performances."

37. Ertz, *Das Lalebuch*, 105.

38. Ibid., 106.

39. Emmelius, "History, Narration, Lalespil," 229.

40. Ertz, *Das Lalebuch*, 32.

41. Ibid., 106.

42. Ibid.

43. Ibid., 105.

44. Foucault, *History of Madness*, 28–29. The equation of *folie* with madness in the English translation of Foucault is not a little problematic.

45. Ertz, *Das Lalebuch*, 139.

46. Ertz, "Schilda und die Schildbürger."

47. The editions and their variations are compared by von Bahder, *Das Lalebuch (1597)*; Hesse, *Das Schicksal des Lalebuches in der deutschen Literatur*; Wunderlich, "*Schildbürgerstreiche*"; Ertz, *Fischart und die Schiltburgerchronik*, 5–12; Dicke, "Lalebuch," 22–23.

48. Filtzhut does no more to shed light on the facts of his life in the almanacs, apart from describing himself there as a "well-known worm-tailor and highly experienced provider of medical services to the young women of Calabria." See Filtzhut, *Ein poßierlich- jedoch warhafftig- und immerwehrender Hauß-Calender und Practica.*

49. Citations in German in this book from Filtzhut's revised *Schildbürgerbuch* rely on the British Library copy, titled *Wunderseltzame Abentheuerliche / lustige und recht lächerliche Geschichte und Thaten der Welt-bekanten Schild-Bürger in Misnopotamia / hinter Utopia gelegen* (1698). The title page includes "Peter Sqentz" as editor. The Jagiellonian University Library, Cracow, holds another edition from around 1698, which is presumably the earliest Filtzhut edition, since it does not mention Peter Squenz, who is apperently a later addition.

50. Filtzhut, *Schildbürgerbuch* (1698), 70. The legend of the Pied Piper was very popular in the early modern period, long before it was published along with the Grimms' other collected tales. See Uther, "Rattenfänger von Hameln."

51. Filtzhut, *Schildbürgerbuch* (1698), 16.

52. Ibid.

53. *Das lustige und lächerliche Lalen-Buch.*

54. This is based on a miscalculation of the Hebrew year [5]487 given in the second extant Yiddish translation of the *Schildbürgerbuch*, printed in Amsterdam in 1727 and mistakenly believed on the basis of this miscalculation to be the first Yiddish edition.

55. *Vielerley lustige Historien und Geschichte / Oder Zeit-Verkürtzer.*

56. Copies of the editions of circa 1698 are in the collections of the Jagiellonian University Library, Cracow (formerly Berlin Yt 7501), and the British Library (12555. aa.28.(1)). The Jagiellonian University Library, Cracow (formerly Berlin Yt 7550), and the Staats- und Universitätsbibliothek Hamburg (A/536119) both have a copy of an undated edition from around 1750. Two copies of an 1800 edition are held by the Staatsbibliothek zu Berlin (Yt 7571 and Yu 2514). There is also one undated edition in the Universitätsbibliothek Basel (Wack 1707c:1).

## CHAPTER 4. GENTILE FOOLS SPEAKING YIDDISH

1. The pseudonym Pomponius Filtzhut is given as the author's name in all editions of the Yiddish *Shildburger bukh*. The titles of the four surviving editions vary (see bibliography), but for convenience, I use the short title *Shildburger bukh* for each of them, with the date in parentheses to differentiate between editions.

2. On the different names and their ideological implications, see Frakes, *Politics of Interpretation.*

3. On Weinreich, see Schwarz, *Survivors and Exiles*, 147–151.

4. Paucker, "Di yidishe nuskhoes fun *Shildburger bukh*."

5. For more on *galkhes*, see Weinreich, *History of the Yiddish Language*, 1:A164–A165. See also Turniansky, "Yiddish and the Transmission of Knowledge."

6. Filtzhut, *Shildburger bukh* (1727), fol. 62r.

7. Ibid.

8. On the spread of reading, see Cavallo, Chartier, and Cochrane, *History of Reading.*

9. Turniansky, "Yiddish and the Transmission of Knowledge," 9.

10. Turniansky, "Old Yiddish Language and Literature."

11. Fagius, *Die fünff bücher Mosis,* fol. 3r. On Fagius in Strasbourg, see Kaplan, *Beyond Expulsion,* 121–140.

12. Goethe, *Aus meinem Leben,* 134. Independently of this conservatism, there were factors peculiar to the Jewish community, such as the manner of teaching the Bible to children, that had a powerful impact on spoken Yiddish, too. See Timm, *Historische jiddische Semantik.*

13. Wagenseil, *Belehrung der Jüdisch-Teutschen Red- und Schreibart,* fol. 2r.

14. Ibid.

15. Weinreich, *History of the Yiddish Language,* 1:A166.

16. Levi, *Ayn nay lid ouf der megile* (1649), quoted in Shmeruk, *Prokim fun der yidisher literatur-geshikhte,* 41.

17. Ibid.

18. Gerson, *Der Jüden Thalmud Fürnembster Inhalt vnd Widerlegung,* 239.

19. Beer, "Über die Nothwendigkeit einer Sammlung von Lebensbeschreibungen," 259. See Sadowski, *Haskala und Lebenswelt,* 50–51.

20. Elchanon Paulus von Prag to the Holy Roman Emperor, Rudolf II, August 9, 1583, Vienna, Diözesanarchiv, Protocollum Episcopatus Viennensis Anni 1581–1587 (WP 7), fol. 392v. On Paulus of Prague, see von Bernuth, "Zu Gast bei Nikolaus Selnecker."

21. Maimon, *Solomon Maimon,* 90.

22. Timm, "Jiddische Literatur." For an introduction to Old Yiddish literature, see Erik, *Di geshikhte fun der yidisher literatur;* Zinberg, *History of Jewish Literature,* vol. 7; and Baumgarten, *Introduction to Old Yiddish Literature.*

23. Ruderman, *Early Modern Jewry,* 99–132.

24. The 1700 edition of the Yiddish *Shildburger bukh* survives in seven documented copies: Bibliotheca Rosenthaliana, University of Amsterdam; Bodleian Library, University of Oxford; British Library, London; Jewish Theological Seminary, New York; Hebrew Union College, Cincinnati; and National Library of Israel, Jerusalem (two copies). There are four documented copies of the 1727 edition: Bibliotheca Rosenthaliana; Austrian National Library, Vienna (previously miscatalogued as dating from 1637); State and University Library of Saxony-Anhalt, Halle; and National and University Library, Strasbourg. The 1777 and the 1798 editions are each represented by a single documented copy only, both in the British Library.

25. Paucker, "Di yidishe nuskhoes fun *Shildburger bukh,*" 67.

26. Filtzhut, *Shildburger bukh* (1700), title page; and Filtzhut, *Shildburger bukh* (1727), title page.

27. Filtzhut, *Schildbürgerbuch* (1698), fol. A 2v.

28. Filtzhut, *Shildburger bukh* (1700), fol. 1v. See also Filtzhut, *Shildburger bukh* (1727), fol. 1v.
29. Filtzhut, *Shildburger bukh* (1700), fol. 8r; and Filtzhut, *Shildburger bukh* (1727), fol. 8v.
30. Filtzhut, *Schildbürgerbuch* (1698), 16.
31. Berger, "Selling Books in Eighteenth-Century Amsterdam." See in addition Berger, *Producing Redemption in Amsterdam*, 205–209.
32. The eighteenth-century scholars Johann Christoph Wolf and Johann Christian Schöttgen each had access to a Yiddish *Shildburger bukh*—Wolf presumably consulting the copy of the 1700 edition in the Oppenheim collection, on which he based his bibliographic magnum opus, while Schöttgen seems to have consulted a copy of the 1727 edition.
33. Wolf, *Bibliotheca hebraea*, 3:1060, no. 631b: "Schildbvrger, i.e. Seltsame und kurtzweilige Geschichte, seu ridicula de Schildburgensibus narrationes, Lingva Judaeo-Germanica, Amstelodami sine anno."
34. Schöttgen, *Vertheidigung der Stadt Schilda*, 38.
35. Ibid., 11–12.
36. For a brief summary, see Richter, *Die Sprache jüdischer Figuren in der deutschen Literatur*, 61–63.
37. Von der Hagen, "Die romantische und Volks-Litteratur," 11. Von der Hagen gave his lecture on August 18, 1853.
38. Lotze, "Zur jüdisch-deutschen Literatur," 90.
39. See Matut, "Steinschneider and Yiddish."
40. Steinschneider, "Jüdisch-Deutsche Literatur," 47, no. 288.
41. Avé-Lallemant, *Das deutsche Gaunerthum*, 477–484.
42. Ibid., 323.
43. Zarncke, "Des Paulus Aemilius Romanus Uebersetzung der Bücher Samuelis," 225. He was disputed by Richard Gosche (1824–1889), a professor of Oriental languages at Halle. On the dispute, see B. Simon, *Jiddische Sprachgeschichte*, 70–73.
44. Jeep, *Hans Friedrich von Schönberg*, 142.
45. Ibid.
46. Ibid.
47. Ibid.
48. Ibid., 144. Jeep was also of the opinion that Filtzhut himself was a Jew. This contention, based on Filtzhut's elimination of occasional anti-Jewish idioms present in the older versions of the *Schildbürgerbuch*, is persuasively discounted by Paucker, who shows that Filtzhut introduced more of such terms than he eliminated. See Paucker, "Yiddish Versions of the German Volksbuch," 257–260.
49. Hesse eventually emigrated to South Africa and taught at the University of Witwatersrand for some time.
50. Hesse, *Das Schicksal des Lalebuches in der deutschen Literatur*, 48, 50; see also 33–34.
51. Ibid., 50.

52. Schüler, "Beiträge zur Kenntnis der alten jüdisch-deutschen Profanliteratur," 116–122.
53. Ibid., 122.
54. Paucker, "Yiddish Versions of the German Volksbuch"; Paucker, "Das deutsche Volksbuch bei den Juden"; Paucker, "Di yidishe nuskhoes fun *Shildburger bukh*."
55. Paucker, "Das deutsche Volksbuch bei den Juden," 316.
56. Paucker, "Di yidishe nuskhoes fun *Shildburger bukh*," 70.
57. A typographical error, however, is introduced in the second Yiddish edition, where two consecutive sections are each numbered chapter 26, making it appear that there are only forty-four chapters.
58. Paucker, "Yiddish Versions of the German Volksbuch," 260. Thus, the first-person-plural object pronoun "wir" (us) appears even in the 1700 Yiddish version of the *Shildburger bukh* as "mir," and the preposition "ohne" (without) appears as "zunder." Prefixes are sometimes changed into their more conventional Yiddish equivalent and often written with word separation between the two components: "unruhig" (fretful) translates into "um ruik"; "empfangen" (to welcome) translates into "ant fangen"; and "Unglück" (bad luck) translates into "um glik." For some nouns, the more conventional Yiddish form replaces the German form: instead of "Meister" (master), the Yiddish form "maynster" is used, and similarly with verbs, so that "lesen" (to read) is always rendered as "leyenen" in all the Yiddish editions. Inflection, too, is adapted to Yiddish customary use, so that, for instance, the German "bei ihnen" (with them) becomes throughout the text "bay zey," and "von den Schildbürgern" (from the Schildburgers) translates as "fun di Shildburger." The verb "zayn" (to be) is given the Yiddish inflection so that, for instance, the plural of the German "sie sind" (they are) is translated as "zi zayn." Conspicuous differences between the Yiddish of the 1700 edition and the language of the German editions exist in the area of tenses, especially the preterite, which not only vanishes in modern Yiddish but is sometimes replaced even in the highly German Yiddish *Schildbürgerbuch* of 1700, so that "worden" (became) is translated as "gevorden var." In addition, the weak conjugation is preferred to the strong, so that the German "traten" (to convene) becomes "tretetn."
59. In many cases, it substitutes Yiddish variant forms of German-derived words, so that the German "derowegen " (therefore), which appears as "dero vegn" and as "des vegn" in the 1700 Yiddish edition, is often "dest vegn" in the 1727 edition. The German "Ankunft" (arrival) is converted to "an kunft" in 1700 and finally into "an kumst" in 1727; "erkennen" (to recognize) becomes "der kenen" in 1727; and "ouf ayn tsayt" (once upon a time) becomes "amol." The word for "is," still written "izt," corresponding to the German "ist," in the Yiddish of 1700, drops the last letter and becomes the conventional Yiddish "iz" in the 1727 edition. Frequently the genitive, which does not exist at all in modern Yiddish, is avoided in the 1727 version, so that "Abschrift des Briefes" (copy of the letter) is translated as "ab shrift fun den briv." *Shildburger bukh* (1727), fol. 8r.
60. Filtzhut, *Schildbürgerbuch* (1698), 27.

61. Filtzhut, *Shildburger bukh* (1700), fol. 27r.

62. Ibid., fol. 30r–v.

63. Filtzhut, *Schildbürgerbuch* (1698), 18; Filtzhut, *Shildburger bukh* (1700), fol. 9r.

64. Hampson, *Medii Ævi Kalendarium*, 164.

65. The interchangeability of the terms is demonstrated by the fact that the German text itself, which uses the phrase "Sankt Velten" on three occasions, uses the form "Potz Velten" on another occasion. The self-consciously diplomatic third Yiddish edition (1777), followed by the fourth (1798), omits the obsolescent imprecation altogether.

66. See Paucker, "Di yidishe nuskhoes fun *Shildburger bukh*," 64; and Paucker, "Yiddish Versions of the German Volksbuch," 267.

67. Filtzhut, *Shildburger bukh* (1727), fol. 1v.

68. Filtzhut, *Shildburger bukh* (1700), fol. 8r.

69. Ibid., fol. 21r; Filtzhut, *Shildburger bukh* (1727), fol. 18r.

70. Thus, there are such bracketed Hebraisms as "milkhome" (war), "sholem" (peace), "koved" (respect), and "kharote" (regret) and such bracketed Romance-language-derived words as "reverents" (reference) and "kompliment" (compliment), along with such proper nouns as the names Aesop and Pomponius.

71. Filtzhut, *Shildburger bukh* (1727), fols. 50v, 57r.

72. Ibid., fol. 31v. On Dutch influences on Yiddish, see Aptroot, "Dutch Impact on Amsterdam Yiddish Prints."

73. Filtzhut, *Shildburger bukh* (1700), fol. 10r.

74. Ibid., fol. 31v.

75. Ibid., fol. 49r: "ayn gut fet khazer." Filtzhut, *Shildburger bukh* (1727), fol. 48v: "ayn gute fete ku"; and ibid., fol. 26v: "ayn partey gents."

76. The "frid" element is a play on the classic German forename ending, as in Alfried or Gottfried, plus *Sau* (sow), yielding a given name vaguely reminiscent of Siegfried or Seyfried. The last name Lödel indicates a slovenly fellow. See Staub and Tobler, *Schweizerisches Idiotikon*, 1101.

77. Filtzhut, *Shildburger bukh* (1700), fol. 29v; and Filtzhut, *Shildburger bukh* (1727), fol. 27v.

78. Filtzhut, *Shildburger bukh* (1700), fol. 30r. Filtzhut, *Shildburger bukh* (1727), fol. 28v, keeps "shvayn" (pig).

79. Filtzhut, *Shildburger bukh* (1700), fol. 29v.

80. Filtzhut, *Shildburger bukh* (1727), fol. 28v.

81. Some of the numerous minor verbal changes involve shortening the length of expressions previously used so as to make them snappier, while others involve lengthening a form of words used in the original to make it more ludicrously overblown. Thus, the German versions and the 1700 Yiddish version refer to the peasant bread as "brot" of a kind so "black and coarse and baked from raw bran" that one of the shepherds of Schildburg has to teach the emperor how to eat it, when they offer it to him on the occasion of his state visit, whereas the Yiddish of 1727 replaces all this description with the single word "pumper nikl" (pumper-

nickel), saving space and cashing in at the same time on the comic mood that the word dependably creates. See Filtzhut, *Shildburger bukh* (1727), fol. 33v. For the editor's countervailing proclivity—his fondness, sometimes, for a jocular heightening of verbosity—it should be sufficient to refer to his transmutation of the 1700 edition's title words "highly amazing" into "highly, broadly, and deeply amazing"; the Schildburgers, who were "nit venig mesameyekh" (not a little happy) in the 1700 edition, were more than not a little happy by 1727—in fact, they were "considerably, greatly, profoundly, expansively, and extremely happy." See Filtzhut, *Shildburger bukh* (1700), fol. 27v; and Filtzhut, *Shildburger bukh* (1727), fol. 42r.

82. Filtzhut, *Shildburger bukh* (1727), fol. 58r.

83. Ibid., fol. 55v.

84. Ibid., fol. 56r.

85. Ibid., fol. 56v.

86. Ibid.

87. Montanus, *Das Ander theyl der Gartengeselschafft*, fol. 5r–v, no. 9. He tells the story about a farmer and his son.

88. Filtzhut, *Shildburger bukh* (1727), fol. 56v.

89. Paucker, "Das deutsche Volksbuch bei den Juden," 316.

90. Martin Luther, however, grossly exaggerated the extent of the evidence for such influence, making a polemic out of it by unjustifiably ascribing primary responsibility for the invention of Rotwelsch to the Jews. See Luther's preface to the *Book of Vagabonds and Beggars*, 3: "Truly, such beggars' cant has come from the Jews, for many Hebrew words occur in the vocabulary, as anyone who understands that language may perceive."

91. Filtzhut, *Shildburger bukh* (1700), fol. 30v.

92. Filtzhut, *Shildburger bukh* (1727), fol. 28r.

93. Ibid.

94. Ibid.

95. On riddling in the early modern period, see Gvozdeva, "Spielprozess und Zivilisationsprozess."

96. See Pagis, "Toward a Theory of the Literary Riddle," 97.

97. Filtzhut, *Shildburger bukh* (1727), fol. 40r. See Bernstein, *Jüdische Sprichwörter und Redensarten*, 6: "Ahin un aher, un in der mit a lokh—vos-zshe vartst du nokh?—Makh a shtokh!" (Back and forth and a hole in the middle—why do you still wait? Make a stitch!)

98. Filtzhut, *Shildburger bukh* (1727), fol. 40r.

99. Ibid., fol. 33r.

100. For more on this practice, see Meuli, "Charivari"; and Dieterich, "Eselritt und Dachabdecken."

101. Bässler, *Sprichwortbild und Sprichwortschwank*, 307–308.

102. K. Wander, *Deutsches Sprichwörter-Lexikon*, 3:1200–1202.

CHAPTER 5. THE ENLIGHTENMENT GOES EAST

1. Wieland, "Ein paar Goldkörner," 97. The translation follows for the most part Wieland, "Couple of Gold Nuggets."
2. Wieland, "Ein paar Goldkörner," 98.
3. Ibid., 99.
4. Auerochs, "Was ist Wahrheit?"
5. Schulz uses the pseudonym Heinrich Ringwald.
6. Röcke, "Joseph Görres' *Teutsche Volksbücher* (1807) und Rebmanns *Empfindsame Reise nach Schilda.*"
7. Wieland used the title *Die Abderiten: Eine sehr wahrscheinliche Geschichte* in *Der Teutsche Merkur. Wahrscheinlichkeit* meant at the time "verisimilitude" in addition to "probability." See Zedler, *Grosses vollständiges Universal-Lexicon*, 1020–1063. Wieland changed the title to *Die Geschichte der Abderiten* for the book publication.
8. On the history of the publication, see K. Manger, "Wielands *Geschichte der Abderiten*" (2003).
9. It was said that the Athenians disparaged the people of Abdera in Thrace as what Robert Burton, in his *Anatomy of Melancholy* (1621), renders as "fools and madmen." Cicero in the first century BCE and Galen in the second century CE make reference to this idea, and the late third- or fourth-century CE grammarians Hierocles and Philagrius present a whole collection of fully-fledged numbskull tales about Abdera, briefly told in a few pages of their *Philogelos*. Thus, according to them, an Abderite was once aboard a ship that became becalmed. Having heard that onions and leeks were liable to produce wind, he filled a bag with these vegetables and tied it to the mast. See Hierocles, *Philogelos*, 70–75. See also Fuchs, *Geistiger Gehalt*; Bülow, "Das historische Vorbild für Wielands Abdera."
10. K. Manger, "Universitas Abderitica."
11. The translation follows for the most part Wieland, *History of the Abderites*, 45. The "oyster nymph" is not a real concept, just a term coined by Wieland for this specific context. In pure Schildburger style, the Abderites' column accomplished exactly the opposite of what they intended. Rather than increasing the number of people who were able to admire the beauty of their life-sized Venus Anadyomene, now it was perched so far away that no one could make out more than that the subject was evidently female and mounted on a scallop.
12. Wieland, *History of the Abderites*, 50.
13. Schiller, "Preface," xvi; Kant, *Conflict of the Faculties*, 146–147.
14. Manuel, *Shapes of Philosophical History*, 73. On Mendelssohn and his alleged Abderitism, see also Shell, *Kant and the Limits of Autonomy*, 321–322.
15. Christoph Martin Wieland to Catharina Elisabeth Goethe, Mannheim, December 23, 1777, in Gibbs, *Goethe's Mother*, 52.
16. Wieland, *History of the Abderites*, 41.
17. Ibid.

18. Martini, "Wieland," 73; Klotz, *Die erzählte Stadt*, 83.

19. K. Manger, "Wielands *Geschichte der Abderiten*" (2008).

20. Wieland, "Nachricht von Sebastian Brand"; Wieland, "Ueber Sebastian Brands Narrenschiff."

21. Paul, "Kleine Nachschule zur ästhetischen Vorschule," 469–470.

22. Ertz, *Das Lalebuch*, 12.

23. Wieland, "Auszug aus einem Schreiben an einen Freund in D***," 243: "Man kann nicht sagen, hier ist Abdera, oder da ist Abdera! Abdera ist allenthalben."

24. Ibid., 246.

25. Wieland, *History of the Abderites*, 44.

26. See Martini, "Wieland," 76–77.

27. On Wieland's critique of the intellectual fashions of the late eighteenth-century German-speaking elite, see Lann, "Christoph Martin Wieland and the German Making of Greece." See also Edelstein, *Wielands "Abderiten"*; and Clark, "Wieland and Winckelmann."

28. Wieland, *History of the Abderites*, 44.

29. Shookman, *Noble Lies*, 117.

30. Wieland, *History of the Abderites*, 118.

31. Ibid., 41. The dictionary, published in many subsequent editions, was also available in German in the translation of Johann Gottfried Gottsched, assisted by his wife, Luise Gottsched, which appeared in print in 1741–1744. See Brown, *Luise Gottsched the Translator*. On Bayle's reception in Germany, see Sauder, "Bayle-Rezeption in der deutschen Aufklärung." Wieland had access to Bayle's dictionary from the age of fourteen, when he began attending Kloster Berge, the Pietist school near Magdeburg. See Zaremba, *Christoph Martin Wieland*, 35.

32. Wieland, *History of the Abderites*, 43.

33. Ibid., 303. The year 1753 is when Wieland started to publish.

34. On Wieland and Sterne, see Michelsen, *Laurence Sterne*, 177–224.

35. Sterne, *Life and Opinions of Tristram Shandy*, 4:2.

36. Wieland, *History of the Abderites*, 306.

37. Ibid.

38. Ibid., 307.

39. Brant, *Das Narrenschiff*, 3.

40. Wieland, *History of the Abderites*, 307.

41. Kleingeld, *Kant and Cosmopolitanism*, 14.

42. See also Wieland, "Das Geheimniß des Kosmopolitenordens."

43. Ibid., 107.

44. See Wieland's "Key to the History of the Abderites" and the letter of a fictitious mayor, written by Goethe's brother-in-law, Johann Georg Schlosser, "Schreiben an Herrn Hofrath Wieland."

45. Wieland, *History of the Abderites*, 119: "We all recognize and admit as with one voice that Democritus is an eccentric, a visionary, a crank."

46. For more on Mendel Lefin, see Gelber, "Mendel Satanower"; Yisroel Vaynlez, "R. Menaḥem Mendel Lefin mi-Satanov"; Klausner, *Historiyah shel ha-sifrut ha-ivrit ha-ḥadashah*, 199–225; Sinkoff, *Out of the Shtetl*; Wodziński, *Haskalah and Hasidism*, 22–27.

47. On the Lefin-Czartoryski relationship, see Sinkoff, *Out of the Shtetl*, 50–112. For a more general consideration of the relationship between Jews and the nobility, see Rosman, *Lords' Jews*.

48. Vaynlez, "R. Menaḥem Mendel Lefin mi-Satanov," 800.

49. See Sinkoff, *Out of the Shtetl*, 116. The remnants are in the Abraham Schwadron Collection of Jewish Autographs and Portraits and in the Joseph Perl Archive, both in the National Library of Israel, Jerusalem.

50. Vaynlez, "R. Menaḥem Mendel Lefin mi-Satanov," 800; Vaynlez, "Mendl Lefin-Satanover."

51. Czartoryski, *Memoirs of Prince Adam Czartoryski*, 46.

52. Ibid.

53. Vaynlez, "R. Menaḥem Mendel Lefin mi-Satanov," 800.

54. Sinkoff, *Out of the Shtetl*, 113–167. See also Wodziński, *Haskalah and Hasidism*; Dynner, *Men of Silk*.

55. On the Baal Shem Tov in Międzybóż, see Rosman, "Miedzyboz and Rabbi Israel Ba'al Shem Tov"; Rosman, *Founder of Hasidism*.

56. Sinkoff, *Out of the Shtetl*, 33.

57. On *Essai d'un plan de réforme*, see Sinkoff, *Out of the Shtetl*, 81–95; Wodziński, *Haskalah and Hasidism*, 22–27.

58. Sinkoff, *Out of the Shtetl*, 85.

59. Lefin Satanover, "Essai d'un plan de réforme," 411, nos. 20–22, and 15, no. 76.

60. Sinkoff, *Out of the Shtetl*, 275.

61. Vaynlez, "Mendl Lefin-Satanover," 348.

62. Sinkoff, *Out of the Shtetl*, 33.

63. Werses, "Ha-dei ha-satira shel Lukianus be-sifrut ha-haskala ha-ivrit."

64. Perl's *Megale temirin* was translated as *Joseph Perl's Revealer of Secrets* by Dov Taylor.

65. Roskies, *Bridge of Longing*, 58–60.

66. On *Megale temirin*, see Taylor, introduction to *Joseph Perl's "Revealer of Secrets"*; Dauber, *Antonio's Devils*, 252–310.

67. Meir, "New Readings in Joseph Perl's *Boḥen tsadik*," 561.

68. On *Boḥen tsadik*, see Zinberg, *History of Jewish Literature*, 10:87–92; Frieden, "Joseph Perl's Escape"; Meir, "New Readings in Joseph Perl's *Boḥen tsadik*"; and Meir, *Ḥasidut medumah*.

69. J. Perl, *Boḥen tsadik*, 57–68.

70. Ibid., 60.

71. Ibid., 62–66. The translation follows Zinberg, *History of Jewish Literature*, 10:90.

72. Perl, *Boḥen tsadik*, 56.

73. Meir, "New Readings in Joseph Perl's *Boḥen tsadik*," 577–578.

74. Ibid., 576–586.

75. An anonymous six-page manuscript in Perl's library, whose plot strongly resembles that of *Boḥen tsadik* and may be its inspiration, is conceivably material composed by Lefin, who bequeathed his library and papers to Perl. See Meir, *Ḥasidut medumah*, 183–195.

76. Dik, *Sipurey khokhmey Yovn*, 18. This is one of the publications from the brief period during which Dik used the pseudonym Avrom Aba KaB.

77. The consonant is vocalized in the text with a *segol*, the short *e* sound.

78. Sherman, "Dik, Ayzik Meyer," 407: "Dik's books . . . were readily accessible not only to his 'dear lady readers' but also to the learned, who valued them for their use of ethnography, folklore, innovative intertextuality, and clever narrative strategies—all of which strongly influenced subsequent Yiddish fiction. Sholem Aleichem described Dik as 'the richest belletrist' in Yiddish, and Shmuel Niger noted that Dik 'sometimes forgot that he was a reformer and told a story for its own sake.'"

79. On Dik's biography, see Zinberg, *History of Jewish Literature*, 12:78–90; Roskies, "Ayzik-Meyer Dik"; Roskies, *Bridge of Longing*, 56–98; and Sherman, "Dik, Ayzik Meyer." On the use of Yiddish in his family, see Paulauskienė, *Lost and Found*, 31. On Dik and Haskalah, see Caplan, *How Strange the Change*, 90–96.

80. Sherman, "Dik, Ayzik Meyer."

81. Roskies, *Bridge of Longing*, 63.

82. Dik, *Blitsende vitsen oder lakhpilen*, no. 29, 18–19.

83. F. Friedman, "Tsu der geshikhte fun di yidn in Khelm," 35–36.

84. Ibid.

85. Ibid.

86. Roskies, "Ayzik-Meyer Dik and the Rise of Yiddish Popular Literature," 290.

87. "You deserve the rope," i.e., you deserve to be hanged.

88. Presumably eating on alternate days doubles the quantity previously consumed daily.

89. He would inquire about buying back the moon.

90. Lieb, "Spiegelbild im Wasser." See also Uther, *Animal Tales, Tales of Magic, Religious Tales, and Realistic Tales*, type 1335: "Catching the Moon."

91. Hirsh Lion Dor, *Yidish brivnshteler* (1851), quoted in Sadan, "Arum Khelem un der Khelmyade," 102.

92. Neumann, "Sonnenlicht im Sack." See Uther, *Animal Tales, Tales of Magic, Religious Tales, and Realistic Tales*, 83, type 1245: "Sunlight Carried in a Bag."

93. Dik, *Blitsende vitsen*, 19.

94. Dröse, "Formen und Funktionen politischer Rhetorik."

95. This story belongs to folk motif "Carrying the Horse." See Uther, *Animal Tales, Tales of Magic, Religious Tales, and Realistic Tales*, 73, type 1201. In documented worldwide stories featuring this motif, the purpose of preserving snow is unique to Jewish tellings, all of which, it is likely, ultimately derive from an innovation on

Dik's part in "The Wisdom of a Certain Town Khes." For the Jewish version, see Jason, "Jewish–Near Eastern Numskull Tales," 36.

96. Manger's 1937 story "Der 'Khelemer' zatsa'l" was printed in *Naye folkstsaytung* and was reprinted in abridged form in *Noente geshtaltn* (1938) but restored to full length (under the title "Der Khelemer") in *Noente geshtaltn un andere shriftn* (1961). The longer version was also translated by Leonard Wolf: I. Manger, "Rabbi of Chelm."

97. Pryłucki, "Khelemer naronim," 198, no. 29; Kipnis, *Khelemer mayses*, 99.

98. Dik, *Di orkhim in Duratshesok*, 27.

99. Gintsburg, *Tikun Lavan ha-Arami*. On Gintsburg (Günzburg), see Bartal, "Mordechai Aaron Günzburg," 138.

100. Glupsk is an invented place name often used by Abramovitsh. See, for instance, *Dos vintshfingerl*. On the influence of Saltykov on Abramovitsh, see Krutikov, "Berdichev in Russian-Jewish Literary Imagination," 95.

101. Dik, *Di orkhim in Duratshesok*, 1.

102. Ibid., 3.

103. Ibid., 27.

104. Ibid.

105. See chapter 14 of any edition of the *Schildbürgerbuch*.

106. Uther, *Animal Tales, Tales of Magic, Religious Tales, and Realistic Tales*, 72, type 1200: "Sowing Salt." The *Schildbürgerbuch*'s precursor, the *Lalebuch* of 1597, is the oldest source to report the story.

107. See chapter 36 of any edition of the *Schildbürgerbuch* and chapter 35 in the Yiddish edition of 1727.

108. Kumove, *More Words, More Arrows*, 53.

109. Roskies, *Bridge of Longing*, 78; Bartal, "Mordechai Aaron Günzburg," 138.

110. See Himka, *Religion and Nationality in Western Ukraine*.

111. Dik, *Der shivim moltsayt*, 46.

112. F. Friedman, "Tsu der geshikhte fun di yidn in Khelm," 35.

113. The fact that Friedman does not mention the idea tends to relegate to the status of urban legend, for example, the notion, eminently plausible but apparently unfounded, although not far from the truth, that the Chelm stories were invented by maskilim of the nearby town of Zamość to ridicule the pious Torah scholars of Chelm, distinctly different at that period in its fervent religious atmosphere from Zamość (as reported via Yissochor Marmorstein, London, by Yosef Becher, also London, from parents raised in early twentieth-century Lublin).

114. K. Wander, *Deutsches Sprichwörter-Lexikon*, 3:930, no. 1173.

115. The book's ownership stamp in the National Library of Israel indicates that it was formerly in the possession of the folktale researcher, rabbi, and bibliophile Moses Gaster in London.

116. On the Ehrenpreis family, see Rovner, *"Please Help Me Tithe unto You."*

117. On Jacob Samuel Bik, see Werses, "Bein shnei olamot."

118. On the shtetl as a place in Jewish fiction, see Miron, "The Literary Image of the Shtetl," chap. 1 in *Image of the Shtetl*.
119. Bik, *Der Khelemer khokhem*, 16.
120. Uther, *Animal Tales, Tales of Magic, Religious Tales, and Realistic Tales*, 2, type 1275: "Sledges Turned." See Schwarzbaum, *Studies in Jewish and World Folklore*, 189–190; Rausmaa, "Die verkehrte Richtung."
121. Bik, *Der Khelemer khokhem*, 3.
122. Ibid.
123. Schwarzbaum, *Studies in Jewish and World Folklore*, 189.
124. Frishman's polemic titled "Ḥemah" (Butter) tells how the Chelmites built an oven of butter. Some parts of the piece bear a close resemblance to the thirteenth chapter of the *Schildbürgerbuch*, in which the Schildburgers construct their oven outside the town hall. See Frishman, "Ḥemah." See also Mierowsky, "David Frishman."
125. Peretz, "In Eyrope un bay unz untern oyvn."
126. See Mahalel, "We Will Not Be Silent."
127. A notable exception is David Roskies's chapter on Peretz, which includes a discussion of "Iber a shmek tabak," in which he connects the story with that of the fifteenth-century kabbalist Joseph della Reina and his downfall, brought on by his accession to a request from the demon Samael for a pinch of frankincense and the destructive forces that this act unleashes. See Roskies, *Bridge of Longing*, 137–138. Khone Shmeruk mentions only in passing Peretz's "In alt Khelem" and its influence on "tens of Yiddish writers," among them most importantly Trunk and Glatshteyn. See Shmeruk, "Yitskhok Bashevis," 261.
128. On Peretz, see Roskies, *Bridge of Longing*, 99–146.
129. Peretz, "Der Khelmer melamed."
130. The idea goes back to an Aggadic passage in the Babylonian Talmud (Yoma 69b), according to which the sages once managed to imprison the *yeytser hore*. Three days later, however, they searched for a freshly laid egg and could not find one in the entire Land of Israel. The sages realized that if they did not free the *yeytser hore* at once, the world would be destroyed.
131. Peretz, "Der Khelmer melamed," 9.
132. See chapter 1.
133. Peretz, "Pinch of Snuff," 258.
134. Peretz, "Der shabes-goy," 185; Peretz, "Shabbes Goy," 132.
135. Peretz, "Shabbes Goy," 133.
136. Ibid., 135.
137. Ibid.
138. Ibid., 136.
139. Peretz, "Der shabes-goy," 194.
140. A contrary view is expressed by Yitskhok Yanosovitsh in his short essay on the Khelemer mayses in the Chelm *Yizker-bukh* (1954). There, he names Peretz as deviating from rather than advancing the cause: "Others have linked their pieces to

Chelm. However, the stories themselves, such as Y. L. Peretz's 'Khelmer melamed,' have no connection with the Chelm material [proper]. Other Chelm stories, therefore, await their great genius who will do justice to the Chelm corpus. Until this happens, it is our unremitting obligation to record every nuance, every variation of the Chelm story, as it travels among Jews all around the world." Yanasovitsh, "Di 'Khelemer mayse' un di yidishe literatur," 52.

CHAPTER 6. THE GEOGRAPHY OF FOLLY

1. Burt, *Friedrich Salomo Krauss*; Daxelmüller, "Friedrich Salomo Krauss."
2. Burt, *Friedrich Salomo Krauss*, 48.
3. Fabian, "Keep Listening," 81.
4. The journal was first published under the title *Am Urdsbrunnen* (At the Fountain) starting in 1881.
5. Segel, "Abderiten von heute unter den Juden."
6. Hobsbawm, introduction to *Invention of Tradition*, 1.
7. The same is true of Laleburg in the *Lalebuch* (1597), precursor of the *Schildbürgerbuch*, discussed in chapter 2.
8. Some scholars have argued at length that Schilde, used in the later chapters of the *Schildbürgerbuch* as a briefer synonym for Schildburg, is in fact Schilda, but the book clearly uses Schildburg or Schilde as alternative names for a fictional foolish town. See Ertz, "Schilda und die Schildbürger."
9. Blaschke and Baudisch, *Historisches Ortsverzeichnis von Sachsen*, 2:664.
10. Zeiller, *Itinerarium Germaniae Nov-antiquae*, 666; Zeiller, *Topographia Superioris Saxoniae Thüringiae*, 166; and Zeiller, *Topographia Superioris Saxoniae Thüringiae*, 2nd ed., 157. More examples from scattered sources can be found in Schmitz, "Das 'Volksbuch' von den Schildbürgern."
11. On Schöttgen, see Eigenwill, "Schöttgen, Johann Christian."
12. The journal, issued weekly, appeared during 1742 only and dealt mainly with topics in such areas of Hebrew literature as rabbinics and kabbalah, but Schöttgen also included translations of Yiddish literature, including excepts from the *Mayse bukh* (Book of stories, 1602) and a Yiddish version of the travels of Eldad ha-Dani. On this journal, see Riemer, "*Der Rabbiner*."
13. Schöttgen and Kreysig, *Diplomatische und curieuse Nachlese*, 261.
14. Schöttgen, *Vertheidigung der Stadt Schilda*, title page.
15. Ibid., 3–4.
16. Ibid., 4.
17. Ibid., title page.
18. Ibid., 11.
19. Ibid., 13.
20. Schöttgen makes the serious point that the vocabulary of the *Schildbürgerbuch* is not that of Saxony. Rather, the author appears to him to have been "from Swabia or somewhere else in the [Holy] Roman Empire" and as such most unlikely to have been out to lampoon a place as inconsequential as Schilda. The compa-

rable *flößlen* is used in Rotwelsch, German underground slang, and listed in the most common editions of the *Liber vagatorum* (1510) and many other books that feature Rotwelsch word lists, including the *Schildbürgerbuch*'s sequel, *Grillenvertreiber* (1603). For more on *flößlen*, see S. Wolf, *Wörterbuch des Rotwelschen*, 102, no. 1492; *Liber vagatorum*, fol. c iir; Agyrta von Bellemont (pseud.), *Hummeln*, 33.

21. On the ambiguity of early modern foolish culture, see Gvozdeva, "Rituale des Doppelsinns"; Gvozdeva, "Karnevaleske Statuten."

22. See, for instance, Schildau's hiking guide: Cernik, *Schildbürgerwanderweg Schildau*.

23. The one exception among these titles is Karl Arnold Kortum's (1745–1824) rhymed satire of the bildungsroman *Leben, Meynungen und Thaten von Hieronimus Jobs dem Kandidaten, und wie Er sich weiland viel Ruhm erwarb auch endlich als Nachtswächter zu Sulzburg starb* (1784). An English translation by Charles T. Brook appeared in 1863 as *The Jobsiad: A Grotesco-Comico-Heroic Poem: The Life, Opinions, Actions, and Fate of Hieronimus Jobs the Candidate, a Man Who Whilom Won Great Renown, and Died as Night-Watch in Sulzburg.* The second German edition, 1799, changed the title to *Jobsiade* and the name of the location from Sulzburg to Schildburg, reflecting the resurgent fame of the *Schildbürgerbuch* during the Enlightenment. For reasons of rhyme, Kortum could not change the name to Schilda. Other authors used names besides Schildburg or Schilda for their foolish towns, such as Scheppenstedt in Johann Gottlieb Schummel's *Die Revolution in Scheppenstedt* (1794), a made-up name that later gave rise to a claimed foolish tradition on the part of Schöppenstedt near Hanover, or Krähwinkel (Crow's corner), or, most prominently, Abdera in Wieland's *History of the Abderites*. On Krähwinkel, see for instance Thümmel, *Wilhelmine, ein prosaisch komisches Gedicht*, 29.

24. Paul, *Titan: A Romance*, 152; Paul, *Titan*, 1:255–256.

25. On works by Campe translated in Hebrew and Yiddish, by Mendel Lefin and others, see Zohar Shavit, "From Friedländer's Lesebuch to the Jewish Campe"; Shavit, "Literary Interference"; Frieden, "Neglected Origins of Modern Hebrew Prose"; Wolpe, "Judaizing *Robinson Crusoe*."

26. Campe, *Wörterbuch der deutschen Sprache*, 4:137. Campe also doubts that Schilda was originally the place of the Schildbürger.

27. Campe, *Wörterbuch zur Erklärung und Verdeutschung*, 74.

28. Ibid. In addition, he suggests *Abderiteneinfalt* (Abderite simple-mindedness), *Abderitenstumpfsinn* (Abderite ignorance), and *Abderitendummheit* (Abderite stupidity).

29. Ibid.

30. On the differentiation between Abdera for the intellectuals and Schilda and other German towns for ordinary people, see Campe's contemporary the German patriot Ernst Moritz Arndt (1769–1860), who, in his *Reisen durch einen Theil Teutschlands, Ungarns, Italiens und Frankreichs in den Jahren 1798 und 1799*, 350, describes a "truth is stranger than fiction" scenario in which Paris in the after-

math of the French Revolution was more foolish than anything the poets write of Abdera or "the limited imagination of the novelists" tells us of Schilda, Reutlingen, and Polkwitz.

31. DeNoël, "Skizze des Plans für die Feier des Karnevals 1825," 12nii.
32. See chapter 2.
33. Woltersdorf, *Jahrbuch der gesammten Literatur und Ereignisse*, 78. A review of the latter mentions the foolish towns again in "Review of E. G. Woltersdorf, *Jahrbuch der gesammten Literatur und Ereignisse*." See also Hackländer, *Künstlerroman*, 181.
34. Schlegel, *Geschichte der romantischen Litteratur*, 153. On Romantic aesthetics and *Volksbücher*, see Grossman, *Discourse on Yiddish*, 115–117; Kreutzer, *Der Mythos vom Volksbuch*.
35. Görres, *Die teutschen Volksbücher*, 185.
36. Von der Hagen, *Narrenbuch*, v. On von der Hagen, see Grunewald, *Friedrich Heinrich von der Hagen*; Röcke, 'Erneuerung' des Mittelalters oder Dilettantismus?"
37. Von der Hagen, *Narrenbuch*, 425.
38. Ibid., 440.
39. Ibid., 430.
40. Jacob Grimm to Joseph Görres, August 12, 1811, in Görres, *Joseph von Görres gesammelte Briefe*, 232. See also Grunewald, *Friedrich Heinrich von der Hagen*, 301–303.
41. On the long-running rivalry between the brothers Grimm and von der Hagen, see Martus, *Die Brüder Grimm*.
42. Grimm and Grimm, "Review of Friedrich Heinrich von der Hagen's *Narrenbuch*," 1283.
43. Ibid., 1287.
44. Uhland, *Uhlands Schriften*, 621.
45. Gervinus, *Geschichte der poetischen National-Literatur der Deutschen*, 345–347; Rosenkranz, *Geschichte der deutschen Poesie*, 409–412.
46. Goedeke, *Grundrisz zur Geschichte der deutschen Dichtung*, 420. On the *Schildbürgerbuch*, see 424–425.
47. Schwab, *Buch der schönsten Geschichten und Sagen*, v.
48. Marbach, *Der Schildbürger*; Simrock, *Wunderseltsame, abenteuerliche und bisher unbeschriebene Geschichten und Thaten*. Another such collection is that of Felix Bobertag, *Volksbücher des 16. Jahrhunderts*.
49. Ude-Koeller, "Kirche verschieben."
50. Aurbacher, "Historia von den Lalenbürgern."
51. Freud, *Der Witz und seine Beziehung zum Unbewussten*, 43. Freud mentions the *Fliegende Blätter* as his only source.
52. Simrock, *Die deutschen Sprichwörter*, iii.
53. Körte, *Die Sprichwörter und sprichwörtlichen Redensarten der Deutschen*, 383, no. 5316.
54. Simrock, *Die deutsche Sprichwörter*, 425, no. 9016.

55. Reinsberg-Düringsfeld, *Internationale Titulaturen*, 105–106. Another collector was the popular, now-forgotten writer George Hesekiel (1819–1874), who published a series of lists of places with their epithets in *Deutsche Roman-Zeitung* in 1866, subsequently published in book form as *Land und Stadt im Volksmunde*. Foolish towns are listed on 27.

56. Heine, *Ideen*, 96.

57. Heine, *Heinrich Heine über Ludwig Börne*, 209–211.

58. Heine, "Anno 1839," 122–123.

59. Ibid.

60. Ibid.

61. Ibid., 124–125.

62. Von Wurzbach, *Glimpf und Schimpf in Spruch und Wort*, 49. Von Wurzbach follows Schöttgen in denying Schilda as the prototype for Schildburg, bizarrely introducing as evidence for his position the fact that Schilda was the birthplace of the anything-but-foolish Prussian field marshal August von Gneisenau (1760–1831). Von Wurzbach is best known for his sixty-volume work *Biographisches Lexikon des Kaisertums Oesterreich* (Biographical dictionary of the Austrian Empire, 1857–1892). See Lebensaft and Reitterer, *Wurzbach-Aspekte*.

63. Von Wurzbach, *Glimpf und Schimpf*, 49.

64. Tendlau, *Sprichwörter und Redensarten deutsch-jüdischer Vorzeit*, 43–44, no. 120.

65. Tendlau, *Das Buch der Sagen und Legenden jüdischer Vorzeit*. On Tendlau, see Glasenapp, "Popularitätskonzepte jüdischer Folklore." On Tendlau's father and grandfather, see Brocke and Carlebach, *Die Rabbiner der Emanzipationszeit*, 850.

66. Tendlau, *Sprichwörter und Redensarten*, 43.

67. Earlier sources, such as Moritz Blass's *Jüdische Sprichwörter* (Jewish proverbs, 1857), include no such references.

68. Tendlau, *Sprichwörter und Redensarten*, 44, 346–347, no. 986.

69. On the emergence of German Jewish literature, see Hess, *Middlebrow Literature*.

70. Tendlau, *Sprichwörter und Redensarten*, vi.

71. K. Wander, *Deutsches Sprichwörter-Lexikon*, 3:931, no. 1188. The Jewish foolish towns are listed once more, along with the German towns, under the keyword "Schildbürgerstreich" in Wander, *Deutsches Sprichwörter-Lexikon*, 4:179.

72. Wander, *Deutsches Sprichwörter-Lexikon*, 3:930, no. 1173.

73. Ibid., 3:934, no. 1278.

74. Ibid.

75. On Maimon's autobiography, see Weissberg, "Salomon Maimon Writes His *Lebensgeschichte*."

76. Maimon, *Solomon Maimon*, 209.

77. Wander, *Deutsches Sprichwörter-Lexikon*, 3:934, no. 1278.

78. Ibid.

79. Bernstein and Segel, *Jüdische Sprichwörter und Redensarten*, 199\*. The page with the asterisk is in Yiddish, whereas the page in the German transcription bears the same number without the asterisk. The second edition of Bernstein's collection

was published in a different format in which each proverb was organized according to keywords accompanied by a transcription on the opposite page. Segel mainly deserves credit for this work. See Segel, "Meine Beichte," 149.

80. Bernstein and Segel, *Jüdische Sprichwörter und Redensarten*, 106: "Ale khazonim zenen naronim" (All cantors are fools). For turkeys, see ibid., 13: "Az men seyet indikes, vaksn naronim" (If you sow turkeys, you reap fools).

81. Indeed, so closely was the penis associated with folly in German culture that *Schwanz* had its extended sense of "penis" extended yet again, so that to call someone a *Schwanz* was (empathically) to call him a fool. The Grimms document this sense as far back as the Middle High German of the fifteenth century. The word had the same tertiary meaning in Yiddish, as demonstrated in Gottfried Selig's early Yiddish textbook and dictionary, which includes the Yiddish sentence "Du bist ein goduler Sonof" and the German translation "du bist ein großer Schwanz (Narr)"—you are a big tail (i.e., fool). See Selig, *Lehrbuch zur gründlichen Erlernung*, 176. For the German, see Grimm and Grimm, *Deutsches Wörterbuch*, 2263. For the Yiddish, see Tendlau, *Sprichwörter und Redensarten*, 43, no. 118. For the use in Yiddish also of *zonov*, the Hebrew for "tail," in both extended senses of German *Schwanz* / Yiddish *shvants*, see Assaf and Bartal, "The Metamorphosis of Zanav."

82. Bernstein and Segel, *Jüdische Sprichwörter und Redensarten*, 104; Wander, *Deutsches Sprichwörter-Lexikon*, 3:930, no. 1175.

83. Von Bernuth, *Wunder, Spott und Prophetie*, 133, 212.

84. The word is not Germanic, not Slavic, and thus, evidently, Hebrew derived.

85. Maimon, *Solomon Maimon*, 134.

86. Lütke, *Kurtze und gründliche Anweisung*, 15. This dictionary is an interesting source insofar as it provides a German-Yiddish dictionary, as against the more common Yiddish-German variety.

87. Kipnis, *Khelemer mayses*, 88.

88. Weinreich records another variant of the saying, namely, that Khoyzek did not recognize his own father. See M. Weinreich, *History of the Yiddish Language*, 1:A293.

89. Bernstein and Segel, *Jüdische Sprichwörter und Redensarten*, 110*. The scholar of Yiddish Alfred Landau published his collection as a supplement to Bernstein's work. In his preface, he claims that the sayings that he includes were in circulation in Brody in the mid-nineteenth century. On Khoyzek, see Landau, "Sprichwörter und Redensarten," 338. He conjectures that the name comes from the Hebrew phrase *be-ḥozek yad* (with strength of hand), not on account of the intrinsic meaning of word *ḥozek*, i.e., strength, but because it is the word with which the Passover Haggadah begins its response to the question as to the meaning of the holiday that it imagines being posed by a hypothetical "simple son," who, as described in chapter 1 of this book, is often construed as a fool. For more on the word *khoyzek*, used in modern Yiddish to denote joking around or playing the fool, see Weinreich, *History of the Yiddish Language*, 1:A293.

90. Bernstein and Segel, *Jüdische Sprichwörter und Redensarten*, xv.

91. Scherman and Krauss, *Allgemeine Methodik der Volkskunde*, 133.

92. Krauss, "Beiträge zur Geschichte der Volkskunde," 284. On Grunwald, see Daxelmüller, "Jüdische Volkskunde in Deutschland."

93. Krauss, "Beiträge zur Geschichte der Volkskunde," 284.

94. Andree, "Abderiten von heute."

95. Ibid., 117.

96. Ibid.

97. Here I rephrase an expression coined in a different context by Rosman, "Categorically Jewish, Distinctly Polish."

98. On the vast research literature, which has identified thousands of *Schildbürgerorte* (Schildburger towns), see Bausinger, "Schildbürgergeschichten"; H. Moser, *Schwäbischer Volkshumor*; Straßner, "Schildbürgerorte in Franken"; Lixfeld, "Ostdeutsche Schildbürgergeschichten."

99. See three articles "Abderiten von heute" by H. Volksmann, Ralf Ofterding, and Ferdinand Höft in *Am Ur-Quell*.

100. Fränkel, "Neutlateinische Abderitenschwänke"; Fränkel, "Zu den Mitteilungen über neuere Abderiten."

101. Segel, "Abderiten von heute unter den Juden."

102. For biographical information, see Hödl, "Segel, Benjamin"; Krah, "Mit den Waffen der Aufklärung"; and, with a partial bibliography of his works, Vaynig, "Benyomin Volf Zegel."

103. Brenner, *Marketing Identities*, 29, 45–52, 62–68, 132–137.

104. See for instance Segel's series on Jews in Russia in *Der Morgen*: Segel, "Die Juden in Rußland unter Nikolaus I."; Segel, "Die Flucht aus der Wirklichkeit."

105. Segel, "Abderiten von heute unter den Juden," 28.

106. Ibid., 29.

107. See Ude-Koeller, "Kirche verschieben."

108. For Swabia, see H. Moser, *Schwäbischer Volkshumor*, 61–66. For Franconia, see Straßner, "Schildbürgerorte in Franken," 160.

109. Segel, "Abderiten von heute unter den Juden," 28.

110. Charap, "Abderiten von heute."

111. Krause, "Abderiten von heute."

112. Segel, "Philosophie des Pogroms," 91; translated in Brenner, *Marketing Identities*, 166.

113. Segel, *Die Entdeckungsreise*, 47.

114. Aschheim, *Brothers and Strangers*, 109.

115. Segel, "Die Tätigkeit der Frankfurter 'Weiblichen Fürsorge.'" On Pappenheim and Segel, see Loentz, *Let Me Continue to Speak the Truth*, 133–135.

116. Segel, *Die Protokolle der Weisen von Zion kritisch beleuchtet*; Segel, *Welt-Krieg*. The latter was translated into English: Segel, *Lie and a Libel*. See also Krah, "Mit den Waffen der Aufklärung."

117. Bloch, "Benjamin Wolf Segel." See also Hirschberg, "Binjamin Segel gestorben."

118. Segel, *Die polnische Judenfrage*, 19–20.

119. Ibid., 37–38.

120. Ibid.

121. Segel, "O mieście Chełmie."

122. Lew, "Nasza Abdera."

123. Grunwald, "Aus unseren Sammlungen," 61–63.

124. Segel, "Das Brillantendiadem," 5.

125. Binjamin Segel to the Centralverein, October 1926, Fond: 721, Opis: 1, HM 2/8739, Delo 1838, Frame 1504–1514, Osoby Archives, Center for the Preservation of Historical Documentary Collections, Moscow.

126. Segel, "Das Brillantendiadem," 5.

127. It served already as a source in Leo Wiener's groundbreaking *History of Yiddish Literature in the Nineteenth Century* (1899). See p. 52.

128. Vaynig, "Benyomin Volf Zegel," 91. On Vaynig and his role as an ethnographer, see Gottesman, *Defining the Yiddish Nation*, 166–168.

129. Weiser, *Jewish People, Yiddish Nation.*

130. Gottesman, "Man in the Brimmed Hat."

131. Borokhov, "Noyekh Prilutskis zamlbikher."

132. Levi, "Volkslieder der Juden," 143.

133. Borokhov, "Noyekh Prilutskis zamlbikher," 349.

134. Ibid., 348.

135. Pryłucki, "Khelemer naronim" (1917), 202. On Pryłucki's collection, see Gottesman, *Defining the Yiddish Nation*, 49.

136. Pryłucki, "Khelemer naronim" (1917), 195–196, nos. 21, 22, 23.

137. Ibid., 193, no. 17.

138. Ibid., 195, no. 23; 200, no. 34.

139. Ibid., 194, no. 20.

140. Genesis Rabba 50.

141. Pryłucki, "Khelemer naronim" (1917), 187, no. 1.

CHAPTER 7. CHELM TALES AFTER WORLD WAR ONE IN GERMAN AND YIDDISH

1. Olsvanger, *Rosinkess mit Mandlen*, 173–175, nos. 280, 281.

2. Ibid., 174, no. 281.

3. On the "Cult of the Ostjuden," see Aschheim, *Brothers and Strangers*, 185–214.

4. Gottesman, *Defining the Yiddish Nation*. A much-discussed article on this question is for instance Mendelsohn, "Interwar Poland."

5. Bloch's books are often characterized as forgeries, since he tends to blur the sources of his writing. His highly successful German version of the golem stories was first published in serial form as "Aus dem Leben des hohen Rabbi Löw" (From the life of the great rabbi Loew) in *Dr. Blochs oesterreichische Wochenschrift* in 1917 and 1918 and a year later in book form as *Der Prager Golem*. It is in fact a translation from Hebrew into German of Yudl Rozenberg's *Sefer nifla'ot Maha-*

*ral* (1909). See Scholem, *On the Kabbalah and Its Symbolism*, 189; Idel, *Golem,* 251–258; and Baer, *Golem Redux*, 33–35. Rozenberg's book was translated by Curt Leviant as *The Golem and the Wondrous Deeds of the Maharal of Prague.*

6. See Bloch's extensive correspondence held at YIVO, RG 513. On his golem, see also Gelbin, *Golem Returns*, 90–94.

7. The book depicts Hershele as court fool at the Hasidic court of Barukh ben Yeḥiel of Mezhbizh (ca. 1756–1811), a grandson of the Baal Shem Tov. Bloch's imaginative literary text is often quoted as if it were a historical source, but the stories are in fact a loose translation from Yiddish into German of *Dos freylekhe Hershele Ostropolyer oder der volveler teater shtik* (1892) by A. M. Sh. The National Library of Israel identifies the acronym as Shmuel Mordkhe Ostrovski, but Ben-Amos identifies him as A. M. Shuman. See Ben-Amos, *Folktales of the Jews*, 575.

8. Bloch, *Hersch Ostropoler*, 7–8.

9. Loewe, *Schelme und Narren*, 55–56.

10. See Druyanov, *Sefer ha-bediḥah veha-ḥidud*, 217, no. 511; and Kipnis, "XXVI: A zeltene hamtsoe."

11. Loewe, *Schelme und Narren*, 51.

12. Loewe, *Die jüdischdeutsche Sprache der Ostjuden*, 2.

13. Loewe, *Die Sprachen der Juden*, 43.

14. Ibid., 64.

15. Loewe, *Schelme und Narren*, 51.

16. Ibid.

17. "Aus dem Buche der Narrheiten," *Menorah* 1, no. 2 (1923): 28.

18. On attempts to differentiate for young readers of Yiddish between the German non-Jewish Schildburgers and the Jewish Chelmites, see Toybin, "Khelm iz nit di eyntsike shtot fun naronim."

19. Agnon and Eliasberg, "Chelmer Geschichten."

20. Kohn and Davidsohn, "Jüdischer Humor und Witz," 1691. On Kohn, see Kowalzik, *Das jüdische Schulwerk in Leipzig*, 281.

21. The entry refers to the Fürth edition of 1798 but misrepresents "E. Schildburger" as the author's name.

22. Berkowicz, "Chelmer Narronim."

23. Wischnitzer, "Chelm," 408. On the history of the German *Encyclopedia Judaica*, see Engelhardt, *Arsenale jüdischen Wissens.*

24. On Carlebach, see Finkelshteyn, "Geshikhte," 180–182.

25. See the letter in which Carlebach describes his life to Khayim Finkelshteyn: "Lomir zikh dermonen," in ibid., 363–367.

26. Ezriel Carlebach, "Vollständige Historie der ehrenwerten Stadt Chelm," 155.

27. Ibid.

28. Ibid. On Jewish humor in general, see Ben-Amos, "The 'Myth' of Jewish Humor," 120.

29. Ezriel Carlebach, "Vollständige Historie der ehrenwerten Stadt Chelm," 156.

30. Landmann, *Der jüdische Witz*, 214–221. Another collection in German with a chapter on Chelm was published by Aleksander Drożdżyński, based on his earlier

Polish edition but with additional stories. See Drożdżyński, "Die Weisen von Chelm" and "O chełmskich mędrcach."

31. F. Wander, *Der siebente Brunnen*, 64: "'But if I returned to Chelm,' a Galician Jew lisped feverishly, 'what would I say? How would I stand there, alone? The windows would not be illuminated on Shabbes by lights nor by the children's eyes. If I returned to Chelm . . .' 'Nobody will return to Chelm,' another Galician Jew said, 'because Chelm is no longer located in this world!'" The 2005 English translation *The Seventh Well* by Michael Hofmann mistakenly supposes Wander to be referring to Chelmno, the site of a death camp with no connection to Chelm.

32. Singer, *Die Narren von Chelm und ihre Geschichte.*

33. See Nalewajko-Kulikov, *"Di Haynt-mishpokhe."* On *Haynt* and Yiddish literature, see Cohen, "Yiddish Press and Yiddish Literature," 154–155.

34. Finkelshteyn, "Geshikhte," 220.

35. Kon, "Menakhem Mendl Kipnis."

36. Gottesman, *Defining the Yiddish Nation*, 56–57.

37. Ibid., 58.

38. Kon, "Menakhem Mendl Kipnis."

39. Goldshteyn, "A bintl zikhroynes fun mayn arbet in *Haynt*," 377.

40. There are several mistakes in the numbering of the stories: some numbers are used twice, others are missing.

41. Kipnis, *Khelemer mayses.* A selection was published in Polish in 2013 by Bella Szwarcman-Czarnota. See Kipnis, *Rabin bez głowy i inne opowieści z Chełma.*

42. Kipnis, "II: Der Khelemer barg."

43. Ibid.

44. Ibid.

45. Gebhard, *Lublin*, 32.

46. Kipnis, "VI: Di shul mit ladens."

47. Kipnis, "XVII: Der nakht shoymer."

48. Kipnis, "XIX: Khelmer 'shomrim leboker.'" A much-less-elaborate version appeared already in *Der morgn zshurnal* in 1911; see Oguz, "A khokhme fun Khelemer kahal."

49. Kipnis, "IV: Di podloge fun Khelmer alter bod" and "V: Khelmer beys-oylem."

50. Gottesman, *Defining the Yiddish Nation*, 59.

51. Ibid., 63.

52. Ravnitski, *Yudishe vitsn*, 199–207.

53. Druyanov, *Sefer ha-bedihah veha-ḥidud*, 219, no. 517; and Kipnis, "Khelemer pozsharne-shpritser un der shtot-shames," in *Khelemer mayses*, 91–92.

54. Kipnis, *Khelemer mayses*, 123–124.

55. Miron, *Image of the Shtetl*, 15. On the Kasrilevke cycle, see also Caplan, "Neither Here nor There."

56. Kipnis, "XLVI: Vu zenen ahingekumen di Khelmer naronim."

57. Ibid.

58. This story is based in part on older folktale, as recorded, for example, in Leo Wiener's *History of Yiddish Literature in the Nineteenth Century* as "The Fool Is Wiser than the Wise," 45–49.
59. Kipnis, "XLVI: Vu zenen ahingekumen di Khelmer naronim."
60. Yakubovitsh, "Alter Ayzenshlos."
61. Kipnis, "LVIII: Vi azoy Khelmer tselen."
62. Stampfer, "1764 Census of Lithuanian Jewry."
63. Kipnis, "LI: Khelmer beys-akvores: A mayse in fersen."
64. Kipnis, "LIX: Di 2 Khelmer mitn ferdl."
65. Kipnis, *Khelemer mayses*, 3.
66. Kipnis, "XXVIII: Di beheyme oyfn boydem."
67. See also Miler's chapter on "Yosl der Khelmer," published in Canada in 1937.
68. Mirer, "Khelmer geshikhtes," 94.
69. See for instance Shteynbarg's "Khoykerl-hoykerl" (1936), in which he reworked the Yiddish proverb about the Chelm cantor's turkey into a story.
70. On Bastomski, see Gottesman, *Defining the Yiddish Nation*, 86–108.
71. Ibid., 107.
72. His name appears also as Halperin or Helpern.
73. On Shaye Faygenboym, see Portnoy, "Creation of a Jewish Cartoon Space," 201.
74. Roskies, *Bridge of Longing*, 245.
75. Ibid., 265, following Manger's self-description to Shloyme Bikl (1896–1969).
76. See also D. Lerer's article "In kenigraykh fun naronim," published in the same journal a month later.
77. Keller, *Die Leute von Seldwyla*.
78. I. Manger, "Di Khelemer mayses," 377.
79. Ibid., 376. For more on Jesus in modern Yiddish literature, see Stahl, *Other and Brother*, 170–171.
80. Von Bernuth, "Folly and Fool, Christianity."
81. I Cor. 1:18.
82. I. Manger, "Di Khelemer mayses," 377. See also the version in which the Chelmites seek out truth: Kipnis, "XXIX: Khelemer emes."
83. I. Manger, "Di Khelemer mayses," 377.
84. This line is quoted at the beginning of Yosl Lerner's poem "Khelem di shtot," one of a series of twenty-seven Chelm poems by Lerner published in 1975 in Tel Aviv. See Lerner, "Khelemer khakhomim."
85. On Manger's concept of *folkstimlekhe baladn*, see Roskies, *Bridge of Longing*, 236–237.
86. I. Manger, "Khelemer balade," in *Lamtern in vint*, 58.
87. Ulinover, "Fun Khelem keyn Lublin"; Ulinover, "Di nekome on di vantsn"; Ulinover, "Khelem oyf der mape"; Ulinover, "Di telegraf-drotn"; Ulinover, "Der tsvayer"; Ulinover, "Tey un tilim"; Ulinover, "Umet"; Ulinover, "Der ganef un der shoymer"; Ulinover, "Di antlofene levone"; Ulinover, "Lomir helfn dreyen di erd"; Ulinover, "Oysgemishte fislekh."

88. Ulinover, "Tey un tilim."
89. I. Manger, foreword to *Noente geshtaltn*, 3.
90. I. Manger, "Der 'Khelemer' zatsa'l" (1938), 195.
91. Ibid.
92. For the publication history of the story, see note 93 to chapter 5.
93. I. Manger, "Rabbi of Chelm," 223. See also Roskies and Wolf, introduction to *World According to Itzik*.
94. I. Manger, "Rabbi of Chelm," 223.

EPILOGUE

1. U. Weinreich, *College Yiddish*.
2. Prager, "Yiddish in the University"; and Shandler, *Adventures in Yiddishland*, 86.
3. Wiecki, "*Untervegs*," 56.
4. Weiman, review of *College Yiddish*, 99.
5. Weinreich, *College Yiddish*, chap. 20.
6. Ibid., 148.
7. Ibid., 16.
8. Eight Chelm stories and jokes are included in Weinreich's *College Yiddish* in chapters 16, 20, 22, 23, and 27.
9. Ibid., 193.
10. See for instance on tsarist Russia, Edwards, "Sketches and Studies in Russia," 276; and in post-Soviet Russia, Montaigne, *Reeling in Russia*, 111–112.
11. Weinreich, *College Yiddish*, 186.
12. Sheinkin, "The Treasure under the Pickles," chap. 4 in *Rabbi Harvey Rides Again*; and Sheinkin, "Wolfie the Wise," chap. 5 in *Rabbi Harvey vs. the Wisdom Kid*.
13. Driz, *Khelomskie mudretsy*. See Dymshits, "Ili-ili . . . K stoletiyu Ovseya Driza"; and Pivovarov, "Yevo golos."
14. This might be a reference to David Frishman's polemic "Ḥemah."
15. See for instance Lorch, "Ḥakhmei Ḥelem."
16. Ashkenazy, "Why 'Chelm'???"
17. See for instance the production *Ḥakhmei Ḥelem* of the Mikro Theater in Jerusalem.
18. Singer's "Zlateh the Goat" and the "Lantuch," for instance, are not set in Chelm but are part of the film's plot.
19. The Yiddish newspaper *Haynt* had at least forty-five thousand readers in the interwar period. See Stein, *Making Jews Modern*, 49. See also Cohen, "Yiddish Press and Yiddish Literature," 155.
20. On the golem, see Gelbin, *Golem Returns*.
21. See A. Schachter, *Diasporic Modernisms*, 152–157.
22. Shandler, *Adventures in Yiddishland*, 22.
23. Taback, *Kibitzers and Fools*.
24. *Village of Idiots* was written by John Lazarus and directed by Eugen Fedorenko and Rose Newlove.

# BIBLIOGRAPHY

Abramovitsh, Sholem Yankev [Mendele Moykher-Sforim, pseud.]. *Dos vintshfingerl.* Warsaw: Lebenzon, ca. 1865.

Adler, David. *Chanukkah in Chelm.* New York: Lothrop, 1997.

Agnon, S. J., and Ahron Eliasberg, eds. "Chelmer Geschichten." In *Das Buch von den polnischen Juden,* 229–230. Berlin: Jüdischer Verlag, 1916.

Agyrta von Bellemont, Conrad [pseud.]. *Grillenvertreiber / Das ist: Neuwe wunderbarliche Historien / seltzame abentheurliche Geschichten / Kauderwelsche Rathschläg vnd Bedencken / So wol von den Witzenbürgischen als auch Calecutischen Commissarien vnd Parlaments Herren vnterschiedtlich vorgenommen / beschlossen / vnd ins Werck gesetzt.* 2 vols. Frankfurt: Johann Spieß und Johann J. Porsch, 1603.

———. *Hummeln: Oder Grillenvertreiber: Von dero Witzenburgischen vnd Calecutischen Wunderbarlichen / beydes Närrischen vnd Viesierlichen / wie dann auch zugleich witzigen vnd nachdencklichen Rathschlägen.* Vol. 3 of *Grillenvertreiber.* Frankfurt: Johann Spieß und Johann J. Porsch, 1605.

Aksenfeld, Yisroel. *Dos shterntikhl oder shabes-khaneke in Mezibiz.* Leipzig: Vollrath, 1861.

Alkvit, B. "A mayse mit a shteyn: Fun di Khelmer mayses." *Kinder zshurnal* 5 (1925): 7–10.

Allen, Woody, "Hassidic Tales, with a Guide to Their Interpretation by the Noted Scholar." *New Yorker,* June 20, 1970, 31–32.

Allison, Alida. *Isaac Bashevis Singer: Children's Stories and Childhood Memoirs.* New York: Twayne, 1996.

American Business Consultants, ed. *Red Channels: Report of Communist Influence in Radio and Television.* New York: Counterattack, 1950.

A. M. Sh. *Dos freylekhe Hershele Ostropolyer oder der volveler teater shtik.* Warsaw: Unterhendler, 1892.

Andree, Richard. "Abderiten von heute." *Am Ur-Quell* 2 (1891): 117–119.

Aptroot, Marion. "Dutch Impact on Amsterdam Yiddish Prints." *Language & Communication* 8 (1988): 7–11.

Arndt, Ernst Moritz. *Reisen durch einen Theil Teutschlands, Ungarns, Italiens und Frankreichs in den Jahren 1798 und 1799.* Rev. ed. Vol. 3. Leipzig: Gräff, 1804.

"Arn Tsaytlin vegn zayn nayer pyese 'Khelemer naronim.'" *Literarishe bleter,* February 17, 1933, 126.

Aschheim, Steve. *Brothers and Strangers: The East European Jew in German and German Jewish Consciousness, 1800–1923*. Madison: University of Wisconsin Press, 1982.

Ashkenazy, Daniella. "Why 'Chelm'???" *Chelm-on-the-Med* (blog). http://chelm-on-the-med.com/index.php?option=com_content&view=article&id=84&Itemid=106 (accessed March 10, 2016).

Assaf, David, and Israel Bartal. "The Metamorphosis of *Zanav* (Tail) from Hasidic Courts to Israeli Slang." *Leshonenu La'am* 44 (1993): 73–79.

Atkinson, Brooks. "Three Short Plays: 'World of Sholom Aleichem' Makes Art Out of Simple Things about People." *New York Times*, September 20, 1953.

Auerochs, Bernd. "Was ist Wahrheit? Oder Einsichten und Schreibweisen: Wielands philosophische Prosa und die menippeische Satire." In *Wissen, Erzählen, Tradition: Wielands Spätwerk*, edited by Walter Erhart and Lothar van Laak, 139–152. Berlin: de Gruyter, 2010.

Aurbacher, Ludwig. "Historia von den Lalenbürgern." *Fliegende Blätter* 5, nos. 108–114, (1847): 89–93, 100–101, 109, 117, 133, 142; 6, nos. 122, 133 (1847): 13–14, 97–100.

"Aus dem Buche der Narrheiten." *Menorah* 1, no. 2 (1923): 28.

———. *Menorah* 1, no. 4 (1923): 23.

———. *Menorah* 2, no. 6 (1924): 18.

———. *Menorah* 2, no. 8 (1924): 32.

———. *Menorah* 2, no. 10 (1924): 24.

Ausubel, Nathan. *Treasury of Jewish Folklore*. New York: Crown, 1948.

Avé-Lallemant, Friedrich Christian Benedict. *Das deutsche Gaunerthum in seiner social-politischen, literarischen und linguistischen Ausbildung zu seinem heutigen Bestande*. Vol. 3. Leipzig: Heinrich Brockhaus, 1862.

*Aylen-shpigl*. Prague: Bakshe bukh drukray, 1735.

*Aylen-sphigl*. Bad Homburg, 1736.

Bachorski, Hans-Jürgen. *Irrsinn und Kolportage: Studien zum Ring, zum Lalebuch und zur Geschichtklitterung*. Trier, Germany: Wissenschaftlicher Verlag Trier, 2006.

Bachorski, Hans-Jürgen, and Werner Röcke. "Narrendichtung." In *Von der Handschrift zum Buchdruck: Spätmittelalter, Reformation, Humanismus, 1320–1572*, edited by Ingrid Bennewitz and Ulrich Müller, 203–213. Reinbek, Germany: Rowohlt, 1991.

Baer, Elizabeth R. *The Golem Redux: From Prague to Post-Holocaust Fiction*. Detroit: Wayne State University Press, 2012.

Bahder, Karl von, ed. *Das Lalebuch (1597), mit den abweichungen und erweiterungen der Schiltbürger (1598) und des Grillenvertreibers (1603)*. Halle, Germany: Niemeyer, 1914.

———. Introduction to *Das Lalebuch (1597), mit den abweichungen und erweiterungen der Schiltbürger (1598) und des Grillenvertreibers (1603)*, v–lxxvii. Halle, Germany: Niemeyer, 1914.

Bakaltshuk-Felin, Melekh, ed. *Yizker-bukh Khelm*. Johannesburg, South Africa: Khelmer landsmanshaft, 1954.

Bakhtin, Mikhail. *Problems of Dostoevsky's Poetics*. Translated by Caryl Emerson. Minneapolis: University of Minnesota Press, 1984.

————. *Rabelais and His World*. Translated by Hélène Iswolsky. Bloomington: Indiana University Press, 1984.

Bartal, Israel. "Mordechai Aaron Günzburg: A Lithuanian Maskil Faces Modernity." In *From East and West: Jews in a Changing Europe, 1750–1870*, edited by Frances Malino and David Sorkin, 126–147. Oxford, UK: Blackwell, 1990.

Bässler, Andreas. *Sprichwortbild und Sprichwortschwank: Zum illustrativen und narrativen Potential von Metaphern in der deutschsprachigen Literatur um 1500*. Berlin: de Gruyter, 2003.

Bastomski, Solomon. *Mayselekh vegn Khelemer naronim*. 3 vols. Vilna: Grininke beymelekh, 1938.

Baumgarten, Jean. *Introduction to Old Yiddish Literature*. Translated by Jerold C. Frakes. Oxford: Oxford University Press, 2005.

Bausinger, Hermann. "Schildbürgergeschichten: Betrachtungen zum Schwank." *Deutschunterricht* 13 (1961): 18–44.

Bayle, Pierre. *Dictionnaire historique et critique*. 2 vols. Rotterdam: Leers, 1697.

Beer, Peter. "Über die Nothwendigkeit einer Sammlung von Lebensbeschreibungen gelehrter und sonst rühmlich sich auszeichnender Männer in Israel." *Sulamith* 3 (1810): 234–266.

Belkin, Ahuva. "*Habit de Fou* in Purim Spiel?" *Assaph* 2 (1985): 40–55.

————. *Ha-purim shpil: 'Iyunim ba-te'atron ha-yehudi ha-'amami*. Jerusalem: Mosad Bialik, 2002.

————. "*Zmires purim*: The Third Phase of Jewish Carnavalistic Folk-Literature." In *Politics of Yiddish: Studies in Language, Literature, and Society*, edited by Dov-Ber Kerler, 149–156. Walnut Creek, CA: AltaMira, 1998.

Ben-Amos, Dan. *Folktales of the Jews*. Vol. 2. Philadelphia: JPS, 2007.

————. "The 'Myth' of Jewish Humor." *Western Folklore* 32 (1973): 112–131.

Ben Mordekhai. *Khelmer naronim: Geklibene mayselekh*. New York: Hebrew Publishing Company, 1929.

Berger, Shlomo. *Producing Redemption in Amsterdam: Early Modern Yiddish Books in Paratextual Perspective*. Leiden, Netherlands: Brill, 2013.

————. "Selling Books in Eighteenth-Century Amsterdam: A Yiddish Sale Advertisment from circa 1760." *Zutot* 5 (2008): 129–134.

Berkley, Miriam. "Isaac Bashevis Singer." In *Isaac Bashevis Singer: Conversations*, edited by Grace Farrell, 208–212. Jackson: University Press of Mississippi, 1992. Originally published in *Publishers Weekly*, February 18, 1983.

Berkowicz, Michael. "Chelmer Narronim." In *Jüdisches Lexikon*, edited by Georg Herlitz and Ismar Elbogen, vol. 1, 1355. Berlin: Jüdischer Verlag, 1927.

Bernstein, Ignatz. *Jüdische Sprichwörter und Redensarten: "Erotica" und "Rustica."* N.p.: n.p., 1908.

Bernstein, Ignatz, and Binjamin Segel. *Jüdische Sprichwörter und Redensarten*. Frankfurt: Kauffmann, 1908.

Bernuth, Ruth von. "The Carnivalesque in Early Modern Ashkenaz: Yuspa Shammes's *Minhagim* and the Oxford Old Yiddish Manuscript Songbook." In *Worlds of Old*

*Yiddish Literature*, edited by Diana Matut and Simon Neuberg. Leeds, UK: Maney, forthcoming.

———. "Folly and Fool, Christianity." In *Encyclopedia of the Bible and Its Reception*, edited by Dale C. Allison, vol. 9, 359–362. Berlin: de Gruyter, 2014.

———. "*Das jischev fun Nar-husen*: Jiddische Narrenliteratur und jüdische Narrenkultur," *Aschkenas* 25 (2015): 133–144.

———. *Wunder, Spott und Prophetie: Natürliche Narrheit in den "Historien von Claus Narren."* Tübingen, Germany: Niemeyer, 2009.

———. "Zu Gast bei Nikolaus Selnecker: Der jüdische Konvertit Paulus von Prag in Leipzig," *Jahrbuch des Simon-Dubnow-Instituts* 13 (2014): 15–36.

[Bible] *Die gantze Bibel der vrsprünglichen Ebraischen vnd Griechischen Waarheyt nach, Die / auffs aller treüwlichest verteütschet.* Zurich: Froschauer, 1531.

Bik, Herts. *Der Khelemer khokhem.* Lemberg: J. Ehrenpreis, 1887.

Billington, Sandra. *A Social History of the Fool.* Brighton, UK: Harvester, 1984.

Binder, Mark. *The Brothers Schlemiel.* New York: Jewish Publication Society, 2008.

———. *A Hanukkah Present!* Providence, RI: Light Publications, 2007.

———. *Matzah Mishugas: Eight Passover Tales.* Providence, RI: Light Publications, 2010.

Blaschke, Karlheinz, and Susanne Baudisch, eds. *Historisches Ortsverzeichnis von Sachsen.* 2 vols. Leipzig: Universitätsverlag, 2006.

Blass, Moritz. *Jüdische Sprichwörter.* Leipzig: Gerhard, 1857.

Bloch, Chajim. "Aus dem Leben des hohen Rabbi Löw: Neue Golem-Sagen." In *Dr. Blochs oesterreichische Wochenschrift*, 1917: 593–595, 614, 630–632, 666–667, 682–683, 697–699, 713–715, 730–731, 747–748, 762–764, 778–779, 794–795, 811–812, 827–828; 1918: 14–15, 30–31, 46–47, 62–63, 78–79, 94–96, 110–111.

———. "Benjamin Wolf Segel: Ein Blatt des Gedenkens." *Die Wahrheit* 47, no. 12 (1931): 2–3.

———. *Hersch Ostropoler, ein jüdischer Till-Eulenspiegel des 18. Jahrhunderts, seine Geschichten und Streiche.* Berlin: B. Harz, 1921.

———. *Der Prager Golem: Von seiner "Geburt" bis zu seinem "Tod."* Vienna: Dr. Blochs Wochenschrift, 1919.

Bobertag, Felix. *Volksbücher des 16. Jahrhunderts: Eulenspiegel, Faust Schildbürger.* Berlin: W. Spemann, 1887.

Boorde, Andrew. *Merie Tales of the Mad Men of Gotam: Gathered to gether by A.B. of Phisike Doctour.* London: Thomas Colwell, 1565.

Booth, Wayne C. *The Rhetoric of Fiction.* Chicago: University of Chicago Press, 1983.

Borokhov, Ber. "Noyekh Prilutskis zamlbikher far yidishn folklor." In *Der pinkes: Yorbukh far der geshikhte fun der yidisher literatur un shprakh, far folklor, kritik un bibliografye*, edited by Shmuel Niger, 347–351. Vilna: Kletskin, 1913.

Botanshanski, Yankev. "Di Khelemer khakhomim viln lebn . . . ." *Di prese*, September 10, 1957.

Bracht Branham, Robert, and Marie-Odile Goulet-Cazé. *The Cynics: The Cynic Movement in Antiquity and Its Legacy.* Berkeley: University of California Press, 1996.

Brant, Sebastian. *Das Narrenschiff: Nach der Erstausgabe (Basel, 1494) mit den Zusätzen der Ausgaben von 1495 und 1499.* Edited by Manfred Lemmer. 3rd ed. Tübingen, Germany: Niemeyer, 1962.

Brednich, Rolf Wilhelm, ed. *Enzyklopädie des Märchens: Handwörterbuch zur historischen und vergleichenden Erzählforschung.* 14 vols. Berlin: de Gruyter, 1977–2014.

Brenner, David A. *Marketing Identities: The Invention of Jewish Ethnicity in Ost und West.* Detroit: Wayne State University Press, 1998.

Brocke, Michael, and Julius Carlebach, eds. *Die Rabbiner der Emanzipationszeit in den deutschen, böhmischen und großpolnischen Ländern, 1781–1871.* Arranged by Carsten Wilke. Vol. 1 of *Biographisches Handbuch der Rabbiner.* Munich: K. G. Saur, 2004.

Brown, Hilary. *Luise Gottsched the Translator.* Rochester, NY: Camden House, 2012.

Buber, Martin. *Die chassidischen Bücher.* Hellerau, Germany: Hegner, 1928.

———. *Tales of the Hasidim.* Translated by Olga Marx. 2 vols. New York: Schocken, 1947–1948.

Bülow, Gerda von. "Das historische Vorbild für Wielands Abdera." In *Christoph Martin Wieland und die Antike: Eine Aufsatzsammlung,* edited by Max Kunze, 95–99. Stendal, Germany: Winckelmann-Gesellschaft, 1986.

Burke, Peter. *Popular Culture in Early Modern Europe.* Farnham, UK: Ashgate, 2009.

Burrows, Edwin G., and Mike Wallace. *Gotham: A History of New York to 1898.* New York: Oxford University Press, 1999.

Burt, Raymond L. *Friedrich Salomo Krauss (1859–1938): Selbstzeugnisse und Materialien zur Biobibliographie des Volkskundlers, Literaten und Sexualforschers mit einem Nachlassverzeichnis.* Vienna: Verlag der Österreichischen Akademie der Wissenschaften, 1990.

Büttner, Wolfgang. *Sechs hundert / sieben vnd zwantzig Historien / Von Claus Narren: Feine schimpffliche wort vnd Reden / die Erbare Ehrenleut Clausen abgemerckt / vnd nachgesagt haben / Zur Bürgerlichen vnd Christlichen Lere / wie andere Apologen / dienstlich vnd förderlich.* Eisleben, Germany: Urban Gaubisch, 1572.

Butzer, Evi. *Die Anfänge der jiddischen "purim shpiln" in ihrem literarischen und kulturgeschichtlichen Kontext.* Hamburg: Buske, 2003.

Butzer, Evi, Nathanja Hüttenmeister, and Wolfgang Treue, "*Ich will euch sagen von einem bösen Stück . . .* : Ein jüdisches Lied über sexuelle Vergehen und deren Bestrafung aus dem frühen 17. Jahrhundert," *Aschkenas* 15 (2005): 25–53.

Cahan, Abraham. "*Khelemer khakhomim* fun Arn Tseytlin in Moris Shvarts's kunst teater." *Forverts,* October 20, 1933.

Callenberg, Johann Heinrich. *Anderer Theil der dritten Fortsetzung seines Berichts an einige Christliche Freunde von einem Versuch das arme Jüdische Volck zur Erkäntniß der Christlichen Wahrheit anzuleiten.* Halle, Germany: Krottendorf, 1732.

———. *Bericht an einige Christliche Freunde von einem Versuch das arme Jüdische Volck zur Erkäntniß und Annehmung der Christlichen Wahrheit anzuleiten.* 18 vols. Halle, Germany, 1728–1744.

Campe, Joachim Heinrich. *Wörterbuch der deutschen Sprache*. 5 vols. Braunschweig, Germany: Schulbuchhandlung, 1807–1811.

———. *Wörterbuch zur Erklärung und Verdeutschung der unserer Sprache aufgedrungenen fremden Ausdrücke*. Braunschweig, Germany: Schulbuchhandlung, 1813.

Caplan, Marc. *How Strange the Change: Language, Temporality, and Narrative Form in Peripheral Modernism*. Stanford, CA: Stanford University Press, 2011.

———. "Neither Here nor There: The Critique of Ideological Progress in Sholem Aleichem's Kasrilevke Stories." In *Modern Jewish Literatures: Intersections and Boundaries*, edited by Sheila E. Jelen, Michael P. Kramer, and L. Scott Lerner, 127–146. Philadelphia: University of Pennsylvania Press, 2011.

Carlebach, Elisheva. *Palaces of Time: Jewish Calendar and Culture in Early Modern Europe*. Cambridge, MA: Harvard University Press, 2011.

Carlebach, Ezriel. "Lomir zikh dermonen." In *Haynt: A tsaytung bay yidn 1908–1939*, edited by Khayim Finkelshteyn, 363–367. Tel Aviv: Peretz, 1978.

———. "Vollständige Historie der ehrenwerten Stadt Chelm." In *Jüdischer Almanach*, edited by Felix Weltsch, 155–175. Prague: Selbstwehr Jüdisches Volksblatt, 1935–1936.

Cavallo, Guglielmo, Roger Chartier, and Lydia G. Cochrane, eds. *A History of Reading in the West*. Oxford, UK: Polity, 1999.

Cernik, Wigand. *Schildbürgerwanderweg Schildau: Auf den Spuren der Schildbürger durch die Stadt Schildau; ein Wanderführer*. Schildau, Germany: Geschichtsverein, 1994.

Charap, J. A. "Abderiten von heute." *Am Ur-Quell* 3 (1892): 169–170.

Christiani, Friedrich Albrecht. *Amme seudat Purim, Das ist: Kurtze Beschreibung von den Jüdischen Fast-Nachten*. Leipzig: Gunther, 1677.

Clark, William. "Wieland and Winckelmann: Saul and the Prophet." *Modern Language Quarterly* 17 (1956): 1–16.

Cohen, Nathan. "Isaac Bashevis-Singer's Attitude to the Yiddish Theater as Shown in His Works." In *Jewish Theater: A Global View*, edited by Edna Nahon, 49–61. Leiden, Netherlands: Brill, 2009.

———. "Yiddish Press and Yiddish Literature." *Modern Judaism* 28 (2008): 149–172.

———. "Yitskhok Bashevis-Zinger and the Writers' and Journalists' Association in Warsaw." In *Isaac Bashevis Singer: His Work and His World*, edited by Hugh Denman, 169–181. Leiden, Netherlands: Brill, 2002.

Czartoryski, Adam Jerzy. *Memoirs of Prince Adam Czartoryski*. New York: Arno, 1971.

Daston, Lorraine, and Katharine Park. *Wonders and the Order of Nature, 1150–1750*. New York: Zone Books, 1998.

Dauber, Jeremy. *Antonio's Devils: Writers of the Jewish Enlightenment and the Birth of Modern Hebrew and Yiddish Literature*. Stanford, CA: Stanford University Press, 2004.

———. *The Worlds of Sholem Aleichem: The Remarkable Life and Afterlife of the Man Who Created Tevye*. New York: Schocken Books, 2013.

Davidson, Israel. *Parody in Jewish Literature*. New York: Columbia University Press, 1907.

Davis, Barry. "Yehiel Yeshaia Trunk." In *Writers in Yiddish*, edited by Joseph Sherman, 314–322. Detroit: Gale, 2007.

Davis, Natalie Zemon. "The Reasons of Misrule." In *Society and Culture in Early Modern France*, 97–123. Stanford, CA: Stanford University Press, 1975.

Daxelmüller, Christoph. "Friedrich Salomo Krauss (1859–1938)." In *Völkische Wissenschaft: Gestalten und Tendenzen der deutschen und österreichischen Volkskunde in der ersten Hälfte des 20. Jahrhunderts*, edited by Wolfgang Jacobeit, Hannjost Lixfeld, and Olaf Bockhorn, 463–476. Vienna: Böhlau, 1994.

———. "Jewish Popular Culture since the Middle Ages." In *In and Out of the Ghetto: Jewish-Gentile Relations in Late Medieval and Early Modern Germany*, edited by Po-Chia R. Hsia and Hartmut Lehmann, 29–48. Washington, DC: German Historical Institute, 1995.

———. "Jüdische Volkskunde in Deutschland zwischen Assimilation und neuer Identität: Anmerkungen zum gesellschaftlichen Bezug einer vergessenen Wissenschaft." In *Völkische Wissenschaft: Gestalten und Tendenzen der deutschen und österreichischen Volkskunde in der ersten Hälfte des 20. Jahrhunderts*, edited by Wolfgang Jacobeit, Hannjost Lixfeld, and Olaf Bockhorn, 87–114. Vienna: Böhlau, 1994.

Decter, Midge. "Belittling Sholom Aleichem's Jews: Folk Falsification of the Ghetto." *Commentary* 17 (1954): 389–392.

Demonet-Launay, Marie-Luce. "Le nom de Bacbuc." *Bulletin de l'Association d'étude sur l'humanisme, la réforme et la renaissance* 34 (1992): 41–66.

Denman, Hugh, ed. *Isaac Bashevis Singer: His Work and His World*. Leiden, Netherlands: Brill, 2002.

DeNoël, Matthias Joseph. "Skizze des Plans für die Feier des Karnevals 1825." *Der Sieg der Freude oder Carnevals-Almanach* 2 (1824–1825): 9–19.

Deutsch, Yaacov. *Judaism in Christian Eyes: Ethnographic Descriptions of Jews and Judaism in Early Modern Europe*. Oxford: Oxford University Press, 2012.

———. "Polemical Ethnographies: Descriptions of Yom Kippur in the Writings of Christian Hebraists and Jewish Converts to Christianity in Early Modern Europe." In *Hebraica Veritas? Christian Hebraists and the Study of Judaism in Early Modern Europe*, edited by Allison P. Coudert and Jeffrey S. Shoulson, 202–233. Philadelphia: University of Pennsylvania Press, 2004.

Dicke, Gerd. "Lalebuch (Schildbürgerbuch; Grillen-, Hummelnvertreiber)." In *Frühe Neuzeit in Deutschland 1520–1620: Verfasserlexikon*, edited by Wilhelm Kühlmann, Jan-Dirk Müller, Michael Schilling, Johann Anselm Steiger, and Friedrich Vollhardt, vol. 4, 13–26. Berlin: de Gruyter, 2015.

———. "Morus und Moros—*Utopia* und *Lalebuch*: Episteme auf dem Prüfstand lalischer Logik." In *Erzählen und Episteme: Literatur im 16. Jahrhundert*, edited by Beate Kellner, Jan-Dirk Müller, and Peter Strohschneider, 192–224. Berlin: de Gruyter, 2011.

Dieterich, Julius Reinhard. "Eselritt und Dachabdecken." *Hessische Blätter für Volkskunde* 1 (1902): 87–112.

Dik, Ayzik Meyer. *Blitsende vitsen oder lakhpilen*. Vilna: Dvorzets, 1867.

———. *Di orkhim in Duratshesok.* In *Geklibene verk*, vol. 1, no. 4, 1–36. Vilna: Sh. Shreberk, [1922]. First published 1872 by Rom in Vilna.

———. *Oyzer Tsinkes un di tsig.* Vilna: Fin Rozenkrants, 1868.

———. *Der shivim moltsayt.* Vilna: Rom, 1877.

———. *Sipurey khokhmey Yovn: O divrey khakhomim.* Vilna: Dvorzets, 1864.

Driz, Ovsei. *Khelomskie mudretsy.* Translated by Genrikh Sapgir. Kemerovo, Russia: kn. izd., 1969.

Dronke, Peter. *Verse with Prose from Petronius to Dante: The Art and Scope of the Mixed Form.* Cambridge, MA: Harvard University Press, 1994.

Dröse, Albrecht. "Formen und Funktionen politischer Rhetorik im *Lalebuch* von 1597." *Daphnis* 33 (2004): 683–708.

Drożdżyński, Aleksander. "O chełmskich mędrcach." In *Mądrości żydowskie*, 87–101. Warsaw: Wiedza Powszechna, 1960.

———. "Die Weisen von Chelm." In *Jiddische Witze und Schmonzes*, 194–209. Düsseldorf: Droste, 1976.

Druyanov, Alter. *Sefer ha-bediḥah veha-ḥidud.* Frankfurt: Omanut, 1922.

Dymshits, Valery, ed. *Evreĭskie narodnye skazki: predaniî͡a, bylichki, bylichki, rasskazy, anekdoty sobrannye E.S. Raĭze.* Saint Petersburg, Russia: Symposium, 2000.

———. "Ili-ili . . . K stoletiyu Ovseya Driza." *Narod knigi v mire knig*, nos. 73–74 (2008), http://narodknigi.ru/journals/73/ili_ili_k_stoletiyu_ovseya_driza1/.

———. "Les nigauds de Khelm, de Tipchichok et de Koulikov." In *Contes populaires juifs d'Europe orientale*, edited by Valery Dymshits and translated by Sophie Benech, 375–387. Paris: José Corti, 2004.

Dynner, Glenn. *Men of Silk: The Hasidic Conquest of Polish Jewish Society.* Oxford: Oxford University Press, 2006.

Edelstein, Ludwig. *Wielands "Abderiten" und der deutsche Humanismus.* Berkeley: University of California Press, 1950.

Edwards, Henry Sutherland. "Sketches and Studies in Russia." *National Magazine* 5 (1859): 275–282.

Eidelberg, Shlomo. *R. Juspa, Shammash of Warmaisa (Worms): Jewish Life in 17th Century Worms.* Jerusalem: Magnes, 1991.

Eigenwill, Reinhardt. "Schöttgen, Johann Christian." In *Sächsische Biografie*, edited by Institut für Sächsische Geschichte und Volkskunde and Martina Schattkowsky. http://saebi.isgv.de/biografie/Johann_Christian_Schöttgen_(1687–1751) (accessed October 21, 2015).

Elswit, Sharon B. *The Jewish Story Finder: A Guide to 688 Tales Listing Subjects and Sources.* Jefferson, NC: McFarland, 2012.

Elyada, Aya. *A Goy Who Speaks Yiddish: Christians and the Jewish Language in Early Modern Germany.* Stanford, CA: Stanford University Press, 2012.

Emmelius, Carolina. "'History, Narration, Lalespil': Erzählen von Weisheit und Narrheit im *Lalebuch.*" In *Erzählen und Episteme: Literatur im 16. Jahrhundert*, edited by Beate Kellner, Jan-Dirk Müller, and Peter Strohschneider, 225–254. Berlin: de Gruyter, 2011.

Engelhardt, Arndt. *Arsenale jüdischen Wissens: Zur Entstehungsgeschichte der "Encyclopaedia Judaica."* Göttingen, Germany: Vandenhoeck and Ruprecht, 2014.

Englander, Nathan. "The Tumblers." In *For the Relief of Unbearable Urges*, 25–55. New York: Knopf, 1999.

Epstein, Abraham. "Die Wormser Minhagbücher: Literarisches und Culturhistorisches aus denselben." In *Gedenkbuch zur Erinnerung an David Kaufmann*, edited by Marcus Brann and F. Rosenthal, 288–317. Breslau: Schlesische Verlags-Anstalt, 1900.

Erasmus, Desiderius. *Praise of Folly.* Translated by Betty Radice. London: Penguin Books, 1993.

Erik, Maks. *Di geshikhte fun der yidisher literatur fun di eltste tsaytn biz der haskoletfuke.* Warsaw: Kultur-lige, 1928.

Erlikh, Borekh Mordkhe. *Khelemer dertseylungen.* Tel Aviv: Mikhal, 1977.

Ertz, Stefan, ed. *Das Lalebuch: Nach dem Druck von 1597 mit den Abweichungen des Schiltbürgerbuchs von 1598 und zwölf Holzschnitten von 1680.* Stuttgart: Reclam, 1998.

———. *Fischart und die Schiltburgerchronik: Untersuchungen zum Lale- und Schildbürgerbuch.* Cologne: Gabel, 1989.

———. "Schilda und die Schildbürger." In *Wunderseltsame Geschichten: Interpretationen zu Schildbürgern und Lalebuch*, edited by Werner Wunderlich, 59–87. Göppingen, Germany: Kümmerle, 1983.

Fabian, Johannes. "Keep Listening: Ethnography and Reading." In *The Ethnography of Reading*, edited by Jonathan Boyarin, 80–97. Berkeley: University of California Press, 1993.

Fagius, Paulus. *Die fünff bücher Mosis sampt dem Hohenlied Salomonis / Ruth / Claglied Hieremie / Prediger Salomonis / und Esther: Auch der Juden Euangelien / die sie Haphtaroth nennen / vnd all Sabbath jn iren Schulen lesen / auß Hebraischer sprach nach Jüdischer Art / von wort zu wort ins Teutsch verdolmetschet / vnd mit Hebraischer schrifft / deren sich die Juden in irem Teutsch schreiben gemainlich gebrauchen / gedruckt.* Konstanz, Germany: [Paul Fagius und Jakob Froschesser], 1544.

Faierstein, Morris M. Introduction to *Poems of the Holocaust and Poems of Faith*, by Aaron Zeitlin, xi–xvii. New York: iUniverse, 2007.

Farrell, Grace, ed., *Isaac Bashevis Singer: Conversations.* Jackson: University Press of Mississippi, 1992.

Fay, Rolf D. "'Mannskopf in Arabesken': Zur Frage nach Provenienz und Priorität der ältesten 'Schildbürger'- und 'Lalebuch'-Drucke." In *"Ist zwîfel herzen nâchgebûr": Günther Schweikle zum 60. Geburtstag*, edited by Rüdiger Krüger, Jürgen Kühnel, and Joachim Kuolt, 225–240. Stuttgart: Helfant-Ed., 1989.

Filtzhut, Pomponius [pseud.]. *Ein poßierlich- jedoch warhafftig- und immerwehrender Hauß-Calender und Practica: Auf dieses jetzige / und alle folgende Jahre / Monat und Wochen / mit sonderbahren Fleisse gerichtet / daß der günstige Leser grosses belieben und lustige Kurtzweil wie auch seinen Nutzen daraus haben kan.* N.p.: n.p., 1662.

———. *Shildburger zeltsame unt kurtsvaylige geshikhte: Vunder zeltsame kurtsvaylige lustige un rekht lekherlikhe geshikhte un datn der velt bekantn Shild burger*. Amsterdam: n.p., ca. 1700.

———. *Vunder zeltsame kurtsvaylige lustige unt rekht lakherlikhe geshikhte unt daten der velt bekantn shild burger*. Amsterdam: n.p., 1727.

———. *Wunderseltzame Abentheuerliche / lustige und recht lächerliche Geschichte und Thaten der Welt-bekanten Schild-Bürger in Misnopotamia / hinter Utopia gelegen*. N.p.: n.p., ca. 1698.

Finkelshteyn, Khayim. "Geshikhte." In *Haynt: A tsaytung bay yidn 1908–1939*, 23–329. Tel Aviv: Peretz, 1978.

Flender, Harold. "An Interview with Isaac Bashevis Singer." In *Isaac Bashevis Singer: Conversations*, edited by Grace Farrell, 36–48. Jackson: University Press of Mississippi, 1992. Originally published in *National Jewish Monthly* 82 (March–April 1968).

Foer, Jonathan Safran. *Everything Is Illuminated*. Boston: Houghton Mifflin, 2002.

Foucault, Michel. *History of Madness*. Edited by Jean Khalfa. Translated by Jonathan Murphy and Jean Khalfa. London: Routledge, 2006.

Frakes, Jerold C. *The Politics of Interpretation: Alterity and Ideology in Old Yiddish Studies*. Albany: State University of New York Press, 1989.

Fränkel, Ludwig. "Neutlateinische Abderitenschwänke." *Am Ur-Quell* 4 (1893): 180–182.

———. "Zu den Mitteilungen über neuere Abderiten." *Am Ur-Quell* 3 (1893): 124–126.

Freedman, Florence B. *It Happened in Chelm: A Story of the Legendary Town of Fools*. New York: Schapolsky, 1990.

Freud, Sigmund. *Der Witz und seine Beziehung zum Unbewussten*. Leipzig: Franz Deuticke, 1905.

Frieden, Ken. "Joseph Perl's Escape from Biblical Epigonism through Parody of Hasidic Writing." *AJS Review* 29 (2005): 265–282.

———. "Neglected Origins of Modern Hebrew Prose: Hasidic and Maskilic Travel Narratives." *AJS Review* 33 (2009): 3–43.

Friedman, Filip. "Tsu der geshikhte fun di yidn in Khelm." In *Yizker-bukh Khelm*, edited by Melekh Bakaltshuk-Felin, 13–38. Johannesburg, South Africa: Khelmer landsmanshaft, 1954.

Friedman, Mira. "The Four Sons of the Haggadah and the Ages of Man." *Journal of Jewish Art* 11 (1985): 16–40.

Frishman, David. "Ḥemah." In *Kol kitve u-mivḥar targumav*, vols. 12–13, 72–77. Warsaw: Merkaz, 1914.

Frommer, Myrna Katz, and Harvey Frommer. *It Happened on Broadway: On Oral History of the Great White Way*. New York: Harcourt Brace, 1998.

Fuchs, Albert. *Geistiger Gehalt und Quellenfrage in Wielands Abderiten*. Paris: Les Belles Lettres, 1934.

Gebhard, Jörg. *Lublin: Eine polnische Stadt im Hinterhof der Moderne (1814–1914)*. Cologne: Böhlau, 2006.

Gelber, Nathan Michael. "Mendel Satanower der Verbreiter der Haskalah in Polen und Galizien: Ein Kulturbild aus dem jüdischen Polen an der Wende des XVIII. Jahrhunderts." *Mitteilungen der Gesellschaft für Jüdische Volkskunde* 17 (1914): 41–55.

Gelbin, Cathy. *The Golem Returns: From German Romantic Literature to Global Jewish Culture, 1808–2008.* Ann Arbor: University of Michigan Press, 2011.

Gerson, Christian. *Der Jüden Thalmud Fürnembster Inhalt vnd Widerlegung.* Helmstedt, Germany: Behme, 1609.

Gervinus, Georg Gottfried. *Geschichte der poetischen National-Literatur der Deutschen.* Vol. 2, *Vom Ende des 13ten Jahrhunderts bis zur Reformation.* Leipzig: Wilhelm Engelmann, 1836.

Gibbs, Alfred S., ed. *Goethe's Mother.* New York: Dodd, Mead, 1880.

Gintsburg, Mordekhai Aharon. *Tikun Lavan ha-Arami: Shir sipuri neged ha-ḥasidim.* Vilna: Rozenkrants, 1864.

Glasenapp, Gabriele von. "Popularitätskonzepte jüdischer Folklore: Die Prager Märchen, Sagen und Legenden in der Sammlung Sippurim." In *Populäres Judentum: Medien, Debatten, Lesestoffe,* edited by Christine Haug, Franziska Mayer, and Madleen Podewski, 19–45. Tübingen, Germany: Niemeyer, 2009.

Glaser, Linda. *Stone Soup with Matzoh Balls: A Passover Tale in Chelm.* Chicago: Albert Whitman, 2014.

Glatshteyn, Yankev. *Yosl Loksh fun Khelem.* New York: Machmadim, 1944.

Goedeke, Karl. *Grundrisz zur Geschichte der deutschen Dichtung aus den Quellen.* Vol. 1, *Von der ältesten Zeit bis zum Dreiszigjährigen Kriege.* 2nd ed. Dresden: L. Ehlermann, 1862.

Goethe, Johann Wolfgang von. *Aus meinem Leben: Dichtung und Wahrheit.* Edited by Peter Sprengel. Vol. 16, *Sämtliche Werke nach Epochen,* edited by Karl Richter. Munich: Hanser, 1985.

Goldberg, Alter. *Khelmer mayses: Vitsn un folks vertlekh.* Biłgoraj, Poland: Kronenberg, 1931.

Goldshteyn, Yoysef-Shimen. "A bintl zikhroynes fun mayn arbet in *Haynt.*" In *Haynt: A tsaytung bay yidn 1908–1939,* edited by Khayim Finkelshteyn, 374–379. Tel Aviv: Peretz, 1978.

Gorny, Yosef. *Converging Alternatives: The Bund and the Zionist Labor Movement, 1897–1985.* Albany: State University Press of New York, 2006.

Görres, Joseph. *Die teutschen Volksbücher: Nähere Würdigung der schönen Historien-, Wetter- und Arzneybüchlein, welche theils innerer Werth, theils Zufall, Jahrhunderte hindurch bis auf unsere Zeit erhalten hat.* Heidelberg: Mohr und Zimmer, 1807.

———. *Joseph von Görres gesammelte Briefe.* Vol. 8, II, *Freundesbriefe 1802–1821.* Edited by Franz Binder. In *Joseph von Görres gesammelte Schriften,* edited by Marie Görres. Munich: Literarisch-artistische Anstalt, 1874.

Gottesman, Itzik Nakhmen. *Defining the Yiddish Nation: The Jewish Folklorists of Poland.* Detroit: Wayne State University Press, 2003.

———. "The Man in the Brimmed Hat: The Fieldwork Narratives of the Warsaw Yiddish Folklorists." *Jewish Folklore and Ethnology Review* 15, no. 1 (1993): 2–4.

Grimm, Jacob, and Wilhelm Grimm. *Deutsches Wörterbuch*. Vol. 9. Leipzig: Hirzel, 1899.

———. "Review of Friedrich Heinrich von der Hagen's *Narrenbuch*." *Leipziger Literatur-Zeitung* 161–163 (1812): 1281–1301.

Gross, Naftoli. *Mayselekh un mesholim*. New York: Forverts, 1955.

Grossman, Jeffrey A. *The Discourse on Yiddish in Germany from the Enlightenment to the Second Empire*. Rochester, NY: Camden House, 2000.

Grunewald, Eckhard. *Friedrich Heinrich von der Hagen, 1780–1856: Ein Beitrag zur Frühgeschichte der Germanistik*. Berlin: de Gruyter, 1988.

Grunwald, Max. "Aus unseren Sammlungen." *Mitteilungen der Gesellschaft für Jüdische Volkskunde* 1, no. 1 (1898): 1–116.

Güdemann, Moritz. *Geschichte des Erziehungswesens und der Cultur der abendländischen Juden während des Mittelalters und der neueren Zeit*. 2nd ed. 3 vols. Vienna: Hölder, 1880–1888.

Gurjewitsch, Aaron. "Bachtin und der Karneval: Zu Dietz-Rüdiger Moser, Lachkultur des Mittelalters? Michael Bachtin und die Folgen seiner Theorie." *Euphorion* 85 (1991): 423–429.

Gvozdeva, Katja. "Hobbyhorse Performances: A Ritual Attribute of Carnivalesque Traditions and Its Literary Appropriation in Sottie Theatre." In *Genre and Ritual: The Cultural Heritage of Medieval Rituals*, edited by Eyolf Østrem, Mette Birkedaal Bruun, Nils Holger Petersen, and Jens Fleischer, 65–86. Copenhagen: Museum Tusculanum Press, 2005.

———. "Karnevaleske Statuten im spätmittelalterlichen und frühneuzeitlichen Frankreich." In *Von der Ordnung zur Norm: Statuten in Mittelalter und Früher Neuzeit*, edited by Gisela Drossbach, 347–365. Paderborn, Germany: Schöningh, 2010.

———. "La procession charivarique en texte et image: Les recueils lyonnais de la chevauchée de l'âne–La Nef des fous de Sebastian Brant–Le Quart Livre de François Rabelais–Les Songes drolatiques de Pantagruel." In *Medialität der Prozession: Performanz ritueller Bewegung in Texten und Bildern der Vormoderne*, edited by Katja Gvozdeva and Hans Rudolf Velten, 323–357. Heidelberg: Winter Universitätsverlag, 2011.

———. "Rituale des Doppelsinns: Zur Ikonologie der Charivari-Kultur im Spätmittelalter und in der Frühen Neuzeit." In *Ikonologie des Performativen*, edited by Christoph Wulf and Jörg Zirfas, 133–150. Munich: Fink, 2005.

———. "Spielprozess und Zivilisationsprozess: Emotionales Rätsel in Italien und Frankreich zwischen 1475 und 1638." In *Scham und Schamlosigkeit: Grenzverletzungen in Literatur und Kultur der Vormoderne*, edited by Katja Gvozdeva and Hans Rudolf Velten, 363–395. Berlin: de Gruyter, 2011.

———. "Spiel und Ernst der burlesken Investitur in den *sociétés joyeuses* des Spätmittelalters und der Frühen Neuzeit." In *Investitur- und Krönungsrituale: Herrschaftseinsetzungen im kulturellen Vergleich*, edited by Marion Steinicke and Stefan Weinfurter, 177–199. Cologne: Böhlau, 2005.

Hackländer, Friedrich Wilhelm. *Künstlerroman*. Vol. 3. Stuttgart: Adolph Krabbe, 1866.

Hadda, Janet. "Bashevis at *Forverts*." In *The Hidden Isaac Bashevis Singer*, edited by Seth L. Wolitz, 173–181. Austin: University of Texas Press, 2001.

———. *Isaac Bashevis Singer: A Life*. New York: Oxford University Press, 1997.

Hagen, Friedrich Heinrich von der. "Die romantische und Volks-Litteratur der Juden in Jüdisch-Deutscher Sprache." In *Philologische und historische Abhandlungen der Königlichen Akademie der Wissenschaften zu Berlin aus dem Jahre 1854*, 1–11. Berlin: Königliche Akademie der Wissenschaften, 1855.

———. *Narrenbuch*. Halle, Germany: Rieger, 1811.

Hamburger, Benjamin Salomon, and Eric Zimmer, eds. *Minhagim de-Kehilat kodesh Vermaysa* (=Worms). Vol. 1. Jerusalem: Makhon Yerushalayim, 1988.

Hampson, R. T. *Medii Ævi Kalendarium, or, Dates, Charters, and Customs of the Middle Ages*. Vol. 1. London: Kent, 1841.

Harris, Max. *Sacred Folly: A New History of the Feast of Fools*. Ithaca, NY: Cornell University Press, 2011.

Heilpern, Falk. *Ḥakhme Ḥelm: Bediḥot ve-halatsot 'amamiyot*. Warsaw: Ahisefer, ca. 1926.

———. *Ḥelm ve-ḥakhameh: Meḥubar be-ḥelko lefi mekorot 'amamiyim*. Tel Aviv: Yisra'el, 1937.

Heine, Heinrich. "Anno 1839." Translated by Walter Arndt. In *Songs of Love and Grief: A Bilingual Anthology in the Verse Forms of the Originals*, 122–125. Evanston, IL: Northwestern University Press, 1995.

———. *Heinrich Heine über Ludwig Börne*. Hamburg: Hoffmann und Campe, 1840.

———. *Ideen: Das Buch Le Grand*. In *Reisebilder I: 1824–1828*, edited by Fritz Mende, 86–137. Berlin: Akademie-Verlag, 1970.

Herlitz, Georg, and Ismar Elbogen, eds. *Jüdisches Lexikon*. 4 vols. Berlin: Jüdischer Verlag, 1927–1930.

Hesekiel, George. *Land und Stadt im Volksmunde: Beinamen, Sprüche und Spruchverse*. Berlin: Janke, 1867. Originally published 1866 in *Deutsche Roman-Zeitung*.

Hess, Jonathan M. *Middlebrow Literature and the Making of German-Jewish Identity*. Stanford, CA: Stanford University Press, 2010.

Hesse, Walter. *Das Schicksal des Lalebuches in der deutschen Literatur*. Ohlau: Hermann Eschenhagen, 1929.

Hierocles. *The Philogelos, or, Laughter-Lover*. Translated by Barry Baldwin. Amsterdam: J. C. Gieben, 1983.

Himka, John-Paul. *Religion and Nationality in Western Ukraine: The Greek Catholic Church and Ruthenian National Movement in Galicia, 1867–1900*. Montreal: McGill-Queen's University Press, 1999.

Hirschberg, Alfred [A.H.]. "Binjamin Segel gestorben." *C. V.-Zeitung: Blätter für Deutschtum und Judentum*, March 20, 1931, 143–144.

Hobsbawm, Eric. Introduction to *The Invention of Tradition*, edited by Eric Hobsbawm and Terence Ranger, 1–14. Cambrigde: Cambridge University Press, 1983.

Hödl, Klaus. "Segel, Benjamin." In *Österreichisches Biographisches Lexikon 1815–1950*, edited by Österreichische Akademie der Wissenschaften, vol. 12, issue 1, 110–111. Vienna: Österreichischen Akademie der Wissenschaften, 2001.

Höft, Ferdinand. "Abderiten von heute." *Am Ur-Quell* 2 (1891): 154–155.

Holdes, O. *Mayses, vitsn un shpitslekh fun Hershl Ostropoler.* Warsaw: Yidish bukh, 1960.

Honegger, Peter. *Die Schiltburgerchronik und ihr Verfasser Johann Fischart.* Hamburg: E. Hauswedell, 1982.

Horowitz, Elliott. *Reckless Rites: Purim and the Legacy of Jewish Violence.* Princeton, NJ: Princeton University Press, 2006.

Howard, John A. "A Little Known Version of *Til Eulenspiegel.*" *Amsterdamer Beiträge zur älteren Germanistik* 15 (1980): 127–142.

——. *Wunderparlich und seltsame Historien Til Eulen Spiegels.* Würzburg, Germany: Königshausen and Neumann, 1983.

Hundert, Gershon, ed. *The YIVO Encyclopedia of Jews in Eastern Europe.* 2 vols. New Haven, CT: Yale University Press, 2008.

Idel, Moshe. *Golem: Jewish Magical and Mystical Traditions on the Artificial Anthropoid.* Albany: State University of New York Press, 1990.

Isaacs, Edith J. R. "Good Playing A-Plenty: Broadway in Review." *Theatre Arts Monthly* 18 (1934): 9–20.

Jason, Heda. "Jewish–Near Eastern Numskull Tales: An Attempt at Interpretation." *Asian Folklore Studies* 31 (1972): 1–39.

Jeep, Ernst. *Hans Friedrich von Schönberg, der Verfasser des Schildbürgerbuches und des Grillenvertreibers: Eine litterarische Untersuchung über das Schildbürgerbuch und seine Fortsetzungen.* Wolfenbüttel, Germany: J. Zwißler, 1890.

Kaftal, Gustav. *Naye oysdervelte Khelmer mayses,* Warsaw: Goldfarb, 1929.

Kalkofen, Rupert. "*Lalebuch* oder *Schiltbürger,* Anonymus oder Fischart? Die buchgeschichtlichen Untersuchungen von Peter Honegger und Stefan Ertz im Vergleich." *Wirkendes Wort* 41 (1991): 363–377.

Kanc, Shimon, ed. *Sefer ha-zikaron li-kehilat Ḥelem.* N.p., 1981.

Kant, Immanuel. *The Conflict of the Faculties = Der Streit der Fakultäten.* Translated by Mary J. Gregor. New York: Abaris Books, 1979.

Kaplan, Debra. *Beyond Expulsion: Jews, Christians, and Reformation Strasbourg.* Stanford, CA: Stanford University Press, 2011.

Katz, Judith. *Running Fiercely toward a High Thin Sound.* Ithaca, NY: Firebrand Books, 1992.

Kazin, Pearl. "The Wisdom of Fools." *Commentary,* January 1, 1946, 94–95.

Keesing, Roger M. *Kwaio Religion: The Living and the Dead in a Solomon Island Society.* New York: Columbia University Press, 1982.

Keller, Gottfried. *Die Leute von Seldwyla.* 4 vols. Stuttgart: Göschen'sche Verlagshandlung, 1874.

Kellner, Beate, Jan-Dirk Müller, and Peter Strohschneider, eds. *Erzählen und Episteme: Literatur im 16. Jahrhundert.* Berlin: de Gruyter, 2011.

"A Khelemer maysele." *Forverts,* July 8, 1928.

Kimmel, Eric. *The Chanukkah Tree.* New York: Holiday House, 1988.

———. *Jar of Fools: Eight Hanukkah Stories from Chelm*. New York: Holiday House, 2000.

Kipnis, Menakhem. *Khelemer mayses*. Warsaw: S. Tsuker, 1930.

———. *Rabin bez głowy i inne opowieści z Chełma*. Translated by Bella Szwarcman-Czarnota Cracow: Austeria, 2013.

———. "II: Der Khelemer barg." *Haynt*, July 14, 1922, 5.

———. "IV: Di podloge fun Khelmer alter bod." *Haynt*, July 21, 1922, 5.

———. "V: Khelmer beys-oylem." *Haynt*, July 21, 1922, 5.

———. "VI: Di shul mit ladens." *Haynt*, July 21, 1922, 5–6.

———. "XVII: Der nakht shoymer." *Haynt*, August 25, 1922, 5.

———. "XIX: Khelmer 'shomrim leboker.'" September 29, 1922, 4.

———. "XXIII: Khelmer keyser in goldene shikh." *Haynt*, October 13, 1922, 4.

———. "XXVI: A zeltene hamtsoe." *Haynt*, October 13, 1922, 4.

———. "XXVIII: Di beheyme oyfn boydem." Haynt, October 20, 1922, 4.

———. "XXIX: Khelmer emes." *Haynt*, October 20, 1922, 4.

———. "XLVI: Vu zenen ahingekumen di Khelmer naronim." *Haynt*, December 8, 1922, 5.

———. "LI: Khelmer beys-akvores: A mayse in fersen." *Haynt*, January 26, 1923, 5.

———. "LVIII: Vi azoy Khelmer tselen." *Haynt*, March 16, 1923, 5.

———. "LIX: Di 2 Khelmer mitn ferdl." *Haynt*, March 16, 1923, 5.

———. "LX: Farmishpet dem fish . . ." *Haynt*, March 23, 1923, 5.

Klatzkin, Jakob, and Ismar Elbogen, eds. *Encyclopedia Judaica: Das Judentum in Geschichte und Gegenwart*. 10 vols. Berlin: Eschkol, 1928–1934.

Klausner, Joseph. *Historiyah shel ha-sifrut ha-ivrit ha-ḥadashah*. Vol. 1. Jerusalem: Hebrew University, 1939.

Kleingeld, Pauline. *Kant and Cosmopolitanism: The Philosophical Ideal of World Citizenship*. Cambridge: Cambridge University Press, 2012.

Klotz, Volker. *Die erzählte Stadt: Ein Sujet als Herausforderung des Romans von Lesage bis Döblin*. Munich: Hanser, 1969.

Kogman-Appel, Katrin. "The Illustrations of the Washington Haggadah." In *The Washington Haggadah: Copied and Illustrated by Joel ben Simeon*, edited by David Stern and Katrin Kogman-Appel, 52–113. Cambridge, MA: Harvard University Press, 2011.

Kohn, Jakob Pinchas, and Ludwig Davidsohn. "Jüdischer Humor und Witz." In *Jüdisches Lexikon*, edited by Georg Herlitz and Ismar Elbogen, vol. 2, 1686–1694. Berlin: Jüdischer Verlag, 1928.

Kon, Henekh. "Menakhem Mendl Kipnis, folks-zinger." *Der tog-Morgn zshurnal*, August 25, 1967, 9.

Könneker, Barbara. *Satire im 16. Jahrhundert: Epoche–Werke–Wirkung*. Munich: Beck, 1991.

———. *Wesen und Wandlung der Narrenidee im Zeitalter des Humanismus: Brant–Murner–Erasmus*. Wiesbaden, Germany: Steiner, 1966.

Koon, Jon. *Confused Hanukkah: An Original Story from Chelm.* New York: Dutton, 2004.

Körte, Friedrich Heinrich Wilhelm. *Die Sprichwörter und sprichwörtlichen Redensarten der Deutschen: Nebst der Redensarten der deutschen Zech-Brüder und aller Praktik Großmutter, d. i. d. Sprichwörter ewigem Wetter-Kalender.* Leipzig: Brockhaus, 1837.

Kortum, Karl Arnold. *The Jobsiad: A Grotesco-Comico-Heroic Poem: The Life, Opinions, Actions, and Fate of Hieronimus Jobs the Candidate, a Man Who Whilom Won Great Renown, and Died as Night-Watch in Sulzburg.* Translated by Charles T. Brooks. Philadelphia: Leypoldt, 1863.

———. *Die Jobsiade: Ein komisches Heldengedicht.* Dortmund, Germany: Mallinckrodt, 1799.

———. *Leben, Meynungen und Thaten von Hieronimus Jobs dem Kandidaten, und wie Er sich weiland viel Ruhm erwarb auch endlich als Nachtswächter zu Sulzburg starb.* Münster, Germany: Perrenon, 1784.

Kowalzik, Barbara. *Das jüdische Schulwerk in Leipzig: 1912–1933.* Cologne: Böhlau Verlag, 2002.

Krah, Franziska. "Mit den Waffen der Aufklärung gegen den Antisemitismus: Leben und Wirken Binjamin W. Segels." *Zeitschrift für Religions- und Geistesgeschichte* 63 (2011): 122–144.

Krause, Norbert. "Abderiten von heute." *Am Ur-Quell* 2 (1891), 231–232.

Krauss, Friedrich Salomon. "Beiträge zur Geschichte der Volkskunde." *Der Urquell* 1 (1897): 284–285.

Kreutzer, Hans Joachim. *Der Mythos vom Volksbuch: Studien zur Wirkungsgeschichte des frühen deutschen Romans seit der Romantik.* Stuttgart: J. B. Metzler, 1977.

Krutikov, Mikhail. "Berdichev in Russian-Jewish Literary Imagination: From Israel Aksenfeld to Friedrich Gorenshtein." In *The Shtetl Image and Reality: Papers of the Second Mendel Friedman Conference on Yiddish,* edited by Gennady Estraikh and Mikhail Krutikov, 91–114. Oxford, UK: Legenda, 2000.

———. "A Postmodern Yiddish Satire Set in Nowhere, Arizona." *Forward,* February 7, 2011.

Krutikov, Mikhail, and Shachar Pinsker. "Zeitlin Family." In *The YIVO Encyclopedia of Jews in Eastern Europe,* vol. 2, 2116–2118. New Haven, CT: Yale University Press, 2008.

Kugelmass, Jack and Jonathan Boyarin, eds. *From a Ruined Garden: The Memorial Books of Polish Jewry,* 2nd ed. Bloomington: Indiana University Press, 1998.

———. Introduction to *From a Ruined Garden: The Memorial Books of Polish Jewry,* 2nd ed., edited by Jack Kugelmass and Jonathan Boyarin, 1–50. Bloomington: Indiana University Press, 1998.

Kumove, Shirley. *More Words, More Arrows: A Further Collection of Yiddish Folk Sayings.* Detroit: Wayne State University Press, 1999.

Lahr, John. "Bring Back the Clowns." *New Yorker,* July 11, 1994, 75.

Landau, Alfred. "Sprichwörter und Redensarten." *Mitteilungen der Gesellschaft für Jüdische Volkskunde,* n.s., 25 (1923): 335–361.

Landmann, Salcia. *Der jüdische Witz: Soziologie und Sammlung.* Olten, Switzerland: Walter, 1960.

Lann, James M. van der. "Christoph Martin Wieland and the German Making of Greece." *Germanic Review* 70 (1995): 51–56.

Lappenberg, Johann Martin. *Dr. Thomas Murners Ulenspiegel.* Leipzig: T. O. Weigel, 1854.

Lebensaft, Elisabeth, and Hubert Reitterer. *Wurzbach-Aspekte.* Vienna: Österreichisches Biographisches Lexikon, 1992.

Lefin Satanover, Mendel. "Essai d'un plan de réforme ayant pour objet d'éclairer la nation Juive en Pologne et de redresser par là ses mœurs." In *Materiały do dziejów Sejmu Czteroletniego,* edited by Artur Eisenbach, Jerzy Michalski, Emanuel Rostworowski, and Janusz Wolański, 409–421. Wrocław, Poland: Zakład Narodowy im. Ossolińskich, 1969.

Le Goff, Jacques, and Jean Claude Schmitt. *Le charivari.* Paris: Mouton, 1981.

Leib, Mani. "Der Barg." In *Lider un baladn,* vol. 2, 175–179. New York: CYCO, 1955.

———. "Litvishe mayz." In *Lider un baladn,* vol. 2, 180–198. New York: CYCO, 1955.

———. "Dos vunder-ferd." In *Lider un baladn,* vol. 2, 163–174. New York: CYCO, 1955.

Lerer, D. "In kenigraykh fun naronim." *Literarishe bleter,* June 28, 1930, 501.

Lerner, Yosl. *Fun Khelemer pinkes.* Tel Aviv: Peretz, 1975.

———. "Khelem di shtot." In *Fun Khelemer pinkes,* 17–18. Tel Aviv: Peretz, 1975.

———. "Khelemer khakhomim." In *Fun Khelemer pinkes,* 13–88. Tel Aviv: Peretz, 1975.

Lessing, Theodor. *Eindrücke aus Galizien.* Edited by Wolfgang Eggersdorfer. Hannover, Germany: Hohesufer.com, 2014.

Levi, G. "Volkslieder der Juden." *Ost und West* 12, no. 2 (1912): 143–150.

Lew, Henryk. "Nasza Abdera." In *Żydowski humor (ludowy), żydowscy dowcipnisie ludowi,* 51–70. Warsaw: H. Cohn, 1898.

*Liber vagatorum: Der betler orden.* Strasbourg: Matthias Hupfuff, 1510.

Lieb, Ludger. "Spiegelbild im Wasser." In *Enzyklopädie des Märchens: Handwörterbuch zur historischen und vergleichenden Erzählforschung,* edited by Rolf Wilhelm Brednich, vol. 12, 1023–1031. Berlin: de Gruyter, 2007.

Lindow, Wolfgang, ed. *Ein kurtzweilig lesen von Dyl Ulenspiegel: Nach dem Druck von 1515.* Stuttgart: Reclam, 1978.

Liptzin, Sol. "Ostropoler, Hershele." In *Encyclopaedia Judaica,* edited by Michael Berenbaum and Fred Skolnik, vol. 15, 512–513. Detroit: Macmillan Reference USA, 2007.

Lixfeld, Hannjost. "Ostdeutsche Schildbürgergeschichten." *Jahrbuch für ostdeutsche Volkskunde* 17 (1974): 87–107.

Loentz, Elizabeth. *Let Me Continue to Speak the Truth: Bertha Pappenheim as Author and Activist.* Cincinnati: Hebrew Union College Press, 2007.

Loewe, Heinrich. *Die jüdischdeutsche Sprache der Ostjuden.* Berlin: Komitee für den Osten, 1915.

———. *Die Sprachen der Juden.* Cologne: Jüdischer Verlag, 1911.

———. *Schelme und Narren mit jüdischen Kappen.* Berlin: Welt-Verlag, 1920.

Lorch, Amnon. "Ḥakhmei Ḥelem." *Maʾariv*, November 1, 2015.

Lotze, Hermann. "Zur jüdisch-deutschen Literatur." *Archiv für Litteraturgeschichte* 1 (1870): 90–101.

*Das lustige und lächerliche Lalen-Buch, das ist: Wunderseltsame, abentheurliche uner-hörte, und bißher unbeschriebene Geschichten und Thaten der Lalen zu Lalenburg, in Misnopotamia, hinter Utopia gelegen.* N.p.: n.p., n.d.

Luther, Martin. Preface to *The Book of Vagabonds and Beggars with a Vocabulary of Their Language and a Preface by Martin Luther* (*The Liber Vagatorum*), translated by John Camden Hotten, 3–5. London: Hotten, 1860.

Lütke, J. P. [PhilogLotto, pseud.]. *Kurtze und gründliche Anweisung zur Teutsch-Jüdischen Sprache.* Freiberg, Germany: Christoph Matthäi, 1733.

Mahalel, Adi. "We Will Not Be Silent: I. L. Peretz's 'Bontshe the Silent' vs. 1950s McCarthyism in America and the Story of the Staging of the World of Sholom Aleichem." *Studies in American Jewish Literature* 34 (2015): 204–230.

Maimon, Salomon. *Solomon Maimon: An Autobiography.* Translated by J. Clark Murray. 1888. Reprint, Urbana: University of Illinois Press, 2001.

Mandelbaum, Allen. *Chelmaxioms: The Maxims, Axioms, Maxioms of Chelm.* Boston: David R. Godine, 1977.

Manger, Itsik. "Di balade fun Hershele Ostropoler mit der levone." In *Lid un Balade*, 201–202. New York: Itsik-Manger-komitet, 1952.

———. Foreword to *Noente geshtaltn*, 3–4. Warsaw: Brzoza, 1938.

———. "Khelemer balade." In *Lamtern in vint*, 58–59. Warsaw: Turem, 1933.

———."Di Khelemer mayses." *Literarishe bleter*, May 17, 1929, 376–378.

———. "Der 'Khelemer' zatsaʾl." In *Noente geshtaltn*, 193–201. Warsaw: Brzoza, 1938.

———. "Der 'Khelemer' zatsaʾl." In *Noente geshtaltn un andere shriftn*, 113–120. New York: Itsik Manger yoyvl-komitet, 1961.

———. "The Rabbi of Chelm: May His Memory Be Blessed." In *The World According to Itzik: Selected Poetry and Prose*, edited and translated by Leonard Wolf, 218–224. New Haven, CT: Yale University Press, 2002.

Manger, Klaus. "Universitas Abderitica: Zu Wielands Romankomposition." *Euphorion* 77 (1983): 395–406.

———. "Wielands *Geschichte der Abderiten.*" In *Wieland-Handbuch: Leben, Werk, Wirkung*, edited by Jutta Heinz, 295–305. Stuttgart: Metzler, 2008.

———. "Wielands *Geschichte der Abderiten*: Vom Fortsetzungsroman im 'Teutschen Merkur' zur Buchfassung." In *"Der Teutsche Merkur": Die erste deutsche Kulturzeitschrift?*, edited by Andrea Heinz, 131–152. Heidelberg: Universitätsverlag Winter, 2003.

Manuel, Frank Edward. *Shapes of Philosophical History.* Stanford, CA: Stanford University Press, 1965.

Marbach, Gotthard Oswald, ed. *Der Schildbürger wunderseltsame, abenteuerliche, unerhörte und bisher unbeschriebene Geschichten und Thaten.* Leipzig: Wigand, 1838.

Mart, Krystyna, ed. *Żydzi w Chełmie.* Chełm, Poland: Muzeum Ziemi Chełmskiej im. Wiktora Ambroziewicza, 2010.

Martini, Fritz. "Wieland: Geschichte der Abderiten." In *Der deutsche Roman: Vom Barock bis zur Gegenwart*, edited by Benno von Wiese, vol. 1, 64–94. Düsseldorf: August Bagel Verlag, 1963.

Martus, Steffen. *Die Brüder Grimm: Eine Biographie*. Berlin: Rowohlt, 2009.

Matthaei, Adam Rudolph Georg Christoph. *Beschreibung des Jüdischen Purim-Festes: Nach ihrer Lehre und gewöhnlichen Gebräuchen aus den talmudischen und rabbinischen Schriften*. Nürnberg: Felssecker, 1758.

Matut, Diana. *Dichtung und Musik im frühneuzeitlichen Aschkenas: Ms. opp. add. 4 136 der Bodleian Library, Oxford (das so genannte Wallich-Manuskript) und Ms. hebr. oct. 219 der Stadt- und Universitätsbibliothek, Frankfurt a. M.* 2 vols. Leiden, Netherlands: Brill, 2011.

———. "Steinschneider and Yiddish." In *Studies on Steinschneider: Moritz Steinschneider and the Emergence of the Science of Judaism in Nineteenth-Century Germany*, edited by Reimund Leicht and Gad Freudenthal, 383–409. Leiden, Netherlands: Brill, 2012.

Meir, Jonatan. *Ḥasidut medumah: ʻIyunim bi-khetavav ha-satiriyim shel Yosef Perl*. Jerusalem: Mosad Bialik, 2013.

———. "New Readings in Joseph Perl's *Boḥen tsadik*." *Tarbiz* 76 (2008): 557–590.

Mendelsohn, Ezra. "Interwar Poland: Good for the Jews or Bad for the Jews?" In *The Jews in Poland*, edited by Chimen Abramsky, Maciej Jachimczyk, and Antony Polonsky, 130–139. Oxford, UK: Basil Blackwell, 1986.

Merks, Benjamin. *Vunderparlikh und zeltsame historien Til Aylen-shpigelz*. Bayerische Staatsbibliothek Munich, Cod. hebr. 100, fols. 134r–191r.

Merkur, Volf. *Di velt iz Khelem*. Buenos Aires: Tsentral-farband fun poylishe yidn in Argentine, 1960.

Metzger, Mendel. *La Haggada enluminée*. Leiden, Netherlands: Brill, 1973.

Meuli, Karl. "Charivari." In *Gesammelte Schriften*, edited by Thomas Gelzer, vol. 1, 471–484. Basel: Schwabe, 1975.

Michelsen, Peter. *Laurence Sterne und der deutsche Roman des 18. Jahrhunderts*. Göttingen, Germany: Vandenhoeck and Rupprecht, 1962.

Mierowsky, David [Ben Eliezer, pseud.]. "David Frishman." In *Letters of a Jewish Father to His Son*, 80–86. London: Murray, 1928.

Miler, Sholem. "Yosl der Khelmer." In *Funem yidishn kval*, 65–78. Winnipeg, MB: Dos yidishe vort, 1937.

Miller, David Neal. "Reportage as Fiction, I: Singer's Pseudonymous Personas." In *Fear of Fiction: Narrative Strategies in the Works of Isaac Bashevis Singer*, 39–70. Albany: State University of New York Press, 1985.

Mirer, Sholem. "Khelmer geshikhtes." In *Antiklerikale folks-mayses*, 93–104. Moscow: Der emes, 1940.

Miron, Dan. *The Image of the Shtetl and Other Studies of Modern Jewish Literary Imagination*. Syracuse, NY: Syracuse University Press, 2000.

Montaigne, Fen. *Reeling in Russia*. New York: St. Martin's, 1998.

Montanus, Martin. *Das Ander theyl der Gartengeselschafft*. Strasbourg: Messerschmidt, 1560.

Moser, Dietz-Rüdiger. "Lachkultur des Mittelalters? Michail Bachtin und die Folgen seiner Theorie." *Euphorion* 84 (1990): 89–111.

Moser, Hugo. *Schwäbischer Volkshumor: Die Necknamen der Städte und Dörfer in Württemberg und Hohenzollern, im bayrischen Schwaben und in Teilen Badens sowie bei Schwaben in der Fremde mit einer Auswahl von Ortsneckereien.* Stuttgart: Kohlhammer, 1950.

Müller, Hermann-Josef. "Eulenspiegel bei den Juden: Zur Überlieferung der jiddischen *Eulenspiegel*-Fassungen." *Eulenspiegel-Jahrbuch* 30 (1990): 33–50.

———. "Eulenspiegel im Land der starken Weiber, der Hundsköpfe und Anderswo: Fünf unbekannte Eulenspiegelgeschichten in einem jiddischen Druck von 1735." In *Jiddische Philologie*, edited by Walter Röll, 197–226. Tübingen, Germany: Niemeyer, 1999.

Nalewajko-Kulikov, Joanna. *"Di Haynt-mishpokhe*: Study for a Group Picture." In *Warsaw: The Jewish Metropolis: Essays in Honor of the 75th Birthday of Professor Antony Polonsky*, edited by Glenn Dynner and François Guesnet, 252–170. Leiden, Netherlands: Brill, 2015.

Neuberg, Simon. *Pragmatische Aspekte der jiddischen Sprachgeschichte am Beispiel der Zenerene.* Hamburg: Buske, 1999.

Neugroschel, Joachim. "Five Stories about Till Eulenspiegel." In *No Star Too Beautiful: Yiddish Stories from 1382 to the Present*, 92–96. New York: Norton, 2002.

Neumann, Siegfried. "Sonnenlicht im Sack." In *Enzyklopädie des Märchens: Handwörterbuch zur historischen und vergleichenden Erzählforschung*, edited by Rolf Wilhelm Brednich, vol. 12, 888–892. Berlin: de Gruyter, 2007.

Niborski, Yitskhok, and Bernard Vaysbrot. *Yidish-frantseyzish verterbukh.* Paris: Bibliothèque Medem, 2011.

Norich, Anita. *Writing in Tongues: Translating Yiddish in the 20th Century.* Seattle: University of Washington Press, 2013.

Ofterding, Ralf. "Abderiten von heute." *Am Ur-Quell* 2 (1891): 191–192.

Oguz, A. D. "A khokhme fun Khelemer kahal." *Der morgn zshurnal*, November 28, 1911, 5.

Olsvanger, Immanuel. *L'Chayim! Jewish Wit and Humor.* New York: Schocken Books, 1949.

———. *Rosinkess mit Mandlen: Aus der Volksliteratur der Ostjuden: Schwänke, Erzählungen, Sprichwörter und Rätsel.* Basel: Verlage der Schweizerischen Gesellschaft für Volkskunde, 1920.

———. *Röyte Pomerantsen.* New York: Schocken Books, 1947.

Oppenheimer, Paul. Introduction to *Till Eulenspiegel: His Adventures*, edited and translated by Paul Oppenheimer, xxi–xcv. New York: Routledge, 2001.

———, ed. and trans. *Till Eulenspiegel: His Adventures.* New York: Routledge, 2001.

Pagis, Dan. "Toward a Theory of the Literary Riddle." In *Untying the Knot: On Riddles and Other Enigmatic Modes*, edited by Galit Hasan-Rokem and David Shulman, 81–108. Oxford: Oxford University Press, 1996.

Paucker, Arnold. "Das deutsche Volksbuch bei den Juden." *Zeitschrift für deutsche Philologie* 80 (1961): 302–317.

———. "The Yiddish Versions of the German Volksbuch." PhD diss., University of Nottingham, 1959.

———. "Di yidishe nuskhoes fun *Shildburger bukh*." *YIVO bleter* 44 (1973): 59–77.

Paul, Jean. "Kleine Nachschule zur ästhetischen Vorschule." In *Jean Paul: Sämtliche Werke*, vol. 5, *Vorschule der Aesthetik*, edited by Norbert Miller, 459–514. Munich: Hanser, 1980.

———. *Titan*. 4 vols. Berlin: Matzdorff, 1800–1803.

———. *Titan: A Romance*. London: Trübner, 1863.

Paulauskienė, Aušra. *Lost and Found: The Discovery of Lithuania in American Fiction*. Amsterdam: Rodopi, 2007.

Peretz, Yitskhok-Leyb. "Iber a shmek-tabak." In *Di verk*, vol. 7, *Folkstimlekhe geshikhtn*, edited by Dovid Pinski, 266–276. New York: Farlag Yidish, 1920.

———. "In Eyrope un bay unz untern oyvn." In *Ale verk fun Y. L. Peretz*, vol. 8, *Oyfzatsn un felyetonen*, 279–291. Vilna: Kletskin, 1922. Originally published 1894 in *Yontef-bletlekh*.

———. "Der Khelmer melamed." In *Ale verk fun Y. L. Peretz*, vol. 2, *Dertselungen, mayselekh, bilder*, edited by Shmuel Niger, 6–9. New York: CYCO, 1947. Originally published 1889 in *Di yudishe folks-bibliotek*.

———. "A Pinch of Snuff." Translated by Maurice Samuel. In *The I. L. Peretz Reader*, edited by Ruth R. Wisse, 251–258. New York: Schocken Books, 1990.

———. "The Shabbes Goy." Translated by Etta Blum. In *The I. L. Peretz Reader*, edited by Ruth R. Wisse, 131–138. New York: Schocken Books, 1990.

———. "Der shabes-goy." In *Di verk*, vol. 4, *Ertselungen*, edited by Dovid Pinski, 184–194. New York: Farlag Yidish, 1920. Originally published 1911 as "In alt Khelem: A Khelemer maysele" in *Der fraynd*.

Perl, Arnold. *The World of Sholom Aleichem: Acting Edition*. New York: Dramatists Play Service, 1953.

Perl, Joseph. *Boḥen tsadik*. Prague: M. J. Landau, 1838.

———. *Joseph Perl's Revealer of Secrets: The First Hebrew Novel*. Translated and edited by Dov Taylor. Boulder, CO: Westview, 1997.

———. *Megale temirin*. Edited by Jonatan Meir. 2 vols. Jerusalem: Mosad Bialik, 2013.

Pivovarov, Viktor. "Yevo golos." In *Velikiĭ Genrikh: Sapgir o Sapgire*, edited by Tatiana Mikhaĭlovskaia, 323–330. Moscow: RGGU, 2003.

Portnoy, Edward. "The Creation of a Jewish Cartoon Space in the New York and Warsaw Yiddish Press, 1884–1939." PhD diss., Jewish Theological Seminary, 2008.

———. "Wise Men of Chelm." In *YIVO Encyclopedia of Jews in Eastern Europe*, edited by Gershon Hundert, vol. 2, 2017. New Haven, CT: Yale University Press, 2008.

Prager, Leonard. "Yiddish in the University." In *Never Say Die! A Thousand Years of Yiddish in Jewish Life and Letters*, edited by Joshua A. Fishman, 529–545. The Hague: Mouton, 1981.

Prose, Francine. *The Angel's Mistake: Stories of Chelm*. New York: Greenwillow Books, 1997.

Pryłucki, Noah, and Shmuel Lehman. "Khelemer naronim." In *Zamlbikher far yidishn folklor, filologye un kulturgeshikhte*, vol. 1, 40–41, nos. 491–499. Warsaw: Nayer farlag, 1912.

———. "Khelemer naronim." In *Zamlbikher far yidishn folklor, filologye un kulturgeshikhte*, vol. 2, 187–210. Warsaw: Nayer farlag, 1917.

———. *Zamlbikher far yidishn folklor, filologye un kulturgeshikhte*, vol. 1. Warsaw: Nayer farlag 1912.

———. *Zamlbikher far yidishn folklor, filologye un kulturgeshikhte*, vol. 2. Warsaw: Nayer farlag, 1917.

Pryłucki, Noah, Yekhiel Yeshaye Trunk, and Yisroel Rabon, eds. *Untervegns: Almanakh far yidisher literatur*. Vilna: Pakelyje, 1940.

Rausmaa, Pirkko-Liisa. "Die verkehrte Richtung." In *Enzyklopädie des Märchens: Handwörterbuch zur historischen und vergleichenden Erzählforschung*, edited by Rolf Wilhelm Brednich, vol. 11, 662–665. Berlin: de Gruyter, 2004.

Ravnitski, Yoshue Khone. *Yudishe vitsn*. Berlin: Moria, 1922.

Rebmann, Andreas Georg Friedrich von. *Empfindsame Reise nach Schilda*. Leipzig: Heinsius, 1793.

———. *Leben und Thaten des jüngern Herrn von Münchhausen, wohlweisen Bürgermeisters zu Schilda: Zweiter Theil der empfindsamen Reise nach Schilda*. Thorn: Gottfried Vollmer, 1795.

Reinsberg-Düringsfeld, Otto von. *Internationale Titulaturen*. Vol. 1. Leipzig: Hermann Fries, 1863.

"Review of E. G. Woltersdorf, *Jahrbuch der gesammten Literatur und Ereignisse*." *Allgemeine Literatur-Zeitung*, no. 180, July 1827, 593–596.

Richman, Jacob. *Jewish Wit and Wisdom: Examples of Jewish Anecdotes, Folk Tales, Bon Mots, Magic, Riddles, and Enigmas since the Canonization of the Bible*. New York: Pardes, 1952.

Richter, Matthias. *Die Sprache jüdischer Figuren in der deutschen Literatur (1750–1933): Studien zu Form und Funktion*. Göttingen, Germany: Wallstein-Verlag, 1995.

Riemer, Nathanael. "*Der Rabbiner*: Eine vergessene Zeitschrift eines christlichen Hebraisten." *PaRDeS: Zeitschrift der Vereinigung für Jüdische Studien* 11 (2005): 37–67.

Röcke, Werner. "'Erneuerung' des Mittelalters oder Dilettantismus? Friedrich Heinrich von der Hagen (1780–1856) und die Anfänge der Berliner Germanistik." *Zeitschrift für Germanistik N.F.* 20 (2010): 48–63.

———. *Die Freude am Bösen: Studien zu einer Poetik des deutschen Schwankromans im Spätmittelalter*. Munich: Fink, 1987.

———. "Joseph Görres' *Teutsche Volksbücher* (1807) und Friedrich Rebmanns *Empfindsame Reise nach Schilda*: Zur widersprüchlichen Deutungsgeschichte eines 'Volksbuches.'" *Daphnis* 33 (2004): 745–757.

Rogovin, Or. "Chelm as Shtetl: Y. Y. Trunk's *Khelemer Khakhomim*." *Prooftexts* 29 (2009): 242–272.

Römer, Nils H. *German City, Jewish Memory: The Story of Worms*. Waltham, MA: Brandeis University Press, 2010.

Rosenberg, Felix. "Ueber eine Sammlung von Volks- und Gesellschaftsliedern in he-bräischen Lettern." *Zeitschrift für die Geschichte der Juden in Deutschland* 2 (1888): 232–296.

——. "Ueber eine Sammlung von Volks- und Gesellschaftsliedern in hebräischen Let-tern." *Zeitschrift für die Geschichte der Juden in Deutschland* 3 (1889): 14–28.

Rosenkranz, Karl. *Geschichte der deutschen Poesie im Mittelalter.* Halle, Germany: Anton und Gelbcke, 1830.

Roskies, David G. "Ayzik-Meyer Dik and the Rise of Yiddish Popular Literature." PhD diss., Brandeis University, 1974.

——. *A Bridge of Longing: The Lost Art of Yiddish Storytelling.* Cambridge, MA: Har-vard University Press, 1995.

Roskies, David G., and Leonard Wolf. Introduction to *The World According to Itzik: Selected Poetry and Prose*, edited by Leonard Wolf, xiii–xlvi. New Haven, CT: Yale University Press, 2002.

Rosman, Moshe. "Categorically Jewish, Distinctly Polish: The Museum of the History of Polish Jews and the New Polish-Jewish Metahistory." *Jewish Studies: An Internet Journal* 10 (2012): 361–387.

——. *Founder of Hasidism: A Quest for the Historical Ba'al Shem Tov.* Berkeley: Uni-versity of California Press, 1996.

——. *How Jewish Is Jewish History?* Oxford, UK: Littman Library of Jewish Civiliza-tion, 2007.

——. "Hybrid with What? The Relationship between Jewish Culture and Other People's Cultures." In *How Jewish Is Jewish History?*, 82–110. Oxford, UK: Littman Library of Jewish Civilization, 2007.

——. *The Lords' Jews: Magnate-Jewish Relations in the Polish-Lithuanian Common-wealth During the Eighteenth Century.* Cambridge, MA: Harvard University Press 1990.

——. "Miedzyboz and Rabbi Israel Ba'al Shem Tov." In *Essential Papers on Hasidism: Origins to Present*, edited by Gershon David Hundert, 209–225. New York: NYU Press, 1991.

Rossel, Seymour. *The Wise Folk of Chelm.* Houston: Rossel, 2013.

Rovner, Jay Evan. *"Please Help Me Tithe unto You": The Ma'sar Kesafim (Income Tithe) Ledger of Mordecai Zeev Ehrenpreis of Lvov.* New York: Jewish Theological Seminary of America, 2003.

Rozenberg, Yudl. *The Golem and the Wondrous Deeds of the Maharal of Prague.* Edited and translated by Curt Leviant. New Haven, CT: Yale University Press, 2007.

"Ruby Dee Heads Yiddish Play Cast: Has Role of Defending Angel." *Afro-American*, May 9, 1953.

Ruderman, David B. *Early Modern Jewry: A New Cultural History.* Princeton, NJ: Princeton University Press, 2010.

Sachs, Hans. "Die Lappenhewser bawren." In *Hans Sachs*, edited by Adelbert von Keller, vol. 9, 380–383. Tübingen, Germany: Laupp, gedruckt für den Litterarischen Verein in Stuttgart, 1875.

Sadan, Dov. "Arum Khelem un der Khelmyade." In *Yidish–tokh un arum: Mekhkarim, eseyen, maymorim*, 85–116. Tel Aviv: Yisroel-bukh, 1986.

———. "Ḥakhmei Ḥelem." *Yeda Am* 2 (1954): 229–232.

Sadowski, Dirk. *Haskala und Lebenswelt: Herz Homberg und die jüdischen deutschen Schulen in Galizien 1782–1806*. Göttingen, Germany: Vandenhoeck and Ruprecht, 2010.

Saltykov-Shchedrin, Mikhail. *The History of a Town; or, The Chronicle of Foolov*. Translated and edited by Susan Brownsberger. Ann Arbor, MI: Ardis, 1982.

Saltzman, Roberta. *Isaac Bashevis Singer: A Bibliography of His Works in Yiddish and English, 1960–1991*. Lanham, MD: Scarecrow, 2002.

Samuel, Maurice. *The World of Sholom Aleichem*. New York: Knopf, 1943.

Sandler, Boris. *Keynemsdorf*. New York, 2010.

Sandrow, Nahma. *Vagabond Stars: A World History of Yiddish Theater*. Syracuse, NY: Syracuse University Press, 1996.

Sanfield, Steve. *The Feather Merchants and Other Tales of the Fools of Chelm*. New York: Orchard Books, 1991.

Sapir, Marc. *The Last Tale of Mendel Abbe: Sonny Bush and the Wise Men of New Chelm*. New York: iUniverse, 2004.

Sauder, Gerhard. "Bayle-Rezeption in der deutschen Aufklärung (Mit einem Anhang: In Deutschland verlegte Bayle-Ausgaben und deutsche Übersetzungen Baylescher Werke)." *Deutsche Vierteljahresschrift für Literaturwissenschaft und Geistesgeschichte* 49 (Sonderheft 18, 1975): 83–104.

Schachter, Allison. *Diasporic Modernisms: Hebrew and Yiddish Literatures in the Twentieth Century*. Oxford: Oxford University Press, 2012.

Schachter, Stanley J. *Laugh for God's Sake: Where Jewish Humor and Jewish Ethics Meet*. Jersey City, NJ: Ktav, 2008.

Schack, William. "Genial Lunacy in Theatre." *New York Times*, October 18, 1933, 24.

———. "Yiddish Season Ends: The Local Playhouses Have Had a Far from Successful Year." *New York Times*, March 11, 1934.

Schaechter, Rukhl. "Absurdity Returns to Chelm." *Forward*, December 1, 2006.

Scherman, Lucian, and Friedrich Salomon Krauss. *Allgemeine Methodik der Volkskunde: Berichte über Erscheinungen in den Jahren, 1890–1897*. Erlangen, Germany: Junge, 1899.

Schiller, Friedrich. "Preface, as Prefixed to the First Edition of *The Robbers* Published in 1781." In *The Works of Frederick Schiller*, vol. 2, *Early Dramas and Romances*, translated by Henry G. Bohn. London: H. G. Bohn, 1849.

Schlegel, August Wilhelm. *Geschichte der romantischen Litteratur*. Vol. 3 of *Vorlesungen über schöne Litteratur und Kunst*. Stuttgart: Göschen'sche Verlagshandlung, 1884.

Schlosser, Johann Georg. "Schreiben an Herrn Hofrath Wieland in Weimar über die Abderiten im deutschen Merkur." *Deutsches Museum* 1 (1776): 147–161.

Schmitz, Heinz-Günter. "Consuetudo und simulatio: Zur Thematik des Lalebuchs." In *Wunderseltsame Geschichten: Interpretationen zu Schildbürgern und Lalebuch*, edited by Werner Wunderlich, 121–141. Göppingen, Germany: Kümmerle Verlag, 1983.

———. "Die melancholischen Schildbürger: Das *Lale-* oder *Schiltbürgerbuch* im Licht der zeitgenössischen Anthropologie und Medizin." *Eulenspiegel-Jahrbuch* 39 (1999): 79–93.

———. "Das 'Volksbuch' von den Schildbürgern: Beobachtungen zur Wirkungsgeschichte." *Daphnis* 33 (2004): 661–681.

Schnyder, André. "Bibliographie zum Prosaroman des 15. und 16. Jahrhunderts." In *Eulenspiegel trifft Melusine: Der frühneuhochdeutsche Prosaroman im Licht neuer Forschungen und Methoden*, edited by Catherine Drittenbass and André Schnyder, 557–609. Amsterdam: Rodopi, 2010.

Scholem, Gershom. *On the Kabbalah and Its Symbolism.* Translated by Ralph Manheim. New York: Schocken Books, 1965.

Schöttgen, Johann Christian. *Inventarium diplomaticum historiae Saxoniae superioris: Das ist, Verzeichnis derer Uhrkunden der Historie von Ober-Sachsen.* Halle, Germany: Waysenhaus, 1747.

Schöttgen, Johann Christian [Johann Christoph Langner, pseud.]. *Vertheidigung der Stadt Schilda, Wider die gemeinen doch ungebührlichen Auflagen bey müßigen Stunden entworffen.* Frankfurt, 1747.

Schöttgen, Johann Christian, and Georg Christoph Kreysig. *Diplomatische und curieuse Nachlese der Historie von Ober-Sachsen und angräntzenden Ländern.* Vol. 2. Dresden: Hekel, 1730.

Schudt, Johann Jacob. *Jüdisches Franckfurter und Prager Freuden-Fest / Wegen der höchst-glücklichen Geburth des Durchläuchtigsten Kayserlichen Erb-Printzens.* Frankfurt: Matthias Andreä, 1716.

Schüler, Meier. "Beiträge zur Kenntnis der alten jüdisch-deutschen Profanliteratur." In *Festschrift zum 75jährigen Bestehen der Realschule mit Lyzeum der Israelitischen Religionsgesellschaft Frankfurt am Main*, 79–132. Frankfurt: Hermon-Verlag.

Schulz, Johann Gottlob [Heinrich Ringwald, pseud.]. *Die neuen Schildbürger oder Lalenburg in den Tagen der Aufklärung.* Nuremberg, Germany, 1791.

Schummel, Johann Gottlieb. *Die Revolution in Scheppenstedt: Eine Volksschrift.* Germanien [Breslau]: Gutsch, 1794.

Schwab, Gustav. *Buch der schönsten Geschichten und Sagen für Alt und Jung wieder erzählt.* Stuttgart: Liesching, 1836.

Schwartz, Amy. *Yossel Zissel and the Wisdom of Chelm.* Philadelphia: Jewish Publication Society, 1986.

Schwarz, Jan. *Survivors and Exiles: Yiddish Culture after the Holocaust.* Detroit: Wayne State University Press, 2015.

———. "Trunk, Yekhiel Yeshaye." In *The YIVO Encyclopedia of Jews in Eastern Europe*, edited by Gershon Hundert, vol. 2, 1908–1909. New Haven, CT: Yale University Press, 2008.

Schwarzbaum, Haim. *Studies in Jewish and World Folklore.* Berlin: de Gruyter, 1968.

Seelbach, Ulrich. "*Die newe Zeitungen auß der gantzen Welt*: Der Anhang des *Lalebuchs* und die Logik der Lügendichtung." *Eulenspiegel-Jahrbuch* 39 (1999): 95–111.

Segel, Binjamin [Benjamin Wolf Schiffer, pseud.]. "Abderiten von heute unter den Juden." *Am Ur-Quell* 3 (1892): 27–29.

———. "Das Brillantendiadem: Eine Geschichte aus Chelm." *Die Wahrheit* 40, no. 43 (1924): 5–6.

———. *Die Entdeckungsreise des Herrn Dr. Theodor Lessing zu den Ostjuden.* Lemberg: Hatikwa, 1910.

———. "Die Flucht aus der Wirklichkeit." *Im deutschen Reich: Zeitschrift des Centralvereins Deutscher Staatsbürger Jüdischen Glaubens* 25 (1919): 145–159.

———. "Die Juden in Rußland unter Nikolaus I.: Ein Kapitel aus der jüdischen Martyrologie." *Der Morgen: Monatsschrift der Juden in Deutschland* 3 (1927): 251–269.

———. *A Lie and a Libel: The History of the Protocols of the Elders of Zion.* Translated by Richard S. Levy. Lincoln: University of Nebraska Press, 1995.

———. "Meine Beichte." *Ost und West* 13 (1913): 149–152.

———. "O mieście Chełmie, którego mieszkańcy słyną z głupoty." In *Materyał do etnografii żydów wschodnio-galicyjskich,* 43–45. Cracow: Nakładem Akademii Umiejtności, 1893.

———. "Philosophie des Pogroms." *Ost und West,* nos. 3–4 (1923): 59–92.

———. *Die polnische Judenfrage.* Berlin: Georg Stilke, 1916.

———. *Die Protokolle der Weisen von Zion kritisch beleuchtet, eine Erledigung.* Berlin: Philo Verlag, 1924.

———. "Die Tätigkeit der Frankfurter 'Weiblichen Fürsorge' in Galizien," *Frankfurter Israelitisches Familienblatt* 9, no. 22 (June 1, 1911): 1–2; no. 23 (June 9, 1911): 1–2.

———. *Welt-Krieg, Welt-Revolution, Welt-Verschwörung, Welt-Oberregierung.* Berlin: Philo Verlag, 1926.

Selig, Gottfried. *Lehrbuch zur gründlichen Erlernung der jüdischdeutschen Sprache für Beamte, Gerichtsverwandte, Advocaten und insbesondere für Kaufleute.* Leipzig: Voß und Leo, 1792.

Shammes, Yuspa. *Seyfer mayse nisim.* Amsterdam: Asher Anshel ben Elieser, 1696.

Shandler, Jeffrey. *Adventures in Yiddishland: Postvernacular Language and Culture.* Berkeley: University of California Press, 2006.

Shatin, Leo. *Simple Wisdom: Modern Tales from Chelm.* Minneapolis: Syren, 2007.

Shatzky, Jacob. "Review of Yizker Books—1955." In *Memorial Books of Eastern European Jewry: Essays on the History and Meaning of Yizker Volumes,* edited by Rosemary Horowitz, 68–80. Jefferson, NC: McFarland, 2011.

Shavit, Zohar. "From Friedländer's Lesebuch to the Jewish Campe: The Beginning of Hebrew Children's Literature in Germany." *Leo Baeck Institute Year Book* 33 (1988): 385–415.

———. "Literary Interference between German and Jewish-Hebrew Children's Literature during the Enlightenment: The Case of Campe." *Poetics Today* 13 (1992): 41–61.

Sheinkin, Steve. *Rabbi Harvey Rides Again: A Graphic Novel of Jewish Folktales Let Loose in the Wild West.* Woodstock, VT: Jewish Light, 2008.

———. *Rabbi Harvey vs. the Wisdom Kid: A Graphic Novel of Dueling Jewish Folktales in the Wild West.* Woodstock, VT: Jewish Light, 2010.

Sheil, Susan Meld. *Kant and the Limits of Autonomy*. Cambridge, MA: Harvard University Press, 2009.

Sherman, Joseph. "Dik, Ayzik Meyer." In *The YIVO Encyclopedia of Jews in Eastern Europe*, edited by Gershon Hundert, vol. 1, 405–407 New Haven, CT: Yale University Press, 2008.

———. "Isaac Bashevis Singer." In *Writers in Yiddish: Dictionary of Literary Biography*, edited by Joseph Sherman, 345–350. Detroit: Gale, 2007.

Shiper, Yitskhok. *Geshikhte fun yidisher teater-kunst un drame: Fun di eltste tsaytn biz 1750*. Warsaw: Kultur-lige, 1923.

———[Ignatz Schipper]. "Jiddische Literatur." In *Encyclopaedia Judaica: Das Judentum in Geschichte und Gegenwart*, edited by Jakob Klatzkin and Ismar Elbogen, vol. 9, 127–171. Berlin: Eschkol, 1932.

Shmeruk, Khone. *Prokim fun der yidisher literatur-geshikhte*. Tel Aviv: Peretz, 1988.

———. "Yitskhok Bashevis: Der mayse-dertseyler far kinder." *Oksforder yidish* 3 (1995): 233–280.

Sholem Aleichem. "The Bewitched Tailor." Translated by Bernard Isaacs. Moscow: Foreign Languages Publishing House, 1958.

———. "The Enchanted Tailor." Translated by Julius Butwin and Frances Butwin. In *The Old Country*, 93–137. New York: Crown, 1946.

———. "Der farkishefter shnayder." In *Ale verk*, vol. 13, *Mayses un monologn*, 3–51. Warsaw: Progres, 1913.

———. "A frier peysekh." *Der fraynd*, April 9 and 12, 1908, 2; April 13, 1908, 2–3.

———. "The Haunted Tailor." Translated by Leonard Wolf. In *The Best of Sholom Aleichem*. edited by Irving Howe and Ruth R. Wisse, 2–36. Washington, DC: New Republic Books, 1979.

———. "A Premature Passover." Translated by Adda Birman. In *Sholem Aleichem Panorama*, edited by Melech W. Grafstein, 109–122. London, ON: Jewish Observer, 1948.

Shookman, Ellis. *Noble Lies, Slant Thruths, Necessary Angels: Aspects of Fictionality on the Novels of Christoph Martin Wieland*. Chapel Hill: University of North Carolina Press, 1997.

Shtern, M. *Hershele Ostropoler un Motke Khabad: Zeyere anekdotn, vitsn, stsenes un shtukes*. New York: Star Hibru buk kompani, 1925.

Shteynbarg, Eliezer. "Khoykerl-hoykerl." In *Mayselekh*, 153–178. Cernăuti, Romania: Komitet af aroystsugebn Eliezer Shteynbargs shriftn, 1936.

Sidon, Ephraim. *Maʾaleh Karaḥot*. Tel Aviv: Am Oved, 1980.

Simon, Bettina. *Jiddische Sprachgeschichte: Versuch einer Grundlegung*. Frankfurt: Jüdischer Verlag, 1993.

Simon, Solomon [Shloyme Seymon]. *Di helden fun Khelm*. New York: Matones, 1942.

———. *Khakhomim, akshonim un naronim: Mayses fun alerley felker*. Buenos Aires: Alter Rozental-fond far yidishe kinder-literatur, 1959.

———. "Der kligster fun ale naronim: An indishe Khelem mayse." In *Khakhomim, akshonim un naronim: Mayses fun alerley felker*, 57–59. Buenos Aires: Alter Rozental-fond far yidishe kinder-literatur, 1959.

———. *More Wise Men of Helm and Their Merry Tales.* Edited by Hannah Grad Good-man. New York: Behrman House, 1965.

———. "An ofene tir: An indishe Khelem mayse." In *Khakhomim, akshonim un naronim: Mayses fun alerley felker,* 33–36. Buenos Aires: Alter Rozental-fond far yidishe kinder-literatur, 1959.

———. "Shir an umglik in Khelem." In *Khakhomim, akshonim un naronim: Mayses fun alerley felker,* 119–123. Buenos Aires: Alter Rozental-fond far yidishe kinder-literatur, 1959.

———. *The Wise Men of Helm and Their Merry Tales.* Translated by Ben Bengal and David Simon. New York: Behrman House, 1945.

Simrock, Karl, ed. *Die deutschen Sprichwörter.* Frankfurt am Main: Brönner, 1846.

———, ed. *Wunderseltsame, abenteuerliche und bisher unbeschriebene Geschichten und Thaten der Schildbürger in Misnopotamien, hinter Utopia gelegen.* Berlin: Vereins-Buchhandlung, 1843.

Singer, Isaac Bashevis [D. Segal, pseud.]. "Bolvan der ershter un zayn ayzerne hant." *Forverts,* February 27, 1967.

———. "Dalfunka, di shtot vu gvirim lebn eybig." *Forverts,* March 7, 1974.

———. "Dalfunka Where the Rich Live Forever: A Story for Children." *New York Times,* March, 28, 1976.

———. *The Fools of Chelm and Their History.* Translated by the author and Elizabeth Shub. New York: Farrar, Straus and Giroux, 1973.

———. "The Fools of Chelm and the Stupid Carp." Translated by the author and Ruth Schachner Finkel. *Cricket,* November 1973, 77–84. Reprinted in *Stories for Children,* 69–76. New York: Farrar, Straus and Giroux, 1984.

———[D. Segal, pseud.]. "Der groyser zets un di antshteyung fun Khelm." *Forverts,* October 11, 1966.

———[Yitskhok Varshavski, pseud.] "A kapitel Khelmer geshikhte." *Forverts,* September 27, 1967.

———[D. Segal, pseud.]. "Kapitlekh fun der Khelmer geshikhte." *Forverts,* October 19, 1966.

———[D. Segal, pseud.]. "Khelm bashlist tsu firen milkhome." *Forverts,* October 25, 1966.

———[D. Segal, pseud.]. "Di Khelmer revolutsye un vos zi hot gebrakht." *Forverts,* February 8, 1967.

———[D. Segal, pseud.]. "Khelm un Mazl-Borsht." *Forverts,* January 12, 1967.

———. *Naftali the Storyteller and His Horse, Sus and Other Stories.* New York: Farrar, Straus and Giroux, 1976.

———[D. Segal, pseud.]. "Der narishe khosn un di farbitene fis." *Forverts,* November 16, 1965.

———. *Die Narren von Chelm und ihre Geschichte.* Translated by Rolf Inhauser. Aarau, Switzerland: Sauerländer, 1975.

———. [D. Segal, pseud.]. "A naye epokhe in Khelm." *Forverts,* December 27, 1966.

———[D. Segal, pseud.]. "Di naye partey fun di Khelmer komitetn." *Forverts*, January 4, 1967.

———[Yitshok Bashevis, pseud.]. "Nokh vegn di Khelmer khakhomim: A fish an azes-ponem." *Forverts*, February 12, 1972.

———[Yitshok Bashevis, pseud.]. "Nokh vegn di Khelmer khakhomim: Der Khelmer barg." *Forverts*, February 18, 1972.

———[D. Segal, pseud.]. "Di parteyen in vaysen Khelm un zeyere makhlokesn." *Forverts*, March 9, 1967.

———[D. Segal, pseud.]. "Di 'politishe ekonomye' fun Khelm." *Forverts*, March 10, 1966.

———[D. Segal, pseud.]. "Di revolutsye in Khelm." *Forverts*, November 30, 1966.

———[D. Segal, pseud.]. "Der sakh-hakl fun der geshikhte fun Khelm." *Forverts*, March 16, 1967.

———. *Stories for Children*. New York: Farrar, Straus and Giroux, 1984.

———[D. Segal, pseud.]. "Di tseteylung fun Khelm un di rezultatn derfun." *Forverts*, February 21, 1967.

———[D. Segal, pseud.]. "Tsores in Khelm un a kluge eytse." *Forverts*, November 22, 1966.

———[D. Segal, pseud.]. "Vi azoy es hot gearbet di Khelmer demokratye." *Forverts*, January 30, 1967.

———[Yitskhok Varshavski, pseud.] "Vi azoy Khelm iz geblibn on gelt." *Forverts*, September 28, 1967.

———. *When Shlemiel Went to Warsaw and Other Stories*. New York: Farrar, Straus and Giroux, 1968.

———. *Zlateh the Goat and Other Stories*. Translated by Isaac Bashevis Singer and Elizabeth Shub. New York: Harper and Row, 1966.

Sinkoff, Nancy. *Out of the Shtetl: Making Jews Modern in the Polish Borderlands*. Providence, RI: Brown Judaic Studies, 2004.

Solomon, Alisa. *Wonder of Wonders: A Cultural History of "Fiddler on the Roof."* New York: Metropolitan, 2013.

Spitz, Leon. "Chelm—The City of Fools: A Humorous Chapter of Jewish Folk Lore." *American Hebrew*, May 3, 1940.

Stahl, Neta. *Other and Brother: Jesus in the 20th-Century Jewish Literary Landscape*. Oxford: Oxford University Press, 2013.

Stallybrass, Peter, and Allon White. *The Politics and Poetics of Transgression*. Ithaca, NY: Cornell University Press, 1986.

Stampfer, Shaul. "The 1764 Census of Lithuanian Jewry." Working paper. Duke-UNC Jewish Studies Seminar, November 16, 2014.

Staub, Friedrich, and Ludwig Tobler, *Schweizerisches Idiotikon: Wörterbuch der schweizerdeutschen Sprache*. Vol. 3. Frauenfeld, Germany: Huber, 1895.

Stein, Sarah Abrevaya. *Making Jews Modern: The Yiddish and Ladino Press in the Russian and Ottoman Empire*. Bloomington: Indiana University Press, 2004.

Steinschneider, Moritz. "Jüdisch-Deutsche Literatur nach einem handschriftlichen Katalog der Oppenheim'schen Bibliothek (in Oxford)." *Serapeum* 3 (1849): 42–48.

———. "Jüdische Litteratur und Jüdisch-Deutsch: Mit besonderer Berücksichtigung auf Avé-Lallemant." *Serapeum* 25 (1864): 33–104.

Sterne, Laurence. *The Life and Opinions of Tristram Shandy, Gentleman.* 9 vols. London: R. and J. Dodsley, 1760–1768.

Straßner, Erich. "Schildbürgerorte in Franken." *Bayerisches Jahrbuch für Volkskunde,* 1966–1967, 155–171.

Sulzbach, A. "Ein alter Frankfurter Wohltätigkeitsverein." *Jahrbuch der Jüdisch-Literarischen Gesellschaft* 2 (1904): 241–266.

Szeintuch, Yechiel. "Aharon Tsaitlin ve-hate'atron be-yidish: al maḥazotav beyn shtey milḥamot ha-olam." In *Brener, Esterkeh, Vaitsman ha-sheni: Shelosha maḥazot,* 11–56. Jerusalem: Magnes, 1993.

———. *Bi-reshut ha-rabim uvi-reshut ha-yaḥid: Aharon Tsaitlin ve-sifrut yidish.* Jerusalem: Magnes, 2000.

Taback, Simms. *Kibitzers and Fools: Tales My Zayda (Grandfather) Told Me.* New York: Viking, 2005.

Tango, Jenny. *Women of Chelm.* N.p.: Akko, 1991.

Taylor, Dov. Introduction to *Joseph Perl's "Revealer of Secrets": The First Hebrew Novel,* by Joseph Perl, xix–lxxv. Boulder, CO: Westview, 1997.

Tenberg, Reinhard. *Die deutsche Till-Eulenspiegel-Rezeption bis zum Ende des 16. Jahrhunderts.* Würzburg, Germany: Königshausen and Neumann, 1996.

Tendlau, Abraham M. *Das Buch der Sagen und Legenden jüdischer Vorzeit.* Stuttgart: J. F. Cast, 1842.

———. *Sprichwörter und Redensarten deutsch-jüdischer Vorzeit: Als Beitrag zur Volks-, Sprach- und Sprichwörter-Kunde.* Frankfurt: Kauffmann, 1860.

Tenenbaum, Samuel. *The Wise Men of Chelm.* New York: T. Yoseloff, 1965.

Thompson, Edward P. "'Rough Music': Le charivari anglais." *Annales: Economies, sociétés, civilisations* 27 (1972): 285–312.

Thümmel, Moritz August von. *Wilhelmine, ein prosaisch komisches Gedicht.* Leipzig: Weidmanns Erben und Reich, 1773.

Tieck, Ludwig. *Denkwürdige Geschichtschronik der Schildbürger, 1796.* In *Schriften,* vol. 9, 1–82. Berlin: Reimer, 1828.

Timm, Erika. *Historische jiddische Semantik: Die Bibelübersetzungssprache als Faktor der Auseinanderentwicklung des jiddischen und deutschen Wortschatzes.* Tübingen, Germany: Niemeyer, 2005.

———. "Jiddische Literatur." In *Literaturlexikon,* edited by Walther Killy, vol. 13, 457–460. Berlin: de Gruyter, 1992.

Toybin, B. "Khelm iz nit di eyntsike shtot fun naronim." *Der khaver,* May 1, 1930, 361–374.

Tozman, Naomi. "Kinder zshurnal: A Microcosm of the Yiddishist Philosophy and Secular Education Movement in America." PhD diss., McGill University, 1993.

Trunk, Yekhiel Yeshaye. *Der freylekhster yid in der velt oder Hersheles lern-yorn.* Buenos Aires: Yidbukh, 1953.

———. *Khelemer khakhomim oder yidn fun der kligster shtot in der velt.* Buenos Aires: Yidbukh, 1951.

———. *Kvaln un beymer: Historishe noveln un eseys.* New York: Unzer tsayt, 1958.

———. *Meshiekh-geviter: Historisher roman fun di tsaytn fun Shabse Tsvi; Yidn kukn aroys fun di fentster: Elf mayses fun Bal Shem.* New York: CYCO, 1961.

———. *Poyln: Zikhroynes un bilder.* 7 vols. New York: Unzer tsayt, 1944–1953.

———. *Sholem-Aleykhem: Zayn vezn un zayne verk.* Warsaw: Kultur-lige, 1937.

———. *Yidishe kultur-fragn un der sotsyalizm.* Warsaw: Kultur-lige, 1935.

Turniansky, Chava. "Old Yiddish Language and Literature." In *Jewish Women: A Comprehensive Historical Encyclopedia.* Jewish Women's Archive, March 1, 2009. http://jwa.org/encyclopedia/article/old-yiddish-language-and-literature.

———. "Yiddish and the Transmission of Knowledge in Early Modern Europe." *Jewish Studies Quarterly* 15 (2008): 5–18.

Tyrnau, Isaac. *Seyfer minhogim.* Translated by Simon Levi Ginzburg. Prague: Ortits, 1610–1611.

Ude-Koeller, Susanne. "Kirche verschieben." In *Enzyklopädie des Märchens: Handwörterbuch zur historischen und vergleichenden Erzählforschung,* edited by Rolf Wilhelm Brednich, vol. 7, 1380–1384. Berlin: de Gruyter, 1993.

Uhland, Ludwig. *Uhlands Schriften zur Geschichte der Dichtung und Sage.* Vol. 7. Edited by Wilhelm Ludwig Holland, Adelbert von Keller, and Franz Pfeiffer. Stuttgart: Cotta, 1868.

Ulinover, Miryam. "Di antlofene levone." *Inzl* 4 (1938): 5.

———. "Fun Khelem keyn Lublin." *Inzl* 2 (1938): 8.

———. "Der ganef un der shoymer." *Haynt,* March 25, 1938, 7.

———. "Khelem oyf der mape." *Haynt,* March, 18, 1938, 6.

———. "Lomir helfn dreyen di erd." *Haynt,* April 1, 1938, 7.

———. "Di nekome on di vantsn." *Inzl* 2 (1938): 8.

———. "Oysgemishte fislekh." *Haynt,* April 1, 1938, 7.

———. "Di telegraf-drotn." *Haynt,* March, 18, 1938, 6.

———. "Tey un tilim." *Haynt,* March 25, 1938, 7.

———. "Der tsvayer." *Haynt,* March, 18, 1938, 6.

———. "Umet." *Haynt,* March 25, 1938, 7.

Uther, Hans-Jörg. *Animal Tales, Tales of Magic, Religious Tales, and Realistic Tales.* Vol. 2 of *The Types of International Folktales.* Helsinki: Suomalainen Tiedeakatemia, 2004.

———. "Rattenfänger von Hameln." In *Enzyklopädie des Märchens,* edited by Rolf Wilhelm Brednich, vol. 11, 300–307. Berlin: de Gruyter, 2004.

Vaynig, Naftole. "Benyomin Volf Zegel (1866–1931)." *YIVO-bleter* 3 (1932): 91–93.

Vaynlez, Yisroel. "Mendl Lefin-Satanover." *YIVO bleter* 2 (1931): 334–357.

———. "R. Menaḥem Mendel Lefin mi-Satanov." *ha-'Olam* 13 (1925): 39: 778–779; 40: 799–800; 41: 19–20; 42: 39–40.

Velten, Hans Rudolf. "Die verbannten Weisen: Zu antiken und humanistischen Diskursen von Macht, Exil und Glück im Lalebuch (1597)." *Daphnis* 33 (2004): 709–744.

*Vielerley lustige Historien und Geschichte / Oder Zeit-Verkürtzer bey allerhand lustigen Gesellschafften / Reisen / auch bey Frauen-Zimmer sehr lustig und kurtzweilig zu lesen und zu erzehlen.* N.p.: n.p., 1698.

"Vodevil vitsn." *Forverts*, February 25, 1923.

Volksmann, H. "Abderiten von heute." *Am Ur-Quell* 2 (1891): 169–170.

Voß, Rebekka. "Entangled Stories: The Red Jews in Premodern Yiddish and German Apocalyptic Lore." *AJS Review* 36 (2012): 1–41.

*Vunderlikhe und komishe geshikhte fon Ayln-shpigl.* Nowy Dwór, Poland: Johan Anton Kriger, 1805–1806.

Wagenseil, Johann Christoph. *Belehrung der Jüdisch-Teutschen Red- und Schreibart.* Königsberg, Germany: Rhode, 1699.

Wander, Fred. *The Seventh Well.* Translated by Michael Hofmann. New York: Norton 2005.

———. *Der siebente Brunnen.* Berlin: Aufbau, 1974.

Wander, Karl Friedrich Wilhelm. *Deutsches Sprichwörter-Lexikon: Ein Hausschatz für das deutsche Volk.* 5 vols. Leipzig: Brockhaus, 1867–1880.

Weiman, Ralph. Review of *College Yiddish. Commentary*, January 1, 1950, 98–100..

Weinreich, Beatrice Silverman, ed. *Yiddish Folktales.* New York: Pantheon Books, 1988.

Weinreich, Max. *History of the Yiddish Language.* Edited by Paul Glasser. Translated by Shlomo Noble, with the assistance of Joshua A. Fishman. 2 vols. New Haven, CT: Yale University Press, 2008.

Weinreich, Uriel. *College Yiddish: An Introduction to the Yiddish Language and to Jewish Life and Culture.* New York: YIVO, 1949.

Weiser, Keith Ian. *Jewish People, Yiddish Nation: Noah Prylucki and the Folkists in Poland.* Toronto: University of Toronto Press, 2011.

Weissberg, Liliane. "Salomon Maimon Writes His *Lebensgeschichte* (Autobiography): A Reflection on His Life in the (Polish) East and the (German) West." In *Yale Companion to Jewish Writing and Thought in German Culture: 1096–1996*, edited by Sander L. Gilman and Jack Zipes, 108–115. New Haven, CT: Yale University Press, 1997.

Welsford, Enid. *The Fool: His Social and Literary History.* London: Faber and Faber, 1935.

Werses, Shmuel. "Bein shnei olamot: Yaakov Shmuel Bik bein haskalah le-ḥasidut—iyun meḥudash." In *Megamot ve-tsurot be-sifrut ha-haskala*, 110–159. Jerusalem: Magnes, 1990.

———. "Ha-dei ha-satira shel Lukianus be-sifrut ha-haskala ha-ivrit." In *Megamot ve-tsurot be-sifrut ha-haskala*, 223–248. Jerusalem: Magnes, 1990.

Wiecki, Evita. "*Untervegs*: A Journey with the Yiddish Textbook." *European Judaism* 42 (2009): 47–61.

Wieland, Christoph Martin. *Die Abderiten: Eine sehr wahrscheinliche Geschichte. Der Teutsche Merkur*, January 1774, 33–112; February 1774, 145–220; May 1774, 125–165;

July 1774, 35–46; July 1778, 26–59; August 1778, 128–144; September 1778, 218–240; October 1778, 37–46; November 1778, 117–136; August 1780, 81–131; September 1780, 183–214.

———. "Auszug aus einem Schreiben an einen Freund in D*** über die Abderiten im 7ten St. des T. M. d. J." *Der Teutsche Merkur*, September 1778, 241–259.

———. "A Couple of Gold Nuggets, from the . . . Wastepaper, or Six Answers to Six Questions." Translated by Kevin Paul Geiman and James Schmidt. In *What Is Enlightenment? Eighteenth-Century Answers and Twentieth-Century Questions*, edited by James Schmidt, 78–83. Berkeley: University of California Press, 1996.

———. "Das Geheimniß des Kosmopolitenordens." *Der Teutsche Merkur*, August 1788, 97–115; November 1788, 121–143.

———. *Geschichte der Abderiten*. In *Christoph Martin Wieland Werke*, edited by Fritz Martini and Hans Werner Seiffert, vol. 2, 121–445. Munich: Hanser, 1966.

———. *History of the Abderites*. Translated by Max Dufner. Bethlehem, PA: Lehigh University Press, 1993.

———. "Nachricht von Sebastian Brand." *Der Teutsche Merkur*, January 1776, 71–76.

———. "Ein paar Goldkörner aus – Makulatur oder Sechs Antworten auf sechs Fragen." *Der Teutsche Merkur* 2 (April 1789): 94–105.

———. "Ueber Sebastian Brands Narrenschiff und D. Johann Gaylers v. Kaysersbergs Weltspiegel." *Der Teutsche Merkur*, February 1776, 168–174.

Wiener, Leo. *The History of Yiddish Literature in the Nineteenth Century*. New York: Charles Scribner's Sons, 1899.

Wischnitzer, Mark. "Chelm." In *Encyclopaedia Judaica: Das Judentum in Geschichte und Gegenwart*, edited by Jakob Klatzkin and Ismar Elbogen, vol. 5, 407–408. Berlin: Eschkol, 1930.

Wisse, Ruth R. *The Schlemiel as Modern Hero*. Chicago: University of Chicago Press, 1971.

Wodziński, Marcin. "Chełm." In *YIVO Encyclopedia of Jews in Eastern Europe*, edited by Gershon Hundert, vol. 1, 309–310. New Haven, CT: Yale University Press, 2008.

———. *Haskalah and Hasidism in the Kingdom of Poland: A History of Conflict*. Oxford, UK: Littman Library of Jewish Civilization, 2005.

Wolf, Johann Christoph. *Bibliotheca hebraea*. 4 vols. Hamburg: Liebezeit, 1715–1733.

Wolf, Siegmund A. *Wörterbuch des Rotwelschen: Deutsche Gaunersprache*. Hamburg: Buske, 1985.

Wolitz, Seth L. "*Der yid fun bovl*: Variants and Meanings." In *Isaac Bashevis Singer: His Work and His World*, edited by Hugh Denman, 31–47. Leiden, Netherlands: Brill, 2002.

———, ed. *The Hidden Isaac Bashevis Singer*. Austin: University of Texas Press, 2001.

Wolpe, Rebecca. "Judaizing *Robinson Crusoe*: *Maskilic* Translations of *Robinson Crusoe*." *Jewish Culture and History* 13 (2012): 42–67.

Woltersdorf, Ernst Gabriel. *Jahrbuch der gesammten Literatur und Ereignisse betreffend die Erdbeschreibung, Geschlechter-, Wappen-, Münz- und Staatenkunde, die Staatswissenschaft, Zeitrechnung, Politische Geschichte und Archäologie von 1824 und 1825*. Berlin: Oehmigke, 1826.

Wunderlich, Werner. "*Schildbürgerstreiche*: Bericht zur Lalebuch- und Schildbürger-forschung." *Deutsche Vierteljahresschrift für Literaturwissenschaft und Geistesge-schichte* 56 (1982): 641–685.

Würfel, Andreas. *Historische Nachricht von der Judengemeinde in dem Hofmarkt Fürth unterhalb Nürnberg*. Frankfurt, 1754.

Wurzbach, Constantin von. *Glimpf und Schimpf in Spruch und Wort: Sprach- und sit-tengeschichtliche Aphorismen*. Vienna: R. Lechner, 1864.

Yakubovitsh, Avrom-Leyb. "Alter Ayzenshlos." In *Leksikon fun der yidisher literatur, prese un filologye*, edited by Zalmen Reyzen, vol. 1, 73–75. Vilna: Kletskin, 1926.

Yanasovitsh, Yitskhok. "Di 'Khelemer mayse' un di yidishe literatur." In *Yizker-bukh Khelm*, edited by Melekh Bakaltshuk-Felin, 45–52. Johannesburg, South Africa: Khelmer landsmanshaft, 1954.

Zaremba, Michael. *Christoph Martin Wieland: Aufklärer und Poet*. Cologne: Böhlau, 2007.

Zarncke, Friedrich. "Des Paulus Aemilius Romanus Uebersetzung der Bücher Samu-elis." In *Berichte über die Verhandlungen der Königlich Sächsischen Gesellschaft der Wissenschaften zu Leipzig*, 212–226. Leipzig: Hirzel, 1871.

Zedler, Johann Heinrich. *Grosses vollständiges Universal-Lexicon aller Wissenschafften und Künste*. Vol. 52. Leipzig, 1747.

Zeiller, Martin. *Itinerarium Germaniae Nov-antiquae*. Strasbourg: Zetzner, 1632.

———. *Topographia Superioris Saxoniae Thüringiae*. Frankfurt: Merian, 1650.

———. *Topographia Superioris Saxoniae Thüringiae*. 2nd ed. Frankfurt: Merian, 1690.

Zeltser, Chaim. *Shtern oyfn yarid oder di festung fun khokhme*. Tel Aviv: Israel-Book, 1985.

Zinberg, Israel. *A History of Jewish Literature*. 12 vols. Cincinnati: Hebrew Union Col-lege Press, 1972–1978.

Zirlin, Yael. "Joel Meets Johannes: A Fifteenth-Century Jewish-Christian Collaboration in Manuscript Illustration." *Viator* 26 (1995): 265–282.

# INDEX

Page numbers in italics refer to illustrations and maps.

Abbaye de Conards, 44, 69

Abbaye de Cornards, 44

Abbaye de Liesse, 44

abbot of misrule, 44, 55, 71

Abdera, 21, 112, 114–115, 120, 122, 130, 135, 151, 157, 158, 159; in ancient literature, 243n9; in *Bohen tsadik* (Perl), 128–130, 176; and Brody, 129–130, 176; and Chelm, 171, 174, 177, 183, 211; as foolish town, 21, 114, 116–118, 121, 123, 127, 130, 151, 157, 159, 172, 174, 176, 177, 180, 183, 211; as literary topic, 115, 116; and "Oyzer Tsinkes un di tsig," 21; and Schildburg/Schilda, 116, 118, 121–122, 151, 157, 250n30, 183. See also *History of the Abderites; Nachlass eines Sonderlings zu Abdera*

*Die Abderiten: Eine sehr wahrscheinliche Geschichte* (Wieland). See *History of the Abderites*

"Abderiten von heute unter den Juden" (Segel), 151, 171, 173–176, 177, 178–179, 183, 184, 190; and Chelm, 151, 171, 174–175, 176, 177, 179; and *Schildbürgerbuch*, 174–175, 177, 179, 184

*Abderitenstreich* (Abderite antics), 157–158

Abderitism, 116, 157–158

Abolafia, Yossi, 217

Abraham Joshua Heschel of Apt, 144

Abramovitsh, Sholem Yankev, 19, 137

Adler, David, 215, 224n6

Agnon, Shmuel Yosef, 194

*agune*, 139

Aksenfeld, Yisroel, 137

Aleichem, Sholem. See Sholem Aleichem

Alexander II, Tsar of Russia, 140

Alkvit, B., 14

Allen, Woody, 9

*Allgemeine Zeitung des Judentums* (Berlin), 178

Almi, A., 182

alphabet: Hebrew, 77, 81, 83, 84, 91; Jews and Western script, 79–80, 82–84, 167, 194; Jews' disapprobation of Roman script, 82–83; Latin characters, 79, 82. See also *galkhes*

Alteration (Netherlands), 102

*Am Urdsbrunnen* (Rendsburg), 249n4. See also *Am Ur-Quell*

*Am Ur-Quell* (Hamburg), 151, 171–174, 176–177, 180; Chelm tales in, 174–177, 179, 183, 184

Amsterdam, 7, 78, 82, 85, 90, 102, 108, 152

*Anatomy of Melancholy* (Burton), 243n9

Andree, Richard, 172–173, 177, 184

Angel of Death, 12–13, 21, 227n80

*The Angel's Mistake* (Prose), 31

*Annalen der Universität zu Schilda* (Laukhard), 157

"Anno 1839" (Heine), 164–165

anti-Zionism, 171, 180

*Antiklerikale folks-mayses* (Mirer), 206

antisemitism, 91, 151, 177, 178, 209
Argentina: Yiddish literature in, 17, 24, 30;
    Yiddish theater in, 16, 17
Arndt, Ernst Moritz, 250n30
*Ars poetica* (Horace), 96
Ashkenazy, Daniella, 216
Association of Jewish Writers and
    Journalists in Warsaw. *See* Fareyn
    fun yidishe literatn un zhurnalistn in
    Varshe
Athens, 28; as literary place, 118
Atkinson, Brooks, 17, 23
Atticus, Titus Pomponius, 74
Aurbacher, Ludwig, 162–163
"Aus dem Leben des hohen Rabbi Löw"
    (Bloch), 255n5
Austrian National Library, 238n24
Austro-Hungarian (Habsburg) Empire,
    102, 113, 127, 131, 141, 142, 177, 178
Ausubel, Nathan, 17; "The Chelm Goat
    Mystery," 22; *Treasury of Jewish Folk-
    lore*, 17, 19, 22–23, 214
Avé-Lallemant, Friedrich Christian
    Benedict, 92
*Ayn nay lid ouf der megile* (Efrayim bar
    Yuda Levi), 82
Ayzenshlos, Alter, 204
Ayzenshlos, Rokhl Leye, 204

Baal Shem Tov, Israel, 126, 256n7
*badkhn* (pl. *badkhonim*), 45, 58
Bakhtin, Mikhail, 43–44
"Di balade fun Hershele Ostropoler mit
    der levone" (Manger), 233n51
Barnai, Yossi, 217
Barry Sisters, 212
Basel, 67
Bässler, Andreas, 68
Bastomski, Shloyme, 207
Baumgarten, Jean, 46, 48
Bavarian State Library, 52, 226n58
Bayle, Pierre, 120, 122
Bebel, Heinrich, 67

Becher, Yosef, 247n113
Beer, Peter, 83
Beireis, Gottfried Christoph, 90
*Belehrung der Jüdisch-Teutschen Red- und
    Schreibart* (Wagenseil), 81–83
Belkin, Ahuva, 46, 48
Belorussia as literary place, 198
Ben Mordekhai, 14, 15
ben Ze'ev, Judah Leib, 130
Bengal, Ben, 30
Berdichev, 182
*Berdychiv. See* Berdichev
Berkowicz, Michael, 194–195
Berlin, 92, 125, *152*, 159, 173, 194, 225n35,
    237n56; Haskalah in, 116, 123–124, 130,
    168–169
Berlin Wall, 32, 38
Bernstein, Ignatz, 141, 168, 169–171, 183,
    195
Bialik, Ḥayim Naḥman, 202
Biberach, 116
Bible, Hebrew, 53, 238n12, 147, 162, 186;
    Esther 9:7, 229n128; Song of Songs, 147;
    in Yiddish, 81
*Bibliotheca Hebraea* (Wolf), 52, 90–91
Bibliotheca Rosenthaliana, 238n24
*Bibrka. See* Bóbrka
Bick, Herz. *See* Bik, Herts
Big Bang, 33–34
Bik, Herts, 141, 142; *Der Khelemer
    khokhem*, 142–145, 146, 148, 179
Bik, Jacob Samuel, 142
Biłgoraj, 206
Binder, Mark, 224n6
Birnbaum, Nathan, 78
*Blass, Moritz*, 167, 252n67
*Blitsende vitsen oder lakhpilen* (Dik), 131,
    132, 141
*Bloch, Chajim*, 178, 189–190
Bloch, Jan, 146
Blum, Eliezer. *See* Alkvit, B.
Bobertag, Felix, 162n48
Bóbrka (as foolish town), 176

Bockum (as foolish town), 164

Bodleian library, 92, 231n12, 237n24; Oppenheim collection, 92, 239n32

*Bohen tsadik* (Perl), 128–130; Abdera in, 128–130, 176; folly in, 128, 130; and Margulies, 129; maskilim in, 128–129; source of, 246n75

Boissard, Jean-Jacques, 117

"Bolvan der ershter un zayn ayzerne hant" (Singer), 36

"Bontshe Shvayg" (Peretz), 18–19

Boorde, Andrew, 60

Borokhov, Ber, 183

Botashanski, Yankev, 16

Boyarin, Jonathan, 223n8

Brachfeld, Paul, 73

Brant, Sebastian, 117, 212; *Ship of Fools* (*Narrenschiff*), 44, 49, 117, 122–123

"Das Brillantendiadem" (Segel), 180–182

British Library, 62, 65, 75, 89, 237n56, 238n24

Broder singers, 12, 225n34

Brody, 123, 127, 129–130, 152, 253n89, 176; as Abdera, 129–130, 176; fools of, 176

Brook, Charles T., 250n23

*The Brothers Schlemiel* (Binder), 224n6

Buber, Martin, 9, 189

*Buch der schönsten Geschichten und Sagen* (Schwab), 162

*Das Buch von den polnischen Juden* (Agnon and Eliasberg), 194

Bund (Der Algemeyner Yidisher Arbeter Bund; The General Union of Jewish Workers), 24, 182

Burton, Robert, 243n9

Büsum, 152; as foolish town, 173, 176–177, 184

Büttner, Wolfgang, 52n40

Butwin, Frances, 22–23

Butwin, Julius, 22–23

Buxtehude, 152; as foolish town, 161

Cahan, Abraham, 12, 31

Callenberg, Johann Heinrich, 52

*Campe, Heinrich, 157–158*

capitalism, 32, 34–35

Carlebach, Ezriel, 195–196

Carnival plays, 46–48

Carnival, 43–44, 47–48, 235n2; Christian, 231n18; in Cologne, 158–159; and Purim, 46–48

carnivalesque, 43–44, 48, 54–55, 57; culture, 43, 48, 57; institutions, 159; performances, 45, 158–159

Carnovsky, Morris, 18

Centralverein deutscher Staatsbürger jüdischen Glaubens, 173, 181

"Chad Gadya" (song), 216

*Chanukah in Chelm* (Adler), 224n6, 215

*Chanukkah Tree* (Kimmel), 215

chapbook (*Volksbuch*), 68, 159, 162

Charap, J. A., 176

charivari, 45, 57–58, 70, 109

Chelm, xiii, 1, 3, 4, 45, 130, 131–132, 140, 143, 146, *152*, 183, 184, 195, 197, 205, 206; as Abdera, 171, 174, 177, 183, 211; Basilica of the Birth of the Virgin Mary, 199; Christian community of, 140–141, 199–200; and folly, 2, 5, 9, 13, 14, 16, 19, 27, 130, 132, 133, 137, 138–142, 147, 149, 167, 179, 194, 216, 222; as foolish town, 1–2, 5, 10, 130, 135, 137–142, 151, 168, 174–180, 183, 190, 194–195, 206, 211, 219; Jewish community of, 3–5, 140, 195; as Jewish Abdera, 177; as Jewish Schilda, 165–166, 168, 191, 194, 195–196, 211; in Polish culture, 1, 174; in proverbs, 2, 140, 141, 168, 170–171, 183, 213; as representative of Polish Jewish community, 25, 26, 37, 153, 188, 190, 191, 190; and Schilda, 168, 189, 191, 194, 195–196, 211; and Schildburg, 193, 210; and *Shildburger bukh*, 108, 110, 133; spelling of, 134, 224n11. *See also* wise men of Chelm; *specific Chelm literature*

Chelm characters: *daytsh*, 12, 147, 150, 184; *indik* (turkey), 170, 258n69; *khazn* (cantor), 170, 258n69; Khoyzek, 28, 170–171; king, 26, 34, 218; Litvak, 20, 26, 29, 60; *melamed* (teacher), 14, 20–21, 23, 25–26, 146–147, 149, 185–186, 203; *melamed's* wife, 20, 25–26, 185–186; night watchman, 200–201; rabbi, 9, 13, 20, 22, 23, 38, 40, 132, 136, 139, 143–145, 146, 147–149, 171, 175, 179, 185, 186, 204, 206, 210, 211–212; rebbetzin (rabbi's wife), 22, 37–38, 136, 139, 143–145, 175, 204; Shabbes goy, 26, 148–149; *shammes* (beadle), 22, 43, 132–133, 136, 139, 174, 179, 180, 185, 188, 190, 192, 203, 204, 211; *shulkloper*, 134, 138; *yishuvnik* (villager), 204–205

Chelm tales: angelic distribution of souls, 2, 14, 19–20, 28–29, 186–187, 199; arithmetic in Chelm, 184, 205; attempting to buy justice/truth, 210, 211–212; beautifying the synagogue, 180, 184, 211; building a synagogue, 174–175, 178, 180, 184, 193, 199, 214; buying a goat, 21–23; carrying logs sideways, 13, 171; carrying vs. rolling logs/stones, 14, 20, 60, 61, 175, 176–177, 178–179, 199, 214; cow in the hayloft, 206; destruction of Chelm, 30, 184, 188, 204–205, 217–218; disoriented by travel, 228n105, 144–145, 171, 179–180, 215, 221–222; eating on alternate days, 132, 134; fish standing trial, 37–38, 40–41; floorboards in the bathhouse, 202–203; headless rabbi, 139, 175, 179, *185*; hiring a night watchman, 200–201; *melamed* and his wife in the trunk, 25–26, 185–186; mistaken identity, 203; mousehound/cat of Chelm, 184, 188, *189*, 192, 194, 216; moving the synagogue/hill, 14, 38, 163, 175, 177, 178–179, 184, 199, 206; oven made of butter/ice, 248n124, 216;

oven protected from theft, 168; pig in the mikveh, 185; protecting the snow, 41, 132–133, 134, 135–136, 138–139, 174, 179, 180, 211; *shammes* and the shutters, 190; shoveling sunlight into a bag, *62, 77*, 175; sowing salt, 138, 206; synagogue without windows, 77, 175, 178; trapping the moon, 13, 25, 29, 110, 132–134, 174, 176, 180, 193, 194, 206, 207, *208*, 210; using the fire hose, 203

*Chelm-on-the-Med* (blog), 216

"The Chelm Goat Mystery" (Ausubel), 22

Chełm, xiii, 152. *See also* Chelm

*Chelmaxioms* (Mandelbaum), 224n6

Chelmer Narronim. See *Khelmer naronim*

Chelmer Narrunim. See *Khelmer naronim*

Chelmno, 257n31

children's literature, 2, 51–52, 54; and Chelm tales, 2, 224n6, 11, 30–31, 192, 207, 215–217, 219, 221; and Isaac Bashevis Singer, 6, 31, 37, 38–41, 221; and *Lalebuch/Schildbürgerbuch*, 60, 162, 177

China, 36, 133

Chmielnik, 135

Christian Hebraism, 91

Christian Hebraists, 47, 81, 90

Christmas, 44, 215

Christmas, Henry, 119

Cicero, 243n9, 120

Cockaigne, land of, 35, 112

*College Yiddish* (Weinreich), 213–215

Cologne, 50, 158–159

*Commentary* (New York), 17–18, 23, 30

communism, 32, 34

*Confused Hanukkah* (Koon), 215, 224n6

conversion of Jews, 82–83

converts to Christianity, 47, 83, 85; their attitude to Roman script, 83

cosmopolitanism, 123

"A Couple of Gold Nuggets, from the . . . Wastepaper, or Six Answers to Six Questions," (Wieland), 112–113 court jesters, 45, 232n32, 71; of Gros-selfingen, 159. *See also* fools; Hershele Ostropoler

Cracow, 152, 166, 237n56, 239n49

Cremona, 50

*Cricket* (La Salle, Illinois), 39–40

Czartoryski, Adam Jerzy, 125

Czartoryski, Adam Kazimierz, 124, 125, 126

Czartoryski, Izabela Fleming, 124

Dachau concentration camp, 17

Dalfn, 35

Dalfon. *See* Dalfn

"Dalfunka, Where the Rich Live Forever," (Singer), 31, 230n153

"Dalfunka, di shtot vu gvirim lebn eybig" (Singer), 230n153

*David y el gigante de piedra* (animated film). *See The Real Shlemiel*

Davidsohn, Ludwig, 194

Days of Awe, 197

Debuskey, Merle, 18

Decter, Midge, 18–19, 23

Ded Moroz (Father Frost), 216

Dee, Ruby, 18

Democritus, 115, 120, 126, 130; as literary figure, 115, 123, 124, 125, 126

*Denkwürdige Geschichtschronik der Schild-bürger* (Tieck), 113–114, 157

*Deutsche Roman-Zeitung* (Berlin), 252n55

*Deutsches Sprichwörter-Lexikon* (Wan-der), 2, 141, 142, 167–168, 170

*Deutsches Wörterbuch*, 253n81

*Dictionnaire historique et critique* (Bayle), 120, 122; German translation of, 244n31

Dijon (as foolish town), 159

Dik, Ayzik Meyer, 21, 130–131, 135, 139–141, 146, 174, 176, 190, 201–202, 210, 211, 220; and Abdera, 21, 130; *Blitsende vitsen oder lakhpilen*, 131–132, 141; and Chelm as foolish town, 132, 138, 141;

*Di orkhim fun Duratshesok*, 2, 137–138, 140–142, 202; "Oyzer Tsinkes un di tsig," 21, 23; and Poland, 131, 140, 141; and *Schildbürgerbuch*, 134, 137, 138–139; *Der shivim moltsayt*, 140, 142; *Sipurey khokhmey Yovn*, 246n76; "The Wis-dom of a Certain Town Khes," 131–136, 138, 140, 174, 180

Diogenes, 28, 120

Doubting Thomas, 174, 181

*Dr. Blochs oesterreichische Wochenschrift* (Vienna), 255n5

Dresden, 90, 154

Driz, Shike, 216

Drożdżyński, Aleksander, 256n30

Druya, 202

Druyanov, Alter, 202–203

Dülken (as foolish town), 159, 164

Duratshesok (foolish town), 2, 130, 137–138, 142; and Chelm, 138. *See also Di orkhim fun Duratshesok*

Düsseldorf, 163

dystopia, 2, 32

Easter, 231n19

Edels, Samuel, 3

Efrayim bar Yuda Levi, 82

Efroyim Greydiger, 29, 190, 206

Efroyim Greydiker. *See* Efroyim Grey-diger

Ehrenpreis, Jacob, 142

"Eindrücke aus Galizien" (Lessing), 178

Einstein, Albert, 26, 29

Elchanon Paulus of Prague, 83

*Eldad ha-Dani*, 249n12

Eliasberg, Ahron, 194

Elijah of Vilna (Vilna Gaon), 127

Elijah, Baal Shem of Chelm, 3

*Empfindsame Reise nach Schilda* (von Rebmann), 113, 156–157

*Encyclopedia Judaica*, 195

England, 16, 60, 159, 161, 173

Englander, Nathan, 10

Enlightenment, 3, 83, 112–113, 114, 119, 124, 131, 158, 169, 220; in Berlin, 116, 168; literature of, 7, 113–114, 120, 127, 131, 156–157, 158, 220; Polish, 124; and *Schildbürgerbuch*, 113–114, 151, 156–158, 162. *See also* Haskalah

*Die Entdeckungsreise des Herrn Dr. Theodor Lessing zu den Ostjuden* (Segel), 178

Erasmus, Desiderius, 44, 212

Erfurt, 116, 232n7

Erik, Maks, 46, 47–48, 232n37

Erlikh, Borekh Mordkhe, 217

Ertz, Stefan, 235n17

"Essai d'un plan de réforme" (Lefin), 126–127

ethnography, 150–151, 172; Jewish, 172, 182; polemical, 47

Euripides, 115

*Everything Is Illuminated* (Foer), 10

evil, 112, 147, 148

*Evreiskaia entsiklopediia*, 194

*Facetiae* (Bebel), 67

Fagius, Paulus, 81

*Fareyn fun yidishe literatn un zhurnalistn in Varshe*, 10

"Der farkishefter shnayder" (Sholem Aleichem), 21–23

Fast of Av. *See* Tish'ah be-Av

*Fastnacht. See* Carnival

*Fastnachtsnarren. See* fools

*Fastnachtspiel. See* Carnival plays

Faygenboym, Shaye, 185, 189, 207, 208

Feast of Asses, 44

Feast of Fools, 44

Feast of St. Nicholas, 55

*The Feather Merchants* (Sanfield), 31, 224n6

Fedorenko, Eugen, 221n24

Feibush Ashkenazi. *See* Joel ben Simon

Filtzhut, Pomponius (pseudonym), 73, 74, 85, 101, 155–156; as Jew, 239n48. See also *Schildbürgerbuch*

Finkelshteyn, Khayim, 195n25, 197

First Cincinnati Haggadah, 51

"The First Shlemiel" (Singer), 41, 230n152

"The First Snow," (Singer), 41, 230n152

Fischart, Johann, 235n9, 117

Flender, Harold, 33

*Fliegende Blätter* (Munich), 162–163

Fockbek, 152; as foolish town, 173

Foer, Jonathan Safran, 10

Foillet, Jacob, 67

folkist party, 182

folklore, 151, 163, 172, 217; and Chelm, 16, 151, 213, 215; English, 16; Jewish, 53, 146, 171, 188, 215; Yiddish, 5n10, 29, 131, 182

folly, 40, 44–45, 48, 53, 57, 59, 61, 65, 68–69, 72, 108, 113, 121–123, 147, 149, 151, 161, 165; in Chelm tales, 2, 5, 9, 13, 14, 16, 19, 27, 130, 132, 133, 137, 138–142, 147, 149, 167, 179, 194, 216, 222; Christian, 45, 210; for Christ's sake, 209–210; Jewish, 19, 46, 49–59; natural, 51; and reason, 72. *See also* fools

folly literature, 7, 25–26, 43, 56, 105, 107, 116–117, 212, 231n13, 233n40; early modern, 25, 68, 117, 147, 149; German, 3, 60, 160; Jewish, 29, 56; medieval, 25, 147

fool societies, 44–45, 55, 57, 69, 74, 109–110, 156, 159; Abbaye de Conards, 44, 69; Abbaye de Cornards, 44; Abbaye de Liesse, 44; in Jewish culture, 55–57; in *Lalebuch*, 69–72; and maleness, 69, 72; and marriage, 44, 69, 72; in *Schildbürgerbuch*, 74, 109–110, 156; and sexual relations 44, 57, 69, 72

foolish culture, 43, 45–46, 48, 54–56, 61, 64, 69, 74, 100–101, 104, 107–109, 123, 250n21, Christian, 47–49; Jewish, 45, 47–49, 54–56, 110, 179; scholarship on, 43–44, 45–48; shared, 48, 56, 58–59, 108, 110

foolish performances, 57, 69–71, 121

foolish symbols, 48, 50, 55, 57–59, 69

foolish towns, 151, 152, 157, 158–159, 161, 163–164, 168, 172–173, 174, 177, 179, 180; German, 156, 158, 160–162, 164, 168, 179, 191, 250n23, 252n71; Jewish 2n2, 130, 137, 151, 165–167, 174, 176, 183, 191. *See also specific towns*

fools, 46, 69, 144; artificial, 170, 232n32; carnival 44, 158–159; Christian, 43–45, 46, 48, 173, 177, 190; holy, 210; Jewish, 45–59, 190, 192; natural, 170, 232n32; professional, 45–46; and Purim, 49; in Yiddish folklore, 29, 170. *See also* court jesters; fool societies; wise men of Chelm

fool's mirror, 122–123, 149

"The Fools of Chelm and the Stupid Carp" (Singer, 40), 230n153

*The Fools of Chelm and Their History* (Singer), 31, 39–40, 196

fools of Posen, 168–169, 180

*Forverts* (New York), 11, 12, 16, 31, 37; and Chelm tales, 11, 31–33, 37, 38, 39, 40, 221, 225n27

Foucault, Michel, 72

four sons, 50–51

France, 44, 159, 161, 164

Franconia, 90, 254n108

Fränkel, Ludwig, 173

Frankfurt (am Main), 45, 53, 73, 85, 90, 94, 152, 174, 178, 234n54; as foolish town, 165–166

Frankfurt (an der Oder), 154

Freedman, Florence, 224n6

Freud, Sigmund, 151, 163

Frey, Jakob, *Gartengesellschaft*, 67

*Dos freylekhe Hershele Ostropolyer* (A. M. Sh.), 256n7

*Der freylekhster yid in der velt oder Hersheles lern-yorn* (Trunk), 54

Friedländer, David, 124

Friedman, Filip, 131–132, 141

"A frier peysekh" (Sholem Aleichem), 226n60

Frishman, David, 145, 259n14

*Froyim Greydiger. See* Efroyim Greydiger

"Fun der kluger shtot" (Kipnis), 196–206, 225n26; narrative style of, 201; sources of, 201–202

*Fun Khelemer pinkes* (Lerner), 217

Fürth, 7, 58, 85, 90, 103, 108, 152; as foolish town, 165–167

Galen, 243n9

Galicia, 10, 127, 129, 131, 141, 142, 166, 174, 176, 177, 178, 179, 183, 191, 194. *See also* Austro-Hungarian (Habsburg) Empire

*galkhes*, 79–80, 82, 84, 98

*Gartengesellschaft* (Frey), 67

*Gartengesellschaft* (Montanus), 104

Gaster, Moses, 247n115

Geiler von Kaysersberg, Johann, 117

*Gemeindeblatt der Israelitischen Gemeinde Frankfurt am Main* (Frankfurt), 173–174

Genesis Rabba, 186

Georgievsky, Eulogius (bishop), 200

German language, 81, 113, 157; Early New High, 60, 75, 78, 97; *Hochdeutsch* (High German), 77–79, 81, 82; and Jews, 82; Middle High, 78, 97, 253n81; and Yiddish, 77–79, 81, 99, 167, 191. *See also* Yiddish language

German studies, 91–92, 95, 151, 159, 161, 163; and Yiddish, 91–92

Germany, 11, 50, 90, 91, 105, 124, 158–159, 160, 161, 164–165, 172, 177, 195; Jewish communities of, 58, 167, 181; as literary place, 27, 124, 164; as successor to ancient Greece, 119, 158. *See also specific foolish towns*

Gershenzon, Moyshe, 216

Gerson, Christian, 83

Gersonides, 56

Gervinus, Georg Gottfried, 161

*Geschichte der poetischen National-Literatur der Deutschen* (Gervinus), 161

Gesellschaft für jüdische Volkskunde, 172
*Di geshikhte fun der yidisher literature*
    (Erik), 46, 47–48, 232n37
*Geshikhte fun yidisher teater-kunst un
    drame* (Shiper), 45–46, 56
Gintsburg, Mordekhai Aharon, 137
Glaser, Linda, 215, 224n6
Glatshteyn, Yankev, 30, 248n127
*Glimpf und Schimpf in Spruch und Wort*
    (von Wurzbach), 165–166
Glupov (foolish town), 137
Glupsk (foolish town), 137
Gneisenau, August von, 251n32
Goedeke, Karl Friedrich, 161
Goethe, Catharina Elisabeth, 116
Goethe, Johann Wolfgang von, 81, 116, 125,
    244n44; and Yiddish, 81
Goldberg, Alter, 184, 206
Goldfaden, Avrom, 211
Goldshteyn, Yoysef-Shimen, 197
golem, 3, 5, 217, 220; of Prague, 189
Görres, Joseph, 68, 159
Gosche, Richard, 239n43
Gotham (Nottinghamshire, England), 16,
    152; as literary place, 6, 16
*Gothelf, Levi. See* Carlebach, Ezriel
Gottesman, Itzik, 202
Göttingen, 164
Gottsched, Johann Gottfried, 244n31
Gottsched, Luise, 244n31
Graubard, Pinkhes, 182
Greece, 115, 135; as literary place, 61, 115,
    118, 135, 158, 211; and Winckelmann, 119
*Grillenvertreiber*, 73–75, 249n20
Grimm, Wilhelm, 67
Grimm, brothers, 160–161, 237n50
*Grininke beymelekh* (Vilna), 207
Gross, Naftoli, 17
"Der groyser zets un di antshteyung fun
    Khelm" (Singer), 33, 38–39
*Grundrisz zur Geschichte der deutschen
    Dichtung aus den Quellen* (Goedeke),
    161

Grunwald, Max, 172, 180, 194
Güdemann, Moritz, 47, 231n14
Gumprekht Levi. *See* Efrayim bar Yuda
    Levi
Gurevich, Aron. *See* Gurjewitsch, Aaron
Gurjewitsch, Aaron, 44
Gvozdeva, Katja, 69

Hadda, Janet, 32
Hagen, Friedrich Heinrich von der, 67, 91,
    159–161; and Grimm brothers, 160–161;
    and *Lalebuch*, 67; and *Schildbürger-
    buch*, 159–160
Haggadah, 46, 49–51, 253n89
*Ḥakhme Ḥelem: Bediḥot ve-halatsot
    ʿamamiyot* (Heilpern), 207
Halle, 52, 93
Hambach Festival, 164
Hamburg, 90, *152*, 172, 195, 237n56
Hanswurst, 47
Hanukkah, 41, 213, 215, 224n6
*A Hanukkah Present!* (Binder), 224n6
Hasid (pl. Hasidim), 22, 110, 124, 126–129,
    137, 141, 170, 212
Hasidic court, 143; court of Barukh ben
    Yeḥiel of Mezhbizh, 256n7; court of
    Zinkover rebbes, 144
Hasidic town, 126, 140, 144, 174
Hasidism, 126–127, 131, 142, 145; anti-
    Hasidism, 22, 124, 126, 129, 131; neo-
    Hasidism, 14. *See also* satire
Haskalah, 7, 83, 113, 123–124, 127, 129, 130–
    131; in Berlin and Prussia, 83, 116, 123–
    124, 130, 168–169; in eastern Europe,
    124, 127, 129. *See also* Enlightenment
"Hassidic Tales, with a Guide to Their
    Interpretation by the Noted Scholar"
    (Allen), 9
*Haynt (Warsaw)*, 195, 220n19; and Chelm
    tales, 10, 37, 153, 189, 195, 196, 197–198,
    202–203, 205–206, 207, 211
Hebrew Union College, 238n24
*Heilpern, Falk*, 185, 189, 207, 208

Heine, Heinrich, 163–165
Di heldn fun Khelm (Simon), 30
Ḥelm ve-ḥakhameh: Meḥubar be-ḥelko lefi
 mekorot 'amamiyim (Heilpern), 207
Helmstedt, 90
"Ḥemah" (Frishman), 248n124, 259n14
Herder, Johann Gottfried, 125
Herodotus, 120
Hersch Ostropoler: Ein jüdischer Till-
 Eulenspiegel des 18. Jahrhunderts
 (Bloch), 189–190
Hershele Ostropoler, 29, 53, 189–190, 211;
 as court fool, 256n7; and Till Eulenspie-
 gel, 53–54, 189–190
Herzl, Theodor, 195
Hesekiel, George, 252n55
Hesse, Walter, 94
Hierocles, 243n9
Hippocrates, 115; as literary figure, 115, 123
Hirschau, 152; as foolish town, 153
Hirschberg (as foolish town), 116
Historien von Claus Narren (Büttner), 52
History of the Abderites (Wieland), 113–125,
 128, 135, 151, 157, 158, 159, 181; and En-
 lightenment, 113, 114, 119, 120, 181; folly
 in, 114, 116–118, 119, 121, 122–123; and
 Wahrscheinlichkeit, 243n7; wisdom in,
 115, 118, 122–123; and Schildbürgerbuch/
 Lalebuch, 116–120, 121–122, 123; sources
 of, 117, 120–121; and Tristram Shandy,
 120–121
History of Yiddish Literature in the Nineteenth Century (Wiener), 258n58
hobbyhorse, 50, 158; in foolish performances; in Rotschild Haggadah, 50;
 in Lalebuch/Schildbürgerbuch, 63, 71,
 74, 89
Hobsbawm, Eric, 151
Hochdeutsch. See German language
Holbein the Younger, Hans, 51
Holocaust, 10, 11, 24, 196, 209, 217–218
holy fools. See fools
Holy Roman Empire, 108, 249n6

Homberg, Herz, 83
Homburg vor der Höhe, 53
Homer, 164
Honegger, Peter, 235n17
Horace, 96, 120, 123
House Un-American Activities Commit-
 tee, 18
Ḥoveve Tsiyon, 145–146
Hrubieszów, 204
Hummelnvertreiber, 249n20
humoral pathology, 68
Hungary, 161

"Iber a shmek tabak" (Peretz), 146–149,
 227n80
Ideen: Das Buch Le Grand (Heine), 163–
 164
Illustrirte vokh (Warsaw), 207
"In alt Khelem: A Khelemer maysele"
 (Peretz). See "Der shabes-goy"
Institutum Judaicum et Muhammedicum,
 52, 93
Internationale Titulaturen (O. von
 Reinsberg-Düringsfeld), 163
Inventarium diplomaticum historiae Sax-
 oniae superioris (Schöttgen), 154
Inzl (Łódź), 211
Irving, Washington, 6
Irving, William, 224n14
Isaacs, Edith J. R., 12
Israel, 1, 5, 202, 207, 216–217; as literary
 place, 27–28
Israelitisches Familienblatt (Hamburg), 195
It Happened in Chelm (Freedman), 224n6
Itinerarium Germaniae Nov-antiquae
 (Zeiller), 153

Janów, 176
Jar of Fools (Kimmel), 31, 224n6
Jeep, Ernst, 93–95
Jesus, 181, 210
Jewish Encyclopedia, 194
Jewish humor, 17, 180, 194, 195, 206, 213, 215

Jewish Theological Seminar, 238n24
*Jewish Wit and Wisdom* (Richman), 17
Job, 148
Jobin, Bernard, 67
*Jobsiade* (Kortum), 250n23
Joel ben Simon, 50
Joseph della Reina, 248n127
*Judenstaat* (Herzl), 195
*Die jüdischdeutsche Sprache der Ostjuden* (Loewe), 191
*Jüdische Sprichwörter* (Blass), 252n67
*Jüdische Sprichwörter und Redensarten* (Bernstein and Segel), 169–171
*Der jüdische Witz* (Landmann), 196
*Jüdischer Almanach* (Weltsch), 195
*Jüdisches Lexikon*, 194–195

kabbalah, 110, 249n12
Kaftal, Gustav, 206
Kaminski, Albert Hanan, 217
Kant, Immanuel, 116, 124, 125; and Abderitism, 116, 157–158; *Der Streit der Fakultäten*, 116, 157–158
"A kapitel Khelmer geshikhte" (Singer), 230n142
"Kapitlekh fun der Khelmer geshikhte" (Singer), 34
Kasrilevke (fictional town), 203–204
Katz, Judith, 10
Kazin, Pearl, 30
Keller, Gottfried, 209
Keren Ha-Yesod (Palestine Foundation Fund), 181
Kerler, Dov-Ber, 223n10
"Key to the History of the Abderites" (Wieland), 120–121, 122–123
*Keynemsdorf* (Sandler), 10, 137
*Khakhomim, akshonim un naronim* (Simon), 30
*Der khaver* (Vilna), 207
"Khelem di shtot" (Lerner), 210n84
"Khelemer balade" (Manger), 210–211
*Khelemer dertseylungen* (Erlikh), 217

*Khelemer khakhomim* (Trunk), 6, 24, 25–30, 36–37; folly in, 27, 28–29; Khoyzek in, 28; wisdom in, 26, 28–29; Yiddish in, 27–28
*Khelemer khakhomim* (Zeitlin), 11–14, 16, 19, 225n34; folly in, 13, 14
*Der Khelemer khokhem* (Bik), 142–145, 146, 148, 179
*Di Khelemer komediye* (Zeitlin), 11–12
*Khelemer mayses* (Kipnis), 22, 37, 198, 203, 205–206
"Di Khelemer mayses" (Manger), 21, 209–210
"Der Khelemer melamed" (Peretz), 14, 146–147, 149, 227n80
"Der Khelemer zatsa'l" (Manger), 211–212
"Khelm bashlist tsu firen milkhome" (Singer), 34
"Khelm un Mazl-Borsht" (Singer), 35
"Khelmer geshikhtes" (Mirer), 206
*Khelmer khakhomim*, 5–6, 43, 176, 212. *See also* wise men of Chelm
*Khelmer khakhomim* (Ben Mordekhai), 225n26
*Di Khelmer khakhomim* (Gershenzon), 216
*Khelmer mayses* (Goldberg), 184, 206
*Khelmer naronim*, 5, 43, 141, 168, 170, 180, 183, 194, 212, 213, 223n3. *See also* wise men of Chelm
*Khelmer naronim* (Ben Mordekhai), 14, 15
"Di Khelmer revolutsye un vos zi hot gebrakht" (Singer), 35
*Khelomskie mudretsy* (Driz/Sapgir), 216
Khes (foolish town), 130, 131, 132–136, 138, 141. *See also* "The Wisdom of a Certain Town Khes"
*kheyder* (Jewish elementary school), 55, 205
Khoyzek, 28, 170–171, 190
*kiddush levanah* (Sanctification of the Moon), 25, 110, 132, 133, 193
Kimmel, Eric, 31, 215, 224n6

*Kinder zshurnal* (New York), 30
*The King of Chelm*, 218
Kipnis, Menakhem, 10, 29–30, 37, 135, 153, 189–190, 195–198, 202; "Fun der kluger shtot," (series in *Haynt*), 196, 197–206, 225n26; *Khelemer mayses*, 22, 37, 198, 203, 205–206; and Singer, 37; "Der melamed in generalske kleyder," 203; and Peretz, 224n9; and Trunk, 10, 29
Kisalon (foolish town), 137
Klotz, Volker, 117
*knel gabbai*, 54–55
Kohn, Jakob Pinchas, 194
Komitee für den Osten (Committee for the East), 178, 191
Kon, Henekh, 197–198
Koon, Jon, 215, 224n6
Körte, Wilhelm, 163
Kortum, Karl Arnold, 250n23
Kozodoyevke (fictional town), 21
Krähwinkel (as foolish town), 250n23, 164
Krause, Norbert, 176
Krauss, Friedrich Salomon, 150–151, 171–172, 175, 177
Kugelmass, Jack, 5n8
*Kurtze und gründliche Anweisung zur Teutsch-Jüdischen Sprache* (Lütke), 170n86

*L'Chayim! Jewish Wit and Humor* (Olsvanger), 225n35
Labor Zionists, 182, 183
*Lalebuch* (1597), 44, 60–73, 75, 95, 103–104, 131, 199, 247n106, 249n7; and feudalism, 236n27; folly in, 61, 65, 66, 68–69, 71–72, 95; deliberation in, 68; fools in, 61, 64, 66, 67, 68, 70–72; fool societies in, 69–72; and gender, 68; and mental afflictions, 68; narrative structure of, 66, 68, 69–71; scholarship on, 66–67, 94; Utopia in, 60, 63; wisdom in, 61, 65, 72. See also *Schildbürgerbuch*

Laleburg (foolish town), 60, 61, 64, 67, 72–73, 249n6
*Lalen-Buch*, 75, 87
*lamed-vovniks*. See thirty-six righteous men
*Lamtern in vint* (Manger), 210
*Land und Stadt im Volksmunde* (Hesekiel), 252n55
Landau, Alfred, 171
Landmann, Salcia, 196
Landowska, Wanda, 180
Langner, Johann Christian. See Schöttgen, Johann Christian
"Die Lappenhewser bawren" (Sachs), 60, 67
*The Last Tale of Mendel Abbe* (Sapir), 224n6
*Laugh for God's Sake* (Schachter), 224n6
Laukhard, Friedrich Christian, 157
*Lazarus, John*, 221n24
*Le Monde est un grand Chelm* (animated film). See *The Real Shlemiel*
*Leben und Thaten des jüngern Herrn von Münchhausen, wohlweisen Bürgermeisters zu Schilda* (von Rebmann), 156–157
*Leben, Meynungen und Thaten von Hieronimus Jobs dem Kandidaten* (Kortum), 250n23
*Lebensgeschichte* (Maimon), 168–169
Lefin, Mendel, 123–127, 130, 142, 176, 250n25; "Essai d'un plan de réforme," 126–127; and Hasidism, 126–127; and Joseph Perl, 125, 127, 246n75; and Wieland, 125. See also *Nachlass eines Sonderlings zu Abdera*
Lehman, Shmuel, 135, 182–184, 187, 190, 202, 205
*Lehrbuch zur gründlichen Erlernung der jüdischdeutschen Sprache* (Selig), 253n81
*Leib, Mani*, 211
Leipzig, 93, 153, 154, 194, 195

*Leipziger Literatur-Zeitung* (Leipzig), 160
Lemberg (Lviv), 141, 142, *152*, 166, 170, 173
"Lemel and Tzipa" (Singer), 230n153
Lent, 43
Leopold von Habsburg, 58
Lerer, Moshe, 197
Lerner, Yosl, 217, 210n84
Lesko, *152*; as foolish town, 174
Lessing, Theodor, 178
Lew, Henryk, 180
*Liber vagatorum*, 249n20
"*Lider fun Khelm*" (Ulinover), 211
Lindeman, Moshe, 204
Lion Dor, Hirsh, 133
*Literarishe bleter* (Warsaw), 14, 209
Lithuania, 130, 142, 144, 174; as literary place, 20, 198. *See also* Poland: Polish-Lithuanian Commonwealth
Löb of Fürth, 58
Łódź, 24, 205
Loewe, Heinrich, 190–192, 195; *Schelme und Narren mit jüdischen Kappen*, 43, 190–191; and *Schildbürgerbuch*, 191, 192; *Die Sprachen der Juden*, 191–192; and Yiddish, 191–192
Łopuszna, 173
Lotze, Hermann, 91–92
Loyhoyopoli (fictional town), 137
Lublin, 247n113, *152*, 183, 184
Lucian, 120
Luther's Bible, 81
Lviv. *See* Lemberg

*Ma'aleh Karaḥot* (Sidon), 217
Magdeburg, 244n31
*Ma'ariv* (Tel Aviv), 195
Maimon, Salomon, 83, 168–170, 176; *Lebensgeschichte*, 168–169
Maimonides, 54
Mandelbaum, Allen, 224n6
Manger, Itsik, 208–209, 211–212; and Abdera, 211; "Di balade fun Hershele Ostropoler mit der levone," 233n51;

and Chelm, 21, 135, 208–212; "Khelemer balade," 210–211; "Di Khelemer mayses," 21, 209–210; "Der Khelemer zatsa'l," 211–212, 247n96; *Lamtern in vint*, 210; *Noente geshtaltn*, 211, 247n96; and Peretz, 146; and *Schildbürgerbuch*, 209, 211; and Sholem Aleichem, 21
Manger, Klaus, 114, 117
Mannheim, 116
Mantua Haggadah, 51
Marbach, Gotthard Oswald, 162
Margulies, Ephraim Zalman, 129–130
Markish, Perets, 209
Marmorstein, Yissochor, 247n113
*marshalik*, 45
Martini, Fritz, 117
*maskil* (pl. *maskilim*), 7, 83, 113, 131, 135, 157, 169, 247n113; in eastern Europe, 113, 123–124, 127, 129, 131, 135, 157, 169, 247n113; and German language, 83, 113; and *History of the Abderites*, 113, 123–124; in *Nachlass eines Sonderlings zu Abdera*, 128–129
*Matzah Mishugas* (Binder), 224n6
*Mayse bukh*, 249n12, 166
*Mayse nisim* (Yuspa Shammes), 166
"Mayse on an ek" (Sholem Aleichem). *See* "Der farkishefter shnayder"
*Mayselekh un mesholim* (Gross), 17
*Mayselekh vegn Khelemer naronim* (Bastomski), 207
*Mayzel, Nakhmen*, 209
Mazl-Borsht (fictional town), 35
*Megale temirin* (Lefin), 127–128
*Megillat setarim*, 56
Mela, Pomponius, 74
"Der melamed in generalske kleyder" (Kipnis), 203
Mendele Moykher-Sforim. *See* Abramovitsh, Sholem Yankev
Mendelssohn, Moses, 116, 124; circle, 123
Menippean satire, 68
*Menorah* (Vienna), 192–194, 195

Merian, Matthäus, 153
*Merie Tales of the Mad Men of Gotam* (Boorde), 60
Merkin, Zalmen. *See* Erik, Maks
Merks, Benjamin ben Joseph, 52
"Merksprüche für Folkloristen" (Krauss), 171–172
Merkur, Volf, 225n34
Messiah, 170
Metz, 152; as foolish town, 165–167
Międzybóż, 126
Mikołajów, 124, 125, 126
*minhagim* books, 46. *See also Seyfer minhogim* (Tyrnau)
Mirer, Sholem, 206
Miron, Dan, 204
*De miseria humanae conditionis* (Poggio Bracciolini), 67
Mishnah, 229n122
*Mitteilungen der Gesellschaft für jüdische Volkskunde* (Hamburg), 180
"The Mixed-Up Feet and the Silly Bridegroom" (Singer), 39
*Moment* (Warsaw), 207
Montanus, Martin, 104
Montbeliard, 67
*More Wise Men of Helm and Their Merry Tales* (Simon), 30
More, Thomas, *Utopia*, 67, 134
*Der Morgen* (Berlin), 173, 255n104
*Moscow*, 206, 216
*Moser, Dietz-Rüdiger*, 231n18
Mostel, Zero, 23
motley, 48, 50, 54
Munich, 232n37, 152, 162

*Nachlass eines Sonderlings zu Abdera* (Lefin), 124–127; and *History of the Abderites*, 125
Nadvirna 152; as foolish town, 174
*Naftali the Storyteller* (Singer), 39
"Der narishe khosn un di farbitene fis" (Singer), 31–32

*Narrenberg* (foolish town), 226n60, 137
*Die Narren von Chelm und ihre Geschichte* (Singer), 196
*Narrenbuch* (von der Hagen), 160
*Narrenliteratur. See* folly literature
*Narrenschiff* (Brant). *See Ship of Fools*
*Narrenspiegel. See* fool's mirror
"*Nasza Abdera*" (Lew), 180
National and University Library Strasbourg, 238n24
National Library of Israel, 50, 238n24, 125, 142, 190
nationalism, 151
"A naye epokhe in Khelm" (Singer), 35
*Naye folkstsaytung* (Warsaw), 211
*Naye oysdervelte Khelmer mayses* (Kaftal), 206
"Di naye partey fun di Khelmer komitetn" (Singer), 229n127
Naye Yidishe Folkshul (printer), 207
Nazareth (as foolish town), 167
Nestler, Volf, 58
Nesvizh, 207
*Die neuen Schildbürger oder Lalenburg in den Tagen der Aufklärung* (Schulz), 113
*New Testament*, 82; I Cor. 1:18, 210
*New York Times*, 12, 17, 23, 39
New York, 6, 10–12, 16–17, 24, 30, 31, 39, 213, 218, 220, 224n5; as Chelm, 224n6, 228n104; as foolish town, 6, 218; as Gotham, 6; as literary place, 6, 213, 215
*New Yorker*, 9
Newlove, Rose, 221n24
Niger, Shmuel, 14, 39, 246n78
"Nokh vegn di Khelmer khakhomim: A fish an azes-ponem" (Singer), 37–38, 40–41
"Nokh vegn di Khelmer khakhomim: Der Khelmer barg," (Singer), 38
Nördlingen, 123
Nowy Dwór (Poland), 53
Nowy Sącz, 176

*Noyekh Prilutskis zamlbikher far yidishn folklor, filologye un kultur-geshikhte* (Warsaw), 37, 150, 183; Chelm tales in, 135, 150, 183–187, 190, 199, 202, 205

Nuremberg, 60, 85, 152

Obadiah ben Petaḥiah (fictional character), 127–129

"O chełmskich mędrcach" (Drożdżyński), 256n30

Odessa, 202

Offenbach, 7, 85, 90, 103, 108

Og, King of Bashan, 26

Oguz, A. D., 14, 201n48

Oldendorf, Menakhem, 45–46

Olsvanger, Immanuel, 225n35, 194

Opitz, Martin, 81

Oppenheim collection. *See* Bodleian library

Oppenheim, David, 90, 92

*Di orkhim fun Duratshesok* (Dik), 2, 137–142, 202; and *Schildbürgerbuch*, 137–139

*Ost und West* (Berlin), 173, 177

*Oxford Old Yiddish Manuscript Songbook*, 55–56, 231n12

"Oyzer Tsinkes un di tsig" (Dik), 21, 23

"Ein paar Goldkörner aus–Makulatur oder Sechs Antworten auf sechs Fragen" (Wieland). *See* "A Couple of Gold Nuggets, from the . . ." (Wieland)

Pacanów, 152; as foolish town, 174

Pale of Settlement, 131, 140, 144, 184, 199, 220

Palestine, 145, 172, 181, 195, 202,

Pappenheim, Bertha, 178

Paris, 250n30, 164, 211; as foolish town, 159

Parma Ashkenazi Haggadah, 51

parody, 9, 112, 124, 164, 218; maskilic, 142, 179

"Di parteyen in vaysen Khelm un zeyere makhlokesn," 36

Passover, 231n19, 50–51, 144, 203, 213, 215; song, 216. *See also* Haggadah

Paucker, Arnold, 85, 87, 94–95, 96, 104, 239n48

Paul (Apostle), 210

Paul, Jean, 117, 157

Paulding, James Kirke, 224n14

Paulus of Prague. *See* Elchanon Paulus of Prague

Peretz, Yitskhok-Leyb, 14, 24, 141–142, 145–149, 202, 224n9, 228n98; "Bontshe Shvayg," 18–19; "Iber a shmek tabak," 227n80, 146–149; "Der Khelemer melamed," 14, 227n80, 146–147, 149; and Kipnis, 224n9; "Der shabes-goy," 146, 148–149; and Trunk, 224n9, 24, 227n80, 146

Perl, Arnold, 17–18, 20; *Tevya and His Daughters*, 18; *The World of Sholom Aleichem*, 17–21, 23

Perl, Joseph, 123, 125, 127–129, 145, 176; archive of, 126; *Boḥen tsadik*, 128–130; and Hasidism, 127, 129; Lefin's influence on, 125, 127; *Megale temirin*, 127–128; "Über das Wesen der Sekte Chassidim," 127

*Phaedon* (Mendelssohn), 125

phallus: and folly, 170; nose as symbol of, 121. *See also* Vayzose

Philagrius, 243n9

*Philogelos* (Hierocles), 243n9

Pickelhering, 47

Pied Piper, 75

Pinczew. *See* Pińczów

Pińczów, 152, 191

*Play of the Week*, 18

Płock, 190

Poale Zion (Labor Zionists), 182, 183

*Podolia*, 124, 126, 127

Poggio Bracciolini, Gian Francesco, 67

Poland, 26, 144, 168, 174, 178, 184, 186, 220; Austrian Poland, 141; Congress Poland, 10, 131, 140, 146, 176, 178, 200; Jewish community of, 25, 153; as literary place, 26, 191, 192; Polish-Lithuanian Commonwealth, 124, 127, 140, 168, 174; Polish Republic (interwar), 11, 24, 29, 153, 188, 190, 191, 192, 196, 209; post-World War II, 1; proverbs, 140, 210; Prussian Poland, 156, 168

"Di 'politishe ekonomye' fun Khelm" (Singer), 32–33, 36

Polkowice. See Polkwitz

Polkwitz, 152; as foolish town, 250n30, 159, 163–164, 165, 168

Die polnische Judenfrage (Segel), 178

Pomerania, 154

Posen (Poznań), 152, 168–169; as foolish town, 132, 168–169, 176, 180

Ein poßierlich- jedoch warhafftig- und immerwehrender Hauß-Calender und Practica (Filtzhut), 74

Poyln: Zikhroynes un bilder (Trunk), 24

Poznań. See Posen

Der Prager Golem (Bloch), 255n5

Prague, 49, 53, 58, 92, 128, 129, 152, 189; Jewish community of, 58; as foolish town, 165–166, 167

Praise of Folly (Erasmus), 44

printing, 84–85; in Yiddish, 84, 96, 98, 102

Proops (printer), 90

Prose, Francine, The Angel's Mistake, 31

Protocols of the Elders of Zion, 178

Prussia, 168; as literary place, 27

Pryłucki, Noah, 29, 132, 135, 182–183, 187; and Chelm, 37, 135, 183–184; Zaml-bikher far yidishn folklor, filologye un kultur-geshikhte, 37, 135, 150, 183–187, 190, 199, 202, 205; and Segel, 182–183; and standardization of Yiddish, 182; and Trunk, 29; Yidishe folkslider, 183

"Pumay, ir libn gezelen," 55–56

Purim king, 56

Purim rabbi, 56

Purim, 43, 45–48, 54–56; plays, 45–48; and Carnival, 46–48

Rabbi Harvey Rides Again (Sheinkin), 215

Rabbi Harvey vs. the Wisdom Kid (Sheinkin), 215

Der Rabbiner (Dresden), 154

Rabinovitsh, Sholem. See Sholem Aleichem

Raïzé, Efim, 223n2

Rapoport, Solomon Judah, 129

Die Räuber (Schiller), 115–116

Ravitsh, Melekh, 209

Ravnitski, Yoshue Khone, 17, 202

The Real Shlemiel (animated film), 217–218

Rebmann, Andreas Georg Friedrich von, 113, 156–157

Red Channels: Report of Communist Influence in Radio and Television, 18

Reinsberg-Düringsfeld, Ida von, 163

Reinsberg-Düringsfeld, Otto von, 163

Reisebilder 31

Reisen durch einen Theil Teutschlands, Ungarns, Italiens und Frankreichs (Arndt), 250n30

Reshumot (Tel Aviv), 202

Reutlingen (as foolish town), 250n30

Die Revolution in Scheppenstedt (Schummel), 113, 250n23

"Di revolutsye in Khelm" (Singer), 35

Reyzen, Avrom, 202

Richardson, Don, 23

Richman, Jacob, 17

Ringwald, Heinrich. See Schulz, Johann Gottlob

Rodfe Tsedakah, 234n54

Rogovin, Or, 6

Rohatyn, 173

Rollenhagen, Georg, 117

Romanticism, 68, 160

"Die romantische und Volks-Litteratur der Juden in Jüdisch-Deutscher Sprache" (von der Hagen), 91

Romm (printer), 131

Rosenberg, Franz, 47, 56, 231n14

Rosenkranz, Karl, 161
Rosenthal, Leeser, 90
Rosh Hashanah, 193
*Rosinkess mit Mandlen* (Olsvanger), 194
Roskies, David, 139, 208, 248n127
Rosman, Moshe, 48
Rossel, Seymour, 224n6
Rothschild Haggadah, *50*, 51
Rotwelsch, 92, 105, 249n20
*Röyte Pomerantsen* (Olsvanger), 225n35
Rozenband, Garel, 204
Rozenberg, Yudl, 189
Rudolf II (Holy Roman Empire), 83
*Running Fiercely toward a High Thin Sound* (Katz), 10
Russian Civil War, 181
Russian Empire, 113, 127, 130, 140, 142, 144, 174, 177, 178, 214; as literary place, 128. *See also* Pale of Settlement; Poland: Congress Poland
Russian Orthodox Church, 140, 200
Russian Revolution, 184, 194
Rylands Ashkenazi Haggadah, 51

Sabbath, 52, 54, 57, 137, 257n31; in *Bohen tsadik* (Perl), 129; in Chelm tales, 37, 150; in "Iber a shmek tabak" (Peretz), 147–148; in *Der Khelemer khokhem* (Bik), 144; and *Shildburger bukh*, 99; in "The Wisdom of a Certain Town Khes" (Dik), 136. *See also* Shabbat ha-Baḥurim
Sachs, Hans, 60, 162, 175; "Die Lappenhewser bawren," 60, 67
Sadan, Dov, 5
"Der sakh-hakl fun der geshikhte fun Khelm" (Singer), 36
*Salmagundi* (New York), 6
Saltykov-Shchedrin, Mikhail, 137
Saltzman, Roberta, 229n109
Sambatyon, 27
Samuel, Maurice, 18

Sanctification of the Moon. See *kiddush levanah*
Sandler, Boris, *Keynemsdorf*, 10, 137
Sanfield, Steve, 31, 224n6
Sapgir, Genrikh, 216, 218
Sapir, Marc, 224n6
Satan, 97, 147, 227n80, 233n40
Satanów (Poland), 124
satire, 32, 35–36, 39; anti-Hasidic, 137, 141–142, 145; and Enlightenment, 116, 131, 250n23, 158, 220; and *Lalebuch*, 67–68; maskilic, 127, 131, 145, 149, 176; political, 11, 158
Saxony, 153, 154, 159, 160, 161, 249n20
Schachter, Stanley, 224n6
*Schelme und Narren mit jüdischen Kappen* (Loewe), 43, 190–191
*Die Schelme von Schelm* (animated film). See *The Real Shlemiel*
Schiffer, Benjamin Wolf. *See* Segel, Binjamin Wolf
Schilda (Brandenburg, Germany), 156
Schilda (Saxony, Germany) 90, 116, *152*, 153–156; and Abdera, 116, 151, 157; and Chelm, 168, 189, 191, 194, 195–196, 211; as German foolish town, 66, 90, 116, 151, 153–165, 191, 211; and Jewish foolish towns, 165–166, 191; in proverbs, 163; vs. Schildburg, 151, 153–154, 156–157, 158, 160–161, 165, 166. *See also* Schildburg; *Vertheidigung der Stadt Schilda*
Schildau (Saxony, Germany), *152*, 153–154, 156n22. *See also* Schilda
Schildberg (Ostrzeszów, Poland), 156
Schildberg (Štíty, Czech Republic), 156
Schildburg (fictional town), 60, 67, 73, 74, 87, 91, 99, 102, 130, 138, 153, 174–175; and Abdera, 116, 118, 121–122, 157, 183; and Chelm, 193, 210; vs. Schilda, 151, 153–154, 156–157, 158, 160–161, 165, 166. *See also* Schilda

*Der Schildbürger wunderseltsame, aben-
teuerliche, unerhörte und bisher unbeschriebene Geschichten und Thaten*
(Marbach), 162
*Schildbürgerbuch*, 2–3, 7, 73–74, 80, 96,
103–104, 107, 111, 113–114, 151, 153,
156–157, 162, 175, 184, 194, 199, 212, 219,
248n124; deliberation in, 118, 134, 201;
folly in, 44, 59, 73, 95, 113; fool societies
in, 74, 109–110, 156; illustrations in, 75,
87; scholarship on, 66–67, 93, 95, 154–
156, 159–161, 163, 173; and *Lalebuch*,
44, 61, 67; *Schildbürgerbuch* (1598), 2,
44, 61, 67, 73, 77, 91, 101, 103, 153, 155;
*Schildbürgerbuch* (Filtzhut), *62*, *65*,
73–76, 85, 87, *89*, 91, 95, 96, 97, 101,
155–156; Utopia in, 107, 118, 153, 160;
wisdom in, 98, 113, 123; and wise men
of Chelm, 137, 138–139, 175, 184, 188,
192–193, 194, 209; Yiddish translations
of, 78, 84, 98–99, 100–101, 110, 131. *See
also* "Abderiten von heute unter den
Juden"; children's literature; *History of
the Abderites*; *Lalebuch*; *Schildbürgerbuch* (Schwab); *Shildburger bukh*
*Schildbürgerbuch* (Schwab), 162
*Schildbürgerstreich* (*Schildburger antics*),
157–158
Schiller, Johann Christoph Friedrich von,
115
Schiltach, 156
*Schlegel, August Wilhelm*, 159
Schlosser, Johann Georg, 244n44
*Schocken, Salman*, 189
Schönberg, Johann von, 235n9
*Schöppenstedt*, 116, 161, 250n23; as fool-
ish town, 116, 161, 163–164, 165, 168,
250n23; and Heine, 164; and *Die Revo-
lution in Scheppenstedt*, 250n23
Schöttgen, Johann Christian, 66, 90–91,
151, 154, 160; *Vertheidigung der Stadt
Schilda*, 66, 90–91, 154–156, 160

Schudt, Johann Jacob, 58
Schüler, Meier, 94
Schulz, Johann Gottlob, 113
Schummel, Johann Gottlieb, 113, 250n23
Schwab, Gustav, 162
Schwabenstreich. *See* Swabian fools
Schwartz, Amy, 224n6
Schwartz, Maurice, 11, 13, 16
Schwarzbaum, Haim, 226n36
Second Nuremberg Haggadah, 51
*Sefer ha-bakbuk*, 56
*Sefer ha-bedihah veha-hidud* (Druyanov),
202–203
*Sefer ha-zemanim* (Book of seasons), 54
*Sefer nifla'ot Maharal* (Rozenberg), 189
Segal, D. *See* Singer, Isaac Bashevis
Segel, Binjamin Wolf, 169, 171, 173–174,
177–179, 181, 183, 184, 190, 194, 201;
"Abderiten von heute unter den
Juden," 151, 171, 173–176, 177, 178–179,
183, 184, 190; on antisemitism, 177–178;
"Das Brillantendiadem," 180–182; and
Chelm tales, 174–182; *Die Entdeckung-
sreise des Herrn Dr. Theodor Lessing
zu den Ostjuden*, 178; on Jewishness,
177–179; pen names of, 173, 174, 181;
*Die polnische Judenfrage*, 178; and
*Schildbürgerbuch*, 174–175; "Sünden-
kauf," 174; and Yiddish, 179; and Zion-
ism, 180–181
Sejm (Polish parliament), 45, 126, 140
Seldwyla (fictional town), 209
Selig, Gottfried, 253n81
Sendak, Maurice, 31
*Serapeum* (Leipzig), 92
*Seyfer minhogim* (Tyrnau), 48, *49*
Shabbat ha-Bahurim, 54–55
Shabbes. *See* Sabbath
"Der shabes-goy" (Peretz), 146, 148–149
Shahn, Ben, 226n37
Shatin, Leo, 224n6
Shaw, George Bernard, 77

Shayke Fayfer, 190

*Shildburger bukh*, 78, 84, 90–96, 108–111, 133, 194; Dutch in, 98–99, 102; folly in, 95, 108, 109–110; Hebraisms in, 95, 97–98, 100; illustrations in, 75, 87; Judaization of, 99–100; language of, 95–99, 241n81; Latin and Romance languages in, 79, 96, 98; rhymes in, 80, 93, 95, 100, 101, 103–106; scholarship on, 94–95; *Shildburger bukh* (1700), 85, 88, 90, 92, 94, 96–101, 102, 105, 109, 242n81; *Shildburger bukh* (1727), 77–80, 84–85, 86, 87, 88, 89, 90, 91, 92, 93, 94, 95–111, 133, 155, 237n54; *Shildburger bukh* (1777), 85, 90, 94, 99, 108, 111; *Shildburger bukh* (1798), 85, 90, 94, 99, 108, 111; as translation, 78–80, 93–94, 96, 98, 105, 110; as transliteration, 79–80, 94, 96; and wise men of Chelm, 108–111, 133, 194, 209; wisdom in, 98, 108. See also *Schildbürgerbuch*

Ship of Fools (Brant), 44, 49, 117, 122–123

Shiper, Yitskhok (Ignacy Schiper), 45–46, 56

*Der shivim moltsayt* (Dik), 140, 142

*shlemiehl*, 31, 39, 41, 215, 217, 218, 221

*Shlemiel the First* (Singer), 31, 215

Shmeruk, Khone, 6, 31, 248n127; *Prokim fun der yidisher literatur-geshikhte*, 47

*Shmuelbukh*, 93

Sholem Aleichem, 18–19, 21, 23, 137, 203–204; and Chelm tales, 19, 21–23, 203–204; and Dik, 246n78; "Der farkishefter shnayder," 21–23; "Iber a hitl," 203–204; and Manger, 21; and Trunk, 23–24

*Sholem-Aleykhem: Zayn vezn un zayne verk* (Trunk), 23–24

*Shtern oyfn yarid oder di festung fun khokhme* (Zeltser), 217

*Dos shterntikhl* (Aksenfeld), 137

shtetl, 26, 143; Chelm as, 1, 6, 26, 40, 134, 143, 179, 216, 221

*Shteynbarg, Eliezer*, 226n56, 257n56

Shub, Elizabeth, 39, 41

Shulevitz, Uri, 31

Sidon, Ephraim, 217

*Der siebente Brunnen* (Wander), 196

Sieniawa, 124, 125, 126

*Silesia*, 159, 167

Silva, Howard da, 18–19

Simon, David, 30

Simon, Solomon, 20, 30, 214

simple son, 51, 253n89

*Simple Wisdom*, 224n6

*Simrock, Karl*, 162, 163

Singer, Isaac Bashevis, 3, 6, 10–12, 31–33, 36–37, 39, 41–42, 216–217, 221; *The Fools of Chelm and Their History*, 31, 39–40, 196; "Der groyser zets un di antshteyung fun Khelm," 33–34, 38–39; and Kipnis, 37; "Der narishe khosn un di farbitene fis," 31–32; "Nokh vegn di Khelmer khakhomim: A fish an azes-ponem," 37–38, 40–41; pen names of, 32, 33, 37; "Di 'politishe ekonomye' fun Khelm," 32–33, 36; scholarship on, 6, 31; *Shlemiel the First*, 31, 215; *Stories for Children*, 31; and Trunk, 10, 36–37; "Di tseteylung fun Khelm un di rezultatn derfun," 35–36; *When Shlemiel Went to Warsaw*, 39; and Zeitlin, 10, 12; *Zlateh the Goat and Other Stories*, 39, 41. See also titles of specific works

Singer, Israel Joshua, 31, 209, 224n8

Sinkoff, Nancy, 126

*Sipurey khokhmey Yovn* (Dik), 246n76

Slawkenbergius, Hafen (fictional character), 121

son who does not know how to ask, 50–51

Soviet Union, 24, 195, 214

*Die Sprachen der Juden* (Loewe), 191–192

*Das Sprichwort als Kosmopolit* (I. von
 Reinsberg-Düringsfeld), 163
*Sprichwörter und Redensarten deutsch-
 jüdischer Vorzeit* (Tendlau), 165–167
St. Petersburg, 124
Stargard, 154
State and University Library of Saxony-
 Anhalt. *See* Universitäts- und Landes-
 bibliothek Sachsen-Anhalt
Steinschneider, Moritz, 92
Sterne, Laurence, 117; *Tristram Shandy*,
 117, 121
*Stone Soup with Matzoh Balls* (Glaser),
 224n6, 215
*Stories for Children* (Singer), 31
Strasbourg, 51, 67, 81, 117; as literary place,
 121
Strassburg, Robert, 215
*Der Streit der Fakultäten* (Kant), 116
*Sukkot*, 193
"*Sündenkauf*" (Segel), 174
Swabia, 156, 159, 254n108
Swabian fools, 156
Switzerland, 58, 194
Szwarcman-Czarnota, Bella, 257n41

*Tales of the Hasidim* (Buber), 9
Talmud, 53, 131, 147n130, 154, 166
Tango, Jenny, 10
Tarnopol, 125, 127, 129, *152*
*taytsh*. *See* Yiddish language
*Tendlau, Abraham*, 165–167
Tenenbaum, Samuel, 31
Teterow, *152*; as foolish town, 161, 165,
 191
*Der Teutsche Merkur* (Frankfurt), 112, 114,
 117, 118
*Tevya and His Daughters* (Perl), 18
"Tey un tilim" (Ulinover), 211
thirty-six righteous men, 147
*Thümmel, Moritz August von*, 250n23
*Tieck, Ludwig*, 113–114, 157

*Till Eulenspiegel*, 51–54, 59, 93, 190, 192;
 folly in, 53; and Hershele Ostropoler,
 53–54, 189–190; in Yiddish, 52–54
Tish'ah be-Av, 136
*Der Titan* (Jean Paul), 157
tobacco, 155–156
*Der tog-Morgn zshurnal* (New York), 197
*Topographia Germaniae* (Zeiller), 153
Torgau, 153
Trachimbrod (as literary place), 10
*Treasury of Jewish Folklore* (Ausubel), 17,
 19, 22–23, 214
Treblinka, 197
Tripstrill (as foolish town), 161
Triptis, *152*; as foolish town, 191
*Tristram Shandy* (Sterne), 117, 121
Trunk, Israel Joshua, 224n8
Trunk, Yekhiel Yeshaye, 10–11, 17, 23–24,
 26, 29, 146; *Der freylekhster yid in
 der velt oder Hersheles lern-yorn*, 54;
 *Khelemer khakhomim*, 6, 24–30, 36–37;
 and Kipnis, 10, 29; and Peretz, 224n9,
 24, 227n80, 146; and Poland, 24, 25,
 26; and Pryłucki, 29; and Sholem
 Aleichem, 23–24; and Singer, 10, 36–
 37; and Yiddish, 24, 28; and Zeitlin, 10,
 227n80
"Di tseteylung fun Khelm un di rezultatn
 derfun" (Singer), 35–36
Tseytlin, Arn. *See* Zeitlin, Aaron
"Tshiribim" (song), 212
"Tsores in Khelm un a kluge eytse"
 (Singer), 35
"The Tumblers" (Englander), 10
Turniansky, Chava, 1, 81
Tyrnau, Isaac, 48–49

"Über das Wesen der Sekte Chassidim"
 (Perl), 127
*Uhland, Ludwig*, 161
*Ulinover, Miryam*, 211
Uniate Church, 140; in Chelm, 140–141

Universitäts- und Landesbibliothek Sachsen-Anhalt, *86, 88, 89*, 238n24
unreliable narrator, 25, 65, 101, 119, 198
*Utopia* (More), 67, 134
Utopia, 2, 219
Uzhmir, 197

Valikh, Ayzik. *See* Wallich, Isaac
Varshavski, Yitskhok. *See* Singer, Isaac Bashevis
*Vaynig, Naftole*, 182
Vaynlez, Yisroel, 125, 127
Vayzose, 35, 38
Velten, Hans Rudolf, 67
*Ven Shlemiel iz gegangen keyn Varshe* (Singer), 228n105
*Vertheidigung der Stadt Schilda* (Schöttgen), 66, 90–91, 154–156, 160, 252n62; and *Schildbürgerbuch*, 154–156
"Vi azoy es hot gearbet di Khelmer demokratye" (Singer), 35
"Vi azoy Khelm iz geblibn on gelt" (Singer), 230n142
Vienna, 78, 90, 130, 150, 151, *152*, 172, 173, 180, 192, 238n20, 238n24; as literary place, 181
*Village of Idiots* (short film), 215, 221–222
Vilna Gaon. *See* Elijah of Vilna
Vilna, 24, 29, 78, 127, 130–131, 132, 142, *152*, 182, 188, 202, 207, 213, 216
Vilnius. *See* Vilna
*Dos vintshfingerl* (Abramovitsh), 247n100
Vladimir-Volinsk, 204
Volhynia, 182, 197; as literary place, 198
*Volksbuch. See* chapbook
"Vollständige Historie der ehrenwerten Stadt Chelm" (Carlebach), 195–196
Volozhin yeshiva, 202

Wagenseil, Johann Christoph, 82–83
*Die Wahrheit* (Vienna), 174, 180, 181

Wallich, Isaac, 45–46, 211
Wander, Fred, 196
Wander, Friedrich Wilhelm, 2, 141, 167–168, 169, 170
Warsaw ghetto, 197
Warsaw, 10, 11, 12, 24, 37, 45, 126, 146, *152*, 153, 168, 182, 188–189, 197, 203, 206, 207, 208, 209, 211, 220; as literary place, 26, 39, 145; Nozyk shul, 197
Washington Haggadah, 51
Weimar, 125
Weinreich, Max, 78, 213, 223n3, 223n10
Weinreich, Uriel, 213–215
"Die Weisen von Chelm" (Drożdżyński), 256n30
Weltsch, Felix, 195
*When Shlemiel Went to Warsaw* (Singer), 39
Wieland, Christoph Martin, 112–123, 125, 127; on Brant, 117; "A Couple of Gold Nuggets," 112–113; "Key to the History of the Abderites," 120–121, 122–123; and Lefin, 125. *See also History of the Abderites*
Wiener, Leo, 258n58
Wiesbaden, 166
Wieser, Salomon, 176
*Wilhelmine, ein prosaisch komisches Gedicht* (Thümmel), 250n23
Winckelmann, Johann Joachim, 119
Winz, Leo, 173
Wischnitzer, Mark, 195
wisdom, 40, 61, 65, 72, 98, 108, 113, 115, 118, 122–123, 128, 147, 212, 222; in Chelm tales, 26, 29, 30, 40, 42, 142, 193, 195, 206, 210, 212
"The Wisdom of a Certain Town Khes" (Dik), 131–136, 140, 174, 180; and *Schildbürgerbuch*, 133–134, 138; and *Shildburger bukh*, 133
*Wise Folk of Chelm*, 224n6
*Wise Men of Chelm* (Tenenbaum), 31

Wise Men of Chelm (Zeitlin). See *Khel-emer khakhomim* (Zeitlin)
wise men of Chelm, 1–2, 5–6, 9, 43, 108, 124, 133–134, 137, 141–142, 168, 171, 175–177, 180, 183, 186, 190, 194, 195, 196, 206, 212, 219; in American Jewish culture, 3, 7, 10–11, 14, 16–17–18, 20, 22–23, 30–31, 41–42, 214–216, 218, 220–221; and deliberation, 32, 38, 40, 132, 134, 138, 145, 201; in encyclopedias, 194–195; in German Jewish culture, 190–194, 195–196; in Israel, 202, 207, 216–217; in Polish Jewish culture, 146, 153, 168, 179–180, 190, 192, 206, 208, 220; and *Schildbürgerbuch*, 137, 138–139, 175, 184, 188, 192–193, 194, 209; scholarship on, 5–6, 21, 131–132, 141, 209–210; and *Shildburger bukh*, 108–111, 133, 194, 209; in Soviet Jewish culture, 206, 216. *See also specific titles*
wise men of Gotham, 6
*The Wise Men of Helm and Their Merry Tales* (Simon), 20, 30, 214
Wisse, Ruth, 6
*Wissenschaft des Judentums*, 78, 173, 195
Witzenburg (foolish town), 73
Woelk, Emma, 229n115
Wolf, Johann Christoph, 52, 90–91
*Women of Chelm* (Tango), 10
*The World of Sholom Aleichem* (Perl), 17–21, 23
*The World of Sholom Aleichem* (Samuel), 18
Worms, 45, 152, 165–166, 211, Christian community of, 55; as foolish town, 165–166; Jewish community of, 46, 54–56
*Wörterbuch der deutsche Sprache* (Campe), 157–158
Wurzbach, Constantin von, 165–166
Wurzen, 154

Yanosovitsh, Yitskhok, 248n140
*Yediot Aḥronot* (Tel Aviv), 195
*yeytser hore*, 14, 26, 147
Yiddish Art Theater, 11–12, 16, 225n34
Yiddish language, 3, 16, 27–28, 81, 85, 91–93, 131, 167–168, 179, 182, 213, 219–220; and German, 77–79, 81, 99, 167, 191; Loewe on, 191–192; names of, 77, 79, 81, 92, 168; and reading, 80–82, 194, 220; scholarship on, 191–192; Segel on, 179. *See also* alphabet
Yiddish literature, 6, 18, 24, 84, 93, 130–131, 137, 249n12, 176, 194, 220; and German literature, 3, 84, 91–93, 167; with German sources, 84, 91, 93; in German studies, 91, 93, 167; Old Yiddish literature, 47–59, 76, 81, 84, 91, 93–94, 249n12; scholarship on, 46–47, 84, 91, 92–95
Yiddish studies, 5–6, 45–47, 92, 94–95
Yiddish theater: in Buenos Aires, 16; in New York, 11–12, 16, 225n34; scholarship on, 45–47, 56; in Vilnius, 216
*Yidishe folkslider* (Pryłucki), 183
Yidisher Visnshaftlekher Institut. See YIVO
Yitskhok Bashevis. *See* Singer, Isaac Bashevis
YIVO (Yidisher Visnshaftlekher Institut; Yiddish Scientific Institute): in Vilna, 182, 197; in New York, 16, 213, 224n14, 225n21, 225n34, 256n6
*Yizker-bukh Khelm*, 5, 141, 248n140
Yom Kippur, 149
*Yosl Loksh fun Khelem* (Glatshteyn), 30
Yossel of Kletsk, 170
*Yossel Zissel and the Wisdom of Chelm* (Schwartz), 224n6
*yudish taytsh. See* Yiddish language
Yuspa Shammes, 54–56, 166

Zakritsh, 183
Zamość, 141, 146, *152*, 204
Zarncke, Friedrich, 93
Zeiller, Martin, 153, 154
Zeitlin, Aaron, 10–12, 14, 146; *Khelemer khakhomim*, 11–14, 16, 225n34, 19; *Di Khelemer komediye*, 11–12; and Peretz, 14, 146; and Singer, 10, 12; and Trunk, 10, 227n80
Zeitlin, Hillel, 14
Żelechów, 183

Zeligfeld, Zimre, 197
Zeltser, Khayim, 217
Zilberman, Boris, 218
Zinkev, 144, as literary place, 144–145
Zionism, 171, 182, 190, 191, 202, 219; and Krauss, 172; and Peretz, 145; and Segel, 178, 180, 181; and Trunk, 28. *See also* anti-Zionism
*Zlateh the Goat and Other Stories* (Singer), 9, 41
Zurich Bible, 51

# ABOUT THE AUTHOR

Ruth von Bernuth is Associate Professor and teaches German and Old Yiddish Literature in the Department of Germanic and Slavic Languages and Literatures at the University of North Carolina at Chapel Hill. She also serves as Director of the Carolina Center for Jewish Studies at the university.